D0884491

HUMOR and SOCIETY

HUMOR and SOCIETY:

Explorations in the Sociology of Humor

Marvin R. Koller

Professor of Sociology
Kent State University

Cap and Gown Press, Inc.
Houston

Copyright © 1988 by Cap and Gown Press, Inc.

All rights reserved.

No part of this work may be reproduced or transmitted
in any form whatsoever, or by any means, electronic
or mechanical, including photocopying, recording, or
by any information storage and/or retrieval system,
without written permission from the Publisher.

Cap and Gown Press, Inc.
Box 58825
Houston, Texas 77258 - U.S.A.

Library of Congress Catalog Card Number 87-24998

Library of Congress Cataloging-in-Publication Data

Koller, Marvin R.
    Humor and Society.

    Bibliography.
    Includes index.
    1. Sociology—Methodology. 2. Wit and humor—Social
aspects. I. Title.
HM24.K615   1987   302.2   87-24998
ISBN 0-88105-017-2

Printed in the United States of America

CONTENTS

List of Figures

Dedicated to my brother,

ED

Preface

Humor is a vital part of human life that has sustained men and women through all their trials and tribulations. It has been expressed in multiple forms, styles, and media. It is part and parcel of individual lives and their respective societies. It is found in antiquity; it delights those living; and it will endure in the future because humor encourages persons to cope with whatever stresses and strains are present in interpersonal relationships.

This book gathers together the efforts of numerous scholars from the widest possible array of disciplines, backgrounds, and persuasions. It provides an opportunity to examine the many facets, functions, and forms of humor in the affairs of individuals and in the groups or associations they create. It seeks to encourage a desire to learn more about humor. It can help in heightening an awareness of humor as an ever-present means to deal with life.

While eclectic in terms of sources of humor, the book focuses on a sociological perspective of humor. It recognizes that sociological concerns are primarily serious, sober, scientific study of unresolved, ongoing issues that trouble humanity. It offers, however, the idea that humor merits attention to balance out the sociological preoccupation with the tragic flaws in social systems, social organizations, and interactive patterns.

The author welcomes any comments, criticisms, and counter-analyses to improve what is offered herein.

MARVIN R. KOLLER
Kent State University

After God created the world, He made man and woman.
Then, to keep the whole thing from collapsing,
He invented humor.

Guillermo Mordillo in
Stuttgarter Zeitung, Germany

PART I:

Humor As Both Sword and Shield, Surviving Pain and Suffering

The multifaceted nature of humor has long captured the attention of scholars. Social historians have examined the human record and traced the development of humor and its protagonists. Social psychologists have begun to unravel the mysteries of humor in terms of how it serves individuals. Sociologists also have entered into studies of humor because they are becoming aware of humor as both an interactive process and a societal product that affects how groups, organizations, institutions, and societies deal with the imperfections and dilemmas of relationships, norms, values, and systems.

In these early chapters, macrotheorists of humor, the functions of humor, the purveyors of humor, the media that both shape and convey humor, and the omnipresence of humor in human affairs are presented and discussed.

An overriding theme is suggested. Humor is viewed as a powerful mechanism to help individuals endure, to cope with, and to move beyond - in a word, *survive* - those difficulties, problems, and issues confronting them because humanity has contrived social systems and procedures that are inadequate and imperfect in meeting human needs.

Chapter 1:

Humor and Its Significance

What is humor? Confident that humor exists and plays a vital part in the fortunes of social affairs and in the personalities of men and women, we need to know what humor is.

At first glance, humor would appear to be easy to define. Humor is that universally human quality that finds events, circumstances, behavior, situations, or the expression of ideas to be funny, joyous, absurd, ludicrous, hilarious, laughable, amusing, clever, and possibly instructive.

This definition, however, is sorely lacking because it opens up a Pandora's box of semantic problems. What is "funny" to some is not "funny" to others. What is "joyous" and "absurd" or "amusing" to the humorist and his or her audience may also be very serious, painful, and degrading to the targets or butts of the laughter. The reinforcement of half-truths or stereotypes often damages and undercuts the character and reputations of individuals and the groups with whom they are associated. There is merit in the perspective of some theorists that humor is essentially hostile. Humor is, in this sense, a weapon, a sharp sword that cuts, thrusts, and demolishes an antagonist.

Two can play the same game, of course. If humor can be symbolized as a sword, then counter-humor is a shield, a defensive device that blunts an attack or makes it ineffective. From the past, we have inherited the expression "hoisted on one's own petard." There is something satisfying about persons caught in their own trap, just as the ancients saw humor in the oaf who went flying through the air instead of the load of stones he had intended to send crashing against an enemy's gates.

The term *humor* is derived from the Latin *humere* which means "to flow or be wet." Humors then were believed by ancient physiologists to be those fluids in the body that affected both physiques and minds. Blood, for example, red, warm and wet, if dominant, meant that a person was healthy or sanguine. Nobility and prelates were said to be sanguine and thus worthy of wielding power. Secretions of the liver, black bile, on the other hand, if dominant, would put the person in a foul, ill-tempered, peevish mood, a state of melancholy or depression that caused a doleful or sourful attitude toward life. The ancient physicians explained that old men and unfortunates were filled with black bile and hence were bitter, unhappy, mournful

3

individuals. It was believed that phlegm, white and colorless, also could dominate the body's fluids. If that condition would occur, persons so affected would become lazy, difficult, or obstinate in their ways. Phlegm was the dominant humor of children and women, said the ancient sages. Finally, there was the humor called choler, which was yellow in appearance. Choler dominance was said to lead to sickness, fever, or violence and explained the behavior of drunkards, traitors, or criminals. The proper balancing of these fluids, the ancient doctors explained, led to a life filled with ''good humor.''

The theory of *humors,* or body fluids has long been discredited as an explanation for human moods. All that remains is the term humor itself that is applied to a phenomenon so complex and multifaceted that it is still difficult to define and comprehend.

The numerous terms applied to *humor* illustrate the variants of humor. A *partial* listing of synonyms for humor might be:

Figure 1-1

Synonyms for Humor (Partial List)

Nouns:	*Verbs:*	*Adjectives:*
Pleasantry	Tease	Merry
Farce	Laugh	Grotesque
Drollery	Snicker	Ludicrous
Wit	Titter	Humiliate
Jocularity	Smile	Scurrilous
Caricature	Titillate	Zany
Burlesque	Divert	Zestful
Travesty	Joke	Wise
Roast	Frolic	Wistful
Whimsy	Banter	Provocative
Waggery	Scoff	Silly
Badinage	Jeer	Nonsensical
Acrimony	Cheer	Sardonic
Parody	Celebrate	Deflating
Jocundity	Quip	Nonserious
Tomfoolery	Pun	Disdainful
Hilarity	Quibble	Trivial
Irony	Taunt	Delightful
Satire	Mock	Joyful
Ricidule	Exaggerate	Amusing
Bon-mot	Castigate	Fanciful
Repartee	Savor	Derisive
Levity	Smirk	Lunatic
Persiflage	Fool	Unconventional
Jest	Fancy	Perspicuous
Gaiety	Pretend	Pointed
Mirth	Humble	Scatological
Buffoonery	Romp	Fumbling
Facetiousness	Vilify	Clumsy
Comedy	Enjoy	Nutty
Lightheartedness	Relax	Crazy
Playfulness	Bamboozle	Jarring
Entertainment	Distort	Pernicious
Glee	Allege	Happy
Hubris	Insult	Pleasant
Absurdity	Giggle	Clowning
Gambol	Kid	Festive
Barb	Triumph	
Slapstick		

Linguists suggest that when something is salient to a people, countless words or terms are used to deal with the nuances, the different shades of meaning, to communicate precisely the particular referent which persons wish to use. Such is the case for snow, which is described in a multiplicity of terms among Eskimos. English speakers can describe snow in such terms as sleet, powder snow, dry snow, wet snow, drifting snow, blizzards, or hail. Eskimos, however, have countless terms for snow variations that can mean the difference between life and death in their lives. The same applies to camels among the Beduin. Camels play no central part in the lives of English speakers, but among nomadic peoples who rely upon camels as their major means of survival, there is a host of terms brought into play to describe a pregnant camel, a mean-tempered camel, an injured camel, a patient camel, a sick camel, and so on.

The presence of hundreds of words in the English language to convey some aspect of humor suggests that humor is also a very significant phenomenon to English speakers. The difficulty of defining precisely what humor is becomes compounded by the effort to place all its variants under the rubric of a single, comprehensive definition.

There is help, however, from such scholars as Arthur Koestler (1964). Koestler envisioned humor as a triptych, a set of three panels side by side that shows a trifold nature of humor. At one extreme there is the purely emotional quality of unequivocal enjoyment expressed in raucous laughter. Koestler identifies it as "Ha-Ha," an observable action and reaction that is represented in a human face wreathed in laughter or a broad smile. The middle screen is labeled "Aha" by Koestler because in this form humor involves a sense of discovery of new, enlightened knowledge. Humor in this context instructs, educates, or enlarges the vision of what life is all about. That which was formerly veiled in mystery or obsfuscation is now made to stand out clearly. The third screen of humor Koestler epitomized as "Ah," that humor which includes the use of the intellect. Those who encounter humor of this sort appreciate, savor, and understand much better than they did previously. Such humor goes far beyond one's self or limited experiences.

Koestler's model corresponds to the sociological usage of a continuum. This conceptual device permits the placing of complex phenomena on a scale between polarities or extremes. Thus, instead of ignoring differences or dichotomizing, data are shown to have shades or degrees of differences between opposing extremes, albeit being linked together in a common pattern. Humor is like a continuum; it is many things to many people, but still a cohesive whole.

A "sense of humor" is generally held to be an admirable quality to have or to develop. But this too is difficult to pinpoint and to have people arrive at some consensus as to what it is. What is "sensed" to be humor again depends upon what criteria are used, who selects the criteria, and why the criteria are used. In short, *humor exists in a social context.* Sociologists recognize this in terms of "the definition of the situation," a conceptualization credited to W. I. Thomas (House, 1936). Defining something as humorous rests heavily upon one's past associations, experiences, values, and overall sociocultural backgrounds. Humor, then, is well within the province and purview of sociology.

Macrotheories of Humor

Macrotheories are those theories that attempt to explain large, overarching portions of a phenomenon as opposed to microtheories, which explain smaller details of the same phenomenon. In more recent years, there has been the advancement of middle-range theories, which organize data and their interpretations around information that is neither global in scope nor dealing in minutia.

In the study of humor, four macrotheories of humor have been put forward: (1) incongruity, (2) relief, (3) ambivalence, and (4) superiority.

Incongruity Theory

For many investigators of humor, its nature is best explained by juxtaposing two or more conceptualizations that do not seem to fit together, but, in the mind of a humorist, are compared and contrasted with considerable profit.

Arthur Schopenhauer [1788-1860] noted the pleasure many derive from finding unexpected connections between ideas. Luigi Pirandello [1867-1936] wrote that humor is essentially a feeling for the opposite. Arthur Koestler [1905-1983] characterized humor as being a matter of bisociation of form and function of a whole or a part. In humorous terms, Koestler wrote, there is a distortion of realities. Many humorists agree that humor consists of looking at things from "a different angle," a perspective not often used by most people. In sum, incongruity theory finds similarity or a connection between dissimilarities.

Application of incongruity theory to humor typically involves the formula of *reductio ad absurdum*, reducing a logical argument to absurdity and hence holding it up to ridicule or laughter. A cartoonist employed this formula when he drew a set of parallel ski tracks going to one side of a tree and the other track going to the other side, and then resumed their parallel paths after having safely passed the tree.

Incongruity humorists, further, derive great satisfaction by leading persons in one direction but, in the end, thrusting their barbs from another angle into an unexpected target. This device of *misdirection* was used by Dorothy Parker when she wrote a satiric appraisal of an author by saying, "He was a writer for the ages... ages four to eight!"

Relief Theory

A number of scholars see humor as a release from restraints or controls whether they are physiological, psychological, or social restrictions. Herbert Spencer (1820-1903) cited the physical relief persons discover when they grasp the contrast between that which is solemn and that which is trivial. Sigmund Freud [1856-1939], renowned for his emphasis upon the struggle between individuals and human society, pointed to the pleasure made possible by being free from keeping forbidden behavior or thoughts repressed and away from one's conscience or social censor. Harvey Mindess (1971) drew upon the same theme of relief when he identified humor as liberation. To be liberated, unchained from the bondage of social conventions, sets up the mood of receptivity toward humor. Poking fun at the social systems that dampen the spirit for self-expression or identity delights those persons or audiences that have suffered too long from these suppressions.

Ambivalence Theory

In the ambivalence theory of humor, there is a struggle between opposing emotions or feeling-states, a type of love-hate, attraction-repulsion commingling. On the one hand, there is some appreciation for social structures or functions, and on the other hand, there is a strong desire to object to these same structures or functions. Related somewhat to the relief theory but not totally, individuals seek to expose those cultural qualities that are filled with sham, pretense, or false pride but never quite reject all the benefits that flow from being conventional and "proper."

The humor portrayed so well on the movie screen by the Marx Brothers is one of outrageous behavior in the face of polite society. The Marx Brothers demolish or completely disrupt high society circles with their shenanigans. In their *Night at the Opera,* seeking to delay the normal renditions of melodious arias, they play catch with a baseball in the midst of the orchestra, which has been slipped copies of *Take Me Out to the Ballgame.* When Groucho wants to lecture his audience on the merits of his ideas, he persists in having a sedate dowager hold one of his legs so he may be more comfortable. The Marx Brothers did poke fun at social posturings, but neither they nor their audience were ever unclear about why they worked as comedians. This was their livelihood and they made their fortunes "laughing all the way to the bank." Wealth and status were held up to laughter, but wealth and status within their profession were also held to be quite desirable and appropriate.

Superiority Theory

Looming large in the analyses of humor are the superiority themes. By degrading others, one can elevate one's own status and so conquer all opposition. Plato [427-347 B.C.] was aware of the contempt persons felt over others' ignorance, vanity, or hypocrisy. By "showing them up" for their shortcomings, humorists and their audiences would demonstrate their superior knowledge, insights, backgrounds, and abilities. Those targeted as butts of jokes were such types as the miser, the glutton, the drunkard, or the authority figures who abused their power. Aristotle (384-322 B.C.) also approved of treating that which was base and ugly as the laughable object or butt of humor.

Perhaps the best known exponent of the superiority theory of humor was Thomas Hobbes [1588-1679], who postulated the "sudden glory" that came over the earliest hominid who stood in triumph over the body of a fellow creature who had tried to defeat him in bloody combat. The realization that he had survived while the other individual was killed made him raise his arms to the sky and throw back his head in an unabashed howl of pure joy and rapture. Life was his to do as he pleased and with great good humor he set about to do just that.

Anthony Ludovici (1932) followed this Hobbesian perspective when he suggested that laughing is a way to show one's fangs in celebrating triumphs over enemies. Likewise, Albert Rapp (1951) discussed "thrashing laughter" in which the tensions of combat give way to high satisfaction in the suddenness of the outcome. Many have witnessed the spontaneous "dancing" and glee of football players who have just carried the ball over the goal line by outwitting the defending team. Don Rickles is a contemporary comedian who has parlayed the superiority theme into prominence through his use of "insult" humor in which he dismisses his hecklers by calling them "hockey pucks."

Henri Bergson's classic, *Laughter: An Essay in the Meaning of the Comic*, (1911) followed the superiority theory closely by observing that there is much humor that has the avowed intention to humiliate, shame, or correct one's neighbors. Such an interactive pattern places superiority humor quite firmly into sociological concerns. In "setting things right," an individual or group of persons draws upon humor to ask others to be reasonable, namely, "to do it our way" rather than "your way." Bergson did not equivocate when he defined a humorist as "a moralist disguised as a scientist."

Relationships Between the Macrotheories of Humor

The four macrotheories of incongruity, relief, ambivalence, and superiority are not to be taken as totally comprehensive or exhaustive of explanations of humor. Each makes a contribution because each reveals a portion of humor that might otherwise escape our attention. Nor are they mutually exclusive. The macrotheories overlap each other so that humor consists of combinations of these qualities. A given bit of humor may incorporate bisociation of dissimilarities, triumph over adversity, and be self-satisfying at the same time.

These theories serve chiefly as baselines or beginning points to assess the nature of humor in its multiple forms and styles. As it has been noted, humor has highly aggressive or hostile features. Nevertheless, humor also may be harmless, free from trying to attack others, and may be basically a liberating, celebrating, expressive action among associates and friends.

The common thread that seems to run through all the macrotheories of humor is *survival.* A person, a group, a subsociety, or a total society endures, continues, or seeks to move on to a future. The idea of dying, coming to some terminal point when existence for that individual group, subsociety, or total society will no longer continue, is abhorrent to them and is pushed out of consciousness. Rather, there is confidence gained through humor that whatever obstacles, roadblocks, delays, hazards, detours, frustrations, or trials are to be found can be overcome. Nothing is allowed to stop the forward progress of a person or a people. Humor is thus *a vital ingredient* in confronting life.

Antonin Obrdlik (1942) coined the term *gallows humor* during World War II. Gallows humor is that brand of ironic humor that acknowledges certain dehumanizing, life-threatening circumstances and seeks to transform them into something human, delightful, and worthy. Morale-building is essential to confront whatever seeks to subdue the human spirit. Even on the gallows, a prisoner can confront executioners with gallantry, poise, disdain, and high courage. His or her bearing, manner, grace, and self-respect transcends the taking of his or her life.

Obrdlik defined gallows humor as a type of humor that "arises in a precarious or dangerous situation." The dangerous situation to which Obrdlik referred at that time was the occupation of his native country, Czechoslovakia, by the German army. The double-pronged objectives of gallows humor, as Obrdlik explained, was to strengthen the morale of the Czechs while at the same time weakening the resolve of their oppressors. Obrdlik thus lends credence to a survivalist theme of humor in its ability to change painful, tragic circumstances into something hopeful, encouraging, or more positive for the future. He wrote, "The purest form of ironical humor is born out of sad experiences accompanied by grief and sorrow. It is spontaneous and deeply felt...the very necessity of life which it helps to preserve."

One example of gallows humor provided by Obrdlik was the popular story, widely circulated in Czechoslovakia at the time, about an elderly Czech who went about proclaiming his new loyalty to the German authorities. He would tell anyone who would listen, "I would rather work for ten Germans than for one Czech!" When asked what his occupation was, he would quickly reply, "Why, I am a gravedigger, of course."

Another analogy in terms of survival is to view humor as "social grease." It may smooth out a difficult situation or allow "saving grace" for those involved. It becomes a way to cope with a stressful situation. In hospital settings, for example, patients carry out their social roles by submitting their bodies, their privacy, their unique individualities to medical regimens. In the context of this contrived, sterile, medically correct environment, patients hope to move on to a healthier life and so cooperatively accept some degree of pain, discomfort, or even humiliation. They may be stuck with needles, asked if they have had bowel movements, or required to expose their "private parts." Emerson's study (1960) documented how female patients often responded with humor to ease the embarrassed tensions of pelvic probings by their male gynecologists or obstetricians.

Connections Between Sociology and Humor

Connections between sociology and humor may appear, at first glance, to be minimal. Pathologies, problems, tensions, strains, and a host of social ills plague humanity. Sociologists are concerned with these matters because they examine those social forms, relationships, and interactions both when these patterns or systems work well and when they do not.

Within recent decades, the grim historic record includes the Great Depression of the 1930s; the Second World War in the 1940s; "brushfire wars" in the 1950s; assassinations, riots, civil disobedience, and campus violence in the 1960s; political scandal and corruption, environmental pollution, runaway inflation, widespread unemployment, generational distrust, and energy crises in the 1970s; and major moves toward conservatism and consolidation in the 1980s. Such events are seemingly devoid of humor and would encourage chiefly a sobering appraisal by scholars in almost every discipline.

Yet humor prevailed throughout these times and continues to flourish. The ubiquity of humor, its omnipresence, is inescapable. Humor operates in both bad and good times; it sustains humanity in its darkest moments and emerges full-blown during times of celebration and rejoicing. Humor speaks to survival, to approach life with courage and hope instead of despair or submission.

Thus, even in the midst of the most calamitous events, there is humor. *To share a laugh together is a major social bond.* The common denominator of humanity is its vulnerability, its frailty, and its predilection to make mistakes. To move past our troubles, we resort to humor. President Ronald Reagan's comment to his wife after an attempted assassination, "I forgot to duck," is an example.

Humor is an integral part of societal and cultural life, and thus some sociologists regard humor as a legitimate area in which to conduct significant sociological research (Emerson, 1969; Adams, 1983).

This seems related to the willingness of sociologists to poke fun at their own discipline and to see the connectedness between the unfunny and the funny, the tragic and the comic, the sublime and the ridiculous. One sociologist wrote, "One of the funniest things about sociologists is that they are so afraid of being funny. I am sure that this is the basic reason they changed the name of the national organization from the American Sociological Society to the American Sociological Association" (Cameron, 1963).

There is much in humor to place it well within the discipline of sociology. Humor is based strongly upon shared symbols - a fundamental concern of symbolic interactionists. Humor emerges from patterned interactions, norms, values, attitudes, and relationships - concerns of structural-functionalists. Humor involves rewards and punishments, positive and negative sanctions - matters of major interest to the exchange theorists among sociologists. Humor can be very hostile, aggressive, or judgmental - behavior that conflict theorists emphasize. Humor criticizes the *status quo* and makes clear that present conditions are far from acceptable in meeting social needs. Problem-oriented sociologists recognize in humor its ability to forthrightly expose social conditions so that corrections can be made. Humor can also be used in social control to induce people to conform to social conventions. It makes an excellent defensive mechanism to preserve the dignity and cohesion of various groups or whole societies. In brief, humor can be understood and valued from a sociological perspective.

Humor operates within human affairs, sometimes castigating humanity for grave errors of judgment, sometimes congratulating people for their achievements, sometimes alerting people to mend their ways, sometimes mocking the stupidity that defeats purposes, and always encouraging humanity to move beyond human folly. Humor is a highly significant phenomenon that helps us to survive our own shortcomings and those of others. Through humor, people are able to persevere.

Summary and Conclusions

In this opening chapter, we conclude that humor exists and operates in significant ways in terms of a sociological perspective. When it came to a definition of humor in order to know what it is, we resorted to a working definition: "Humor is that universally human quality that finds events, circumstances, behavior, situations, or the expression of thoughts to be funny, joyous, absurd, ludicrous, hilarious, laughable, amusing, clever, and possibly instructive." Such a definition, however, is only tentative because the semantics of what is "funny," "absurd," or "laughable" depends upon what criteria are brought into use, who selects the criteria, and why the criteria are employed. Indeed it will require this entire book to delineate the nature of humor without doing damage to its components. More likely, a single volume cannot definitively treat humor in all of its shades of meaning or applications. A whole literature of humor has developed and we can sample it to great advantage.

The abundance of terminology to express what humor is indicates that humor is multifaceted and replete with a broad spectrum of interpretations. As both sword and shield, humor thrusts at targets and fends off attacks. In a threefold way, humor allows for gleeful expression, surprise and pleasure in discovering new ideas, and the unfolding of human wit. The macrotheories of incongruity, relief, ambivalence, and superiority are useful explanations of the nature of humor. We can, at least, start with them and determine later on if these are sufficient explanatory theses to draw upon.

The suggestion is made that perhaps the best capsulation of humor is that it is a mechanism for survival. To be able to cope with all the stresses that human beings encounter, particularly those that human beings themselves bring into being, humor offers tremendous support and comfort.

Lastly, the interfaces of humor and the concerns of sociologists are interconnected. Humor is a distinctly human quality and manifests itself in human relationships, human organizations, and human interactive processes. Whether sociologists identify themselves as symbolic interactionists, structural-functionalists, conflict- or exchange-oriented, problem-oriented, or applied sociologists, such scholars will find much that is relevant and significant when they turn their attention to humor. Moreover, there is every reason to believe that sociological expertise can be brought to bear upon humor with considerable benefits for students of sociology and for students of the vital entity called humor.

STUDY QUESTIONS

1. Critique the definition of humor suggested by the author. Improve upon it by developing a definition of humor that satisfies your criticisms.

2. Keep a record of the number of times you observe people using humor spontaneously in their daily, weekly, or monthly activities. To what extent can you ascertain that such humor was used to cope with stressful situations?

3. In what ways have you used humor to your own advantage? In what ways can you recall humor being used to your disadvantage?

4. From a select number of leading sociology textbooks, determine whether or not humor is utilized in any form or style.

5. Is humor a legitimate topic for sociological investigation and analysis? What makes any topic "legitimate" in terms of scientific disciplines?

6. While some sociologists study humor, what explains why the vast majority of sociologists do not?

7. Can you agree or disagree that humor is both a group product and a group process?

8. What is humorous about noncompliance with social norms?

9. Who are the targets for humor and what is accomplished by attacking them humorously?

10. What part do values, attitudes, and socialization play in the development of a "sense of humor"?

Suggested Readings

Adams, David S., *Teaching Sociology Through Humor*. Washington, DC: American Sociological Association, 1983.

Bates, Alan P., *The Sociological Enterprise*. Boston: Houghton Mifflin, 1967.

Bergson, Henri, *Laughter: An Essay in the Meaning of the Comic*. N.Y.: Macmillan, 1911.

Cameron, William B., *Informal Sociology, A Casual Introduction to Sociological Thinking*. N.Y.: Random House, 1963.

Emerson, Joan P., *Social Functions of Humor in a Hospital Setting*. Unpublished doctoral dissertation. Berkeley, CA: University of California, 1960.

Emerson, Joan P., "Negotiating the Serious Import of Humor." *Sociometry*, 32 (1969).

House, Floyd N., *The Development of Sociology*. N.Y.: McGraw-Hill, 1936.

Inkeles, Alex, *What Is Sociology? An Introduction to the Discipline and Profession*. Englewood Cliffs, NJ: Prentice-Hall, 1964.

Koestler, Arthur, *The Act of Creation*. N.Y.: Macmillan, 1964.

Ludovici, Anthony, *The Secret of Laughter*. London: Gordon Press, 1932.

McNall, Scott G., *The Sociological Experience, A Modern Introduction to Sociology*. Boston: Little, Brown, 1969.

Mindess, Harvy, *Laughter and Liberation*. Los Angeles, Nash, 1971.

Obrdlik, Antonin, "Gallows Humor, A Sociological Phenomenon." *American J. of Sociology*, 47 (March, 1942): 709-716.

Rapp, Albert, *The Origin of Wit and Humor*. N.Y.: Dutton, 1951.

Rose, Caroline, *The Study of Sociology, Social Science Perspectives*. Columbus, OH: Charles Merrill, 1966.

Turner, Jonathan H., *Sociology, A Student Handbook*. N.Y.: Random House, 1985.

Chapter 2:

Sociological Analyses of Humor

Sociology and humor are inseparably linked. Sociology takes as its unique perspective the intricate relationships between two or more persons, expanding from the dyad, the smallest unit of study, to include the societies of the world. Further, sociology is concerned with the interactions, the dynamic exchanges and behaviors between persons, and the results of these relationships and interactions. Humor itself is a *universal,* an everpresent phenomenon of every known society, a recognizable feature of every cultural inventory. The Human Relations Area Files (HRAF), which monitors an enormous array of known characteristics of the world's cultures, includes constant references to humor whether found in preliterate cultures now vanished from the earth or in the literate cultures from antiquity to the present. Humor is estimated to comprise almost one-half of the total nature of human life, granting that life is both tragic and comic or more likely, tragicomic. Humor is certainly pervasive in human affairs, in human interactions, and in human achievements — the identical items of concern in sociology.

Social Functions of Humor

Sociologists search out patterns, forms, or structures that persist among varied human groups and then ask what purposes are being served. These persistent patterns, forms, and structures operate or function in some manner to serve the objectives of those involved. If they function well, they are maintained and endorsed. If they falter or malfunction, they may be discarded or sharply altered to meet better perceived needs.

The universal presence of humor, a major hallmark of humanity, indicates that humor does indeed serve human groups, human associations, and human social order. A full and complete listing of all of the varied and

17

valued functions of humor awaits the concerted efforts of scholars but certainly a listing of the functions of humor should include the following:

Social bonding
Relief from stress and strain
Expression of aggression or hostility
Celebration of life
Self-effacement
Social correction
Upholding honesty over sham
Provoking thought
Balancing pain
Reinforcing or undermining stereotypes
Therapy or catharsis
Defense against, counter or parry attacks or threats
Survival

Each of the above functions are discussed further in the following:

Social Bonding

Vulnerable, mortal men and women would like to live as long and as well as possible. They will do so as long as they preserve their relationships, their social bonds, their means of mutual assistance. While Charles Darwin's monumental *On the Origin of Species* stressed the process of natural selection that popularized such familiar expressions as "survival of the fittest" and "the weak fall by the wayside," there was another view that emphasized cooperation and the survival of mutual assistance. That perspective was promoted in Petr Kropotkin's *Mutual Aid.* In that classic, Kropotkin painstakingly documented how individually weak or relatively defenseless creatures or members of a specie protect each other by gathering in collectivities such as families or herds to present a united front against whatever enemies threaten their existence. Musk-ox, for example, are well known for their survival on the tundra by forming a circle of formidable bulls, all facing outward against potential dangers while their cows and young huddle behind them. So it is with human beings, according to Kropotkin. No match for claws, fangs, talons, venom, speed, muscles, or body weight of other animals, human beings rely upon each other to work together in mutual aid or assistance. Human beings must be socially tied, socially bonded, in order to continue their individual lives.

Sociologists have pointed to consensus as the "social glue" that keeps diverse and sometimes conflicting elements in human societies, groups, or associations together. Prominent sociologist Louis Wirth stated:

"I regard the study of consensus as the central task of sociology, which is to understand the behavior of men insofar as that behavior is influenced by group life...because the mark of any society is the capacity of its members to understand one another and to act in concert toward common objectives and under common norms..." (Wirth, 1948).

What has humor to do with consensus? Humor is one of the major means to achieve consensus because it signals to individuals that they share common experiences, ideas, themes, or values. Pitchford (1960) identified humor as a "shortcut" to consensus because it quickly shows who may laugh and smile together and, at the same time, who may disagree, quarrel, and reject the qualities that others cherish.

Humorists seek to unite their audiences in some form of fellowship or comradery. To fail to do so, to fall short of the mark, is to, in the language of comedians, "lay an egg," "bomb out," or "fall on one's face." A sickening feeling in the pit of one's stomach is familiar to all those would-be comedians who tried to establish rapport with an audience and who were received instead with stony, cold, indifferent, shocked, or angry stares. "I died out there," says the frustrated comic. "My jokes went sour," says another. A *faux pas,* a blunder, a social indiscretion, a breach of propriety had occurred, and the audience was clearly telling the comic that his or her humor was not acceptable to them. Queen Victoria is reputed to have turned to a person who offered some off-color joke in her presence and figuratively cut him to ribbons with her response, *"We* are not amused."

Humor then is a consensus device that finds accord, a group-leveling effect that puts people on notice that they can laugh together, even for a fleeting moment, because they are bonded by their agreements and commonalities. Again, sociologically, their shared humor identifies them as members of the same "in-group." By the same token, "out-group" members would not laugh, would not view the humor as funny, and so would be set aside.

Relief from Stress and Strain

The Hobbesian figure of an early man exalting over the body of a conquered enemy clearly conveys the unburdening he felt once the stress of battle was over. He laughed, danced, and congratulated himself that he was alive and unscathed, a truly triumphant warrior.

Emerson's gynecological humor displayed this same use of humor to allow patients to deal with the stress of pelvic probings. Emerson wrote concerning the use of humor to maintain human dignity despite the embarrassing posture of the medical examination:

"How convenient to have a mode of communication labelled 'unimportant' in order to discuss important matters of which public significance cannot be publicly acknowledged. How convenient to be exempt from responsibility and free to convey matters for which one does not wish to accept the serious consequences. Behind the smokescreen of the official definition of humor as trivial, humor functions as a mode of indirect communication in the most serious of matters." (Emerson, 1960, p. 10)

By "kidding around," by good-natured banter, the female patients and their male doctors "got through" a stressful situation. Otherwise there would have been a medical impasse such as that reported by Robert Latou Dickinson in the early years of his gynecological practice when patients resisted the need to disrobe in his presence and persisted instead in discussing their "problem" seated in front of his desk (Dickinson & Beam, 1931).

Expression of Aggression or Hostility

Aggression, hostility, or social conflict is held by anthropologists to be a "universal," indicating that it is found in every known society or culture. On the other hand, the means of settling differences are varied and can be held to be "near-universals," those behavioral patterns that are widespread but may be lacking or underplayed in certain cultures. Warfare, for example, is a near-universal because Eskimos, before contact with other cultures, were relatively free from wars and other combative situations. Vilhjamur Stefansson horrified the Eskimos when he described how other people handle their conflicts (Stefansson, 1913). He reported that a number of them came to him after a sleepless night of debating among themselves and offered to send a missionary group of Eskimos to persuade the non-Eskimos to abandon their wars and to become instead converts to Eskimo-styles of handling their differences.

The Eskimos' technique for settling differences was to engage in juridical contests of insults or humorous sallies of wit to humiliate antagonists. The one who could express his contempt for his opponent in the most clever and sustained manner would be declared the winner. Herein humor is functioning effectively as an expression of aggression or hostility. In the vernacular, one has "topped the other" by heaping more insults than the other would muster, and serves as a less physically harmful way to resolve conflict.

The defusing of combative situations through humor is, of course, not confined to the Eskimos. Richard Stephenson (1951) identified such humorous forms of irony, satire, sarcasm, caricature, parody, lampooning, and burlesque as nothing more than "concealed malice." Through such styles, humorists may assault those with whom they disagree and still fall short of an actual physical attack of violence. The ill-will hidden in humor does no physical damage, but it disarms foes by revealing qualities they would much rather keep concealed. There is deep resentment in the cynic who redefined the Golden Rule as "the one who has the gold makes the rules." Such an observation notes that wealth and power are interlinked and the one making the observation lacks both.

Celebration of Life

Exuberance in the form of festivities is another function of humor. The

French, appropriately enough, call it the *joie de vivre,* the joy of life. The celebration of various rites of passage (Van Gennep, 1909) in which one's status is shed for another status such as birthdays, graduations, promotions, weddings, anniversaries, or retirements is a time for merriment and rejoicing. Even in funerals, the Irish wake is an example of celebrating the release of a soul to a happier, eternal life.

When the usual routines of ordinary days are set aside for holidays, people express their glee with parades, fireworks, feasts, dancing, music, drama, costume parties, masquerades, tomfoolery, or sporting events. The French celebrate "Bastille Day;" in Hong Kong and Thailand, there are "Dragon-Boat Races." New Orleans is the scene of the Mardi Gras. Pasadena, California, is the locale for the "Rose Parade" every New Year's Day. Thanksgiving serves as a harvest festival and Christmas, in the midst of winter, ushers in tremendous outbursts of giftgiving and generosity all in a spirit of goodwill and wholesome humor. In short, there is gleeful recourse to humor in celebrating the significant arrival of major events in the lives of individuals or in the lives of an entire society. Even at sea, there are ceremonials known as "Neptune Day," a boisterous initiation of those who have never crossed the Equator.

Self-Effacement

There is something to be said in favor of self-devaluation or self-humiliation rather than engaging in hostility or in indignation directed against others. In this usage of humor, the purveyor of humor makes himself or herself out to be inferior or lacking in sharp contrast to those qualities of superiority assigned to his or her audiences. Some animals lay on their backs and expose their throats to their opponents to indicate an acceptance of defeat or an unwillingness to fight. Fighting is thus avoided and each may go their way, satisfied that one is subordinate and the other is superordinate.

The late comedian, Jimmy Durante, used this style when he referred to himself as the "schnozzola." His audiences were alleged to be handsome - he was not. By such self-degradation, others were elevated to higher levels of respect or esteem. Charlie Chaplin's famous characterization of "The Little Tramp" allowed millions to identify with this humble man who, while inferior in status, was dignified and strong in meeting unbelievable odds stacked against him.

Self-effacement is a safe technique for comedians because it leaves audiences unscathed and safe from criticism while the comic suffers "the slings and arrows of outrageous fortune." Those who "play the fool" free their audiences from slipping on the banana peels of life. It serves both audiences and comics well to practice self-effacement.

Social Correction

Imperfection is a hallmark of humanity. Somehow, despite the presence of geniuses and brilliance among men and women, there are the nagging shortcomings, the failures to achieve utopias in social systems. Humor functions to correct human errors so that humanity may get back on course and steer toward greater heights and accomplishments.

From the perspective of the comic, there is grave need to call attention to the foolishness of current conditions lest they continue to some disastrous point of no return. To be sure, a humorist may be self-appointed, but he or she does not hesitate to give voice to ways and means to amend ongoing circumstances or actions before they destroy individuals or even total ways of life. This is an admirable use of humor, albeit not necessarily appreciated by those profiting from the *status quo* in the short run. For the many, however, humor that calls for change is warmly welcomed in many quarters and, for the comic, wins admiration and respect from many audiences for courageous behavior.

Social criticism then occurs in the guise of humor. It was the *Pogo* cartoon that had swamp creatures saying, "We have met the enemy and they is us." It was the cartoons of *Doonesbury* with their acidic attacks on prominent political figures that led many newspapers to place them on the editorial pages rather than on the funny pages. Berke Breathed's *Bloom County* takes aim at the foibles and ineptitudes of persons in high and low positions and audaciously exposes them to ridicule (Breathed, 1983). It was the antiwar sentiments of characters in *M.A.S.H.* that appealed to mass audiences of television viewers and earned the series such high marks. These are only some of the modern equivalents of the funny asides that dramatists throughout history have placed in the mouths of their characters. All this effort is meant to be instructive, persuasive, or cajoling in order to warn people to alter their behavior to avert pain or trouble that may yet arrive. Humor, in this function, is a type of "preventive medicine" at its best.

Upholding Honesty Over Sham

Humanity is also very adept at covering up its many mistakes. By a number of devices such as false pride, blind loyalty, or outright chicanery, people resort to deceit, pretense, and trickery to get their way.

Humor counters this sham or posturing by exposing the cover-ups, by tearing away the veils, the obstacles, or the "stonewalling," to endorse honesty and integrity. The child who exclaimed, "But the Emperor has no clothes!" was telling the truth and cutting through the smokescreens of fakery and hypocrisy of adults. Workers in Poland have exposed the pretense of communism that proclaims its dedication to the well-being of the proletariat. There is ironic humor in contemporary Poland that military law and its strictures must be imposed to forbid workers from organizing in their own interests.

This same use of humor is employed by minorities when they seek to make clear that majorities are oppressing them. Some feminists, particularly the more militant, enjoy pointing out how men have kept women subordinated. Blacks take careful aim at whites who speak knowingly about freedom and rights for their countrymen but who ignore the conditions imposed upon "those with color." Hispanics delight in exposing the ignorance of "gringos" who do not share their traditions. Jewish people will employ humor among themselves when they note the centuries of anti-Semitism they have endured at the hands of Christians who have said that love is a central tenet of their faith. Students employ humor when they identify certain "educators" as really "propagandists" for special causes who select supportive information while neglecting other data that may be in conflict.

Many find humor useful in exposing the physicians who harm more patients than they heal. Many workers turn to humor to expose the fumblings and bumblings of mismanagement. Holding these things up to ridicule encourages those involved to rid themselves of deceit eventually.

Provoking Thought

A major function of humor is to provoke thought. While many humorists feel their efforts are rewarded by raucous laughter, there are others who seek to promote thought that does not surface in observable laughter. Instead their objective is to provoke their audiences to weigh information and to consider where it might lead. The result is often quiet, silent, or subtle response that takes considerable time before observable reactions can be detected. The "knowing smile" of the Mona Lisa is a case in point. Whatever brought on this captivating reaction, the painter captured this fleeting, enigmatic smile of a thoughtful lady. Viewers of this portrait have speculated on what evoked that knowledgeable smile. The stimulus, whatever it was, certainly was something that was intellectual in nature. Her secret thoughts were well controlled, but the glimmer of amusement in her face did show through.

Thought processes, of course, are too complex to be necessarily registered on the human face. Those who play poker are familiar with the advantages of maintaining a straight "poker face" that in no way hints what cards a player holds. Nevertheless, behind this facial mask, the mind is busy planning strategic moves to gain the bets on the table. The target of intellectual humor is the mind and not the prolonged laughter or applause of receptive audiences.

Balancing Pain

Humor functions well when it counters pain. Humorists are not naive in the sense of insisting that life is supposed to be pleasant. Rather, they are quite familiar with human anguish and seek instead to remind their audiences that discomforts are tolerable because there are rewards in life as well. Much humor is generated by the desire of comics to lighten human burdens and to encourage persons to deal directly with their difficulties, or at least to put their problems momentarily aside. This is the gist of the lyrics of a popular song, "Eliminate the negative, accentuate the positive."

Reinforcing or Undermining Stereotypes

In journalism, the need to create tremendous numbers of identical pages of print led to the development of stereotypes. Composed type makes an original paper-mache of type metal. This single mold can then make as many copies as a publisher wishes.

Sociologists have adopted the concept of stereotypes for their own purposes. They apply stereotyping to the allegations that a given group of people can be characterized as having certain identical qualities that distinguish them from all other groups. These stereotypes are pictures or ideas carried about in the minds of people that the individuals in a targeted group are "all alike." These "stereotypes" may contain partial truths or half-truths but not necessarily whole truths. They are convenient "short cuts" to thinking that allow members of out-groups to regard members of some in-group as persons "cut from the same cloth." The end result is the assumption by those who accept stereotypes that they have prior knowledge about a given people and can treat them accordingly. Stereotypic thinking plays a major role in the prejudgments or prejudices found in many societies. These assumptions of homogeneity seriously affect the ways in which various groups of people are received or treated.

Humor draws upon this stereotyping in at least two different ways. It may reinforce stereotypes, or it may seek to undercut them. The first function is the most commonly employed. The second function becomes operable when targeted groups or their defenders seek to turn the tables on their detractors and show them to be seriously in error about their conceptions.

In the first and most common application of stereotypes, "the stage is set," so to speak so that humorists do not have to resort to elaborate explanations about the premises of their humor. Audiences are supposedly well-informed about the nature of a given group of people and "make the connections" easily. For example, the stereotype of rich and powerful Texans underlies the one-liner about the Texan who purchased a chemistry outfit for his son for Christmas — DuPont!

In the second application, stereotyping itself becomes the target for ridicule and is satirically undermined by demonstrating that there are exceptions to these widely held myths. The stereotyping of black Americans as "slow" became the object of much humor until Jesse Owens out-ran all competitors at the 1936 Olympic games. In a more recent example of a stereotype becoming the object of ridicule, pro-feminists have popularized the bumper-sticker that reads, "A woman's place is in the House — and in the Senate!" Sociologists expose what is called "the particularistic fallacy," that is, knowing certain particulars about human groups or organizations does not mean that all particulars are known. Whenever perpetrators of sweeping generalizations about a given social group insist that their descriptions and interpretations have universal applications, sociologists need only point out a single case that is an exception to such general rules. In fact, sociologists are able to cite numerous exceptions to stereotypic allegations so that in the end stereotypes are revealed for what they really are: unfair, invalid characterizations that fall short of accurate descriptions of complex, heterogeneous groups.

Therapy or Catharsis

The therapeutic benefits of humor have long been known. In recent years, however, this function of humor has received much more attention through the publications of Raymond A. Moody, Jr. (1978) and Norman Cousins (1979). The remarkable recovery of Cousins from a life-threatening illness by the incorporation of humor into his medical care has brought humor a new respect in medical circles, calling upon Cousins to alert trainees in medical schools to the potential therapeutic value of humor. One hospital has gone so far as to include a "laughing room" in their facilities, just as they routinely offer a chapel for those seeking religious solace. Cousins found that by getting regular "dosages" of film comedies and other bits of humor he gained needed rest and a rallying of his energies to fight his bodily afflictions. Moody, a physician, makes the same point in his book, *Laugh After Laugh, the Healing Power of Humor.* The ancients who spoke of being in "good humors" were not far off the mark when they realized that enjoyment of humor was a good catalyst for digestion, respiration, circulation, and muscle-tone.

Defense Against, Counter, or Parry Attacks or Threats

Tendentious wit has a preselected target, and it attacks this target through humorous assaults. Tendentious wit is "wit with a barb," and it hurls this barb in all the media that conveys humor. The hostile nature of such humor has already been noted. As also noted in the countering of stereotypes, humor can confound would-be enemies and thwart their intentions. Akin to karate or judo, the energy expended by an antagonist is used to trip them up. In the annual celebration of Purim, for example, there is rejoicing among Jewish people over the hanging of the wicked Haman on gallows he had prepared for the execution of Persian Jews. This transformation of a threat into a new lease on life is cause for great good humor. Similar to the popular booing of villains in the melodramas of the past, there is widespread rejoicing as the villain gets his "come-uppance." To this day Jewish children are given hand-held "greggars" or noisemakers to drown out the name of Haman when the story of Esther is recited. Haman is the ancient counterpart of Adolf Hitler who initiated genocide in Germany in the midst of World War II.

Survival

The single concept that subsumes all the social functions of humor is survival. In social bonding, relief from stress and strain, expressing aggression or hostility, celebrating life, self-effacement, social correction, upholding honesty over pretense, provoking thought, balancing pain, reinforcing or undermining stereotypes, therapy, and defense against threats or attacks, humor helps humanity endure. When the substantive areas in which humor operates are examined, the thesis that humor is a survival mechanism can be documented.

Humor as Social Control or Social Conflict

Sociologists have developed a number of macrotheories designed to analyze and synthesize data concerning societies, groups, aggregates, or categories. Each provides a framework that systematically organizes data and suggests what further investigations are needed. Structural-functionalism focuses upon social forms and what services are performed. Symbolic interaction concentrates on the ways persons affect each other through shared symbols and their meanings. Exchange theory deals with the reciprocal nature of human behaviors. An integrated view has been to draw upon each of these theories in terms of their strengths and to avoid wherever possible their weaknesses or shortcomings.

Two particular perspectives have emerged from these theories, however: one is *conflict theory* and the other is *control theory*. Conflict theory takes a critical stance concerning the struggle between various factions within society and reveals the domination of power elites over the exploited masses of people. Control theory, by contrast, is more accepting and less critical of conditions as they currently seem to exist. The former studies clashing interests of opposing groups, and the latter investigates the *status quo* in terms of its stability and predictable effects.

The study of humor from a sociological perspective should take into account whatever theories exist and pay particular attention to conflict and control tendencies. Aggressive or hostile humor falls into the conflict worldview; milder, less quarrelsome, more fun-oriented humor falls into the control model.

One application of control theory is the employment of humor as a "safety valve," a blowing off of steam without doing harm to participants or to established social orders. Authority figures would predictably approve of such "shenanigans." Merchants, for example, whose storefronts were once the targets for candle-waxings have learned during Halloween to sponsor art contests in which budding artists can apply water color designs to front windows. Destructive potentials are thus redirected toward more constructive activities.

Astronauts who are engaged in missions involving millions of dollars and who are carefully screened and intensively trained for their space explorations are not above humorous hijinks. One astronaut, in full view of his earthbound superiors and his television audience, suddenly hit a golf ball while on the surface of the moon. Another astronaut from the U.S. Navy secretly arranged for the playing of the song *Anchors Aweigh* just when he blasted off the lunar surface.

In a more serious context, the conflict and control functions of humor were aptly described by Gustave Dupreel (1928) when he called attention to "the laughter of inclusion and the laughter of exclusion." On the one hand, people enjoy humor that expresses comradery, and on the other hand, they put others on notice that they do not "belong." This in-group versus out-group humor brings into play both conflict between groups and control within groups.

Cameron illustrates the conflict-control duality in humor when he wrote about the loyalties of Protestants, Catholics, and Jews as follows:

"An Irishman was working on a sewer in a red-light district when he noticed a Protestant clergyman enter one of the houses. He turned to his helper and said, 'There now! Isn't that just what I always said about them Protestants, their clergy and all! Oh, the shame of it!' A few moments later a rabbi followed suit. 'Yes,' observed the Irishman, 'and it goes for them, too. Birds of a feather, y'know!' In the course of time, the parish priest appeared and he, too, entered the same house. 'Well, what do you know about that,' said Pat, 'one of the poor girls must be sick!'" (Cameron, 1963, p. 88).

Not all sociologists agree that conflict and control are adequate explanations of humor. Barron (1950), for instance, seriously questioned that humor used against outsiders simultaneously controls the loyalties of those within a group. Rather, he suspected that much of the humor directed against a group was generated, supported, and enjoyed by the targeted group itself.

A remarkable example is found in the humor of "the Irish Bull," a derivative of the ridiculous blunders in speech made by an Obediah Bull, an Irish lawyer who practiced at the English Bar about mid-18th century. Bull is reported to have said such "brilliant" things as "a stone coffin should last a man a lifetime" (Esar, 1952). The unintentional humor of the Bull is significant because it is humor directed against a witless Irishman, generated by Irish people, and enjoyed by Irish people.

Barron's questioning of simultaneous conflict and control usages of humor asked why "victims" of humor invent such humor and even encourage it within their own ranks. One hypothesis worth testing is that while in-groups recognize that out-groups are in conflict with them, they also recognize that they must keep control of the membership under fire. By reminding its membership of out-group antagonisms, in-group solidarity is enhanced against a common foe. The paradox applies to members of families who actually enjoy poking fun at each other but who would resent the same humor if it came from outsiders. Family members are willing to acknowledge their human weaknesses and shortcomings among themselves but they close ranks and present a solid front before nonfamily members. The taunts of enemies directed against the morale of military forces can and have strengthened the resolve of military units rather than destroying the bonds that unite them.

Burns (1953) offered another explanation when he distinguished between *banter* and *irony*. Banter was defined by Burns as humor in which consensus was shared. This is to say that members of a group understood each other well enough to laugh together about their own shortcomings. Irony, by contrast, was defined by Burns as humor in which consensus was withheld. By this means, irony excluded others from social discourse and increased the social distance from outsiders. Banter is used when boys and girls, men and women, engage in the polite fiction of being very interested in each other but, at the same time, withdraw into their own ranks by teasing and by drawing opponents onto unsafe grounds. By this double-pronged maneuver, males and females do not lose favor with representatives of their own sex and yet gain something of value from persons of the opposite sex.

Studies by Middleton and Moland (1959) and Goldwin (1960) confirmed the use of humor among blacks as self-initiated and group-supported humor that results in internal group control. The fabrication of such humor, while for all outward appearances was in conflict with whites, achieved effective control and cohesiveness among blacks themselves.

The same double functioning of humor is observed among professional people or among those engaged in the same occupation. In each instance there is banter, horseplay, or shared humor of a commonality accomplished under a framework of "fun" or nonseriousness. At the same time, there is awareness that those outside a profession or job are critical and that the safest and wisest course is to stand together in mutual support of their activities.

Summary and Conclusions

The concerns of sociologists and humorists are interlinked. Sociologists study human groups and the patterns and processes that they create. A universal, humor is found in all societies and their subgroups and invites sociological analyses, interpretations, and applications because humor is both a group product and a group process. Groups do present serious, even tragic, qualities that require sobering and sensible treatment. Groups, however, also deal in humor, and sociologists have begun to participate in studying humor in terms of its social significance.

Furthermore, humor serves groups well through their social functions. Social bonding, relief from stress and strain, expressing aggression or hostility, celebrating life, self-effacement, social correction, upholding honesty over sham, provoking thought, balancing pain, reinforcing or undermining stereotypes, therapy or catharsis, and defending against attacks or threats are among the major services and actions being taken through humor. These and possibly more are suggested to be a part of the need for human beings and their groups to survive against all odds. People and their social groups are dedicated to the proposition of continuing, of being ongoing, of enduring. It would be difficult to find individuals and groups who seek their own demise.

Finally, sociologists have documented the presence of both conflict and control among human groups. Humor again in terms of these concerns is operative. Humor can be a devastating weapon of attack. It can also be used to keep control of group members by shoring up group morale. The paradox of a group fostering humor that both attacks its own integrity and yet keeps its members from breaking ranks is a fascinating phenomenon. Some studies have attempted to explain why in-groups promote such humor, but more study and analyses are needed.

STUDY QUESTIONS

1. What characteristics of sociology and humor tie them together?

2. Is the assertion of the universality of humor warranted? Could there possibly be some society that is devoid of humor in any form or manifestation?

3. Can you suggest any other social functions of humor that were ignored or neglected in this chapter?

4. Offer a critique of the "survival" theme suggested as the common thread that runs through all of the social functions of humor.

5. Just how does humor help individuals and their groups cope with the exigencies of societal life?

6. Aside from the extrinsic values of humor, is there intrinsic value to humor?

7. How does "self-effacement" become useful to individuals?

8. Granting that humor seeks social corrections or changes, exactly how is this achieved through humor?

9. In what ways does sham or pretense serve those who use it? How much approval or support can be anticipated when humorists seek to expose false appearances?

10. What new information or insights are encouraged through such cartoons as *Doonesbury* or *Bloom County*?

11. Why do humorists derive such satisfaction from their activities?

12. Why do in-groups tolerate humor among their members that is critical of them?

Suggested Readings

Barron, Milton L., "A Content Analysis of Intergroup Humor." *American Sociological Review,* 15 (Feb., 1950): 88-94.

Breathed, Berke, *Bloom County.* Boston: Little, Brown, 1983.

Burns, Tom, "Friends, Enemies, and the Polite Fiction." *American Sociological Review,* 18 (Dec., 1953): 654-662.

Cameron, William Bruce, *Informal Sociology, A Casual Introduction to Sociological Thinking.* N.Y.: Random House, 1963.

Cousins, Norman, *Anatomy of an Illness, Reflections on Healing and Regeneration.* N.Y.: W.W. Norton, 1979.

Darwin, Charles, *On the Origin of Species: A Facsimile of the First Edition with an Introduction by Ernst Mayr.* (Harvard Univ. Press, 1964). N.Y.: Atheneum, 1967.

Dickinson, Robert L. and Laura Beam, *A Thousand Marriages, A Medical Study of Sex Adjustment.* Baltimore, MD: Williams & Wilkins, 1931.

Dupreel, Gustave, "La Problems Sociologique du Rire," *Revue Philosophique,* Annee 53 (1928): 214-248.

Emerson, Joan Paret, *Social Functions of Humor in a Hospital Setting.* Unpublished doctoral dissertation. Berkeley, CA: University of California, 1960.

Esar, Evan, *The Humor of Humor, The Art and Techniques of Popular Comedy Illustrated by Comic Sayings, Funny Stories, and Jocular Traditions Throughout the Centuries.* N.Y.: Horizon Press, 1952.

Goldwin, Morris, *The Sociology of Negro Humor.* Unpublished doctoral dissertation. N.Y: New School for Social Research, 1960.

Kropotkin, Petr, *Mutual Aid, A Factor of Evolution.* Foreword by Ashley Montagu and "Struggle for Existence" by Thomas Huxley. Boston: Extending Horizons Books, 1976.

Middleton, Russell and John Moland, "Humor in Negro and White Subcultures," *American Sociological Review,* 24 (Feb., 1959): 61-69.

Moody, Jr., Raymond A., *Laugh After Laugh, The Healing Power of Humor.* Jacksonville, FL: Headwaters Press, 1978.

Pitchford, Henry Grady, *The Social Functions of Humor.* Unpublished doctoral dissertation. Atlanta, GA: Emory University, 1960.

Roucek, Joseph S., *et al., Social Control.* 2nd edition. Princeton, NJ: Van Nostrand, 1956.

Stefansson, Vilhjamur, *My Life with the Eskimo.* N.Y.: Macmillan, 1913.

Stephenson, Richard M., "Conflict and Control Function of Humor." *American J. of Sociology,* 56 (May, 1951): 569-574.

Van Gennep, A., *Les Rites De Passage.* Paris: Nourry, 1909.

Chapter 3:

Psycho-Social Treatment of Humor

When it comes to the study of humor, psychology has by far demonstrated its willingness to include it as a legimiate topic of investigation. Sociology has lagged behind in its recognition of humor as a substantive specialization within its field but is "catching up" as more sociologists become involved in its study and analysis.

In a summary of studies of humor made by psychologists, sociologists, anthropologists, philosophers, and other scholars since the 1900s, Alford (1979) found that psychology was the leading discipline, with sociology rated as next to last (see Figure 3-1 below):

Figure 3-1
Humor Studies by Discipline and Decade

Decade:	Psychology	Sociology	Anthropology	Philosophy	Other	Total
1970s	257	27	36	5	93	418
1960s	124	22	28	2	106	282
1950s	64	13	9	2	56	144
1940s	43	9	13	2	25	92
1930s	47	2	2	2	27	80
1920s	25	2	0	3	36	66
1910s	12	0	2	1	10	25
1900s	6	0	0	2	4	12
	578	75	90	19	357	1119

Source: Richard Dane Alford, *Humor and the Structures of Responsibility and Play.* Doctoral Dissertation, University of Pittsburgh, 1979; Table A, p. 43. (By permission of the author)

Another source supporting the leadership of psychologists in studying humor over the same period as Alford's is Goldstein and McGhee's work (1972), presenting an annotated bibliography of published research papers on humor over a 70-year period. They continued their work with a two-volume handbook in which basic issues related to the measurement of humor and applied studies are discussed (McGhee & Goldstein, 1983).

"Turf" - The Humor of Disciplinary Boundaries

Among scholars in colleges and universities, disciplinary boundaries are carefully guarded, much as in the geopolitical world where political boundaries are zealously watched. Traditional understandings that certain topics are the exclusive domain of certain disciplinary specialists usually go unchallenged. Those who labor within these disciplinary fields of inquiry have undergone years of training, and they are normatively regarded as the stewards of disciplinary techniques, theories, findings, and applications. All others who have an interest in a given disciplinary field are welcome as long as they do not seek to claim as their own some hard-won data or insights. Interlopers, invaders, or those seeking power and prestige at the expense of those already committed to a specific discipline can expect considerable reactions of indignation or outrage that may well include satiric humor.

Predictably, those disciplines that share close concerns are the academic areas in which disciplinary "turf" becomes the subject of much discussion, negotiations, or disguised hostilities in the form of satire. Griessman (1974) presents such as example in a polite but satiric exchange of memoranda between a mythical psychology and sociology department on some campus over what is exclusively psychological and similarly sociological academic "territory."

Humor itself is an interdisciplinary topic because it cuts across long-established academic boundaries. Each discipline makes major contributions to the study of humor. Specialists in English, comparative literature, drama, speech, forensics, journalism, art, music, history, philosophy, anthropology, recreation, health, telecommunications, political science, education, languages, and business administration are privy to aspects of humor that need to be shared and discussed by those interested in understanding what humor is all about and why it is significant in human affairs.

An eclectic approach to humor does require drawing upon whatever contributions each discipline can make. Within this discourse, however, this exposition stresses a sociological perspective to bring out how the discipline of sociology can specifically enhance the comprehension of humor in human society. And, within this chapter, the common concerns of sociology and psychology are highlighted in the psycho-social analyses of humor.

What are some of the common concerns of the two fields of sociology and psychology that lend themselves to a psycho-social analysis of humor? These involve matters that concern individuals in group or social situations. Unique personality patternings, individuality, and personal health or well-being in the form of mental, emotional, and social health are paramount in such an analysis. Closer examination of these aspects can begin to deepen the understanding of how humor interacts with individuals, one affecting the other.

Humor and Personality

By personality, we mean the subjective reflection of both internal and external environments for a given person. Psychologists deal with the biological, physiological, biochemical, and uniquely individualistic mechanisms that underlie personality traits and patterns. Sociologists deal more with social milieus, the external environments, such as dyadic relationships, small group interactional settings, subcultures, countercultures, or overall sociocultural systems that are internalized or interpreted in positive and negative ways by individuals. Bits and pieces of these external systems are encountered, weighed, evaluated, and selected as significant items to be retained or rejected, to be intepreted in some fashion, and finally to be incorporated into the individual's personality or makeup. In less technical language, experiences, whether they originate from within a person or outside the person, affect persons differently and result in established, well-developed characteristics that affect individual behavior.

Humor and Creative Personalities

Humor is one of the products of creative beings who seem to be more sharply sensitive or "tuned in" to humorous episodes or situations. They call attention to the presence of humor where most people may never have looked or been aware. For their own purposes, they detect in the most commonplace events of the day an opportunity to exercise their keen senses of humor. Or without waiting for some stimulus actually to occur, they can contrive a humorous event out of imaginary circumstances and present it in a delightful, artful, talented way.

All creative personalities do not necessarily attune their talents to recognize humor in interpersonal relationships or feel impelled to concoct some imaginative scenarios. When their concentration is fixed upon serious matters in which humor would be inappropriate and unwelcome, they bring their talents into play in a "no-nonsense," sober, effective way. However, there is empiric evidence that supports the contention that creative personalities do have a keener sense of humor than more prosaic individuals.

Berelson and Steiner (1964) compiled an extraordinary inventory of scientific findings on human behavior, and reported:

"Highly creative people are more likely than others to view authority as conventional rather than absolute; to make fewer black-and-white distinctions; to have a less dogmatic and more relativistic view of life; to show more independence of judgment and less conventionality and conformity, both intellectual and social; to be more willing to entertain and sometimes express their own 'irrational' impulses; *to place greater value on humor and in fact to have a better sense of humor* (emphasis added); in short, to be somewhat freer and less rigidly controlled."

Their summations agree that humor does afford relief, a release from tension, or serves as a liberating force from the shackles of social conventions. Unlike others who plod along, who conform to whatever is required of them, who internalize social expectations through personality rigidity, creative personality types break away from grinding routinization and automatic programming of their lives. They refuse to become what Yablonsky (1972) calls *robopaths*, "walking computers" who display rigid, uncompromising, authoritarian personality attributes, who cannot see humor in any topic of deepest concern to themselves or in the manner in which they conduct their affairs. These robopaths are "machine-made simulations of people," in Yablonsky's terms, who are characterized by their dedication to ritualism, orientation to the past, conformity, image-involvement, "acompassion," hostility, self-righteousness, and alienation.

Because humor is a very human quality, those who divorce themselves from the rest of humanity, those who cannot put themselves into the roles of others, those who cannot imagine the feelings of others brought about by their own actions, those who cannot identify with others, take on the mechanist, machine-like qualities of robopaths and are the most likely candidates to view the world as a cold, unhappy, desolate place in which humor has no reason to exist.

Robopathic personalities become themselves the butts of humor because, once set in gear, they will behave precisely as they were programmed to respond and drive machine-like into a solid wall or over a cliff to their own destruction. Like robots in automobile factories, they will work tirelessly, efficiently, and without complaint. But neither will they smile, joke, relax, enjoy, empathize, or sense the humor of their lives and surroundings.

Psychoanalytic View of Humor

The founder of psychoanalysis, Sigmund Freud, was aware of humor and explained it in relation to the unconscious by use of his constructs of id, ego, and superego (1960). To Freud, that which was held to be comical, witty, or humorous depended largely upon releasing energies usually held in check by the superego. Freud saw comic relief in transforming a painful episode into a pleasurable event through "an economy of thought." Energy buildups that would normally be released through psychic channels are censored by the superego. By *thinking* about forbidden behaviors, the pent-up energies are thereby released and the results are laughter and enjoyment.

Wit, from Freud's perspective, is derived from circumventing the superego's disallowance of either regression or aggression by *comprehension* of situations. This understanding is pleasurable or ego-rewarding to the person (Strachey, 1960). The ego has triumphed over the superego and is celebrating its victory.

Pitchford (1960) built on this psychoanalytic interpretation of humor by distinguishing between wit and the broader field of humor. Wit was defined by Pitchford as "the felicitous association between ideas and words not usually connected to produce amusing surprise." Wit involved "a swift perception of the ludicrous." Further, wit was contrived deliberately, artfully, and with an emotional content that was potentially hostile. Humor, by contrast, was seen by Pitchford to be the "quality of a happening, action, situation, or expression of ideas that appeals to the ludicrous." Humor was "more leisurely executed," used media other than words, such as a picture, a dramatic interaction, an experience, or a feeling-state that situationally evolves into something funny, hilarious, or amusing; it could contain an admixture of affection and tended to be natural and spontaneous.

In these distinctions, Pitchford joins with others who have observed that "brevity is the soul of wit." Many delight in the ability of a wit to cut through long, drawn-out, convoluted, complicated information to arrive at some brilliant capsulation. Audiences say to themselves "how true that is" and store the statement for future reference. It can apply to a variety of personal situations.

The essence of humor, however, may not be in terms of its brevity. Rather there is humor in performances in which the punchline or climax is delayed. All along the recitation of a storyline or plot are strung amusing bits and pieces that please and inform audiences. This is the art of the playwright, raconteur, monologist, speaker, or entertainer who offers a sustained performance with many laughs along the way rather than a single laugh before the conclusion.

The Favorite Joke Hypothesis

The relationship between humor and personality can also be revealed through "the favorite joke hypothesis." This postulates that the type of humor that particularly appeals to an individual reflects or reveals a great deal about that person's personality. If the hypothesis has merit, it would predict, for example, that aggressive persons would gravitate toward frequent usage and appreciation of hostile humor. Further it would anticipate that speakers and writers would be inclined to rely heavily upon word humor or wordplay. It would be vindicated if modest, unassuming persons would favor self-effacement in their humor rather than assaults upon the integrity of others.

The favorite joke hypothesis seems to have logical or face validity, but it does need to be tested before it can find acceptability among scholars. Both humor and personality may be too complex to be revealed through findings that certain types of humor are more appealing to certain types of individuals than other types of humor. Nevertheless, there are persons who make the assumption that personality is mirrored in preferences or choices. Perhaps persons who enjoy a broad spectrum of humor forms or styles can be shown to have multifaceted natures rather some single-minded concerns. This too would suggest that the favorite joke hypothesis can be documented. As the study of humor continues, further research should establish, reject, or qualify the hypothesis.

Humor and Health

Health has been defined by the World Health Organization as a "state of complete physical, mental, and social well-being, not merely the absence of disease or infirmity" (Mangus, 1948). In short, health not only consists of physical fitness and stamina but also mental, emotional, spiritual, and social aspects that are conducive to vigor, vitality, and vivaciousness.

Health undoubtedly is positively correlated with humor. The sounder the health, the more likely greater amounts of humor will be manifested. The weaker the health, the less likely humor will be present.

Correlation, of course, does not prove causation. Further there remains a problem with the complexity of humor and the complexity of health. Is humor still present when a physically sick person makes wry jokes about his or her condition? Is a mentally disturbed individual prone to use bizarre, hypercritical humor against perceived conditions or imaginary enemies? Much depends upon what one means by humor and its manifestations.

Connections between health and humor have been made by a variety of persons. Theologians have said, "Mirth is God's medicine." Folklorists are fond of saying, "Humor is the best medicine" a person can buy. Medical practitioners, too, know that humor is a useful device to maintain or foster homeostasis, the tendency to keep internal stability through a coordinated response to any disruptive assault upon a person's body. Physicians have found that, as a result of being in a state of well-being or good humor, there is a stabilization of blood pressure, oxygenation of the blood, massage for vital organs, stimulation of circulation, improvement of digestion, and a relaxation of the numerous systems of the body. Satchel Paige, one of American baseball's immortals, said it rather ineloquently but well when

he observed, "humor is good for your gizzard!" There is an overall eupho-
ria, or in the language of some, a "high," that humor brings out in individuals.

As discussed earlier in terms of the therapeutic benefits of humor, the
celebrated case of Norman Cousins, who successfully fought off the rare,
degenerative spinal disease known as anklosing spondylitis with a regimen
of comic films and videotapes helped publicize the connection between humor and good health. Cousins (1979) reported that for every hour he could
laugh, he could get a refreshing hour of deep sleep that would help him
fight the disease that was racking his body.

The Cousins case, of course, is not proof positive that humor *per se* cures
disease. Cousins went along with the medical treatment prescribed by his
physician. His "humor dosages" were in addition to established medical
procedures for his illness. Which regimen then was a causative factor in his
recovery? The best that could be said in favor of using humor, as Cousins
did, is that it did not interfere with his medical treatment and may possibly
have served to make him more receptive to medical therapies. Further,
there is the commonsense observation by many that the "bedside manners" of physicians and nurses and the supportive attention and concern of
relatives and friends through pleasant visits or messages go a long way as
catalytic agents in convalescence.

Uncontrolled, Undesirable Laughter

There is other evidence that suggests that what appears to be a response
to humor is, in itself, a symptom of ill health or disease. Laughter that is
uncontrolled, undesirable, or involuntary may be symptomatic of underlying disease or poor health. While hearty, self-controlled, desirable laughter seems to parallel good health, the presence of laughter at inappropriate
times may signal a deterioration of health.

Kuru, for example, is a disease found among the 12,000 members of the
Fore tribe, who live in the highlands of New Guinea. Known as "the laughing death," its victims experience tremors, lack of coordination, and in the
final stages before death, paroxysms of uncontrollable laughter (McElroy
& Townsend, 1979).

Women in the Fore tribe fall prey to *kuru* at a ratio of 25 to one man. The
disease has been attributed to the ritual cannibalism of the Fore whose
women consume the brains of dead relatives. With the stopping of this
practice and the development of a cash crop economy from coffee production under Australian administration that moved the people from their former magical reliance on relatives in a hunting-gathering economy, the
laughing-death cases have been brought under control.

There are diseases other than *kuru* that can led to unprovoked, inappropriate laughter or silly facial expressions as part of their symptomol-
ogy (Moody, 1978). These include pseudobulbar palsy, multiple sclerosis,

amytrophic lateral sclerosis (ALS, - 'Lou Gehrig' disease), Wilson's disease, and epilepsy.

Mood-altering substances also produce uninhibited laughter and unrewarding gaiety. Ingestion or inhalation of alcohol, marijuana, nitrous oxide, manganese, and strychnine can produce such results. Gales of laughter over trivial or even serious matters are easily provoked when such substances have been taken into the body. There is a narcotizing effect described as the "loosening of inhibitions" that seems to occur after these substances are taken. Nightclub comics are aware that some of the responses they evoke in audiences may not be due entirely to their efforts to be funny but are due, rather, to alcohol consumption with its anticipated results.

Lastly, there are the "pre-senile dementias," such as Alzheimer's disease and Pick's disease, that manifest *moria,* a tendency for frivolity that refuses to treat serious matters seriously. In all such cases, the laughing response to humor does not necessarily represent good health but rather a departure from it.

It is important to note that in addition to organic diseases, there are mental or emotional illnesses that are associated with uncontrollable, undesirable, unrewarding, malfunctioning hilarity or departures from normal expectations in response to humor. Among them are depression, schizophrenia, paranoid states, mania, and hysteria. In each of these illnesses, nonhumorous and humorous responses may be symptoms of grave difficulties that require professional treatment.

Humor and Disparagement

One of the puzzles that still confronts those who study humor is why stimuli that make certain individuals laugh, enjoy, savor, delight, or be amused can also produce an opposite reaction in other individuals. This is particularly noticeable in disparagement humor which attacks, denigrates, downgrades, demeans or otherwise devalues persons or their affiliations. The humiliation of some victims or targeted groups is amusing or funny to some individuals but the identical procedure is held to be unfunny, nonhumorous, unacceptable, and even malicious as far as other individuals are concerned.

Disparagement humor would seem to be easily explained by the superiority conferred upon those who are down-grading others and the rejection of such humor by those who are the butts of the laughter or ridicule. But this does not explain why certain individuals who are either in the alleged superior group doing the disparaging or who are not connected with those being disparaged find such humor repugnant or not humorous at all.

A number of studies have tested hypotheses that prior dispositions or affiliation explain the differential reactions to disparagement humor. Wolff,

Smith and Murray (1934) tested the proposition that unaffiliated objects, anything not associated with certain individuals, are acceptable targets for humorous assaults. To poke fun at affiliated objects, however, is tantamount to disparaging one's self and this type of demoralization is far removed from being humorous at least from the point of view of the disparaged. Thus, Wolff and his collaborators found that their prediction that jokes disparaging Jews would be less appreciated by Jews than by non-Jews was confirmed. In addition, they found that men enjoyed humor that down-graded women more than women did. Similarly, women registered higher degrees of appreciation for humor that denigrated men than did men.

La Fave and his collaborators (1961, 1972, 1976) refined this dispositional approach by specifying "unaffiliated objects" to be "negative reference groups" or "negative identification classes." Those that were "objects of affection" were held to be "positive reference groups" or "positive identification classes." As Zillman and Cantor (1976) indicated, these specifications led to the awkward conclusion that seeing good things happen to friendly persons or categories is cause for humor. Such a circumstance may be enjoyable, but is not necessarily funny. There remains the need to explain why some Jews find humor in anti-Jewish sallies, some blacks find humor in disparagment of blacks, or some women find humor in negative judgments of women.

Zillman (1983) suggests that research efforts should concentrate more upon attitudes or personal predispositions to respond to certain stimuli rather than previous studies that concentrated upon broad, overall categories to predict humorous response. Thus, there is reason to believe that the sharing of common labels, categories, or group affiliations does not predict the acceptance or rejection of humor aimed at disparaging one's own group, affiliation, or classification. What may well explain why some Jews, blacks, or women do not necessarily align themselves with all Jews, blacks, and women in rejecting disparagement of their own kind is that they hold attitudes based upon prior socialization that differs markedly from those normatively ascribed to their affiliation. There is thus no monolithic consensus that Jews, blacks, and women think alike or hold to some common view of themselves as above reproach or humorous attacks.

Zillman himself remains skeptical that enjoyment of disparagement qualifies as adequate humor theory. He does note that dispositional analyses, at best, can predict "how funny a disparaging event will be to whom," but fails to predict "whether or not it will be funny in the first place." Questions still remain concerning the nature of humor itself, and these will be posed and eventually answered by ongoing psycho-social research and analyses.

Summary and Conclusions

Psycho-social analyses of humor are concerned with the common ground shared by psychologists and sociologists that deals with relationships between individuals and their respective groups. At times the boundary lines between these disciplines may be disputed seriously, but they also provide the bases for humorous treatment in which the situation is defused and understood to be the result of common concerns. How can groups be studied without ever considering individual members of groups? Or how can individuals be studied without reference to other individuals or the groups in which they operate?

Humor itself is an interdisciplinary field of inquiry and thus draws upon whatever disciplines can contribute through their distinctive theories or research. In this chapter the focus is upon a selection of topics in which social psychologists or psycho-sociologists appear to have a shared interest. These are personality, health and disparagement, which are examined in terms of their relationship to humor.

Creative personalities, for instance, have been found to be more likely than others to treat authority as a matter of social convention rather than one of uncritical acceptance. Such creative types are prone to distinguish shades of meanings rather than more simplistic dichotomies. Finally, because they are less bound by societal demands, they are willing to both entertain and express impulses or ideas that others either suppress or rarely consider.

Those individuals who are robopathic, rigid and unbending about what they believe or have been trained to believe, display a minimal or marginal sense of humor in contrast to the senses of humor so markedly displayed by creative individuals who relish getting off the beaten paths now and then.

Psychoanalytic theory holds that humor is derived from transforming pains into pleasures by an economy of thought. By thinking about forbidden behaviors, energies formerly held in check are released and are vented through laughter and enjoyment. Wit was distinguishable from humor by comprehension of situations, and this understanding ego rewards the individual according to psychoanalytic theory. As Freud put it, the ego has triumphed over the superego and is celebrating its victory.

One means to test or reflect personality attributes is to determine what type of jokes are the favorite styles of individuals. This projective technique can begin to suggest what kinds of individuals prefer certain forms or manifestations of humor over others.

Health and humor appear to be correlated phenomena, but humor has yet to be demonstrated as a causative factor that, in and of itself, cures ill health. It accompanies sound health and may catalytically enhance health. Humor apparently has beneficial effects that help physical, mental, and emotional well-being so that persons may endure stress. This is why it is characterized as a survival mechanism. Psycho-social analyses, however, provide enough room for appropriate caution or the reservation of final judgment until more evidence is accumulated. In addition, uncontrolled, involuntary, undesirable humorous responses such as episodes of uncontrolled laughter are found to be symptomatic of disease such as *kuru*, multiple sclerosis, ALS, and epilepsy. Pre-senile dementias produce *moria* and the intake of certain substances result in heightened sensitivity to humorous outbursts. Finally there are mental or emotional illnesses that manifest responses sometimes called humorous. All of these require professional attention rather than a surface observation that humor is present.

Efforts to explain disparagement humor have focused upon the influence of reference groups, identification classes, and affiliated or nonaffiliated objects. Furthermore, there is growing acknowledgment that there are intra-category differences in sympathies and attitudes that explain why members of the same groups or categories do not unanimously accept or reject disparagement humor directed against their own kind. Humor cues or frameworks still explain what is humorous and what is not. As with most scientific study, there is still much to learn about the nature of humor and its manifestations by individuals in group situations.

STUDY QUESTIONS

1. What accounts for the earlier and sustained interest of psychologists in the study of humor in contrast with sociologists?

2. What examples of duplication of courses by different disciplines exist on your campus? In what ways are these problems of "turf" in academic serious and in what ways do they invite a humorous approach?

3. What analyses or syntheses of humor are contributed by specialized disciplines aside from sociology and psychology?

4. Differentiate between sociological, psychological, and psycho-social analyses of humor.

5. What are the identifying characteristics of creative personalities and how do these explain a heightened awareness of humor?

6. Identify the personality qualities of robopaths and explain how these result in non-receptivity to humor?

7. From a psychoanalytic perspective, what is the source of humor?

8. Freud separated wit from humor by what criteria?

9. What are your favorite jokes and do they reflect much about your personality?

10. What exceptions, if any, can be found to the positive correlations of humor to health?

11. Just how is humor used therapeutically?

12. How does substance abuse increase receptivity to attempts at humor?

13. Why do certain individuals respond favorably to disparagement humor and others detest it?

14. Zillman's view of disparagement humor is that adequate theory explaining it has not yet been developed. Do you support or reject Zillman's view? Why?

15. Aside from personality, health, and disparagement, what other psychosocial phenomena are worth investigating because they, too, are related to the study of humor?

Suggested Readings

Alford, Richard Dana, *Humor and the Structures of Responsibility and Play.* Unpublished doctoral dissertation. Pittsburgh, PA: University of Pittsburgh, 1979.

Berelson, Bernard and Gary A. Steiner, *Human Behavior, An Inventory of Scientific Findings.* N.Y.: Harcourt, Brace & World, 1964.

Cousins, Norman, *Anatomy of an Illness As Perceived by the Patients.* N.Y.: W.W. Norton, 1979.

Goldstein, Jeffrey H. and Paul E. McGhee, *The Psychology of Humor.* N.Y.: Academic Press, 1972.

Griessman, B. Eugene, "Boundary Maintenance and Shiboleths in the Grove of Academe," *ASA Footnotes,* 2 (April, 1974): 3.

La Fave, L., *Humor Judgments As a Function of Reference Groups: An Experimental Study.* Unpublished doctoral dissertation, Norman, OK: University of Oklahoma, 1961.

La Fave, L., J. Haddad and W.A. Maesen, "Superiority, Enhanced Self-Esteem, and Perceived Incongruity Theory," in A.J. Chapman and H.C. Foot, eds., *Humour and Laughter: Theory, Research, and Applications.* London: Wiley, 1976.

La Fave, L., K. McCarthy and J. Haddad, "Humor Judgments As a Function of Identification Classes: Canadian vs. American," *J. of Psychology,* 85 (1973): 53-59.

Mangus, A. R., *Personality Adjustment of School Children.* Columbus, OH: Ohio State University, Ohio State Dept. of Public Welfare, and the Ohio Agricultural Experiment Station, July, 1948.

McElroy, Ann and Patricia K. Townsend, *Medical Anthropology in Ecological Perspective,* North Scituate, MA: Duxbury Press, 1979.

McGhee, Paul E. and Jeffrey H. Goldstein, eds., *Handbook of Humor Research.* N.Y: Springer-Verlag New York, 1983.

Moody, Jr., Raymond A., *Laugh After Laugh, The Healing Power of Humor.* Jacksonville, FL: Headwaters Press, 1978.

Pitchford, Henry Grady, *The Social Functions of Humor.* Unpublished doctoral dissertation, Atlanta, GA: Emory University, 1960, pp. 52-55.

Strachey, James, transl. & ed., *Jokes and Their Relation to the Unconscious* by Sigmund Freud. N.Y.: W.W. Norton, 1960.

Williams, J. M., "An Experimental and Theoretical Study of Humor in Children," *British J. of Educational Psychology,* 16 (1946): 43-44.

Wolff, H.A., C.E. Smith and H.A. Murray, "The Psychology of Humor: I. A Study of Responses to Race-Disparagement Jokes," *J. of Abnormal and Social Psychology* 28 (1934): 341-365.

Yablonsky, Lewis, *Robopaths, People as Machines.* Baltimore, MD: Bobbs-Merrill, Pelican Books, 1972.

Zillmann, Dolf and J.R. Cantor, "A Disposition Theory of Humour and Mirth," in A.J. Chapman and H.C. Foot, *op. cit.*

Zillman, Dolf, "Disparagement Humor," in McGhee and Goldstein, *op. cit.,* vol. I.

Chapter 4:

Social History of Humor

Social history, a specialized field within the discipline of history that focuses on lifestyles within a context of prevailing societal conditions, reveals the presence and enhancement of humor from antiquity to modern times. Certain social types were prominent features of each historical period and provided needed humorous relief. Sometimes these social types catered exclusively to the elite, wealthy and powerful leaders. In other circumstances they drew upon the general population for their audiences.

Social types are sociological constructs that draw upon realistic portrayals of persons in action. They are recognizable types within various groups who perform certain functions and who, once identified, enable others to deal with them effectively (Klapp, 1958).

Buffoons and Fools

Two social types that play central roles in the social history of humor are buffoons and fools. Buffoons are laugh-makers who enjoy a certain amount of prominence by virtue of their audacity to defy societal norms without fear of retaliation. They strip away the veneer of social conventions to reveal the raw truths of human conduct. Fools are those persons who, consciously or unconsciously, exaggerate human qualities that are defective, weak, or lacking in intelligence, courage, or grace (Klapp, 1954).

Klapp offers a typology of fools in terms of their forms or styles in Figure 4-1:

Figure 4-1

Typology of Fools by Theme and Style (Klapp*)

Key Theme	Style to Elicit Humor
The Antic	Overracts to circumstances
The Rash	Takes undue risks
The Clumsy	Stumbles awkwardly
The Deformed	Downgrades physical appearances
The Simple	Approaches situations childishly
The Weak	Copes poorly with challenges
The Small-minded	Approaches life timidly
The Pompous	Pretends to be honored personages
The Comic Butt	Offers self as scapegoat
The Comic Rogue	Poses as a villain
The Mock Hero	Uses thinly disguised or sham heroics

*From Orrin E. Klapp, *Social Types, Process, Structure and Ethos.* By permission.

Each of these types of fools may seek to emphasize, highlight, or dramatize the key themes given in Figure 4-1. There are certain fools, however,
who are versatile enough to combine several of these themes and styles
within their own characterizations. Whichever theme or style is chosen,
fools use themselves as examples with which audiences may identify. Failures, ineptness, frustrations, and heavy burdens are personified by the
fools. By degrading fools, audiences are thereby upgraded, a status they
can thoroughly enjoy. This process of seeing themselves by seeing fools
carry their heavy loads, and of being able to rank themselves above fools
sets the stage for expressions of humor.

Historical Buffoons

Among the historical buffoons are beggars, con artists, and gate-
crashers. Xenophon, the Greek historian who lived about the 4th to the 3rd
century B.C., wrote about a buffoon named Philip who attended a supper
party of Callius, undeterred by the fact that he was not on the guest list.
Rather than making himself inconspicuous, Philip chose to parody some
graceful Syracusan dancers who were the official entertainers at the banquet. Further compounding his audacity and increasing the chances that he
would be forcefully evicted or physically assaulted, Philip dared to engage
in a mock-serious dialogue the great Socrates himself, who was attending
the banquet as an honored guest (Welsford, 1935).

In the second century A.D., Lucian described a similar event at the Feast of Lapithae in which Alcidamus, the Cynic, showed up uninvited and deliberately provoked an argument with the host and one of his household retainers named Satyrion. A ridiculous fight ensued before the astonished guests, who happened to be the heads of prominent philosophical schools. Alcidamus apparently was effective as a buffoon because Lucian reported that the guests agreed "they gave us a good laugh."

Historical Fools

Buffoons tend to be relatively unknown amateurs who are unlikely to be chronicled by social historians. They are more parasitic in their functions and so make a living by contributing very little to those they encounter. By contrast, fools are historically prominent because of their socially redeeming services to their patrons. These are professionals in the arts of humor and earn the support of wealthy households, courts of nobility, retinues of church leaders, or followers of prominent and powerful officials. Court fools or jesters do appear in historical accounts because those who observed their actions found them memorable and worthy.

Perhaps the earliest court fool was a mysterious pygmy named Danga who was part of the entourage of Dadkeri-Assi, a pharaoh of the Fifth Dynasty. Danga was more of a physical curiosity than a wit, an example of the Deformed Fool social type. His small stature automatically conferred height to those who observed him, a feeling of superiority that others found most pleasing.

A dwarf named Knumhotpu, another Deformed Fool, not only was able to benefit others and himself by comparisons with his diminutive size but made himself useful to his pharaoh by serving as superintendent of the royal linen. Knumhotpu's statue is reported to still exist at Gizeh.

In the Roman era, a court fool named Gabba was retained in the court of Emperor Augustus. Gabba did not rely upon some physical abnormality as Danga or Knumhotpu did. Rather, Gabba had a ready wit and used it to generate humor based upon daily court activities. He and other court fools developed routines, surefire formulas, or repertoires guaranteed to provoke laughter. This is not too far removed from contemporary professional comics who spend their careers developing familiar, pleasing, easily recognized mannerisms that become their stock-in-trade. Once these professionals become associated with some hallmark, expression, or identity that has long-run appeal, they have "arrived" at their zenith and can, henceforth, play out their characterizations for the remainder of their careers.

This is precisely what happened in the case of the court fools of ancient Rome. Gabba and those who followed him performed antics and concocted jokes that were thought important enough to be recorded in Roman jest books. These were widely circulated so that the general public, apprentice or would-be court fools and future generations might benefit from the contrived humor.

The fall of the Roman Empire brought on disorder, disunity and despair, a period sometimes called the "Dark Ages." Court fools or professional comics seemed to disappear from the pages of history. They did resurface, however, when times changed and prosperous merchants, powerful nobles, and influential church officials could afford once again to keep professional entertainers within their households. As before, these professional purveyors of humor found employment by brightening up what might otherwise have been prosaic, boring, run-of-the-mill routines or burdensome schedules.

In fourteenth century Italy, for instance, Dolcibene and Gonella were renowned court fools. Gonella's forte was practical joking, humor in which someone is "fooled" with the full knowledge and support of co-conspirators. Dolcibene's strengths lay in his acting skills. Emperor Charles called him "King of the Italian Actors," a title Dolcibene, with his customary aplomb, accepted as well deserved. He is reputed to have once addressed the emperor audaciously by saying, "My Lord, you may well conquer the whole world since you are on such good terms with the Pope and men. You fight with the sword, the Pope with seals, and I with words!"

Pope Leo X could possibly be rated as one of the most appreciative connoisseurs of comical performers. Despite the heavy demands on his time and energies, he left standing orders with his valet-de-chambre that audiences would be granted to fools, buffoons, entertainers, and similar comedians at any time of the day or night.

Not to be outdone by the Pope in his admiration of laughmakers, the Court of Ferrara in 1490 let it be known that it would sponsor a burlesque investiture of buffoon knights. The invitation proved irresistible to both professional and amateur comics, and they gathered in great numbers for the gala event.

While Italy, France, and Germany traditionally had courts that sponsored court jesters, Elizabethan England's court jesters were immortalized in Shakespearian dramas. While such plays had serious plots and subplots, court fools offered comic relief just as they did in the midst of real court intrigues that often occurred around monarchs and nobility.

Court fools had to be aware of the fine line between being humorous and being serious. To transgress the boundaries of that which is viewed as humorous and serious was risky business particularly with personages who wielded power. Social bonding was noted earlier as one of the major functions of humor. If there is consensus or agreement that something is funny and persons can share the humor, then there is recognition or evidence of strong social bonding. Both the initiator of humor and the receiver of humor are signaling that they are members of the same group and can live together in accord or harmony. If however the initiators of attempts at what the initiator believes to be humorous are regarded as serious or non-humorous, then the receiver of such alleged humor signals that the initiators are not members of the same group, are not socially bonded, and instead, are antagonistic or repugnant to each other.

Charles Chester, a jester in the employ of Queen Elizabeth, apparently overstepped the bounds of propriety when he angered Sir Walter Raleigh and other nobles with his ceaseless joking. They ordered him confined to a corner of a room and then brought in stonemasons to brick-in the entire corner. By the time the bricks had been laid high enough to reach his neckline, Chester was begging for mercy. The courtiers finally relented, to Chester's relief, but he had been taught a lesson he would never forget. There are limits to patience and tolerance of what humorists regard as humor and what audiences accept or view as humor. Consensus is what humorists desire, but dissensus is what they may encounter. If dissensus or disagreement occurs, humorists find themselves outlawed, banished, or as Chester discovered to his dismay, possibly faced with injury, discomfort, or even death as retaliation.

Klapp (1954) makes the point that fools, buffoons, clowns, and comedians must endure status reduction by receiving mockery and ridicule from their audiences. He wrote, "Although he is amusing, we do not sympathize with the buffoon, but stand off and laugh at his fate. Even in the professional rewards of clowns and comedians a sanction is hidden, for they must endure humiliation as butt as well as maker of jokes for the sake of the applause of the crowds. 'Clowning' includes the reception of indignities."

In sociological terms, while there are positive sanctions or rewards in offering humor, there are also negative sanctions or punishments if one engages in humorous activities. As Chester found out, there may be dissensus about what constitutes humor. Or, as Klapp indicates, the fool must suffer some indignities in order to win the applause of audiences. In dramaturgical theory, an individual takes on the *persona* or mask of the fool and portrays a character who makes mistakes in social behavior and who must suffer the consequences. This persona of the fool is quite apart from the individual who assumes the part of the fool while on "front stage." "Back stage" or off-stage, when the performer is not in view of audiences, self-respect and dignity which was disguised can be restored, retained and manifested.

There is also the possibility that audiences may empathize with the fool when status reduction is staged. This is to say that audiences may recognize, in the fool's shortcomings, failures and anguish, something that they too have experienced at times. In such instances, audiences may show tremendous sympathy or compassion for the performer who reminds them of their common human frailty.

Tribute paid to the memory of Will Somers, the court fool of Henry VIII, indicates that Will did indeed win the hearts and minds of those who knew him. Beloved by his sponsors, originally Henry VIII and later Edward VI and Queen Mary, his eulogy read in part, "Will...exiled sadness many a time. He was no carry-tale, nor whisperer, nor flattering insinuator to breed discord and dissention, but an honest, plain down-right that could speak home without halting, and tell the truth of purpose to pain the devil, so that his plainess mixed with a kind of facetiousness and tartness with pleasantness made him acceptable into the company of all men.''

A similar tribute was recorded for posterity by the epitaph over the grave of Gilbert, the collaborator with Sir Arthur Sullivan of many world-famed light, comic operas, read "His enemy was folly; his weapon, wit.''

Legendary, Fictitious, or Mythical Buffoons and Fools

While historians verify the lives and accomplishments of buffoons and fools, myth-making is also a part of comedic history. Legendary, imaginary figures emerge from tales told and retold so often that fabrications are difficult to separate from reality. One such mythical, highly improbable figure was Till Eulenspiegel. One of his notorious exploits reported in German folklore is reminiscent of the tale of *The Emperor's Clothes.*

It was said that Eulenspiegel passed himself off as a great painter to the Landgrave of Marburg. Accordingly, he won himself a handsome commission to paint the Landgrave's great hall. He allegedly proceeded to do so behind locked doors with the explanation that no one would be able to disturb his creative, artistic endeavors. When he decided enough time had elapsed, he emerged to announce that his paintings were completed, but because they were specially prepared, they would be invisible to those who were bastards! Relying upon the reluctance of persons to admit that they saw nothing, the cunning Eulenspiegel was said to have carried out his ruse successfully.

The Roman jest books had their counterpart in the Near East. One of the best known collections was *The Jests of Si-Djoha,* which dealt with an intriguing simpleton named Si-Djoha by the Arabs, Juha or Juhi by the Persians, or Khoja by Turkish people. Kohja was alleged to be the court jester for Timur-leng, the conqueror.

Timur is reported in one tale to have caught a glimpse of his face in a mirror and was so appalled by what he saw that he wept for two hours in company with all of his retainers. When everyone had ceased their weeping and wailing, Khoja did not stop but continued to bemoan the sad event. Asked why he continued with such lamentations, Khoja quickly replied, "If you saw yourself in the glass and wept for two hours, is it not surprising that I weep longer since I see you the whole day?" At this audacious reply, Timur was said to burst into inextinguishable laughter. Not only was the brazen Khoja's life spared, but his fame as a comic was even more assured.

One other mythical figure worth mentioning was a balding, hunchbacked peasant named Marcolf. Near Eastern literature contains numerous references to his exploits, particularly his ability to match wits with none other than King Solomon, the Wise.

Marcolf apparently went too far in his ceaseless badgering and constant attempts to be witty. King Solomon became enraged and thoroughly disgusted, leading him to banish Marcolf from his sight forever and ordered his execution by hanging. The only concession that Solomon stipulated was that Marcolf could choose which tree would serve as his gallows. This concession suited Marcolf just fine and proved to be his salvation. Solomon's servants and Marcolf traveled far and wide in search of a suitable gallows -tree, but somehow such an appropriate tree was never found. Marcolf eventually returned home and lived out the remainder of his life quite content that he had outwitted the great King Solomon.

Marcolf's case is strikingly similar to folklore concerning "last requests" prior to executions. One clever prisoner, when asked what his last request was, replied that he should be executed just as soon as he could teach the warden's horse to fly. The duped warden granted the request on the outside chance that such could be done and thus make him famous as the owner of such an amazingly talented horse. Of course, all attempts to teach the horse how to fly were unsuccessful, but the prisoner continued the attempt for the rest of his life.

Demise of Court Fools

Court fools lasted well into the nineteenth century and could be found in the courts of the Russian czars, perhaps the last strongholds of European feudalism. With the collapse of such theories as the divine right of kings, court jesters lost their final base of support. Such professionals were forced to seek out audiences from the general public to make their living. Wherever people gathered, in such places as markets, fairs, festival sites, or streets, there the purveyors of humor could perform their trade.

Playing the fool or buffoon was never the exclusive domain of certain individuals. Masses of people could and did engage in celebrations, festivals, and revelry whenever opportunities arose. Springtime, harvest-time, weddings, or holidays would bring large numbers of people together to relax, rejoice, and refresh themselves, making their daily routine life more tolerable.

The usual norms or group expectations were temporarily suspended or could even be reversed on such occasions. Persons who were socioeconomically lower in society could mock the higher-ups. A commoner could pretend to be a noble. A peasant could pose as a king. A servant would assume the role and mannerisms of a master. A parishioner could be enthroned as a bishop. One could be whatever or whoever he or she wished to be as the chains of social restraints were cast off for a short time, and unrestrained merriment could occur.

For instance, in the Saturnalia, a Roman festival honoring Saturn, the God of Agriculture, there was generaly feasting, dancing, rejoicing, and overall tomfoolery. A mock king ruled over the Saturnalia, in which routines were suspended and make possible an inversion of roles. The same atmosphere of mass revelry prevailed during the New Year festivals. At that time, everyone exchanged gifts, masqueraded as fools, gorged themselves with food and drink, and looked forward to better times in the year ahead.

Churches or cathedrals were also settings for such hilarity and hijinks. Customary decorum, awe, and silent respect were displaced by conferring "titles" upon someone in the crowd and making him "Lord of Misrule," and "Abbot of Unreason," or "Prince of Fools." Such a personage would be duly crowned, paraded, and given homage to the delight of the masses.

A popular version was the Feast of the Ass. In this celebration, townspeople would stage an elaborate parade in imitation of the exodus of Jews from Egypt. A flamboyantly decorated donkey would head the procession that would be welcomed into a local church. A mass was recited, but instead of singing the traditional Latin responses in the ceremony, the congregation would respond to the ritual with brays of "Hee-haw." Such broad humor did not particularly please the clergy, and for many years there were attempts to forbid such sacrilegious behavior. It was a losing battle for the clergy, however, because the celebrations spilled over onto the church grounds and out to the streets where the mockery persisted for many years.

Schools and universities were also settings for outbursts of mass humor. Students would organize fun-oriented societies such as the *Societes Joyeuses* of French academies. These organizations endured for almost two hundred years. Young scholars would dress up as court fools in motley, eared hoods, and they would carry appropriate bells and baubles. Each of these societies dedicated to revelry had their own domains or "kingdoms" ruled over by a "Mother of Fools" or a "Prince of Fools." England and Germany had their own versions of university-based fun societies. In these societies, there would be staged scenes in which young scholars took on the status and roles of expert social critics and, with impunity, mocked their professor or mentors.

In every instance, there could be no "business-as-usual." Participants could shed their usual restraints and enjoy the opportunity to vent their repressed feelings and ideas. Modern counterparts can be found in such diverse settings as the Mardi Gras of New Orleans, St. Patrick's Day celebrations when everyone becomes honorary Irish for a day, or the annual "spring breaks" when thousands of college students flock to the beaches of Florida after the fall term.

Specialization

While buffoons and court fools assumed the broad tasks of inventing humor and presenting it to their sponsors, and while audience participation in mass revelry allowed a populace to rid itself of restraints, there were parallel developments in terms of specialization. This means that over the centuries there were individuals who concentrated on perfecting some special skills or abilities in humorous techniques that would be in demand from many audiences.

Some, like Dolcibene, were consummate actors who could use their talents to portray with great skill the characters, moods, and story lines they wished to present. Others relied upon their ready wit to extemporize clever responses to whatever situation they encountered. Still others trained themselves to become mimes, contortionists, acrobats, dancers, singers, magicians, musicians, poets, jugglers, ventriloquists, puppeteers, or satirists (Dorcy, 1961; Broadbent, 1964; Disher, 1968; Christopher, 1973; Avital, 1977). Each of these specializations required a singleness of purpose and many years of training and experience before there could be some mastery over it.

Their livelihood depended upon reaching paying audiences gathered at town squares, marketplaces, local fairs, weddings, or during festivals and holidays. Wherever they might find an audience, they would set up makeshift, temporary platforms upon which they could stage their specializations and hope to win the largesse of interested passersby. Traveling in small or large groups, they would form companies of entertainers that would reach villages, small towns, and crossroads to ply their specialties.

Another name or label applied to these groups was *commedia di zanni*, because servants or *zanni* were the chief characters who initiated most of the dramatic actions. Audiences could identify with the *zanni*, because they, for the most part, held lowly positions themselves. Audiences would rejoice over the clever machinations of servants who knew how to trick their masters into compromising behaviors. Most of the *zanni* were men, but usually at least one maid-servant was involved in the comedies. This maidservant was known as the *fantessa*, called Columbine, Franceschina, or Smeraldina, typically was portrayed as being very young, plainspoken and romantically involved with one of the male servants.

There were other stock characters or archetypes such as Harlequin and Pierrot. Harlequin was originally a stupid servant who grew more sophisticated as an acrobat, a maturing boy, or a romantic who was constantly in trouble of his own making or those of his master. Pierrot was always gullible, sometimes melancholic, and frequently given to crude actions. Harlequin would make his appearances in a patched costume that eventually became patterned and symmetrical. His face was half-masked, unlike Pierrot whose face was floured or powdered white. The white faces of clowns owe their origins to the character of Pierrot. Their white faces were greasepainted with distinctive styles that proclaimed instantly to all who met them that they are not to be received and understood as normal persons but, rather, as caricatures designed to incite laughter.

Harlequin usually carried a wooden sword, a *batte* or slapstick, that could make a loud clapping noise but did little harm. Broad, physical comedy to this day is known as "slapstick comedy." Comedians appear to do considerable damage to each other, but audiences know that the abuse and violence are staged and that no real harm is done. Punch and Judy puppet shows captivated audiences for centuries with their constant battering of each other.

Clowns are specialists in humor and have a long history all their own. Interestingly, there was no English word for clown until the sixteenth century. The term is said to be a derivative of *colonus* or clod, essentially a farmer, a rustic, or an unsophisticated, roughshod sort of person (Towsen, 1976). They were not, as most persons think, associated with circuses until late in the eighteenth century in England. Instead they would appear as part of a traveling company of players, mainly as characters who could provide comic relief. Their identity with farming had considerable appeal to their rustic audiences, who saw something of themselves in what clowns presented.

Clowns or comical characters began to develop expertise in certain performing techniques. For example, miming consists of conveying moods, feeling-states and ideas by specific body postures and contortions of the face. Most performers are familiar with body language to communicate with audiences, but controlling one's face and body is usually coupled with delivering lines or dialogue as part of a drama. Mimes eventually became "silent actors" and relied exclusively on the remarkable ability of face and body images to express messages of value to those who saw them.

Other performers moved in the opposite direction of the mimes. Not only did they use the spoken voice, but they raised it in song. Singers were known as *scop* and later as *minnesingers* in Germany, as *gleemen* in England, and as *troubadours* in southern France. Coupled with their ability to play musical instruments and the fact that they were well traveled and could relay news from distant places, they were welcomed as *minstrels* in households and locales. In a sense, they were the forerunners of newspapers, keeping people informed about what was going on in the world.

Certain versatile clowns were known as *jongleurs*. These multitalented performers could juggle, do acrobatics, walk on high wires or ropedance, and amaze their audiences with magical tricks. In addition they could keep up a steady flow of comical remarks to enhance their performances.

A specialization of considerable interest was the *mountebank*. The performer would pose as a medical doctor of great skill. He would offer miraculous cures for every ailment and then make sure that he was far out of town when those who had been fooled into purchasing his fake nostrums would try them. His name was said to have originated in the practice of the performer to climb upon some bench (mount-a-bank) in order to make his pitch to assembled crowds. Mountebanks always had an accomplice or servant, and this servant would act as a foil for the mountebank to the amusement of audiences. Sometimes this funny fellow would be called Merry Andrew or Harlequin, but typically he would be addressed by the name of some popular food. In England he was called Jack Pudding; in France he was Jean Potage; in Holland he was Pickleherring; and in Germany he was known as Hanswurst.

The ventriloquist was an entertainer who could "throw his voice" so that it would appear that a large puppet or dummy could speak. Such a specialization is alleged to have originated in the usage of a bauble or scepter carried by a court fool. The fool's bauble often was made to represent a miniaturization of the fool himself, so that the fool was able to hold prolonged conversations with his alter ego. The bauble would supposedly make outrageous and insulting comments to the fool, and of course, the fool would try to suppress his utterances or try to squelch statements that would have been better off unspoken. The disclaimer that the fool and the bauble were two separate identities allowed the fool to take on any target he might choose and then cast any blame on the bauble.

One other specialization fell to the *knockabouts* or *cascadeurs*. Knockabouts were acrobatic clowns who were able to perform amazing leaps, jumps, balancing acts, or contortions. Cascadeurs were those who could take falls or disappear and reappear. Their skills lay in their ability to convince observers that they were being slapped, hit, upset, or pushed around. The knockabouts and cascadeurs were the forerunners of stunt personnel who "stand-in" for main characters when dangerous scenes are portrayed.

Summary and Conclusions

Three developments in the social history of humor are:
(1) the appearance of social types known as buffoons or fools,
(2) mass participation in times of celebration or revelry, and
(3) specialization occurring in the ranks of performers.

Buffoons are identified as amateur humorists because their activities are spontaneous, based upon taking advantage of situations. Their livelihood, however, does not depend upon their humorous outbursts. Fools, on the other hand, became professionals because they attached themselves to households or courts, and their livelihood rested upon their ability to bring humor into the lives of their sponsors. Both historical and legendary buffoons and fools were remembered and appreciated for their talents and amusing exploits.

Buffoons and fools were emulated by mass audiences when there were times for relaxation from work or daily routines of living. Holidays, festivals, celebrations, and revels in which everyone could participate were very popular and widely supported. The temporary suspension of the usual norms allowed a wide latitude of behavior to occur, aggressions to be dissipated harmlessly, and imagination to be expressed. A return to normalcy followed such outbursts. Serious tasks and responsiblities were made a bit more tolerable.

Finally there were those who specialized in some form of humor above and beyond being buffoons or fools. Traveling companies of actors brought comedies to the villages, towns, and cities. Some would convincingly portray some dramatic parts; others could mime, sing, do acrobatic leaps, perform magical acts, dance, juggle, be ventriloquists, clown, or engage in dangerous stunts. The traditions they began continue to offer humor to huge audiences or invite them to participate in the expression of humor and so enjoy its benefits.

STUDY QUESTIONS

1. What is "social history" and how is it helpful in understanding the social significance of humor?

2. What contemporary examples are there of buffoons?

3. What are the distinctions between a buffoon and a fool?

4. What modern examples are there that match the typology of fools devised by Klapp?

5. In what Shakespearian plays do court fools play prominent roles?

6. Is status-reduction the common fate of all buffoons or fools?

7. What buffoons or fools are important characters in comparative literature?

8. In what ways do holidays, celebrations, and mass revelry benefit both participants and their society?

9. What examples are there of organizations associated with the promotion of humor in contemporary schools and universities?

10. Have any specializations among professional humorists been abandoned in human history?

11. What specializations among professional entertainers have gained tremendous support in recent years? What explains their tremendous following and popularity?

12. Why are clowns so appealing in circus and other settings?

13. Why are so many people attracted to spectacles in which performers engage in dangerous, life-threatening acts?

14. Is the survival theme evident in the social history of humor?

SUGGESTED READINGS

Avital, Samuel, *Mime Work Book, Le Centre Du Silence.* Venice, CA: Wisdom Garden Books, 1977.

Broadbent, R.J., *A History of Pantomime* (1901). Reprinted, N.Y.: Benjamin Blom, 1964.

Christopher, Milbourne, *The Illustrated History of Magic.* N.Y.: Thomas Y. Crowell, 1973.

Disher, Maurice Willson, *Clowns and Pantomimes* (1925). Reprinted, N.Y.: Benjamin Blom, 1968.

Dorcy, Jean, *The Mime.* N.Y.: Speller, 1961.

Klapp, Orrin E., "Heroes, Villains and Fools as Agents of Social Control," *American Sociological Review,* 19 (Feb., 1954): 56-62.

Klapp, Orrin E., "Social Types: Process and Structure," *American Sociological Review,* 23 (Dec., 1958): 674-678.

Klapp, Orrin E., *Social Types, Process, Structure and Ethos.* San Diego, CA: Aegis Publishing Co., 1971.

Towsen, John H., *Clowns.* N.Y.: Hawthorn Books, 1976.

Wellsford, Enid, *The Fool, His Social and Literary History.* London: Faber & Faber, 1935.

Willeford, W., *The Fool and His Scepter: A Study in Clowns and Their Audience.* Evanston, IL: Northwestern University Press, 1969.

Chapter 5:

Humor Media

While the social historial record shows the development of humor and humorists, it would be incomplete if it did not also contain some reference to the means by which humor and those who purvey it reached audiences eager to receive it. In this chapter the focus is on the media, the connecting links between humorists and their publics.

Communication is a social interactive process in which there are senders and receivers who "sense" messages, most commonly by sight or by sound. The carriers of messages, the media, are often described as extensions of the eyes and ears of humanity because they enable persons far removed both in time and in place to see and hear performers anywhere in the world at the moment of performance or at some appropriate time. Electronic technology has moved rapidly to the forefront of attention to such an extent that sociologists rate it as an emerging social institution of profound significance. Many wonder if the expansion of technical means of communication literally dominates societal life rather than simply serve as message carriers.

It was Marshall McLuhan (1964) who coined the concept, "the medium is the message." By this McLuhan meant that rather than being inert, passive, mechanistic, technically elaborate devices used to carry message, the very nature of and reliance on media made major changes of scale, pace, and pattern in human affairs. Time and space are contracted by media in such a way that, in McLuhan's view, humanity now lives in "global villages." Where before the history of humanity consisted of the global dispersion of people into their unique enclaves, thanks to available and omnipresent media, people are now able to see and hear each other instantaneously. This "implosion" of societies around the world is a phenomenon of deep social significance. It includes what has happened to humorists and to humor itself enabling humorists to reach mass audiences and bringing humor in all of its forms and functions to serve human needs.

McLuhan distinguished between media that were "hot" and media that were "cold." Hot media were those that extended a single human sense in high definition. By "high definition," McLuhan meant a condition in which so much information was provided that persons who received the data had little to do other than to absorb it or take it all in just as it was presented. Cold media, by contrast, offer a small amount of information so that receivers fill in more data by their interpretations and conceptualizations based on prior knowledge, training, socialization, or experience.

Oral speech or language was an early major step in media that enabled human beings to communicate ideas, subtleties, and shades of meaning far beyond those of other creatures. In oral speech, sounds are "cool" media that can be interpreted in multiple ways by those who speak and understand what they represent. Sociologically, language development was a fundamental breakthrough in symbolic interaction. Words in syntax thus are the first media used to convey humor that this chapter will consider. The "heating up" of these media through printing of books or literature will be followed by successive analyses of other media used by humorists based on technological inventions. Many of these media developments are within the memories of living generations' lifetimes, so that persons living today can verify the drastic changes in societal life that these new technical marvels have provided.

Wordplay or Wordsmithing

Techniques

A wide variety of techniques are available to humorists in which words themselves are the media and the materials of humorous messages.

Acronyms are words formed from the first letters of terms used to represent a program, plan, or organization. The formation of bureaus or agencies authorized to carry out some policy or function has been proliferating to such an extent that programs and systems are often better known by their acronyms than by their full names. The FBI (Federal Bureau of Investigation) and the IRS (Internal Revenue Service) are cases in point. As April 15th annually approaches, in sardonic humor, many distraught taxpayers prefer to call the IRS the "infernal" revenue service. Of more recent vintage is the acronym used by political humorists concerning the program devised by the military advisors for the deployment of the MX missiles. This program is referred to as DUMB, deep underground missile bases, a program that opponents feel strongly is a foolish procedure because it offers an identifiable target if nuclear warfare ever becomes a reality.

Those who are proponents of some program or organization, of course, do not wish to be perceived as being foolish or dumb. Accordingly, acronyms are useful shortcuts to identifying some plan or organization, but they may also be discarded if they can be used in some negative fashion by those determined to give an acronym a humorous twist. For years, the American Sociological Society was the dignified official name for the major professional organization of American sociologists. Its acronym, however, also can be interpreted negatively, and this is widely surmised to be the reason the name was changed to the American Sociological Association.

Alliterations consist of two or more stressed syllables or sounds by repetition of consonants. By referring to politicians as "slimy, slinky, slick" individuals, the "s" sound tends to be heard as a hissing sound, which is associated with snakes. It is an alliteration that politicians would rather not hear or favor because it puts them in a bad light. The words themselves are disparaging, and the possible association with snakes is also pejorative. Herein alliteration becomes a sword or a sharp point used by humorists with considerable effect.

Antanaclasis is the repetition of a word in two different meanings. Better known as puns, this form of wordplay, dual or multiple meanings attached to a single word, is also known technically as the double entendre, paranomasia, metonym, or syllepsis. John Crosbie (1977) provides more than 3,500 entries in his *Dictionary of Puns*. Crosbie, for instance, defines "debate" as that which lures "de fish."

Some call punning "a low form of humor" because one does not have to have high intelligence to figure out that a single word sounds like some totally different term. Groaning long and loud over some attempt at punning is said to be the sole reward a punster seeks. But there are word-conscious persons of high intelligence who also enjoy a well-delivered pun, and these relish the feigned anguish of audiences over some particularly adept bit of antanaclasis. Bennett Cerf, the late distinguished publisher, author, and panelist, thoroughly enjoyed offering some far-fetched bit of paronomasia whenever he had a chance. (See, for example, Bennett Cerf's *Bumper Crop*, vol. 1 and 2, 1956.)

Benedicta are good words with a possible ironic twist. This is a neologism created by Reinhold Aman to counterbalance what he calls *maledicta*, bad words or curses. Aman has been studying for over twenty years the insults, curses, and blasphemies in 220 languages. Annually Aman publishes a scholarly journal on maledicta. Maledicta are excellent devices to relieve tensions and are far better to rely upon than some outright assault. Aman enjoys quoting Sigmund Freud, who said, "The first human who hurled a curse instead of a weapon against his adversary was the founder of civilizations."

Maledicta, curses, slurs, and name-calling are so common that Aman has called for an annual holiday in which maledicta would be consciously displaced by benedicta such as saying "gosh," "fudge," or "shucks." He proposes to call the day "No-Cuss Day," a holiday from foul language (Associated Press, 1985).

Irish Bulls put together words that convey incongruous ideas. Persons who hear them recognized there is some connection between them, but they also know that their juxtaposition is ridiculous and defective by definition. For example, "abstinence must always be practiced with moderation." Or in the same vein, a patient reports to her doctor that she is "a little bit" pregnant.

Clerihews are named for their inventor, Edmund Clerihew Bentley, who created couplets in which the first line always contained the name of some well-known person. For instance, "George, the Third, ought never to have occurred; one can only wonder at so grotesque a blunder."

Cliches are bromides, platitudes, trite, overworked phrases or expressions that have lost their original appeal. Clara Peller's "Where's the beef?" was an advertising gimmick for a hamburger chain that captured the nation's attention for a short time and was even used by a presidential candidate during his political campaign. But the phrase was repeated so often it lost its punch and will be remembered only as a passing word-fad, a dated cliche. The same applies to the expression "Have a nice day."

Epitaphs are humorous references found on tombstones (Spiegel, 1973). They represent the final words of individuals and attempt to typify the deceased buried at some grave. Over a dentist's grave, for example, the epitaph read, "He is filling his last cavity." W.C. Fields was once asked to suggest his own epitaph, and he replied, "Say on it, 'I'd rather be in Philadelphia'."

Euphemisms are attempts to make something that is negative appear to be positive. "Senior citizens" and "golden-agers" are terms used to identify elders as respected personages who are living out their remaining years in well-earned happiness. Gerontologists, however, have long documented the negative state of affairs for large numbers of the elderly who are far removed from the mainstream of society that prides itself more on lip-service than on actual service to its aged. In a similar euphemistic attempt, nuclear bombs are dubbed "peacekeepers" by their proponents while they are seen as weapons of doom by their opponents.

Litotes are understatements that carry a particular punch when a positive perspective is expressed in a negative fashion. This type of incongruity is used sarcastically when persons say something is "not bad at all" and then add after a significant pause that leads listeners to think in one direction, "it was horrible, obnoxious, or abysmally ignorant, however." The rude awakening as to the real intent of the speaker or writer increases the chances that the statement will be remembered.

Limericks are witticisms in verse. For example, the pursuit of special subject matter by scholars is held up to ridicule by the following limerick: "I once had a friend named Guessor whose knowledge grew lesser and lesser. It grew so small, he knew nothing at all. And now he's a college professor!"

Malaprops are bloopers, boners, gaffes, slips, or errors made unintentionally (Schafer, 1973). They please those who know how to avoid them, or they increase a sense of identification with those who have displayed their human proclivities for imperfection. One example of a malaprop is the statement, "Your whole fallacy is wrong!"

Metaphors are figurative but not literal comparisons. To say "that person is a jerk" is to portray the individual as a person unable and unconscious of whatever he or she is doing. The automatic, reflexive action implies the person has little control or understanding of what is occurring.

Oxymorons display an internal contradiction. Two unlikely, often at cross-purposes, terms are put together. Giant shrimp, military intelligence, and student teacher are cases in point. Sociologists are familiar with another oxymoron: the constant variable.

Parodies are spoofs, take-offs, burlesques, or humorous treatment of more serious, sober phenomena. For example, a comic may say of his ladylove, "Her teeth are like stars. They come out at night!"

Spoonerisms occur when the first letter or sounds of words are transposed by sheer accident or unintention. Eddy Peabody, a famed and talented banjoist was once introduced by an over-excited master of ceremonies as follows: "Ladies and Gentlemen, Eddy Playboy will now pee for you!"

The Power of Words

The techniques briefly described above indicate that words are powerful media in communicating humor. Command of the appropriate words for each occasion is the mark of a skillful and well-prepared communicator. Such persons, as speakers or as writers, find they will be well-received and well-rewarded for their ability to delight audiences or readers with their abilities in wordsmithing or word-creations (Rocke, 1972; Lake, 1975).

Print Media

In McLuhan's terms, the "heating up" of the "cooler" oral and written words through printing presses, the gigantic leap in the Guttenberg technology of movable type, was perhaps the most significant movement in media of centuries of human history. The print media of books, newspapers, magazines, or journals were a quantum change in communication, treated matter-of-factly in the present but has continued to enable senders and receivers, regardless of locus or time, to establish contact with each other. Oral speech can be monitoried on the spot, senders and receivers are identifiable to each other, and there can be prompt feedback so that both senders and receivers can modify rather quickly their comprehension of information. Print media stands in sharp contrast with those characteristics of oral communication. Publishing is a much more complex process in which there are many more persons involved in the sending of messages, senders and receivers are not known to each other, and feedback in terms of retention, elimination, or modifying of ideas is much slower in pace or quantity.

Hiebert, Ungurait, and Bohn (1974) offer a model of mass communication that is similar to that of dropping a pebble into a pond, causing ripples that move outward to the shores until the ripples bounce back to the center of where they originated. Their HUB Model of Mass Communication starts at the center with the involvement of teams of communicators. The content of their messages are less personal, less specialized, more rapid, and more transient than interpersonal communication. These substantive message are codified depending upon the nature of the media such as camera angles, freeze frames, and editing for films or typography and design of the printed page. Further, there are "gatekeepers" or editors who creatively evaluate what is communicated and how it is to be communicated. Next there is a complex technology such as the printing processes run by an organization in order to couch the messages. Moreover, there are regulators such as courts, governmental regulators, professional organizations, and public pressure groups that affect the materials through laws, standards, and normative expectations. The audiences are heterogeneous, not necessarily in contact with each other, and prone to be affected by changing conditions in their own locales or perspectives. Finally, there is feedback in which the audiences react to the messages so that the communicators may alter what has been produced.

With print media sending out humor of some quality and quantity, this process of coding, gatekeeping, complex technology, regulating varied audiences or publics, and feedback shapes the final results. Those professional humorists, those who make their living from the production, distribution, and usages of humor, can prosper only if they have learned to deal effectively with all aspects of the mass communication process. From a sociological perspective, professional humorists operate in an elaborate maze of socially imposed systems with which they must deal in order to sustain their performances. Professional humorists must maximize the advantages of these systems and minimize their hazards, pitfalls, or disadvantages.

Sound Media

Music

Certainly one of the historical media to convey moods, feeling-states, and ideas is music. Music may excite listeners, express emotions, soothe their feelings, or truly delight them by the beauty and charm of the harmonic sounds.

As noted earlier in the social history of humor, singers or troubadors and instrumentalists were welcomed visitors in isolated locales because they not only entertained but kept villagers and townspeople informed about events occurring far beyond the daily lives of local residents. In the rapid expansion of mass media, those who could combine the appeal of music with the enjoyment of humor have been able to sustain professional careers that mass audiences find unforgettable. Victor Borge and Jimmy Durante, for example, drew upon their talents as pianists to reach vast audiences. Borge's forte was to bring together audiences primed to listen to his performance of classical music and then deliberately interrupt or delay the musical performance in order to make funny asides and sing with great vigor, deliberately feigning exasperation when someone would try to outshine or upstage him. Durante's "everybody's-tryin'-to-get-inta-da-act" reaction had tremendous appeal because many people experience feelings of inadequacy when competitors push them aside by their devious tactics.

Jack Benny was a master violinist but always portrayed himself as a clumsy beginner. Morey Amsterdam was an accomplished cellist but he used his cello as an excuse to get on stage and offer his comic routines, similarly to Henny Youngman's rarely played violin accompanying his rapid-fire "one-liners." Harpo Marx, a talented harpist, was able to move audiences by demonstrating the fine line humanity treads between the ridiculous and the sublime (Marx & Barber, 1974).

Peter Schickele is still another humorist who draws upon his musicology to convey his brand of humor. As a student at Juilliard School of Music, Schickele's comic flair would sometimes intrude upon the decorum of formal concerts. Reprimands from his professors for his persistence in going off in musical flights of fancy led to his career of satirical musical performances. Alleging that he is a professor at the 'University of Southern Northern Dakota,'' he diligently uncovers the long-lost works of the oddest of Johann Sebastian Bach's alleged 21 children, a fictitious character Schickele named "P. D. Q. Bach." A mysterious personage named "Deep Note" passes on the works of P.D.Q. Bach, who is really a musical idiot, and Schickele is then able to inflict paying audiences with the catastrophic, horrible, but hilarious results. The violations of musical norms please the knowledgeable audiences because they are able to distinguish between the appropriate and the inappropriate, a superiority not granted the uninitiated.

The storage and retrieval of musical humor or the combinations of humor and music have immeasurably increased the outreach and influence of such humorists through such media as phonograph recordings, tapes, films, or video cassette recorders. A single "live" performance can be "canned" for unlimited replays whenever their purchasers wish to hear them (Humphrey, 1971).

Radio

A sound medium that brought on a "Golden Age of Broadcasting" was radio (Campbell, 1976). For almost a quarter of a century prior to World War II, radio was one of the major media to bring humor into the lives of millions of eager listeners. People would gather around their radios to hear such great talents as Fred Allen, George Burns and Gracie Allen, Charles Correll and Freeman Gosden as Amos'n Andy, Mary Livingston and Jack Benny, Gertrude Berg as Molly Goldberg, or Jim Jordan and Marian Driscoll as Fibber McGee and Molly. Through sound alone and imaginative "filling-in" by mass audiences, these radio comics made outstanding humor history.

Sight Media

Art, Caricature, and Cartoons

Those able to visualize some pattern, form, design, symbolism, or concept by their artistic talents in line drawing, shadings, colors, textures, and contrasts also deserve attention in terms of conveying humor. Perhaps one of the best known works of art that offers a subtle reaction to a humorous stimulus is the Mona Lisa painting. Her enigmatic smile can be interpreted in a variety of ways depending upon a viewer's predilections. Some might say her private thoughts dealt with her strong self-assurance in the face of adversity. Others might say she had knowledge not known to persons who would discover soon enough what she already knew. Whatever it was that brought on that fascinating smile, artistry captured the overt reaction to a covert experience, a distinction of concern to sociologists in which observable actions require interpretations.

Artists as well as their interested publics have probably never agreed upon a single philosophical question, namely, whether the medium of art should be realistic, true-to-life in as much detail as possible, or nonrealistic, imaginary, symbolic, unique, impressionistic, or individualistic. Realism in artistic media has many supporters or advocates. But there are many other protagonists of styles such as cubism, Dadaism, or Surrealism. Connoisseurs of one style or artistic school of thought will rave over some artistic piece while the uninitiated will reject the same piece as totally ridiculous. Artists "see" with different "eyes" and persons who can "see" the same perspectives on the nature of life appreciate the message. Those who disagree, and so prefer another perspective, delight in poking fun at the bizarre forms and colors made by "some crazed chimpanzee."

Caricature is derived from the verb *caricare* meaning to load or to exaggerate. Objective reality is transformed into subjective interpretation, an artist's privilege from earliest cave drawings to the scribblings of children to the most accomplished professionals (Hofmann, 1957). By distorting reality through the techniques of emphasizing, overdoing, heavily weighing certain features of the face, body form, or human actions, caricaturists make unmistakably evident the humorous point they wish to make. Heller (1981), for example, offers cross-cultural samples of satiric art over the past twenty years that demonstrate how effectively caricatures skewer their targets.

Cartooning is a special form of drawing of one or more panels, in representational or symbolic style, used to convey both humorous and serious messages. Editorial and political cartoons are particularly adept at visualizing the deeds and misdeeds of newsmakers or powerful officials (Hoff, 1976).

In a classic study by Allport and Postman (1945), the cartoon was used to study the diffusion of rumors. An illustration, for instance, showed an inner view of a subway train in which eight individuals were portrayed, two standing. One of the standing persons was a black man well dressed in hat, suit, and tie, whereas the other man was white, dressed casually in cap, open shirt, and sleeveless sweater. The white man carried an open, straight-edged razor. The black man had his hands down, opened, indicating an effort at being reasonable. The white man, by contrast, was pointing his right-hand finger at the black man and carried the razor in his left hand. Signs advertising "Gosling Soap, 99 44/100 pure—It Floats!" and "Smoke Lucky Rakes—They Satisfy" were in the background.

This illustration and others were shown to a single individual, and then that person was asked to pass on to a second person what he or she saw. The second person was asked to pass on the acquired information to a third person; that person to pass it on to a fourth person; and so on. Allport and Postman noted three processes going on when they questioned the final recipient of the information: leveling, sharpening, and assimilation. In leveling, the data are simplied, made shorter, more concise, and easily related and understood. The eight people became a "crowd" or a "mob." In sharpening, certain details are dropped out while the remainder become more prominent. In the subway scene, the black man and the white man become the star performers. In the assimilation process, the story "made sense" to the receiver of information in terms of their perception of reality.

Leveling, sharpening, and assimilation are the particular processes that cartoonist-communicators use in making their points. Simplified two-dimensional figures are drawn, usually in black and white. Minor features are dropped out such as the body is shrunk and the head and facial features stressed to convey various moods. Finally, assimilation is used by exaggerating and stressing certain features over others. The villain is made even more villainous. The hero is more muscular, handsome, and daring. The heroine is endowed with features far beyond those of normal proportions.

Harrison (1981) notes that the normal human figure is seven heads tall. The head in humor cartoons, however, may account for one-fourth of the total height. In animation the figures is three heads tall, as in "Snoopy" or "Ziggy." This suggests a more appealing, childlike figure that allows the cartoonist to make a point with greater impact than if the message came from an adult, a more threatening symbol. Finally, the cartoonist imitates life by an action line, a thought cloud, and a speech balloon (Becker, 1959; Walker, 1975).

Sight, Motion, Sound, and Color Media

In the twentieth century, two more media emerged to offer the world a combined image of sight, motion, sound, and color, the closest duplication of reality yet devised. These were motion pictures and television.

Films

Silent films, at first, could bring outdoor action scenes to audiences where before comic or tragic drama had to be staged indoors and limited to the traditional dimensions of theatrical stages. Schooled in vaudeville, burlesque, and the stage, some of the greatest comics of all time, Chaplin, Keaton, Lloyd, Langdon, and the Keystone Kops brought unforgettable humorous episodes to millions (Durgnat, 1970). By 1927, sound was syncronized with the images on the screen and the screen projections took on even greater verisimilitude. Color was added later on, with only the "3-D" effect, creating a stereoscopic effect, being the remaining challenge to create an illusion of reality or believability. Talented performers of comedy could become familiar faces, warmly welcomed throughout the world through cinematic arts and technology (Jacobs, 1970; Giannetti, 1976).

Television

The most recent medium dating back to the end of World War II has been television. This medium brought screens into the privacy of homes and has changed family households markedly. Living room furniture is arranged, for example, to face this "window of the world," and family members arrange their time schedules to take advantage of their "magic box." Terms such as "sitcoms" (situation comedies), are neologs well understood by television devotees. Series like "I Love Lucy," "All in the Family," and "M.A.S.H." are already part of television's history. Whole generations have been socialized with television regarded as part of the taken-for-granted facilities available to people.

While news, education, and serious messages are conveyed through television, humor has been an important part of television programming throughout its development.

One other quality associated with the media, but one that has particular significance for television, is insatiability. Television programming for twenty-four hours a day and seven days a week has required the attention of huge numbers of personnel who must use their ingenuity to meet the heavy demand for material to fill the long programming hours. Prior to the advent of television, humorists could offer their repertoires to audiences over and over again. The materials would be old and well-rehearsed, but audiences were new and could support the performances. Television programming calls for fresh materials, new ways of presenting humor, and thus puts tremendous pressure on performers to sustain or surpass their offerings. A loss of ratings, the feedback in contemporary media, foreshadows the displacement of a program in favor of some newer, although untested, program or humor series.

Summary and Conclusions

The media, the connecting links between humor and those who receive it, have become social forces in themselves (Altheide, 1985). First, the spoken word and later on the written and published word, were the chief means of communicating humor. Wordplay or wordsmithing remain fundamental in the symbolic transmission of humor, but sound media such as music and radio are also powerful means to convey humor to vast audiences. Sight media — art, caricature, and cartoons — enlarge the vision not only through realistic portrayal of human behavior but also through departures from reality through artistic license to unmistakably portray circumstances, moods, and ideas worth consideration. Finally, the sensing of sight, sound, motion, and color simultaneously through films and television has brought those who create humor and those who consume it closer together than has ever been possible. Tremendously talented performers have used the media in a most appealing and memorable fashion. At the same time, the media makes demands on human ingenuity that results in the quick rise and fall in popularity of efforts to satisfy the insatiable demand of the public for comic relief.

Life styles are deeply affected by the messages conveyed through mass media. But as McLuhan observed, the media is also the message itself, and humanity has had to adapt to its presence. The sociology of humor must take into account the media by which humor is transmitted and shaped. Media make and break careers. They also call for rethinking how, as Shakespeare put it, "all the world is a stage" and people make entrances and exits.

STUDY QUESTIONS

1. What is "high" and "low" definition in media and how do these distinctions affect covert thought and overt actions of audiences?

2. Do media create audiences of passive consumers or active participants in society?

3. Why is word-humor or wordsmithing so fundamental or basic to humor in media?

4. How have media "heated up" formerly "cool" media so that humor transmissions may be improved?

5. Preferences or tastes in word humor have been said to characterize certain personality types. Can you agree or disagree?

6. Just how does the HUB Model of Mass Communication substantiate the complexities involved in the modern transmission of humor in contrast with the primary group styles used by humorists in the past?

7. Can you find professional humorists whose career was made possible only through one medium or another? How did the characteristics of that medium shape the career?

8. What are the advantages of caricature in art over that of caricatures in literature?

9. What relationships are found between humor conveyed through realism in art and artistic license or symbolism?

10. What occurs in leveling, sharpening, and assimilation in cartooning?

11. What symbolization is used in connection with facial features, body language, or body forms in the transmission of humor?

12. Just how has television transformed human societies? And, in particular, how has humor on television affected viewers?

13. Is there more humor in advertising spots on radio and television than within the content of so-called humorous programs?

14. How does humor help sell products and services in support of radio or television programming?

15. What new mass media may yet displace media currently dominant and so affect the way humor is offered to the public?

16. How do media become more significant than the substantive messages they convey?

Suggested Readings

Allport, G.W. and L.J. Postman, "The Basic Psychology of Rumor," N.Y.: Transactions of the New York Academy of Sciences, Series 118: 61-81, 1945.

Altheide, David L., *Media Power*. Beverly Hills, CA: Sage Library of Social Research, v. 158, 1985.

Becker, Stephen, *Comic Art in America*. N.Y.: Simon & Schuster, 1959.

Calhoun, Richard B., *In Search of the New Old, Redefining Old Age in America, 1945-1970*. N.Y.: Elsevier, 1978.

Campbell, Robert, *The Golden Years of Broadcasting, A Celebration of the First 50 Years of Radio and TV on NBC*. N.Y.: Scribners, 1976.

Cerf, Bennett, *Bennett Cerf's Bumper Crop*. Two volumes. Garden City, N.Y.: Garden City Books, 1956.

Crosbie, John S., *Crosbie's Dictionary of Puns*. N.Y.: Harmony Books, 1977.

Durgnat, Raymond,, *The Crazy Mirror, Hollywood Comedy and the American Image*. N.Y.: Horizon Press, 1970.

Everson, William K., *The American Movie*. N.Y.: McClelland & Stewart, 1963.

Gianneti, Louis D., *Understanding Movies*. Second Edition. Englewood Cliffs, NJ: Prentice-Hall, 1976.

Harrison, Randall P., *The Cartoon, Communication to the Quick*. Beverly Hills, CA.: Sage, 1981.

Heller, Steven, *Man Bites Man, Two Decades of Drawings and Cartoons by 22 Comic and Satiric Artists, 1960-1980*. N.Y.: A & W Publishers, 1981.

Hoff, Syd, *Editorial and Political Cartooning, From the Earliest Times to the Present*. N.Y.: Stravon Educational Press, 1976.

Hofmann, Werner, *Caricature, From Leonardo to Picasso*. N.Y.: Crown, 1957.

Hiebert, Ray Eldon, Donald Ungurait and Thomas Bonn, *Mass Media. An Introduction to Modern Communication.* N.Y.: McKay, 1974.

Humphrey, Laning, *The Humor of Music and Other Oddities in the Art.* Boston: Crescendo, 1971.

Jacobs, Lewis, *The Movies as Medium.* N.Y.: Farrar, Straus & Giroux, 1970.

Lake, Anthony B., *A Pleasury of Witticisms and Word Play.* N.Y.: Bramhall House, 1975.

Marx, Harpo and Roland Barber, *Harpo Speaks!* N.Y.: Freeway Press, 1974.

McLuhan, Marshall, *Understanding Media, The Extensions of Man.* N.Y.: McGraw-Hill, 1964.

Rocke, Russell, *The Grandiloquent Dictionary, A Guide to Astounding Your Friends with Exotic, Curious, and Recherche Words.* Englewood Cliffs, NJ: Prentice-Hall,, 1972.

Schafer, Kermit, *Best of Bloopers.* N.Y.: Avenel Books, 1973.

Schwartz, Tony, *Media: The Second God.* N.Y.: Random House, 1981.

Spiegel, Fritz, ed., *A Small Book of Grave Humor.* N.Y.: Arco, 1973.

Walker, Mort, *Backstage At the Strips.* N.Y.: Mason/Charter, 1975.

PART II:

Social Variables of Humor

Humor varies not only by reason of its structures, styles, functions, specializations, and media, but also by its substance, the content with which it
deals. Age, sex-gender, urban-reality, cross-cultural, and subcultural differences are social variables that affect the substantive nature of what is
presented as humor. Furthermore, those persons who are the subjects of
these variations in humor have much to offer in terms of understanding
what is regarded as humor and what purposes are being served by promoting humor about them. Finally, persons who believe they stand apart from
the targeted group or category feel free to hold them up to ridicule until
such time as they realize that they, too, are deeply involved and strongly
tied to the people selected "in fun."

The initial chapter on race and humor in this second part touches upon
one of the most sensitive variables affecting humanity. Ensuing chapters
deal with age-grades, sex and gender, city-country, and macro- and micro-
cultural differences that shape the destinies of both in-groups and out-
groups who charge these factors or qualities with their own definition of the
situation.

By focusing upon each variable in turn, distinctive humor emerges to
suggest that social forces are constantly at work in building up and tearing
down social structures by which human beings order their lives.

Chapter 6:

Racial Humor

In this chapter the concept of race is analyzed in terms of labeling theory and determining how such a conceptual perspective has been manifested in humor. Changing conceptualizations have led to changing ways of dealing with racial humor. Dominance-submission patterns, holding up bigotry to ridicule, therapeutic effects of racial humor, functions of racial humor, and "black humor" are treated to reveal some of the interconnections between social definitions of race and humor.

The Concept — Race

The etymology of "race" is a fascinating story in itself. Distinctions between peoples that are sociocultural in nature have long been made such as "in-groups" and "out-groups," "we" and "they," "believers" and "nonbelievers," "free persons" and "slaves," "civilized" and "savage," or "nationals" and "foreigners."

The idea of using physical or biological features to distinguish people, however, was a relatively recent historical development. The word *razza* first appeared in Italian literature in the fourteenth century. The word *race* did not appear in the English language until 1570 in Fox's *Book of Martyrs* (Berry, 1958). It first appeared in French in 1684 and in German in 1696. These linguistic additions were made at a time when European expansionism brought Europeans into contact with people around the world. Not only were these people socially and culturally different, but their physical appearances seemed to justify their exploitation by Europeans.

To further compound the meaning of *race,* the term has been confused with religion, nationality, language, or culture. For example, there is no such thing as a Jewish race anymore than there is a Catholic, Protestant, or Buddhist race, with anyone being free to enter or to leave such faiths. Sociologically there is no such thing as a French, German, Italian, or English race, the references being to loyalty to a nation or to those who speak a particular language. Persons of any physical makeup or appearance are free to be loyal to a country and its standards or to choose to communicate in a specific language system. Or persons of various skin pigmentations, of various body forms such as lips, eyes, nose, or body build, or of different textures of hair may choose to favor and conduct their lives within certain life styles, but their selection of cultural options does not mean that they constitute a race. Racial differences cut across religious, nationality, language, or cultural lines rather than being confined within these distinctions.

The ambiguity and lack of clarity has led some scientists to call race a modern fairy story, a fabrication, or a persistent myth. Barzun (1937) called race "the modern superstition" and Montagu (1965) called it "a dangerous fallacy."

What race really is requires an understanding of the sociological construct known as a category, people who are *thought* to be physically, biologically, genetically alike. A category is a *label*, a classification placed on persons that assigns or ascribes to them identical qualities but ignores differences among them or their common qualities with persons who stand outside the category (Garn, 1965). Genetic pooling or inbreeding can produce visible physical differences by reason of physical or social isolation, conditions often brought about by insistence that one category should be kept apart from all other categories. Racial "purity" is itself another myth because there are racial hybrids or mixtures that verify the fact that all humanity belongs to a common specie of creatures. As Pierson(1942) observed, a "black-white" person in Brazil is called "white" whereas a "black-white" in the United States is more likely to be identified as "black." Such conventional views of race make it a substantive phenomenon subject to humorous exploitation.

Labeling, categorizing, classifying, naming, or applying specific names to racial hybrids or those of mixed ancestry is commonly used to identify differential treatment to keep them apart or to control conditions as they currently exist. A partial list of some of the nomenclatures used around the world to rationalize barriers to full participation in society is provided by Thompson and Hughes (1958):

Figure 6-1

Racial Names Around the World

Afro-Asians (South Africa)	*Jibaro* (Puerto Rico)
Anglo-Indians (India)	*Leperos* (Mexico)
Cape Coloured South Africa)	*Melungeons* (eastern Tennessee)
Cariboco (North America)	*Metis* (Brazil)
Cascos (southern U.S.)	*Moors* (Delaware; southern N.J.)
Chino (South America)	*Moplash* (India)
Cholo (Peru)	*Morisco* (Mexico)
Emabasitela (Swaziland)	*Muladis* (Mediterranean Basin)
Eurasian (India)	*Salto Atras* (Mexico)
Griffe (Louisiana)	*Sarakolle* (Senegal)
Griquas (South Africa)	*Turks* (South Carolina)
Guineas (West Virginia)	*Vecinos* (Yucatan)
Jackson White (New York)	*Wesorts* (southern Maryland)

Such terms are used in what is popularly called "put-down" humor so that one group is made "inferior," the butts of jokes, and another group is made "superior," persons who stand outside such categories.

Sociologists have documented that whenever people meet, they tend to mix. This does not mean that everyone interbreeds or that they necessarily merge or blend, but the frequency with which people from so-called races can and do breed common children is testimony that human beings can find more in common with each other than they can when they focus upon "racial differences." Miscegenation is a sociological fact; racial purity is a myth often unmasked by humorous twists or treatment.

"Passing" as a member of one race or another, one category or another, is a familiar practice among persons of mixed ancestry. Once such persons can shed some racial labels, they find barriers to discourse and to opportunities for fulfillment removed. One daring reporter, a white, who passed himself off as a black, found that he was no longer acceptable to persons he had once interviewed successfully but was warmly received by blacks (Griffin, 1961).

The absurdity of racial classifications would be laughable in and of itself if not for the serious consequences of *racism,* the insistence that one race or another is either superior or inferior in intellect, talent, contributions, or virtue. Continuing studies, investigations, and analyses have been carried out to support or refute claims of racial superiority or inferiority (Myrdal, 1944); Count, 1950; UNESCO, 1952; Rose, 1964, 1968; Baughman & Dahlstrom, 1968; Mack, 1968; Goldschmid, 1970; Wilson, 1978). To date, not one study or analysis can verify such assertions.

Racial mythology, of course, needs no scientific proof. It persists on the basis of unverified assumptions and the strengths of personal and shared beliefs. As long as people cling to ideas, substantiated or unsubstantiated, they are reified or "made real" and persons act accordingly. Sociologists have long observed that ideas, right or wrong, are translated into reality.

Definitions of situations are "blueprints for actions" and racism is no exception to the rule. Prejudice, attitudinal prejudgments, and discrimination, overt acts that favor or disfavor persons and their ways, are justified by persons who hold such views or behave as they do because they are convinced they have the facts and their interpretation of these data as proper is well in hand.

The Changing Nature of Racial Humor

The matter-of-fact acceptance of the existence of races and the consequences of such beliefs, racism, has led to humor that seeks to poke fun at visible minorities. Persons from powerless racial minorities have been held as "fair game" for derisive laughter. White comedians could put on "blackface" and entertain locals with their antics and witticisms. Minstrel shows were very popular with their companies of white performers in blackface-greasepaint that featured end men known as "Mr. Tambo" and "Mr. Bones," who were constantly badgering each other or the interlocutor with humorous asides.

In public celebrations of holidays, blackface mummers paraded with their elaborate headgears and strumming banjos. In radio, Amos and Andy were funny characters created by the voices of white comedians.

All that is now past history. Minstrel shows are no longer staged because they would invite outrage from both blacks and whites. Blackface mummers no longer are seen celebrating major holidays because such appearances would denigrate blacks and would be seen as a public insult to the mores of American society. The Amos and Andy Show of oldtime radio had to give way to black actors and actresses who played their parts on television before viewers who no longer would tolerate whites imitating stereotypical portraits of black personalities.

If anyone was to portray some aspects of black life styles or black perspectives humorously acceptable, it would have to be black comics themselves. Talents like Pearl Bailey, Godfrey Cambridge, Nell Carter, Gary Coleman, Bill Cosby, Red Foxx, Dick Gregory, Moms Mobley, Eddie Murphy, Sidney Poitier, Richard Pryor, Nipsey Russell, Jimmy Walker, Slapsey White, and Flip Wilson were given headline positions in the presentation of humor rather than minor, backdoor, servile characterizations that reinforced the subordinate status of blacks in a white world. Their materials could be drawn from experiences with racial prejudice and discrimination, but the humor was often directed at whites rather than blacks. Or better yet, with no particular emphasis upon racial distinctions, black persons could be portrayed in humorous situations familiar to most people. The Cosby Show, in which Bill Cosby plays the part of a medical doctor and his wife is an attorney, portrays a family life delightful to all who know the trials and tribulations of rearing sons and daughters of various ages. The

Cosby Show is not a racially oriented television sitcom, but one with appeal to universal themes.

Humor in Dominance-Submission Patterns

Humor as a survival mechanism was well demonstrated under a dominance-submission pattern based on racism. Those who had to submit to the lowest statuses in society found they could endure by using humor defensively. In such instances, humor was indeed a "shield" that protected people even when they were enslaved.

On plantations of the antebellum South, slave humor consisted of clever ruses to achieve whatever comforts could be coaxed from their reluctant masters. One group of field hands was consistently being underfed by their slaveowner. He, on the one hand, provided very well for his own table. Once, when he was fattening up seven hogs for his own family, his slaves came to him to report that the porkers were found dead in the fields. Sure enough, when the owner inspected the area, the hogs were found lifeless. Demanding an explanation, the slaves told him that his hogs "just up and died from 'malitis'." The master fumed, "we just can't go around wasting hogmeat," and so he ordered that the hogs should be promptly dressed and fed to the slaves. The slaves dutifully prepared the hogs for their own tables and relished the meat, particularly when they explained to each other how one of the strongest slaves had "tapped the hogs 'tween the eyes so that 'malitis' set in mighty quick!" (Mendel, 1970).

Dominance-submission requires a certain finesse by both the dominators and the dominated. They must of necessity be in close proximity and yet keep the appropriate "social distance" between them. This is accomplished "in polite society" by racial etiquettes such as averting one's eyes, taking off one's cap, shuffling one's feet, standing while superiors are seated, entering rear doors, and addressing superiors with acceptable titles (Doyle, 1937). Acting "as if one is a fool" in front of whites was a well-known tactic among slaves. The tears shed at funerals of their owners might have been genuine enough, but the slaves themselves could distinguish between the tears of sorrow and the tears of joy.

Racial humor thus evolves out of these situations because they are ironic, absurd, often silly, and even foolish as ways to use human services. Humor may even serve the purpose of correcting such discriminatory social conditions.

The legality of racial segregation and dominance-submission patterning continues in the Union of South Africa under the policy of *Apartheid.* The racial etiquettes once found by Doyle in regions of the United States can now be found in South Africa when, for instance, taxicabs are prominently marked "For Whites Only," but are driven by blacks. Such etiquettes survive in the sale of stamps at South African postoffices, where a white clerk waits upon customers at a single table that requires one line of blacks to form at one end and another line of whites to form at the other end in order to obtain postal services.

In more recent years whites have been "let in" on racial humor, previously hidden, that forthrightly pokes fun at them. Dick Gregory, for example, (1962) built much of his reputation as a comedian on the exposure of the sham and pretense behind much racial humor. "Wouldn't it be a helluva joke," he told a nightclub audience, "if all this were really burnt cork and you people were being tolerant for nuthin'?"

At Christmastime, Gregory commented, "All the record stores are playing that subversive song again, 'I'm Dreaming of a White Christmas'... It's kinda sad but my little girl doesn't believe in Santa Claus. She sees that white cat with the whiskers and, even at two years old, she knows damn well ain't no white man coming into our neighborhood at midnight."

Concerning baseball, Gregory noted his approval of the game by pointing out, "Baseball is very big with my people. It figures. It's the only time we get to shake a bat at a white man without starting a riot."

Laughing at Bigotry

Bigotry is certainly not a funny phenomenon. Those who are oppressed by bigots may use humor to sustain their morale, but those who are doing oppressive acts, consciously or unconsciously, do not relish being told about it, being "put down," or being the object of satire.

The turnaround in the sense of publicly, openly, forthrightly making bigotry the target for laughter came in the 1960s. In the '70s such a turn-of-affairs was institutionalized or formalized so that media could freely poke fun at those who supported racism with the approval of generalized audiences. It is more difficult to ascertain the mood of the '80s in the United States, but an educated guess would be that the dominant philosophy of conservatism prevails and people tend not to get too excited about racial prejudice or discrimination whenever it is brought to their attention. Many believe that social machinery is in place to guard against any return to the past in which flagrant cases of racism were acceptable under the law of the land. Humorists who use humor for social correction continue to hold racial bigotry up to laughter, but in the current decade, the responses are not as popular, as raucous, or as evident openly as in past decades.

If there could be a single television series that best represented the willingess to confront racial bigotry through a humorous assault, most would likely agree that "All in the Family" starring Carroll O'Connor as the bigoted, benighted character known as Archie Bunker would be the most likely candidate. The program originated in England in 1964 when an arch-reactionary character named Alf Garnett was created for a television series known as "Till Death Us Do Part." Norman Lear and Bud Yorkin bought the rights to the program in 1970 and introduced Archie into American homes with phenomenal success. The Germans came out with a version of the identical theme in a TV series called "Ein Herz and Eine Seale" ("A Heart and a Soul"), starring Heinz Schubert as Alfred Tetzlaff, an anti-Semite, anti-communist, anti-socialist, anti-everything (Shearer, 1974).

The sitcom, now a part of television history, based its comic appeal on the utter foolishness of the biased Archie, himself. Completely convinced that he was right in his red, white, and blue version of "Americanism," Archie flailed away at any who dared to oppose his views. Archie explained his bigotry in outlandish terms and with careless deductive reasoning. With garbled "facts" and shaky logic, Archie, a self-righteous patriarch, took for granted that racial "inferiors" knew their "place" and would contentedly accept their "Godgiven fate."

One of the most memorable segments of "All in the Family" featured a visit to the Bunker household by Sammy Davis, Jr., a prominent black performer, to recover a briefcase left by mistake in Archie's taxicab. The dialogue went as follows:

Sammy: "Now listen, if you were prejudiced you might have thought of me as a coon or a nigger. But you never said that. Instead, you came out clear as a bell and said — colored.

Archie: "That's right.

Sammy: "And if you were prejudiced you'd shut your eyes to what's going on in this great country, but not you. You can tell blacks from whites and I have a feeling you'll always be able to tell black from white. And I know if you were prejudiced you'd go around thinking that you're better than anyone else in the world, Archie. But, having spent this wonderful afternoon with you, I can honestly say you've proven to me that you ain't better than anybody.

Archie: "Can I shake your hand on that? I hope youse heard all that. Coming from no lesser man than Mr. Wonderful himself. Now that oughtta prove to youse once and for all that I ain't prejudiced." (*Wit and Wisdom of Archie Bunker*, 1971).

Archie's total lack of insight is capsulated in such exchanges and humorously captures the character of racial bigots who are convinced of the righteousness of their own disvaluing of persons different from them.

Racial Humor as Therapeutic

Langston Hughes gathered an impressive array of humor of blacks and expressed hope that such an effort would evoke a responsive, constructive effect in the hearts and minds of readers (1966). It was his perspective that the study of racial humor would reveal the common humanity of minority and majority peoples. Hughes wrote:

"Humor is laughing at what you haven't got when you ought to have it.

Of course, you laugh by proxy. You're really laughing at the other guy's lacks, not your own. That's what makes it funny — the fact that you don't know you are laughing at yourself. Humor is when the joke is on you but hits the other fellow first — before it boomerangs. Humor is what you wish in your secret heart were not funny, but it is, and you must laugh. Humor is your own unconscious therapy.''

Thus racial humor has redeeming value from Hughes' point of view. The one who picks up mud dirties his or her own hands. The one for whom the mud was intended does not receive it all and can even empathize with the sullied mud-slingers.

Functions of Racial Humor

Racial humor performs useful services. The manifest functions may well be to establish and maintain superiority on the part of some, but it also has the latent function, the unintended consequences, of affirming the integrity of the so-called inferiors. This is the redemptive value to which Hughes referred.

Expressing Openly That Which was Previously Unspoken

Under the guise of humor, unspoken ideas and feelings about race or racism are given their voice. Proponents can argue that all they are doing is "having a little fun," but what they are really doing is giving substance and content to serious categorical thinking that sustains the mythology of race and racism. Not too many years ago, a joke that made the rounds among whites referred to a black singer who was crooning "Am I Blue?" The punchline was "No, you are not!"

In the turnaround of events in which whites became the targets of derision, Red Foxx once asked increduously of his son who wanted to get engaged to a white woman, "Why would you want to marry an ugly white woman?" His connection between ugliness and whiteness brought gales of laughter from his audience.

Heightened Morale as a Result of Racial Disvaluing

As a case in point, the attitude among blacks toward police officers is that they are enforcers of law and order that exists to keep them subordinated or under control. The reputation of policemen is tainted because they are viewed as supporting laws that are basically unfair to blacks. This does not apply to *all* blacks or to *all* police officers, but it is held by sufficient numbers of blacks to affect the image they believe to be true and whatever behavior flows from it. Spalding (1972) illustrates this view with an anecdote about a little boy named Claude who lives in New York's Harlem.

Claude's elementary school teacher decided that it would be a good idea to have her pupils write about the police as valued friends in the lives of small children. She expected them to tell how police protected them from auto accidents, robberies, muggings, or getting lost. Little Claude, however, had his own notions about the police, and in his essay he wrote, "New York cops is bastards." Horrified by such a response, the teacher promptly arranged a public relations campaign that would change Claude's negative views and held"get-to-know-us" sessions, parties, and picnics with smiling, uniformed policemen telling the children how they loved them and helped them. To evaluate the effectiveness of the campaign, the teacher then had her pupils write another composition about the police. All the children wrote flattering reports except Claude. "New York cops," Claude wrote, "is *sly* bastards!"

Claude's case suggests that deep-seated suspicions are not easily modified, but they are retained for many years inside personalities. Self-respect and strong group-identification dilute overtures of goodwill, as in Claude's example, and suggest that whole generations will have to come and go before the damages done by racism will be healed. And this process will likely be the subject of much humor as it runs its course.

Denigrating Those Who Devalue Others

Racism in the past was instituted as a rationale for the dehumanization of slaves as commodities. Essentially slaves were property to be used to the economic advantage of owners. Legal emancipatiom broke the bondage, but racism continued in subtle forms. The advantages of having a labor force that was relatively uneducated, uninformed, politically unrepresented and unprotected, and out of necessity willing to work for low wages were not lost on those who stood to gain from the situation. Racism, consciously or unconsciously, meant that whites could continue to treat blacks contemptuously or derisively.

Racism then was essentially "white" racism for many years in the United States. To the astonishment of those whites who were unaware, unconcerned, or relatively isolated from direct knowledge or contact with "the black experience," there came a time when whites experienced the discomforts of what they called "black racism." This was unfair and must be changed, they agreed. Such actions as boycotts, sit-ins, demonstrations, marches, voter registration, and strikes were comparatively peaceful, but they sorely inconvenienced many whites who wondered why they were occurring. Unfortunately there were also violent actions such as burnings, lootings, beatings, and bloodshed. These too meant pain and harm for blacks and whites. Efforts to right the wrongs took the form of fair employment practices, fair housing, school integration, and quota systems, and they brought howls of anguish from persons displaced by them or required to make necessary adjustments to them.

These changes in public policy were accompanied by humor — in the main, bitter humor. Long present and frequently disguised, racial humor among blacks that poked fun at "whitey," "ofays," or "honkeys" finally surfaced. Formerly "underground," humor directed against whites became widely known in the mass media. It continues today but returns underground whenever it is expedient to do so. Humor as *symbolic aggression* will predictably continue between so-called races as long as racial inequities and injustices are maintained or rationalized.

Racism's Ridiculous Nature Exposed

Racial criteria include differentiations in skin pigmentation, color, amount and texture of hair, cephalic index, shape of the lips and nose, and the presence or absence of the epicanthic fold. These observable, external forms and appearances are seized upon as proof positive that different races do exist. Further, it is argued by those who "see" these differences that these factors are socially significant, and thus, differential treatment is justified.

The humor formula, *reductio ad absurdum,* refuting a proposition by showing its logical conclusions to be absurd, can be used to demystify the rationale of racism. Ruth Benedict and Gene Weltfish (1943) wrote a classic pamphlet, *The Races of Mankind,* that employed such a formula. Ethel Alpenfels did the same in her *Sense and Nonsense About Race* (1957). What is even more ridiculous is that these publications and their data were known and available at least forty years ago.

The absurdities are compounded by the mistaken beliefs that documented data and education can effectively destroy racial mythologies. The documented data concern the fact that observable differences selected for emphasis are more matters of degree than they are of kind. Furthermore, much depends upon what is understood to be the meaning of "education." To some it means formal education given in schools; to others it means full and complete disclosure of information; to still others it may mean selected information to achieve preconceived ends; finally, to still others it may mean informal training or socialization in families, friendship groups, or in occupations. All of these forms of education may or may not be consistent and operating for the benefit of all humanity.

Racism itself is an irrational, emotional phenomenon and consequently does not yield to rational, intellectual approaches, analyses, or procedures. Skin pigmentation is perhaps the single criterion most people use to distinguish between races. Skin pigmentation, however, is not as simple or reliable a criterion for racial categorization as many people believe. A variety of absurdities result when skin coloring is used to separate people into various racial classifications. And also becomes a source of racial humor.

Humorists as Race Leaders

Because humor applied to race has both an aggressive and a nonaggressive, conciliatory nature, those who employ such humor often find themselves thrust to the forefront of racial movements. A number of entertainers have found that their humor enables them to stand in the spotlight and casts them in the roles of leadership among their people. This is a serious, sobering status, a far cry from their protestations of being nonserious and facetious.

There are those who are not professional entertainers or comics, but who are instead dead serious about their objectives of dignity and respect for all humanity. Such persons will also resort to humor that appeals to both the minds and emotions of their listeners. Their wit and insights, cleverly expressed, arouse the emotions and exhort persons to use their resources to right the innumerable wrongs committed in the name of racism.

Sociologists differentiate between "designated" and "natural" leaders. Designated leaders are those identified as spokespersons for their constituencies. Natural leaders are those who appear out of gatherings, crowds, or masses, even momentarily, to express the ideas and feelings of their groups or associations. Designated leaders may rely upon their own wit and charisma or may hire ghostwriters to embellish their speeches with appropriate humor. Natural leaders have no such support, but their fleeting comments are extremely effective in hitting their targets.

Such a natural leader came forward during a discussion of racism and its consequences when she spontaneously remarked to those uknown persons who hold tenaciously to their prejudices, "If you do not like me because you think I am ignorant, I can get educated. If you do not like me because you think I am dirty, I can cleanse myself. But if you do not like me because of my skin pigmentation, I can only refer you to the Creator who gave it to me." The statement brought gales of laughter, applause, and high approval from the audience.

Optimism Over Pessimism

One other function of humor in terms of racism is to urge those who are embittered and in despair to hold firmly to their courage and inner fortitude that social corrections will occur. The life histories of many persons have been scarred by the effects of racism (David, 1968; Teague, 1968). But in every case these people were sustained by choosing an optimistic view over a pessimistic one. Like sundials, they functioned on the sunny days.

Another Perspective — "Black Humor"

The eternal optimist, however, is also targeted for humor. This is *not* the humor of blacks about their long history of enslavement, emancipation, reconstruction, migration in search of a better life, urban ghettos, militancy, and political-economic struggles for full citizenship. Rather, this is that genre of humor that takes the pessimistic view and sees no way out of the cruelties, degradation, and visciousness visited upon so many people (Davis, 1966).

"Black humor" is that style of humor that carries with it a meaning of derision and despair. Malone (1969) observed in her study of black humor among American writers, "The black humorist avows that the whole business of the human condition is ludicrous, that there is no sane response to the absurdity of man's position other than a desperate and derisive laugh, a laugh which is one way of expressing bitter rage at man's miserable condition."

The use of the term *black* in black humor presents an interesting semantic differential. Embedded in English is the interpretation that black means something that is bad or debased. Words and phrases such as blackball, black market, blacklist, black eye, Black Friday, blackguard, blackmail, or black sheep convey something negative, something derogatory, something to be rejected. The term *white,* however, connotes something positive, constructive, or commendable. A white lie is a good lie. A whitewash covers defects. The White Knight is a symbol of bravery. A white paper is an authoritative governmental document.

In this chapter the most current, acceptable term for a so-called race, is *blacks.* It is a term that has been redefined over the past few decades to mean pride and self-respect for a people rather than the older term *Negro.* Such a term was judged to mean '*negative growth"* and consequently was displaced by the early popularity of another label, *Afro-Americans,* Americans of African origins, until *black* became the approved and proper terminology.

Racial Humor in General

Racial humor in general has much broader connotation than black-white relationships. Black-white relationships were given prominence in this chapter because such relationships are the dominant ones affecting minority-majority patterns in American society. However, there are other racial types within the United States and in the world to whom racial humor also applies.

There are, for instance, the American Indians or Amerinds of North, Central, and South America who have a long history of contacts with white Europeans. This history is filled with a conscious policy of disruption of Amerind cultures, their displacement or their annihilation.

For persons in the Orient or in Oceania, there is still another story of exploitation, prejudice, and discrimination. This tragic record cannot be undone, of course, but humor again will be found to serve both the persecuted and persecutors of Asiatics and Pacific peoples.

In Chapter 10, in the context of cross-cultural humor, there will be an opportunity to examine the humor of Amerinds, Asiatics, and Pacific peoples because, aside from so-called racial distinctions, there are unique cultural factors that provide a dimension that shapes and forms their special styles of humor.

Summary and Conclusions

Racial humor is characterized by the use of labels to set one group of people apart from all others and consequently lay the groundwork and rationale necessary to legitimize differential treatment. Problems occur, of course, when efforts to separate clearly peoples by their phenotypes fail and when alleged racial distinctions are blurred and blended among Homo sapiens. This failure to identify one racial category from another does not deter racists from insisting that one race or another is either superior or inferior to their own. Racial mythology, of course, need not be substantiated by empiric investigations but rests instead upon ideas, beliefs, or fabrications made up out of unsubstantiated, even irrational, ideas, notions or logic based upon false assumptions. The whole phenomenon would be tragic rather than comic, but humor does flourish within the context of race and racism.

Blatant racial humor that assumed that certain people were essentially excellent targets for derision was once publicly accepted and supported. Such is no longer the case, and portrayals of blacks as stupid or lacking in some way or another is no longer tolerated. Humor long underground and hidden within older dominance-submission patterns emerged enough to reestablish the dignity of racial minorities. Bigotry itself becomes the target of humorists within the next context. Humor becomes the therapy that redeems a people and encourages them to participate constructively within society.

Among the redemptive functions of racial humor are the opportunities to express openly that which was previously unspoken, to develop resolve and heightened morale among those who have experienced rejection, to turn the tables on those who detract or devalue people by reason of alleged racial differences, to expose the ridiculous nature of racism, to strengthen the hands of designated or natural leaders, and finally, to secure an aura of optimism rather than to allow pessimism to have the upper hand.

Finally, the semantic difference between black humor and other humor was noted. Black humor, in short, is an outcry directed against the absurdity of human conditions. These conditions need not exist, but they do, and one response is to laugh at them. Within recent decades the redefinition of black to mean pride and self-respect has, once again, shown the ability of humanity to bring about environments more in line with their longings for dignity and harmony.

STUDY QUESTIONS

1. How does labeling theory explain the nature of racial humor?

2. In what way does the sociological definition of race differ from the conventional definition of what constitutes a race?

3. How is it possible to have "black-whites" and "white-blacks"?

4. What local names do you know apply to racial hybrids? Are these terms negative or positive in their usage in minority-majority relationships within your community?

5. Why would members of a given racial category seek "to pass" as a member of another racial category?

6. Why are racial categorizations so absurd?

7. Why does racism persist despite evidence that it is concocted out of sheer myths?

8. How has racial humor itself undergone social change in the United States?

9. What styles are to be found among black entertainers or comedians and in what ways, if any, do they differ from those of white entertainers and comics?

10. Does racial humor fit the model of a survival mechanism?

11. Why is bigotry an excellent target for racial humor?

12. What are the redemptive qualities of racial humor?

13. Are there functions of racial humor not mentioned or discussed in this chapter? If so, what would you add to the list by explaining how they may benefit proponents?

14. In what ways does racism affect the lives of both racial minorities and majorities?

15. Why is skin pigmentation an ineffective criterion to distinguish between so-called races?

16. What part does humor play in the making or breaking of racial leaders?

17. What are the differences between "black humor" and the "humor of blacks"?

18. Why must racial humor be understood within a social context?

19. Racial humor has changed over the years, but can it ever completely disappear or be eradicated?

20. Does racial humor fit better into conflict models of society or into control models?

Suggested Readings

Alpenfels, Ethel J., *Sense and Nonsense About Race.* N.Y.: Friendship Press, 1957.

Barzun, Jacques, *Race, A Study in Modern Superstition.* N.Y.: Harcourt, Brace, 1937.

Baughman, E. Earl and W. Grant Dahlstrom, *Negro and White Children.* N.Y.: Academic Press, 1968.

Benedict, Ruth and Gene Weltfish, *The Races of Mankind.* N.Y.: Public Affairs Committee, 1943.

Berry, Brewton, *Race and Ethnic Relations.* Boston: Houghton Mifflin, 2nd edition, 1958.

Count, Earl W., *This Is Race.* N.Y.: Henry Schuman, 1950.

David, Jay, *Growing Up Black.* N.Y.: Wm. Morrow, 1968.

Davis, Douglas M., *The World of Black Humor.* N.Y.: Dutton, 1967.

Doyle, Bertram Wilbur, *The Etiquette of Race Relations in the South.* Chicago: University of Chicago Press, 1937.

Garn, Stanley M., *Human Races.* Springfield, IL: C.C. Thomas, 1969.

Goldschmid, Marcel L., *Black Americans and White Racism.* N.Y.: Holt, Rinehart & Winston, 1970.

Gregory, Dick, *From the Back of the Bus.* N.Y.: Dutton, 1962.

Griffin, John Howard, *Black Like Me.* Boston: Houghton Mifflin, 1961.

Hughes, Langston, ed., *The Book of Negro Humor.* N.Y.: Dodd, Mead, 1966.

Mack, Raymond W., *Race, Class, and Power.* N.Y.: American Book Co., 1968.

Malone, Gloria, *The Black Humor of Four American Writers.* Unpublished Master's Thesis. Kent, OH: Kent State University, 1969.

Mendel, Werner M., ed., *A Celebration of Laughter.* Los Angeles, CA: Mars Books, 1970.

Montague, Ashley. *Man's Most Dangerous Myth: The Fallacy of Race.* NY: Columbia Univ. Press, 1942.

Myrdal, Gunnar, *An American Dilemma: The Negro Problem and American Democracy.* N.Y.: Harper, 1944.

Pierson, Donald, *Negroes in Brazil.* Chicago, University of Chicago Press, 1942.

Rose, Peter I., *They and We, Racial and Ethnic Relations in the United States.* N.Y.: Random House, 1964.

Rose, Peter I., *The Subject Is Race.* N.Y.: Oxford University Press, 1968.

Shearer, Lloyd, ed., "Intelligence Report," *Parade,* July 4, 1974.

Spalding, Henry D., ed., *Encyclopedia of Black Folklore and Humor.* Middle Village, NY: Jonathan David Publishers, 1972.

Teague, Bob, *Letters to a Black Boy.* NY: Walker, 1968.

Thompson, Edgar T. and Everett C. Hughes, *Race, Individual and Collective Behavior.* N.Y.: Free Press, 1958.

UNESCO, *What Is Race? Evidence from Scientists.* Paris: United Nations, 1952.

Wilson, William J., *The Declining Significance of Race.* Chicago: University of Chicago Press, 1978.

Wit and Wisdom of Archie Bunker. N.Y.: Popular Library, 1971.

Chapter 7:

Age and Humor

In analyzing the relationship between the process of aging and humor, this chapter will examine age as the independent or "causal" variable while holding humor as the dependent or "outcome" factor. We will seek to find what emerges in humor when factors in age or aging are the dominant or primary concern.

Essentially age deals with how time affects all entities whether they be individuals, generations, populations, groups, social systems, or whole societies. Within this chapter, however, the emphasis will be upon age and the aging process from a social psychological perspective, a concern for individuals within social settings, and how this concern is interpreted through humor.

The chief framework of this chapter is based upon the life-course, the various stages of age-statuses through which individuals typically pass from birth to death, and what is selected from these stages for humorous treatment. For purposes of keeping the chapter within manageable limits, the phases of childhood, adolescence, middle age, and old age are explored to reveal how each age-status or phase elicits certain responses in humor and what underlies these manifestations.

Childhood

Childhood covers the period from birth to puberty or, in arbitrary terms, approximately the first dozen years of an individual's life. Sociologists are particularly concerned with the socialization process that is initiated in childhood but continues throughout a lifetime to acquire ways and means to cope with societal demands, ascriptions, or pressures to conform to sociocultural norms (Erikson, 1963; Koller, 1978). In the complex struggles to gain control over their bodies as well as comprehend and react appropriately to social ascriptions, children acquire different levels of sophistication with humor.

Gesell and Ilg (1946) reported that there was a gradient of humor among the fifty children they observed under controlled, laboratory conditions:

Figure 7-1:
Gradient of Humor Among Children 1 - 10 Years Old

Age of Child: *Level of Ability with Humor*

1 Year	Repeats performance laughed at by adults
2 Years	Initiates humor with playmates
3 Years	Laughs and plays with more motor humor (e.g., peek-a-boo and chasing)
4 Years	Engages in silly, boistrous humor; wild laughter at play
5 Years	Enjoys slapstick humor which he/she initiates
6 Years	May not be too responsive to humor
7 Years	Perpetuates hackneyed jokes; little sense of humor; cannot be handled with humor
8 Years	High sense of humor; enjoys humor in stories particularly when one person is fooled by another; dislikes jokes about self
9 & 10 Years	More robust humor; enjoys humor; can laugh off teasing

Source: Arnold Gesell & Francis L. Ilg, *The Child From Five to Ten.* N.Y.: Harper, 1946, pp. 288-291.

This early study indicated that humor was discovered very early in life and languished for a time, but then was rediscovered and thoroughly enjoyed in later childhood. Attempts at humor failed dismally if there was no "playful attitude" on the part of the child. If there was tension and anxiety, humor was most unwelcome. There is apparently a need to have "a fun frame-work" in place before humor can be truly appreciated. Chapman and Speck (1977) spoke to this point when they used in their study of humor respon-siveness in young children a mobile laboratory equipped in such a way that their child-subjects were made to feel uninhibited and relaxed. Gesell and Ilg further suggested that the acquisition of a sense of humor is an import-ant portion of children's socialization. Whatever sense of humor is ac-quired, those who are charged with the responsibilities of rearing children need to be aware that this acquisition is a vital component in the achieve-ment of mental health. Gesell and Ilg referred to it as an absolute necessity "to safeguard sanity."

Martha Wolfenstein (1954) supported Gesell and Ilg's contention that anxiety reduction is a prominent feature of children's humor. By making fun of the adult world with its immensity, power, and prerogatives, children can use humor to trim their environments to manageable sizes. Feeling less threatened, less anxiety-ridden, and less tense resulted in much rejoicing and high humor among the very young. Wolfenstein cited, for example, the case of a five-year-old whose father had died in the past year. The child was waiting after his kindergarten class for a member of his family to pick him up. When the teacher asked little Eugene if his mother or his sister Betty was coming for him, the boy replied, "My mother is coming and Betty is coming and Kay is coming—the whole family is coming except me because I'm already here!" Wolfenstein commented, "The human capacity to transform suffering into an occasion for mirth is already at work in a five-year-old child."

On a less poignant note, Wolfenstein also told of a teacher who was trying to instruct her children how to tell time. She was using a large clockface with hands that she placed in various settings. When she placed the hands for 3:00 p.m., dismissal time for the children, and asked what time it was, the children responded, "Three o'clock! Goodbye, teacher!" and in high glee rushed to put on their hats and coats. The fun of "putting something over" on their teacher was not lost on these youngsters.

Natalie and Morris Haimowitz (1966) postulated the hypothesis that there was a strong correlation between creativity and humor in young children. It was their contention that those childen who had experienced a closed, homogeneous, consistent or convergent set of thought patterns were less inclined toward humor. Those children, however, who had the reverse pattern, given the freedom to experience a variety of viewpoints, open and alert to the world, would have highly developed senses of humor. Their studies affirmed their hypothesis.

In sociological terms, the Haimowitz's hypothesis favors broad exposure to multiple, sometimes conflicting, points of view in order to increase the chances that the ludicrous ways in which people behave will become known. Not only will individual children know more, but such youngsters can experiment and discover which style or styles best suit their expressions of humor within the limits imposed by their own circumstances.

There was a time when the socialization of children was carried on within their families, kinship networks, and immediate surroundings. In urban, industrial, or post-industrial societies, however, the proliferation of mass media, as discussed earlier, not only serves to enlarge the audiences and provides a variety of ways to couch humor, but it has brought into view the "different" styles of secondary groups in terms of conceptualizations of childhood. Children's humor occupies a considerable portion of mass media presentations and appears to be highly influential in assessments of the nature of childhood.

One view of childhood is that some youngsters are precocious, well ahead of other children in social graces. The films of Shirley Temple, for instance, offered the model of a talented, honest, charming little girl who saw "good" in people. Another view is that children are appealing because they have not yet acquired the ways of the world and hence make mistakes or miscalculations that are funny — funny, that is, to "superior" adults who "know better." In this context, children are not trying to be funny but are acting out their inexperience. Allen Funt's "Candid Camera" television show often ran an unrehearsed filming of the forthright responses of children to questions and situations, and vast audiences were amused for many years by the children's spontaneity, creative imaginations, and lack of adult restraints.

Art Linkletter used a similar format in his television program by interviewing panels of children on a variety of themes. In his *Secret World of Kids,* Linkletter (1960) provided countless samples of this same child integrity. His child subjects were not trying to be humorous but were humorous nevertheless because their unintentional errors were frequently accurate or "on the mark." Linkletter, for instance, told of an elementary school child whose teacher, being in the final trimester of pregnancy, had left her classroom temporarily. The child wrote a sympathetic letter as follows: "Dear Teacher, We miss you. We are all fine. How are you filling?"

Conventional wisdom has long held that childhood is a significant, basic stage in the life course, but it must be shed, displaced, or set aside in order to achieve adulthood or full maturity. Ashley Montagu (1981) in his *Growing Young* took a different stance or assessment of childhood. He saw childhood as filled with traits or qualities that should be enhanced, encouraged, and affirmed throughout individual lifetimes. Montagu urged readers to practice neotony, the art of "growing younger," instead of growing older. Montagu had in mind 26 traits of childhood that should never be set aside or abandoned. Paramount, for example, are such characteristics as curiosity, playfulness, imagination, creativity, openmindedness, flexibility, explorativeness, joyfulness, and a sense of humor. It is these qualities that set the tone of a lifetime despite the sometimes devastating or tragic experiences persons encounter.

Adolescence

Adolescent humor reflects those circumstances that place persons who are in their "teens" or early twenties somewhere between the dependencies of childhood and the relative independencies of adulthood. Autonomy seems so close and yet so elusive. Confined by the ascriptions of being "too young" or "not-yet adult," adolescents may revert to behaviors that can and do bring them into conflict with authority figures (Adams & Gullotta,

1983; Sebald, 1984). These authority figures become the targets for the tendentious humor of adolescents. Or playing it safe so as not to alienate those controlling their lives, youngsters resort to a certain amount of self -ridicule. By using such a tactic they seek to make the best of their situation and consequently to have fun within their own ranks or peers.

The longing for autonomy is evident in the tale of a father who sympathized with his son's desire to take his girl to the high school prom, and so he generously helped him secure a tuxedo, loaned him the family car for the evening, and made certain that he would have some extra money to spend. Just as the son reached the front door to leave for the big event, his father spontaneously called out, "Have a nice time!" The son turned on his father and retorted, "Don't tell me how to act!" As many parents have discovered, material or economic aids are gladly received by adolescents, but there is resentment or rebellion when youngsters believe their freedom to do as they please is thwarted or threatened.

Exasperated parental generations who have to deal with such sensitivity over just how "grown up" and "independent" adolescents really are sometimes retaliate in either serious or humorous form. A serious response, for instance, has been the appearance of parental groups such as "Tough Love," which advocate the refusal to let adolescents have their way and so either set definite limits on their behavior or withdraw their support by letting youngsters feel the effects of rash actions. A humorous response can be seen in the bumper stickers that declare, "Live long enough to avenge yourself on your children!" or "We are spending our children's inheritance!" The thinly disguised aggression between generations is expressed through such humorous means and helps vent parental frustrations harmlessly or gives notice that there can be more serious consequences if adolescents press too hard on the good graces of their parents.

What seems particularly to disturb some parents, teachers, or others in contact with adolescents is the "know-it-all" attitudes of some youngsters. They see trouble ahead for those young people. One entrepreneur has capitalized on this theme by offering a sign which humorously advises, "Hire teenagers while they still know everything!"

Many contemporary adolescents, of course, are more aware and better educated than their elders give them credit. Much earlier than their parental generation, considerable numbers of adolescents are alert to the world about them. In the area of sex, for example, there may have been a time when youngsters were "shielded from a 'too-early' introduction to sexuality," but given the presence of a sex-conscious mass media, naivete can no longer be held to be the norm for adolescents. Adolescent humor is bound to reflect this consciousness so grudgingly acknowledged by those who nurtured them. Sex educators, for instance, have used the story of the father who decided the time had come for him to tell his son about sex. Taking his son aside, the father locked the door, pulled down the shades, and solemnly spoke to his son saying, "Now, son, I want to ask you some questions about sex." The nonchalant son agreed, "Sure, Dad. What do you want to know?"

One of the qualities of childhood is the relatively close supervision normatively given them by their caretakers, parents, family members, or teachers. As adolescents, however, such supervision is gradually relaxed, and teenagers and twenty-year-olds are increasingly free to operate "on their own." Indeed the legal age of "emancipation" that began officially at age 21 has been reduced to age 18 in the past fifteen years. Children then are generally highly controlled whereas adolescents are held to be old enough, big enough, socialized enough to act out their ideas and feelings for themselves. This anticipatory socialization process of approaching adulthood may go smoothly and without too much difficulty for many young people, particularly as they adopt the values of adults or older generations and closely identify themselves with such generations. Nevertheless, adolescence is also a time for experimentation, a "trying-out period" when peer pressures run very high and consequently many youngsters find reinforcement, support, and reference groups among their own age groups whose ideas, values, and behaviors run counter to older generations. It is these rebellious adolescents who capture the attention of the mass media and are given prominence in the headlines.

Adolescent humor parallels these developments or takes on a mirror-image patina from them. In recent history, in the '60s' and the early '70s,' young people almost dominated public attention in their vigorous protestations against the Vietnam conflict. Consciously trying to separate themselves from adults who were held responsible for waging this unpopular war, adolescents made efforts to make some kind of statement against the political-economic policies of the times. One way was to wear long hair and outlandish clothing. One story making the rounds then was about a teenager who entered a barbershop to have his hair trimmed. "Where?" asked the barber. "Just a little around the hips," replied the young man.

Such visual humor included "put on" clothing or wearing apparel. Military surplus stores could furnish symbols of protest to make a mockery of the accoutrements of being in the military services. An adolescent could become an "instant" staff sergeant or a lieutenant by donning some military jacket replete with stripes or bars. Or choosing to identify with the underclasses of the poor, the exploited, or laborers, young people would wear patchwork outfits or overalls. These were mainly middle-class youth and the incongruity of wearing the apparel of another social class was to be understood as to where their sympathies were.

The same applies to adolescent music and dance. In these areas, visual and auditory techniques are employed that taunt, make fun of, or otherwise humorously assault the sensibilities of older, more sedate, conventional generations. To adults, music associated with adolescence is outrageously loud, grossly amplified, and simplistic in its lyrics or messages. To adolescents, the whining guitars, heavy drum beats, and stamping rhythms are "groovy," "with it," "out-of-this-world," "where it's at," or similar expressions. Popular groups take on the most absurd names possible such as "The Grateful Dead," "Led Zeppelin," or "Police." The more incongruity in such titles, the wilder the music and the antics accompanying them, the better.

Each musical group develops its own loyal fans or "groupies." They will sport T-shirts that carry some symbol or sign of their favored group or mimic and idolize singers and musicians by wearing clothing and bizarre hair styles identical to these performers. Such groups and their followers can fill huge staging areas and make their "concerts" the settings for tremendous audience participation. Such musical extravaganzas are ways of saying in essence, "We who are young have a place in the world, and this is our way of celebrating life as we see it."

The dancing that accompanies the music is free-flowing, individualistic, gymnastic, and improvised. Dancing "partners" may touch and move together, but in the main, the twosome may be responding to the music in very different ways. By such means young people declare their independence from the more sedate, conventional, or highly stylized dances of their elders. In the name of fun, a serious message is thus given.

Sociological analysis of adolescent humor and its manifestations would be incomplete if it did not also include the more serious consequences of such adolescent expressions or appreciation for the circumstances of their position in industrial-urban society. For example, despite the humor that declares them to be more sophisticated about sexuality than their parental generations, there are still serious matters of illegitimate births, teenage motherhood, or immature marriages that end up in divorces, separations, desertions, or abject bitterness. Aside from the adolescents' strong desire to express their growing autonomy in such fun-filled music, dance, or bizarre clothing and hair styles, sociologists can help assess the "costs" in terms of being "co-opted" or exploited by entrepreneurs, in the possible loss of hearing resulting from music with excessively high decibel levels, or in the collective behavior that has led to patrons at concerts being crushed to death or seriously hurt in the rush for "first come-first served" seating and related deviant conduct such as drug abuse, etc. Such data are sobering when, in the name of having fun and being humorous and in high spirits, youth are seriously injured or damaged for the remainder of their lives. Such a view is not to find fault or be overly critical of the verve and ideals of adolescents, but to be more aware of the thin line that separates comedy from tragedy.

Middle Age

Given the current life expectancy of some 70 years for men and approximately age 80 for women, "middle age" can be said to begin about age 35 to 40. Its chief characteristic is the recognition that an individual's lifetime is finite and that childhood's imagination and adolescent optimism has not necessarily resulted in adult fulfillment. Middle age humor then would bear these hallmarks.

Two types of "joking frameworks" apply to humor associated with middle age. One is a "setting-specific" framework and the other is a "category-routinized" framework (Handleman & Kapferer, 1972).

Setting-specific joking frameworks are those dependent upon unique situations such as being in one's workplace. In these settings, participants did not choose each other but rather were "thrown together" to provide some special services or to create useful products. Workers, employees, staff members were hired by their employers to cooperate as factory workers, office help, sales personnel, hospital staff, or as professionals within the fields of their expertise.

Category-routinized settings differ in the sense that people come together because they are bonded by kinship, deal with each other because they are socially-legally tied, and they are socially-culturally expected to perform social roles over a lifetime with each other. Individuals may come and go in setting-specific situations, but to do so in category-routinized situations is to disrupt seriously the social fabric. In occupations, persons are hired, fired, or retired, but this is a far cry from abandonment, abuse, neglect, avoidance, or death within family settings.

Within both of these frameworks there is "a license to joke," to be funny, to draw upon humor with its vital functions to help people "get through" each day. Humor, as previously noted, becomes the "social grease" that lubricates social machinery to help it work smoothly. In setting-specific conditions, humor must be used with considerable caution because bonding is more fragile or could possibly interfere with productivity or services being rendered. The bonds that bring workers together are allegedly the performance of certain tasks during working hours. A wide range of personality types are brought together and they do not necessarily share common religious, economic, or cultural heritages.

By contrast, in category-routinized settings, men and women may be fathers-daughters, mothers-sons, brothers-sisters, uncles-aunts, or male and female cousins. They are bonded by reason of consanguinity or strong legal affinity. These bonds can either never be broken or can be broken only with maximal, long-standing effects from such actions as divorce or desertion. Humor in category-routinized settings is based upon close, intimate, enduring relationships that tolerate a certain amount of familiarity among the participants much more than humor in setting-specific circumstances.

Radcliffe-Brown (1952) observed, recorded, and discussed "the joking relationship" in category-routinized settings among various preliterate societies. Such a relationship defused what might otherwise become a very serious matter if there ever was, in fact, some actual action such as incest or a violation of the mores. Males and females within a household, an extended family, or kinship structure are "available" to each other but are denied actual access to each other because to do so would play havoc with the agreed-upon statuses and roles. By joking, teasing, bantering, or obviously nonserious remarks, persons can remain bonded and in close touch with each other without causing harm to themselves or to the cultural systems in which they live.

Apropos middle age and urban, literate societies, the middle-aged husbands and wives, for instance, will resort to establishing a joking relationship when they reach a point in their married lives where they have "settled down" to some familiar, well-used patterns. Stopping short of an actual breakup or serious alienation, they have learned to tolerate certain shortcomings, annoyances, or eccentricities in each other and defuse the situation with some well-aimed, but harmless, barbs that come remarkably close to being insulting but are understood to be a blowing off of steam and nothing more. Such couples have learned to laugh at their relationship rather than let something come between them or abandon each other. Hagar, the rapacious Viking comic strip character, once reminisced, "I used to be my most severe critic. Then I got married." His wife agrees with him wholeheartedly.

Whether in setting-specific or category-routinized settings, by mid-life vast numbers of men and women have reached well-established work habits and family routines. Major decisions have been made, and in mid-life the consequences of such decisions are relatively well known. People are deeply enmeshed, committed, or caught up in their occupations and families. While they may long to recapture more youthful, carefree, less responsible days, that time has elapsed and the realities of their careers are upon them. For some, if they derive satisfaction, pride, and contentment with what they have accomplished, they simply continue and enjoy their circumstances. For others, however, there is the onset of what has been called "mid-life crises." These are feelings of malaise, discontent, or psychic anguish that time may be passing them by because they may have missed their "lost youth" or options. Half of their life is over and the remaining half is far from promising. Such a context elicits the need for humor, the need to meet conditions that may not be easily changed, wished away, or avoided and to move confidently through them — to survive them.

For example, a typical bit of mid-life humor has to do with the desire to retain personal appeal or attractiveness:

Two middle-aged women were gossiping about a mutual friend. One woman observed to the other at a houseparty, "Did you see that man over there annoying Mary?" The other woman replied, "Why, he's not even looking at her!'' The first woman snorted, "Of course! That's what is annoying her!''

For workers, there are the many years already invested in their jobs and in mid-career they draw upon humor in whatever form available to them to hold on and endure. They will post signs that acknowledge their routines, tedium, and generalized feelings of entrapment. Such signs might read: "Bless this mess," "I like the pay; it's the work I can't stand," "You want the work done when?'' (accompanied by an illustration of workers collapsing in uncontrollable laughter), or "I'd rather be ... fishing, flying, swimming, etc., check one space.'' Or they might draw upon the myriad references to what time will bring to them such as: "Old teachers never die, they just lose their class,'' "Old soldiers never die, they just smell that way,'' or "Our workers are proof of resurrection. At quitting time, the dead come alive.''

Old Age

The middle-agers become increasingly aware of what changes have occurred to them over time. They comfort themselves with humor. For the persons who have reached "old age,'' however, there is no doubt what time has done to them. The evidence confronts them whenever they glance at a mirror or whenever they draw upon their energy resources and find, as they say, "Their 'get up and go' has got up and went!''

The following illustrates some of the humor generated by older persons themselves or it represents the popular image of the elderly promoted by those who have not yet reached that stage in their lives:

Figure 7-2

How to Know You're Growing Older

Everything hurts and what doesn't hurt, doesn't work.
The gleam in your eyes is from the sun hitting your bifocals.
You feel like the night before, and you haven't been anywhere.
Your little black book contains only names with M.D.
You get winded playing chess.
Your children begin to look middle-aged.
You finally reach the top of the ladder and find it leaning against the
     wrong wall.
Your back goes out more than you do.
A fortune teller offers to read your face.
You're still chasing women, but can't remember why.
A dripping faucet causes an uncontrollable bladder urge.
Your mind makes contracts your body can't meet.
You know all the answers, but nobody asks you the questions.
You look forward to a dull evening.

(Figure 7-2 (continued):

You walk with your head held high, trying to get used to your bifocals.

Your favorite part of the newspaper is 25-years-ago-today.

You turn out the lights for economic rather than romantic reasons.

You sit in a rocking chair and can't make it go.

Your knees buckle and your belt won't.

You're 17 around the neck, 42 around the waist, and 126 around the golf course.

After painting the town red, you have to take a long rest before applying the second coat.

Dialing long distance wears you out.

You remember today that yesterday was your wedding anniversary.

Your pacemaker makes the garage door go up when you watch a pretty girl go by.

The little gray-haired lady you help across the street is your wife.

You have too much room in the house and not enough in the medicine cabinet.

You sink your teeth into a steak and they stay there.

(Anonymous, 1983)

Humor associated with old age then tends to concentrate upon losses over time rather than any gains. Palmore's content analysis of jokes about old age found that they overwhelmingly reflect a negative view, particularly when they concern physical ability, physical appearance, age concealment, unmarried women, and mental abilities (1971). Further, Palmore found a stronger negative attitude toward women than toward men as they grow older.

Palmore's findings of a pejorative view of old age supported and sustained by humor was confirmed by Joseph Richman (1977) and Leland Davies (1977) in their studies. Weber and Cameron (1978), however, did not concur with this conclusion because they questioned the representativeness of edited jokes, the reliability of judges in coding the data, and the validity of jokes as a measure of attitudes toward aging. Finally, Weber and Cameron reserved judgment about just how jokes about old age served to stereotype older persons.

Dwayne Smith (1979) responded to some of the criticisms of Weber and Cameron by attending carefully to the reliability of judges and by using cartoons dealing with older men and women rather than edited jokes. Smith found that cartoon humor about the elderly was far less harsh on older persons than jokes. Nevertheless, he confirmed the earlier findings of Palmore, Richmand, and Davies that there were indeed strong negative attitudes promoted in humor dealing with old age.

Demos and Jache (1980) took a different tack when they studied birthday cards identified as "humorous" in various card shops. They affirmed, once again, that the birthday cards they examined reinforced popular stereotypes concerning the physical and mental deficiencies of elders, drew sharp contrasts between people within different age boundaries, and tended to support the notion that aging is something that happens to other people but not to one's self. Losses in personal attractiveness and sexual prowess were treated humorously in the birthday cards, not so much for the senders of the cards but for the recipients of such messages.

Jokes, cartoons, and birthday cards are not the only media that convey humorous messages that old age is laughable. Theatrical presentations often feature the prototype of "an old man" as being irascible, quick to anger and to oppose the wishes, plans, or actions of younger persons. Such a stock character, the *senex iratus,* always is portrayed as bitter over the past, grumpy over the present, and grim about the future. For him there appears not to be a future in which he will participate and he cares little for those who will have a future. Now and then he may cease being a grouch, but the *senex iratus* is far more likely to complain about existing conditions, to be appalled by what he calls the abysmal ignorance of young people, and to oppose the plans or proposals of enthusiastic youth because he sees them as utterly foolhardy.

There is a counterpart for women who are older. When asked to portray an older woman humorously, actors and some actresses will take on the character of a frail, wrinkled, inane personality. Cliff Arquette, Jonathan Winters, and Dick Van Dyke have amused millions with their taking on the persona of such an old woman. Carol Burnett has done a similar character, all in the name of fun. When Johnny Carson portrayed his version of "Aunt Blabby," a silly old lady with frumpy clothes, out-dated wig, and a habit of incessantly talking sheer nonsense, Maggie Kuhn, founder of the militant "Gray Panthers," then 74 years of age, appeared on his television program and countered his humor by presenting him with a T-shirt to help "liberate" Aunt Blabby from such a demeaning role.

Poking fun at the elderly, laughing at old age, has been going on for a very long time, but the "graying of America" and the growing numbers and proportions of older persons in Western, urban, industrialized societies portend some modifications of this treatment in the future. There is simply more economic and political clout among "senior citizens" as well as a tremendous range of personality types among the elderly to permit humorists from going "too far" in catering to mass audiences when lampooning old age. Richard Calhoun (1978), for instance, carefully documents how old age is being redefined in America in his study, *In Search of the New Old.* Somewhat akin to Montagu's views in *Growing Young,* mass media are disseminating remarkable case histories of older men and women who are light-years away from being a *senex iratus* or frail, inept old women who do not really matter in modern times. Such advanced age individuals have accomplished amazing deeds that serve the needs of all age-groups. They are not "has-beens," marginal to the life of societies, but are indeed active participants in the mainstream of their societies. No doubt, humor associated with old age will continue as before, but with increasing evidence that there are "the new old," people will at least identify such humor as playing upon half-truths or distorted stereotypes. Paul Zopf's *America's Older Population* (1986) presents convincing data in support of the thesis that today's elderly in America are not nearly as impoverished, in dire financial straits, nor dependent, helpless and senile as stereotypes have depicted. It will also be of interest to observe how changing social images of the elderly will affect future humor about this aged population.

Summary and Conclusions

Passage along the life course starting with childhood and adolescence and continuing through middle age and old age has been linked with humor because each age-status has to cope with whatever social characteristics have been ascribed to it. Each age-status then manifests unique qualities that color their distinctive form of humor.

Because childhood is characterized by high dependency upon adults, the humor of childhood fundamentally concentrates on the need to make manageable a grown-up world that dominates this age-status. Socialization has just begun in childhood and childish errors or shortcomings along the way are not only tolerated, understood, and anticipated, but they are also found to be humorous to their adult caretakers.

Adolescence, however, represents a break from childhood and former tolerances, understandings, and appreciation for failures to comply no longer apply. Indeed, they are not necessarily held to be charming or amusing and thus humorous. Instead, adolescence is viewed as an awkward age-status in which persons are asked to shed their childish ways but are still denied full access to adulthood. Adolescent humor may mirror resentment and rebellion against the denial of adult prerogatives or offer some means to share the comradery within their own age-status. When rising expectations are frustrated, adolescents have found refuge, solace, comfort, identification, and status within their own subculture. Within their own reference groups, adolescents may mock or shock their elders by such means as visual or musical humor.

Middle-age humor takes on a different patina than either childhood or adolescence. Within their age-status, the life course has reached its midpoint and is seen to be finite. From a societal viewpoint, life courses overlap and are constantly repeated. Thus, for society, this coming and going of individuals is a renewable resource and is called the life cycle. Time is passing too rapidly for the middle-aged. This age-status has to deal with childhood, adolescence, and young adults in as optimal a manner as possible. Humor helps the middle-aged deal with their problems as relatively independent agents who have made decisions that led to their present circumstances, or they can draw upon humor to aid them as the supportive agencies for dependent youngsters and dependent elderly.

Old-age humor focuses on the decrements or losses in the aging process. In more recent decades, however, old-age humor has been criticized as older people reject being stereotyped as rather funny, superfluous people who are somewhat out of the mainstream of social life. Rather, the new mood is one of redefining old age in terms of more vitality, verve, and vigor as older persons continue to contribute to their own well-being and to the well-being of others.

STUDY QUESTIONS

1. Just how does aging humor aid and abet stereotypic views of various age-statuses?

2. Can humor change whatever qualities are alleged to belong to various age-grades?

3. What functions are performed by the humor of childhood and all subsequent age-statuses?

4. In what ways does age-humor offer a way to engage in symbolic aggression against other age-statuses?

5. How does humor strengthen group identity with one's age-peers? Is it stronger in certain age-groups or does it apply to all age-groups?

6. In what way does incongruity operate in age-humor?

7. What part does precociousness play in children's humor?

8. What are the hallmarks of adolescent humor both from the in-group's perspective and those outside this age-status?

9. In what ways does humor help various age-grades endure whatever indignities are thrust upon them by societal definitions?

10. Does age shape certain manifestations of humor or does humor contribute to the conditions people experience as they move through the life course?

11. What is humorous about growing older?

12. Is age humor universal or is it lacking in certain societies or times?

13. Are there fluctations in aging humor as various age-groups encounter social changes within their society?

14. Do persons have a preference for certain age-humor depending upon where they are, personally, along the life course? Why so or why not so?

15. What are the sobering results of humor that support adolescent contentions that this age-status is indeed ready and able to be autonomous, responsible adults?

16. Has age humor, as you have known it, changed in your lifetime? How would you explain it?

17. How do joking relationships differ in category-routinized or setting-specific situations?

18. What would you predict will happen to humor about old age in the 21st century?

19. Does age humor support the idea that one age-grade or another is, in fact, "the prime of life?"

20. Do self-definitions or social definitions control or affect age humor?

Suggested Readings

Adams, Gerald R. and Thomas Gulltta, *Adolescent Life Experiences*. Belmont, CA: Brooks/Cole, 1983.

Calhoun, Richard B., *In Search of the New Old, Redefining Old Age in America, 1945-1970*. N.Y.: Elsevier North Holland, 1978.

Chapman, Anthony J. and Linda J.M. Speck, "Birth Order and Humour Responsiveness in Young Children," in Anthony J. Chapman and Hugh C. Foot, *It's A Funny Thing, Humour*. Oxford: Pergamon Press, 1977, pp. 219-221.

Davies, J. Leland, "Attitudes Toward Old Age and Aging as Shown by Humor," *The Gerontologist*, v. 17 (June, 1977): 220-226.

Demos, Vasilikie and Ann Jache, "When You Really Care: An Analysis of Attitudes Toward Aging in Humorous Birthday Cards," Paper presented at the annual meeting of the North Central Sociological Association, Dayton, Ohio, May, 1980.

Erikson, Erik H., *Childhood and Society*. 2nd ed. N.Y.: W.W. Norton, 1963.

Gesell, Arnold and Francis L. Ilg, *The Child From Five to Ten*. N.Y.: Harper, 1946.

Haimowitz, Morris L. and Natalie Reading Haimowitz, eds., *Human Development, Selected Readings*. 2nd ed. N.Y.: Crowell, 1966. (See therein "Children's Humor: Joking and Anxiety," by Martha Wolfenstein.)

Handelman, Don and Bruce Kapferer, "Forms of Joking Activity: A Comparative Approach," *American Anthropologist*, v. 74 (June, 1972): 484-517.

Koller, Marvin R. and Oscar W. Ritchie, *Sociology of Childhood*. 2nd ed. Englewood Cliffs, NJ: Prentice-Hall, 1978.

Linkletter, Art, *The Secret World of Kids*. N.Y.: Bernard Geis, Pocket Books, 1960.

Montagu, Ashley, *Growing Young*. N.Y.: McGraw-Hill, 1983.

Palmore, Erdman, "Attitudes Toward Aging as Shown by Humor," *The Gerontologist*, v. 11, Part I (Autumn, 1971): 181-186.

Radcliffe-Brown, A.R., "On Joking Relationships," *Africa*, v. 13, pp. 195-210. Reprinted in *Structure and Function in Primitive Society*. London: Cohen & West, 1952.

Richman, Joseph, "The Foolishness and Wisdom of Age: Attitudes Toward the Elderly as Reflected in Jokes," *The Gerontologist*, v. 19 (June, 1977): 210-219.

Sebald, Hans, *Adolescence, A Social Psychological Analysis*. 3rd ed. Englewood Cliffs, NJ: Prentice-Hall, 1984.

Smith, M. Dwayne, "The Portrayal of Elders in Magazine Cartoons," *The Gerontologist* v. 19 (1979): 408-412.

Weber, Timothy and Paul Cameron, "Humor and Aging - A Response," *The Gerontologist*, v. 18 (1976): 73-75.

Wolfenstein, Martha, *Children's Humor, A Psychological Analysis*. N.Y.: Free Press, 1954.

Zopf, Jr., Paul E., *America's Older Population*. Houston, TX: Cap and Gown Press, 1986.

Chapter 8:

Sexual and Gender Humor

Perhaps the most emotionally charged topics with which humor deals are sex, sexuality, and gender. This chapter examines sexual and gender humor to help explain why they evoke such predictably strong responses, what underlies their attraction-repulsion components, and how they underscore struggles between those who wish to sustain traditional views about the appropriate status and roles of males and females and those who seek to emancipate both men and women from what they believe is social bondage.

Every society acknowledges the presence of males and females and is aware of sexual distinctions based upon anatomical, physiological, genetic, and biochemical differences. When it comes to the ways in which men and women are to express their sexual differences and similarities, their sexuality, societies are prepared to provide certain opportunities and also limitations upon their actions. Furthermore, societies offer structurally-functionally gender ascriptions to males and females as to what constitutes masculinity and femininity and, accordingly, rationale for "acceptable" statuses and roles for men and women. Social order, social control, and social conflict are at stake, and sexual and gender humor call upon protagonists and antagonists to exercise some degree of discretion or caution in using them.

Sensitivity About Sexual Humor

Despite repeated claims that contemporary Western societies at least have learned how to deal with sex, sexuality, and sexual identity in a free, relaxed, nonjudgmental, comfortable, easy, open, and honest way, there remains "a residue of antagonism" against any lighthearted, frivolous, or thoughtless treatment of sex and gender. Sex or anything that has to do with sex, remains a sensitive, volatile, even dangerous matter that can do considerable damage to those who want to joke about it, to make sly references to it, or to use it in the name of humor. Just as dynamite can explode

111

in the face of the careless, sexual humor can become "social dynamite" with painful ramifications for those who promote it or are exposed to it.

There are two theories or schools of thought as to what explains ambivalent reactions to sexual humor. The dominant theory is that within the lifetime of living generations there has been a "sexual revolution" in which profound changes have occurred that radically alter the ways with which sexual topics, including sexual humor, are perceived. A second theory, however, holds that no sexual revolution has occurred and that, instead, whatever has been happening in reference to sex and sexuality is a continuation of old, established, traditional, and even ancient attitudes and styles.

In support of the theory that radical change has occurred in sexual mores, folkways, or codes are Kardiner (1954), Farberow (1963) and Lipton (1965). Lipton wrote about "the erotic revolution," Kardiner wrote about the changes in sexual morality, and Farberow wrote about human sexual behavior as among the "taboo topics" that have become much more open to study, investigation, and analysis than in the past.

John Crosby (1985) lent his support more in behalf of the second theory, that the idea of a new sexual morality or drastic departure from older sensibilities about sexual topics is essentially temporocentric, myopic, premature, or illusionary. Crosby presented data that reply to myths that sex and sexuality are something new under the sun and that support instead the theory that sex and sexuality have always carried with them an aura of attraction-repulsion.

The second theory receives further credibility when investigators of human sexuality encountered considerable resistance from potential informants (Kinsey et al., 1948, 1953; Masters & Johnson, 1966, 1970; Sorensen, 1973; Hite, 1975). In every instance, Kinsey and those who followed him found a majority of potential respondents refused to cooperate with such studies, did not return questionnaires, and did not wish to share their sexual histories even under the cloak of anonymity. The samples of subjects of these researchers have been seriously criticized in scientific circles because they do not represent validly the universe they purport to investigate. These subjects do, of course, represent the sexual attitudes and behaviors of those who did respond frankly and willingly to their probings.

Both theories contain some measure of social reality that reflect back on sensitivities concerning sexual humor. On the one hand, there does appear to be, from the perspective of persons living today, tremendous openmindedness about sex and sexuality, and this tolerance of viewpoints opens the way for more freedom to use sexual humor publicly. On the other hand, sex and sexuality remain for huge numbers of people matters of privacy and not something to be treated by the public as laughable, silly, or foolish. Sex and sexuality are serious matters for many people, and these persons are less receptive to freewheeling sexual humor. In this context a familiar response to attempts at sexual humor is "nervous" laughter that is less of a response to the humor itself as it is to a release of tension, stress, anxiety, and uncertainty over whether or not to enjoy the sexual humor or to reject it because others might interpret the sexual connotations involved.

For those who do promote sexual humor, there are several advantages. They have found that humor can defuse an emotionally charged subject such as sex and sexuality because they are not "serious;" they can symbolically break the rules against improprieties but not actually break them; and they can demonstrate their emancipation or liberation from sexual taboos without necessarily requiring it of others. Audiences or publics may or may not be receptive to attempts at sexual humor, but those who do use sexual humor feel that options should be open and not closed or censored.

Sexual Humor: "Clean" or "Dirty"?

Sexual behavior *per se* is a serious area of scholarly study (Ellis & Abarbanel, 1961; Kogan, 1973; Delora & Warren, 1977; Hyde, 1982). The bulk of these publications, however, devote no space to any consideration of sex as a source for humorous treatment. Such benign neglect makes sense because sexologists want to be taken seriously. Only a few pioneering scholars from a variety of disciplines have begun to recognize that sexual humor is a legitimate field of inquiry.

Aside from its continuing taboo status among many people and their associated groups, the dearth of studies of sexual humor can possibly be explained by the widespread tendency to associate or equate human sexuality with that which is obscene, vulgar, animalistic, and "dirty." Such an association or equating exists, in part, because sexual organs have the dual function of excretion and sexual pleasuring. Masters and Johnson use this precise phrase in describing the "pleasure bond" between men and women as the fullest functioning of their sexuality.

The dilemma as to which assessment should be made about sex and sexuality, whether it is "filthy" or it is "delightful," is rooted in socialization begun in infancy and childhood and reinforced in adolescence and adulthood. Individuals are taught that eliminated body wastes or fluids are odious, ugly, unappetizing materials to be flushed away in privacy. At the same time, sexual organs or anatomy are also held to be "centers of modesty." Public exposure of sexual organs is judged to be indecent, illicit, shameful, and degrading. One must cover up these centers of modesty while in the company of others (Ellis, 1902).

Given this socialization and its constant reinforcement, it is not surprising to find attempts to portray human sexuality in a more positive, forthright, wholesome way have met with considerable resistance. The opposition to sex education in public schools, for instance, still continues by those unconvinced that sex and sexuality are fit subjects for academia.

There is one scholar at least who does not equivocate on humor about sex being "clean" or "dirty" (Legman, 1968). Legman sees sexual humor as being on a continuum with degrees of "dirtiness." In his "First Series," Legman offered what could be called "clean dirty" jokes. These are all "dirty" bits of humor, but they are relatively mild when compared with other substantive topics. Legman chose to place humorous references to children, fools, animals, males' approaches to females, sadism, women, premarital sex acts, marriage, and adultery in this "least dirty" part of his continuum.

In his "Second Series," Legman (1975), so to speak, "drops the other shoe." In this series, Legman turns to "dirty dirty" jokes which fill out the remainder of his continuum. Themes of these jokes concerned homosexuality, prostitution, venereal disease, castration, cursing, and scatology. These were judged by Legman to be "presumably of less ordinary occurrence or of greater psychological danger or violence" and "therefore theoretically of greater anxiety-content."

In this analysis Legman is well within the tradition of Sigmund Freud, founder of psychoanalysis, who made the term *libido* central to his conceptualization of primary motivations for human behavior. The Freudian view is that erotic humor contains a strong element of sexual aggression or exploitation of one sex by the other. Sociologically this aggressive component of sexual humor fits conflict theory in which dominance-submission patterns become the battlegrounds by opposing forces.

For males, for example, to call attention to sexual organs, sexual functions, or overt erotic acts in the presence of women through the vehicle of humor is tantamount from a conflict perspective to "verbal rape," "psychological seduction," or "social undressing" of females. In the New Testament, the symbolism is carried even further when Christ declared to his followers that to even "think about" sexual relations with a woman who is not one's wife is the same as adultery itself and consequently must be held to be reprehensible, sinful, and vicious (Matthew 5: 28).

Women too within the context of social conflict, turn to sexual humor for their own purposes. Some women are apparently quite adept at satirical tongue-lashings of men they judge to be sexually inadequate (Masters & Johnson, 1970). The effects of such sexual humor include "demasculination," humiliation, loss of self-respect, and impotence. Support groups, psychiatric consultations, and sexual therapists have coped with these possibilities for many years. The severity of sexual humor used by women may also be a retaliation for a male-dominated, "macho" culture that has kept women in subordinate, unappreciated, subservient positions for too long. Through humor, women can assault, diminish, and taunt those men who have held them in subjugation and contempt without regard for women's feelings or longings for dignity and appreciation.

Sex, marriage, and family educators are caught up in the same milieu as their clients, and so, despite training that divests them of notions that would be a detriment to their professional services, they too may hold strongly to the idea that somehow sex is tainted by a label of dirtiness, shame, pain, and guilt. Robert and Frances Harper (1957) noted how certain sex educators underplayed, de-emphasized, repressed, avoided, feared, and attempted to by-pass sexual topics. Thus professionals and lay persons alike see sex, and by extention, sexual humor, as a matter best left unattended or unexplored. Or as noted earlier, men and women will turn to sexual humor whenever it suits their purposes quite well.

Wesley Adams (1974), a sex educator, does not fit the characterization of sex educators as persons afraid to come to terms with their own subject matter, as portrayed by the Harpers. Rather, Adams has found another usage for sexual humor that is constructive or helpful for university students. By using cartoons that focused upon such topics as sexuality among older persons, lesbianism, homosexuality, exhibitionism, obscene telephone calls, "turning one" sexually, and new moral codes, Adams found that his students could express their anxieties concerning these and similar sexual topics much more effectively than by the more usual grim approaches. In Adams' approach to sex education, there is further confirmation of humor as a "safety-valve" in letting off harmless steam rather than letting it build up to some destructive end.

According to Legman, national groups tend to react to sexual humor depending upon what degree of "dirtiness" fits their nationalistic paradigms. For example, Legman claims that German and Dutch people are highly entertained and brought to heights of uncontrollable laughter by reference to feces. Their excessively strict discipline and early toilet-training are credited by Legman as the root cause of their anxieties and hence their understandable relief to be able symbolically to ventilate their pent-up feelings through such humor.

The French, who associate sexuality with pleasant experiences and not embarrassment or shame, are far less shocked or intimidated by humorous references to sexuality. Again, according to Legman, French men and women seemingly are highly amused by references to the entrapment of adults caught up in some forbidden sexual liaisons. The cuckold, the archetype in sexual humor in which the husband of an unfaithful wife either never knows about his wife's escapades or is the last to learn about his wife's infidelity, is a favorite of the French.

Legman finds that English men and women rate as disproportionately concerned over homosexuality and incest. The stereotype of conservatism and dedication to "proper" conduct alleged to be part of the British character supposedly explains their anxieties over such deviations from their normative sexual expectations.

Finally, Legman turns to Americans and suggests that their sexual humor is unique because it seems to be preoccupied with racism and oral-genital contacts.

The idea that there is some recognizable "modal personality type" or "national character" for a given nationalistic society has wide currency in popular folklore, but there remains considerable skepticism that a singular descriptive pattern can be applied to fit every individual within that society. Furthermore, the logical connection between alleged modal personality types and their preference, rejection, or preoccupation with selected sexual humor requires far more verification by future research.

There is a form of expression for sexual humor that suggests that there is indeed something that is "dirty," shameful, or unclean about it. That form is graffiti, writings that appear in public restrooms, sidewalks, passageways, walls or seats or anywhere the general public or passersby may see it. These writings with their sexual messages are usually prepared unobserved, under cover of darkness, surreptitiously, anonymously, and untraceable. Apparently originators of sexually oriented graffiti are somewhat aware of how their attempts at sexual humor are perceived as "lowdown," "filthy," and "disgusting," and this technique allows them to broadcast or make public their preferences without fear of personal consequences (Read, 1977). Sociologists recognize in graffiti some elements of Goffman's dramaturgical model (1959), in which "backstage" behavior is brought "frontstage" in a departure from usual norms.

Public morality is not offended, however, when references to sexuality occur in sources judged to be of the highest repute (Brav, 1959). The Old Testament, for example, contains explicit references to a wide variety of sexuality: the nudity of Adam and Eve; the willingness of Abraham to impregnate Hagar, a maidservant in his household in order to assure a male heir; the sexual acts of Sodom and Gomorrah; the incestuous acts of Lot's daughters; the rape of Dinah by Shechem; the lustful King David who willingly sacrificed one of his generals on the battlefield in order to copulate with the general's wife, Bathsheba; the sexual misadventures of Samson and Delilah; and in the Song of Songs, the ecstatic and extravagant praises heaped upon a woman by her lover. One of the most memorable Biblical references to sexual humor itself was the case of Sara, wife of Abraham, who laughed helplessly behind her tent's curtains when she eavesdropped on the message from visitors to her husband that she would have child despite her advanced years.

The rhetoric over "cleanliness" or "dirtiness" or acceptable-unacceptable nature of sex and sexuality continues between those who would uphold their perceptions of "public decency" and those who see no threat to the social order when they pursue their own private responses to sex or sexuality. Either camp includes sexual humor in advancing their views and in detracting from their opposition. A cartoonist, for instance, portrays an old-fashioned, prim and proper, elementary school teacher who tells her children sarcastically, "The Board of Education requires me to give you some basic information on sex, reproduction and other disgusting filth" (Savage, 1967). Mark Twain used a publication called *1601* to expose the false modesty of aristocrats by assembling a fictional cast of famous and imaginary charactaers who exchange sophisticated views about such topics as "breaking the wind," the sexual conduct of widows, the sexual rivalries of women, premarital and nonmarital sexual relations, pregnant brides, the erotic adventures of pious clergy, and curses uttered by the Queen (Kronhausens, 1959).

Gender Humor

Gender humor that has to do with alleged qualities either inherent in the nature of males and females or acquired through normative expectations pits one sex against the other. This "battle of the sexes" is not something that has its origins in the contemporary struggles between men and women over their "proper" statuses and roles. Rather, the exasperation over how each gender can endure the other gender has been expressed in humorous ways since antiquity.

From ancient India, for example, comes the following story of gender conflict couched in humorous terms:

(And the Lord made woman and gave her to man.) But after one week, man came to Him and said, "Lord, this creature that you have given me makes my life miserable. She chatters incessantly and teases me beyond endurance, never letting me alone; and she requires incessant attention, and takes up all my time; and cries about nothing, and is always idle; and so I have come to give her back again, as I cannot live with her."

So the Lord said, "Very well," and He took her back.

Then, after another week, man came again to Him and said, "Lord, I find that my life is very lonely, since I gave you back that creature. I remember how she used to dance and sing to me, and cling to me; and her laughter was music, and she was beautiful to look at, and soft to touch; so give her back to me again."

So the Lord said, "Very well," and gave her back again.

Then, after only three days, man came back to Him again and said, "Lord, I know now how it is; but after all I have come to the conclusion that she is more trouble than a pleasure to me; so please take her back again."

But the Lord said, "Out on you! I will have no more of this. You must manage how you can."

Then the man said, "But I cannot live with her."

And the Lord replied, "Neither could you live without her."

So He turned His back on man and went about His work.

Then man said, "What is to be done? For I cannot live either with her or without her." (Bain, 1905)

In modern form, one finds gender humor that takes as its central theme that little change has been made since that ancient lament from India. Most have heard women sigh, "Just like a man... " or men say, "Just like a woman... " Or perhaps they have encountered the quip that refers to the creation of men and women in engineering terms, "God realized the flaws in the first draft and, consequently, perfected the design in the second draft."

Male dominance and female submission to that dominance is well engrained in societal systems. "Man is head of the household" is a formula still very much alive in the world. *Machismo* is well-entrenched in Latin countries, particularly among lower-class rural families. In the Roman Catholic Church, the male priesthood has been questioned by feminists but shows little signs of changing long-standing male domination or leadership in the church hierarchy. And so it goes on and on. Whether it is in religious circles, within cultural enclaves, family structures, or political-economic systems, persons seeking equity in opportunities to fulfill their lives find themselves stymied. Gender humor reflects this despair that social changes are not occurring fast enough and effectively enough. Pond (1985) sarcastically notes that the feminist future will change, but that it will take until the year 7008 before the Democratic party once again will consider a female vice-presidential candidate.

Naomi Weisstein (1973) offered a withering response to those who castigate women for either lacking a sense of humor or alleging that women have a very inadequate sense of humor because of their militancy and outrage over the *status quo*. She wrote:

"As women, we live in a coercive, threatening, unpleasant world; a world that tolerates us only when we are very young or very beautiful. If we become stupid or slow, jumpy or fast, dizzy or high-pitched, we are simply expressing the pathology of our social condition. So when we hear jokes against women and we are asked why we don't laugh, the answer is easy, simple, and short. Of course we are not laughing, you (bleep). Nobody laughs at the sight of their own blood."

By such a diatribe, Weisstein resorts to humorous thrusts to diminish opposition to feminism and to promote feminist aspirations. Male chauvinism, in her view, has continued too long, and through humor she can encourage women to dismantle it through their collective outrage. Weisstein concluded, "We must construct a women's culture with its own character, its fighting humor, its defiant celebration of our own worth. We must reclaim our history, our rights to self-expression and collective enjoyment. We must create our own humor. The propitiating laugh, the fixed and charming smiles are over. This time, when we laugh, things are going to be funny."

Some years have passed since Weisstein wrote in such militant and strident terms. The "fighting humor" that Weisstein felt was essential may be toned down a bit by changes in strategy by key leaders in the women's movement. Betty Friedan, whose *The Feminine Mystique* (1963) is credited with sparking the women's movement. has called for a "second stage" in which men and women join together to carry out mutually acceptable responsibilities (1983). Such a conciliatory approach probably would call also for gender humor that treats inequalities between men and women with less venom and with more finesse or tact. Indeed such a change may be manifested in a collection of feminine humor by Kaufman and Blakely (1980). In it, one finds a more relaxed mood in which women turn on themselves as humorous targets rather than attacking men in general. Their work, *Pulling Our Own Strings,* is epitomised by an uncaptioned cartoon of two females walking off together toward an unknown future with their tampon strings openly showing.

The messages conveyed by gender humor have helped educate the general public about the many demands placed upon women that can no longer be taken for granted. Couched in humorous mode, the multiple roles of women were made clear by the following item appearing without comment in the newspapers: The State Motor Vehicle Department of Madison, Wisconsin, reported that they returned an application for a driver's license from a woman because she had not filled in the space marked "Occupation." The woman replied by filling in the space with "Mother, maid, cook, ironer, mender, furniture polisher, painter, baby sitter, entertainer (children and adult), unregistered nurse, unlicensed M.D., bottle washer, part-time father, and baby machine." She added, "This is just a partial list, but hope it will be sufficient." The departmental director said it would be.

That some men still have to learn about the division of labor that puts women "inside" a home doing domestic chores and men "outside" their homes doing their jobs is demonstrated by a cartoonist who portrayed a husband rejecting his wife's suggestion that she find a job outside their home by saying, "Stick to your washing, ironing, scrubbing, and cooking. No wife of mine is going out to work!" Women have always worked, instructs this humor. What is changing is the *locale* of women's work. Not only do women continue to work in their homes, but they work outside their homes out of necessity rather than, as many men believe, out of a desire to compete with men or to demonstrate their personal freedom to do whatever they please.

Weddings, of course, are prime times for gender humor because these rituals signal a merging of the two different worlds of men and women. From the male point of view, marriage can be perceived as "entrapment" by wily women. Thus it made sense to the brother of a bridegroom to paint "H E" on the left sole of the groom's shoe and "L P" on the sole of right shoe. Those in attendance had a good laugh when the couple knelt at the altar, exposing the message.

This is in keeping with a priest's experience when he was approached by a young man during a wedding rehearsal. The husband-to-be wanted to tell the priest that he realized at last that marriage was a very serious event. He told the priest, "Father, I know now that marriage is not simply a word. It is a lifetime sentence!" The man was laughing, but through humor he was able to speak of his understanding of marriage as a sobering commitment between a man and a woman.

Comedians and Comediennes

In the context of gender humor it is useful to observe that men have traditionally dominated professional comedy. Comediennes have been around a long time, but in relative numbers and proportions, their ranks are few when compared to that of men. Furthermore, their onstage personae have frequently been based upon some subordinate roles that are based on the social realities of offstage life for women.

Erma Bombeck, for instance, is a columnist and author who has parlayed the image of the harried, ever-suffering suburban housewife and mother into a lucrative and significant career. She effectively portrays for her readers how women carry on bravely and with stiff upper lip despite the thoughtlessness and thanklessness of those womanhood serves so well. Her recent book in reference to motherhood but with tongue in cheek in reference to females being exploited by men was *The Second Oldest Profession* (1983). Other works that have delighted women readers who see in her prose an expression of what their lives are really like are *I Lost Everything in the Post-Natal Depression, The Grass Is Always Greener Over the Septic Tank,* and *If Life Is a Bowl of Cherries—What Am I Doing in the Pits?* Her column, "At Wit's End," appears in some 700 newspapers and speaks directly to millions of women whose lives are alleged to be filled with car pools, P.T.A. meetings, and Tupperware parties. How shall men ever understand the world of women? Bombeck with her self-deprecating prose can help men understand vicariously through the vehicle of gender humor.

Comediennes are probably most effective when they dramatize the place of certain women in the scheme of things. Notable comediennes who drew upon their relationships with their husbands for the substance of their work were Gracie Allen, Portland Hoffa, Mary Livingston, and Marie Driscoll in an earlier generation of performers. Their portrayals were of wives who were "weaker" than their husbands in intellect, training, or worldliness. Their forte lay in making their husbands look good or to appear to be even more amusing than they really were. George Burns, for example, has often told audiences that he lived off the considerable talents of his wife, Gracie Allen, by merely nodding his head, smoking his cigar, and looking nonchalant while Gracie prattled on in a nonstop discussion based on absurdities.

Not all comediennes portrayed inane wives; a number took a different tack by portraying "strong women" who lived with "weaker men" in their comedic lives. Gertrude Berg, Lucille Ball, Marie Dressler, and Phyllis Diller were adept at these characterizations. Jean Stapleton, a consummate actress and comedienne, was able to play both parts in relation to her tyrannical husband's character, Archie Bunker. Her original performances of her character, Edith, was of a totally subservient spouse who would run to meet her husband at the door, accept his views at face-value, and meet his demands for prompt service at the dinner table. Later on, Stapleton earned plaudits for her shifting to an assertive, "stronger" woman when Archie would go too far in pressing his demands. In the spin-off situation comedy series, Maude, Beatrice Arthur gave strong performances of a "liberated wife" and militant feminist. She first appeared in the Archie Bunker television series as a woman who could match or top Archie in audacity.

Other comediennes focused upon characterizations of women who would project the image of helplessness, dumbness, or foolishness. Zasu Pitts, Carol Channing, Goldie Hawn, Judy Holiday, Joan Davis, and Judy Canova were some examples of this persona.

Still other comediennes would exaggerate female sexuality. Mae West was probably best known of this genre, but Sophie Tucker and Bette Middler were also effective in such a posture.

Finally, there are comediennes who did not rely on their identities as women to project their brand of humor. Imogene Coca, Carol Burnett, Beatrice Lillie, Gracie Fields, Moms Mabley, Louise Fazenda, Minerva Pious, and Lily Tomlin were versatile enough to earn well-deserved fame as being funny in their own right (Franklin, 1979).

Summary and Conclusions

Sex and gender are powerful determinants in life histories and sexuality and gender reflect their influences. Whether sexual behavior is rooted in nature or in nurture, sexual humor takes it cues from either school of thought. Gender humor unquestionably deals with social ascriptions assigned to men and women and consequently is used with telling effect by both protagonists and antagonists of the social order. Both sex and gender are capable of arousing deep emotional responses and its follows that a certain amount of caution is needed by humorists in dealing with these highly sensitive subjects.

Two theories or schools of thought explain some of the sensitivity involved in sexual and gender humor. The prevailing thesis is that a sexual revolution has occurred and that sexual humor can be articulated freely and without fear of social condemnation. The second theory holds that nothing really new has occurred and that there is simply a continuation of behaviors and judgments concerning sex and gender extending from ancient times to The second theory holds that nothing really new has occurred and that there is simply a continuation of behaviors and judgments concerning sex and gender extending from ancient times to the present. In this perspective sex and gender assessments are deeply embedded in the social scheme of things, and sexual and gender humor can only continue to represent men and women's socialization in these matters.

STUDY QUESTIONS

1. What underlies the sensitivity associated with sexual and gender humor?

2. Is there greater sensitivity over sexual humor than gender humor?

3. How does structure-functionalism, conflict, or symbolic interactional theory explain the nature of sexual and gender humor?

4. Wherein does sexual humor draw upon dramaturgical models?

5. Why does there appear to be proponents and opponents of sexual and gender humor?

6. Does the weight of available evidence support the thesis of a sexual revolution or a continuation of old, even ancient, patterns of sexual and gender ascriptions that affect the nature of sexual and gender humor as they are currently offered?

7. What, in your judgment, is funny about sex itself, or sexuality?

8. What ends are served by sexual or gender humor?

9. Is Legman's approach to sexual humor as "clean dirty" and "dirty dirty" useful in the study of humor? Why?

10. How are feminists using humor to undercut the "macho" subculture?

11. Do you support or do not support Legman's contention that national modal personality types are preoccupied with certain types of sexual or gender humor?

12. What explanations are there for using graffiti to present sexual or gender humor?

13. Is "false modesty" a legitimate target for sexual satire?

14. How could sociological studies affirm or deny the presence of "community standards" that would accept or reject sexual humor?

15. What are the relationships between gender ascriptions and gender humor?

16. Do men and women have distinctive senses of humor?

17. Why have there been relatively few comediennes in comparison to the predominance of comedians?

18. What aspects of sexual or gender humor have comediennes selected for their "on-stage" personae?

19. How is social power and social control operative in sexual or gender humor?

20. How does sexual and gender humor reflect social changes?

21. Is sexual and gender humor "a sword" or "a shield" in "the battle of the sexes"?

Suggested Readings

Adams, Wesley J., "The Use of Sexual Humor in Teaching Human Sexuality at the University Level," *The Family Coordinator*, v. 23 (October, 1974): 365-368.

Bain, F.W., *A Digit of the Moon.* N.Y.: Putnam's Sons, 1905.

Bombeck, Erma, *Motherhood, The Second Oldest Profession.* N.Y.: McGraw-Hill, 1983.

Brav, Stanley R., *Since Eve, A Sex Ethic Inspired by Hebrew Scriptures.* N.Y.: Pageant Press, 1959.

Crosby, John F., *Reply to Myth, Perspectives on Intimacy.* N.Y.: Wiley, 1985.

Delora, Joann S. and Carol A.B. Warren, *Understanding Sexual Interaction.* Boston: Houghton Mifflin, 1977.

Ellis, Albert and Albert Abarbanel, eds., *The Encyclopedia of Sexual Behavior.* Two volumes. N.Y.: Hawthorn Books, 1961.

Farberow, Norman L., ed., *Taboo Topics.* N.Y.: Atherton Press, 1963.

Franklin, Joe, *Encyclopedia of Comedians.* Secaucus, NJ: Citadel Press, 1979.

Friedan, Betty, *The Feminine Mystique.* N.Y.: W.W. Norton, 1963.

Goffman, Erving, *The Presentation of Self in Everyday Life.* Garden City, NY: Doubleday, 1959.

Harper, Robert A. and Frances R. Harper, "Are Educators Afraid of Sex?", *Marriage and Family Living*, v. 19 (August, 1957): 240-244.

Hite, Shere, *The Hite Report, A Nationwide Study of Female Sexuality.* N.Y.: Macmillan, 1976.

Hyde, Janet Shible, *Understanding Human Sexuality.* N.Y.: McGraw-Hill, 1982.

Kardiner, Abram, *Sex and Morality.* N.Y.: Bobbs-Merrill, 1954.

Kaufman, Gloria and Mary Kay Blakely, eds., *Pulling Our Own Strings.* Bloomington, IN: Indiana University Press, 1980.

Kinsey, Alfred C., Wardell B. Pomeroy and Clyde E. Martin, *Sexual Behavior in the Human Male.* Philadelphia: Saunders, 1948.

Kinsey, Alfred C., Wardell B. Pomeroy and Clyde E. Martin, *Sexual Behavior of the Human Female.* Philadelphia: Saunders, 1953.

Kogan, Benjamin A., *Human Sexual Expression.* N.Y.: Harcourt, Brace, Jovanovich, 1973.

Kronhausen, Eberhard and Phyllis Kronhausen, *Pornography and the Law.* N.Y.: Ballantine Books, 1959.

Legman, G., *Rationale of the Dirty Joke, An Analysis of Sexual Humor.* First Series. N.Y.: Grove Press, 1968.

Legman, G., *No Laughing Matter, Rationale of the Dirty Joke.* Second Series. N.Y.: Bell, 1975.

Lipton, Lawrence, *The Erotic Revolution.* Los Angeles: Sherbourne Press, 1965.

Masters, William H. and Virginia E. Johnson, *Human Sexual Response.* Boston: Little, Brown, 1966.

Masters, William H. and Virginia E. Johnson, *Human Sexual Inadequacy.* Boston: Little, Brown, 1970.

Masters, William H. and Virginia E. Johnson, *The Pleasure Bond, A New Look at Sexuality and Commitment.* Boston: Little, Brown, 1974.

Pond, Mimi, "Future Trends, The Feminist Future," *Ms.,* v. 14 (July, 1985): 96.

Read, Allen Walker, *Classic American Graffiti.* Waukeesha, WI: Maledicta Press, 1977.

Savage, Brian, *Playboy Magazine.* Chicago: HMH Publishing Co., 1967.

Sorensen, Robert C., *Adolescent Sexuality in Contemporary America, Personal Values and Sexual Behavior, Ages 13-19.* N.Y.: World Publishing Co., 1973.

Weisstein, Naomi, "Why We Aren't Laughing Any More," *Ms.,* (November, 1973): 50-51; 88-90.

Yankelovich, Daniel, *The New Morality, A Profile of American Youth in the '70s.* N.Y.: McGraw-Hill, 1974.

Chapter 9:

Urban and Rural Humor

Introduction

In urbanity and rurality the focus is upon the "setting" or community within which humanity conducts its affairs. These settings have long been of sociological concern because not only have they been the products of complex social forces, but they themselves have become active forces in the lives of those residing within them. In this chapter the initial concern will be to indicate the significant contributions of sociological theory and research in both urban and rural communities. The variety of urban-rural environments can then be linked to how these variations in the use of space give rise to humor that enables individuals and their enclaves to endure, to survive, or to carry on their affairs with some semblance of stability.

The earliest developments in sociology occurred in Western Europe during major transitions in communal settings between traditional rural farm and village life to increasing domination by major urban centers based on industrialization and expanding economic systems. These changes in environments were noted by such major sociological pioneers as Ferdinand Toennies and Emile Durkheim and figured prominently in their theories of social cohesion and its consequences. The rural-urban processes continued in America and they captured the attention of American sociologists who brought their own insights and expertise to bear on specialized studies in human ecology, rural and urban sociological analyses.

Toennies: Gemeinschaft and Gesellschaft

Published in 1887, Toennies' *Gemeinschaft and Gesellschaft,* translated as *Community and Society,* (Loomis, 1957) underscored the profound changes that had occurred in European society. Central to these changes was the transition from the close-knit, intimate, familial, enduring, warm relationship found in small, isolated, rural villages, a community spirit or aura Toennies called *Gemeinschaft* to the qualities of diversity in values and norms, transient, impersonal, formal relationships, and wide variations in status, role, and functions characteristic of urban centers he

127

termed as *Gesellschaft* society. This transition indicated to Toennies the demise of small, highly integrated rural communities and being increasingly replaced by the industrialized, specialized, urban aggregates that influenced almost every aspect of societal and personal lives. Family-centered lives, for instance, that were key elements in *Gemeinschaft* life styles were transformed into more individualistic, self-centered lives that fit *Gesellschaft* society. The close bond of kinship was being replaced by the more formal obligations of the contract. Thus, employer-employee relationships made the new system work, not whole kinship networks or intimate friendships.

Durkheim: Mechanical and Organic Solidarity

A contemporary of Toennies, Emile Durkheim shared his concern over the movement of modern society from *Gemeinschaft* to a *Gesellschaft* style of life. Durkheim differed from Toennies, however, by noting that social solidarity continues in the newer communities albeit on different bases than in the historical past. He distinguished between mechanical and organic solidarity, the former characterizing the social bonding occuring in *Gemeinschaft* society and the latter identifying the newer *Gesellschaft* society (Giddens, 1972). In mechanical solidarity, self-sufficient families and their small, rural communities carried on similar task through a division of labor by age, sex, and shared agreements on values, beliefs, and sentiments. In organic solidarity, however, a variety of individuals and collectivities carried on different functions or services, yet formed a cohesive interdependence much like an organism survives through the operations of its different organs and systems. Thus the newer urban clusters did not constitute a breakdown of society in its large sense but represented instead a reorganization of society that could effectively deal with the complexities of emerging cities and their hinterlands.

Park: University of Chicago School of Thought

Under the leadership of Robert Ezra Park at the University of Chicago, the study of cities with their emphases on human ecological zones or "natural areas" such as slums, rooming-house districts, manufacturing and industrial centers, workers' homes, and wealthy suburbs went forward for many years (Schwab, 1982). Classic publications in urban sociology flowed from the University of Chicago Press: Anderson's *The Hobo,* Faris and Dunham's *Mental Disorders in Urban Areas,* Shaw's *Delinquency Areas, The Jack-Roller,* and *Brothers in Crime,* Thrasher's *The Gang,* Wirth's *The Ghetto,* and Zorbaugh's *The Gold Coast and the Slum.* These works tended to focus on the alienation, stress, separations, and disorganization that was said to be associated with urbanity. In more recent studies, these anomic themes have been reconsidered and modified by the detailing of considerable social organization and normative order to be found within, for example, slum neighborhoods. Whyte's *Street Corner Society*, Gan's *The Urban Villagers*, Liebow's *Tally's Corner*, and Suttle's *The Social Order of the Slum* are representative of this later type of studies. Thus there does exist a *Gemeinschaft* type of spirit within subcommunities that are part and parcel of the larger, host, all-encompassing *Gesellschaft* society in which they are located.

Urbanization and Urban Ecological Patterns

Drawing upon the interrelationships of four variables, population, organization, environment, and technology, current urban ecologists divide their attention between two major phenomena, the urbanization processes themselves and the internal structures of cities that deal with how populations, organizations, and activities are distributed over the land-area. Of growing concern is the nature of segregation in terms of social class, race, and ethnicity, whether the separations into distinct neighborhoods are the result of self-segregating or the imposition of other social pressures, and the processes of centralization and dispersion of economic services within and between cities.

Studies in Rural Sociology

Urbanity and rurality are thus "two sides of the same coin." While urbanity seems to be the dominant characteristic of modern life, there is need to understand that rurality was the older, traditional, and original source of societal life for centuries. The surplus of food, supplies and goods, or resources has been regarded as one of the major driving forces behind the development of cities. Further technical improvements meant that fewer persons were needed on the farms and the surplus of rural dwellers found employment within urban enclaves. Markets and commercial activities emerged within cities, but they were dependent upon supplies and persons in the rural areas. The reciprocity between urban and rural locales continues in modern times, sometimes at a gradual pace and other times at a dramatic, quickened pace that drastically changes life styles.

At least seven different indices differentiate rurality from urbanity: (1) occupation — rural residents are usually involved in nurturing or growing things to make their livelihood; (2) size of community — by arbitrary agreement in the United States Bureau of the Census, those communities with less than 2500 population are categorized as rural; (3) population density — rural areas have relatively low density compared to urban areas; (4) environment — such factors as soil, climate, topography, and seasonal growth of plants and animals play vital roles in how rural people operate; sociocultural traditions and sentiments also affect the precise manner with which rural residents conduct their affairs; (5) social differentiation —

homogeneity is more a rural trait in contrast to urban dwellers' hetereogeneity; (6) social stratification — rural communities generally have fewer social class differences, fewer extremes in socioeconomic levels; and (7) social solidarity — the close bonds of family and community are manifested among rural people while urbanites find similar bonds more in enclaves than in the entire urban complex (Smith & Zopf, 1970).

While Americans were experiencing a population shift from rural to urban dominance, rural populations are the dominant mode in Asia and Africa and in many areas of South and Central America, eastern Europe and Scandinavia and in portions of the Near and Middle East.

Urban and Rural "Bias"

Urban and rural communities are the major kinds of settings in which people conduct their lives. They are studied by sociologists in an objective, empiric manner. But there is a subjective side to urban and rural community life from the perspective of those individuals who live within them. Thus there is an urban bias that portrays city life as the most rewarding life style to follow. There is also its counterpart in the rural bias that holds that country life is "the good life." Both biases have corollaries that suggest that both of these life styles also have repugnant features that are scorned and should be avoided at all costs. Hence the groundwork is laid for the emergence of much humor with these contrasting viewpoints playing their part.

Bain (1955) identified a social structure as sociopathic "when its ideology is internally inconsistent; when it interferes with the basic need-satisfaction of the major institutions; when it resists useful technological and ideological change; and when it costs more than necessary in human, physical, and biological resources." Bain chose to illustrate one of the sociopathic conditions in big cities by what he called "The Sociopathy of the Dog Complex," a tongue-in-cheek paper calculated to arouse the ire of dog lovers because he deliberately selected as many negative results from dog ownership in large cities as possible while also ignoring any positive features of dog ownership. In semi-serious analyses, Bain pointed out the expenditure of large sums of money in catering to dogs, money which could have been spent more societally useful; the large number of dog bite cases for children, mail carriers, sales personnel, or business agents; the driving accidents caused by dogs running free, the nuisance of barking and destructive dogs; the health hazards they can create; and the curbing of their natural instincts because they live in cities rather than in the open country where Bain felt they belonged. Bain's rural bias was evident, but he relied upon humor to reveal more information than people may care to know.

Variety of Urban-Rural Environments

Distinctive differences exist in urban-rural environments. There are central cities surrounded by satellite cities. Urban expansion outward in fully developed urban centers entails moving past the political-corporate limits of original cities into suburbs that house upwardly mobile or growing populations. In many instances suburbs serve as "bedroom communities" or "dormitory spaces" for persons who earn their living in the central cities.

Moving outward from different centers, urban expansion also creates massive urban agglomerations called megalopolises (Gottman, 1961) that amount to "wall-to-wall" cities. No sooner has one left some "greater city" than he or she has entered into another urban complex of a center city and its own suburbs or satellite cities. Perhaps the best known megalopolis is "Bosnywash" which refers to the continuous urban-suburban corridor running from Boston, New Haven, New York, Philadelphia, and Baltimore to Washington, D.C. "Chipitts" is the second megalopolis stretching from Pittsburgh north and west to include Youngstown, Akron, Cleveland, and Toledo until it reaches Chicago and beyond into Illinois. "Sanlosdiego" is the third megalopolis, located on the West Coast and reaching from San Francisco south to Fresno and Bakersfield to Los Angeles and San Diego (King & Koller, 1975). There are other megalopolises developing in other parts of the nation such as around the Dallas-Fort Worth "metroplex" or the Florida coastal cities. Depending upon one's urban or rural bias, these developments are held to be positive additions to the quality of life or are to be decried and regretted. In the inconsistencies of pride or disdain, persons can and do turn to humor to support their own value-judgments regarding the urban-rural situations in which they find themselves.

A pattern that has been developing for some time but is now receiving more and more attention is the competition between "Sunbelt" and "Frostbelt" cities (Abbott, 1981). The Frostbelt cities of the North with their troublesome winters have been losing businesses, industry, and populations to the more attractive Sunbelt cities of the South and the West. Blizzards and hazardous driving conditions in the Frostbelt are widely publicized so that Sunbelt cities may profit during the winters. One airline has effectively used this theme of the horrors of winter and the blandishments of warmer weather in southern locations by vignettes in mass media showing snow-covered and shivering citizens crying out pitifully, "I need it bad!"

Aside from the internal movements within cities such as invasion-succession patterns, urban aggregates themselves move out, expand, or encroach upon their surrounding rural communities. Persons who have a rural preference or bias in terms of residence or conducting their affairs find themselves unable to keep creeping urbanization away from their neighborhoods and business enterprises. Ironically, for example, a couple who invested their life savings in a quiet rural area "to escape city-life," found that an interstate highway would be built a few yards away from their home. Or some small, crossroads town with its *Gemeinschaft* ways suddenly finds itself a "boom town" because it is targeted as the hub of a new industrial development. These changes can be viewed as "progressive" or being "modernized," but they also set the stage for conflict in which the aggressive functions of humor can come into play.

Survival Through Humor in Urban-Rural Settings

Building and Rebuilding within Cities

There are relatively few cities that were the result of careful, rational, mutually agreeable planning. Rather, they were the result of multiple forces or socioeconomic pressures often unanticipated or unknown to their earliest residents. Economic and sociopolitical forces that have changed over the years have led to building and rebuilding considerable portions of large and small cities. It is not uncommon to pave a new thoroughfare only to tear it up soon thereafter with installation of a new sewer system, cables, or subway system. It is commonplace to erect large business and professional office buildings only to tear them down to allow room for taller, more elaborate structures that will accommodate more people and different enterprises than in the past.

Some urbanites regard these changes with pride and readily accept the temporary or prolonged inconveniences created during the tearing-down and building-up processes. Those opposed or unfamiliar with these changes approach these circumstances armed with humor to help them endure or comprehend what is going on. A proud urbanite, for instance, showing his city to a visitor pointed out the huge skyscrapers going up on First Street, the tremendous crater being dug on the Square for a multi-tiered parking deck, the miles of deep trenches where a future subway system will go, and the piles of bricks and construction equipment scattered over the site of a future shopping mall. "What do you think of our fair city?" asked the urbanite. "Isn't it just grand!" "Well," drawled the visitor, "it sure should be a nice place to live once they finish building it!"

The discomforts and patience required by these massive urban changes do not necessarily sit well with all urbanites. One wag posted a conspicuous sign near the reconstruction of his town's downtown section. It read, "This way to Chaos."

Personality Types in the City and the Countryside

The heterogeneity or the cosmopolitan nature of cities contrasts with the relatively homogeneous nature of rural communities. Differences then seem to apply to urban centers and sameness appears to be more applicable to rural places. There is some hedging in these generalizations because the differences found in cities may be more illusory than real and the similarities in rural areas may mask the wide variety of people living there.

These qualifiers however are commonly set aside by those who wish to dramatize, highlight, or emphasize their points by turning to half-truths or stereotypes. Urban and rural humor makes good use of partial truths by personifying city dwellers as urbane, sophisticated, wise in ways of dealing with the world. Perhaps the best known of these city types is the "city slicker," who can "sell the Brooklyn Bridge" to strangers several times a day. He or she is manipulative and survives by his or her wits in the midst of crowded cities.

The counter-figure of a rural resident is what the ancients called the "agroikos." Such a person was portrayed as honest, down-to-earth, a "hick," a "rube," or a person who believes in and follows the simple virtues of hard work and honest toil.

Humor does, however, expose "the little lie" found in human relationships and finds a way to delight persons by observing that certain assumptions, like stereotypes, are flawed in the face of new information. Such an instance occurs when a "city slicker" meets an "agroikos" and finds the tables are turned:

An urbanite has somehow lost his way in the countryside and by turning off onto an unpaved side road got his car mired hubcap-deep in a muddy rut. Failing to move his car, the city-man got out of his auto to walk to the nearest town for help. Just as the urbanite had abandoned all hope, a farmer drove over a hill with a sturdy team of horses. The city-man promptly asked the farmer to pull his car onto firmer ground. The farmer obliged and the city-man was overjoyed to pay for his services.

In the next town the urbanite pulled into a gasoline station and recounted his good fortune to the attendant. "That farmer sure was nice to me. I hope his farm brings him good harvests." "Sorry, stranger," replied the attendant, "but that man's farm hardly yields him a penny all summer."

"How could that be?" asked the city-man. "His farm looked pretty big to me."

"No time or energy left to take care of the place," explained the attendant. "He's so durn busy hauling water down to that mudhole he built in the road!"

Such a yarn creates some urban-rural humor out of exposing the naivete of the sophisticated "city slicker" and the slyness of the allegedly honest "agroikos."

Automobiles, Traffic, and Parking

A basic need in major cities is mobility. One must learn how to enter a city, move easily to destinations within the city, and when necessary, exit the complex without too much difficulty. The trouble is that thousands and millions of other individuals have the same needs and get in each other's way as they pursue similar purposes simultaneously, creating traffic, parking, and other problems in the hectic process.

Joey Adams (1968) pointed out that there are more cars in New York City than in England and France combined. There are also more cars in California than in Italy, Germany, and Belgium. Adams' solution is "we will have to park overseas."

Crossing heavily traveled streets present still another problem. Those afoot have to stay alert if they are to survive the ordeal of getting from one side of a street to another. A humorous perspective helps out by confronting this reality and suggesting how to deal with it. As one humorist put it, city pedestrians may be classified as "the quick or the dead.." In another example, the mixing of children's honesty with the dangers of crossing against the flow of traffic is illustrated in the story of a little boy who was waiting almost an hour on the side of a busy avenue. A friendly stranger happened by and asked if he might help the child cross the street. The boy brightly replied, "Oh, no. There's really no problem, thank you. I'm just waiting for any empty space to come along!" In a similar vein, the futility of getting frustrated over the traffic problem in major cities is demonstrated in the remark alleged to be made to the mayor of New York City by his traffic commisioner, who calmly informed him that the only way to get to the West Side is to be born there!

Specialized Cities and "Image" Problems

While most cities are multifaceted and multifunctional, there are certain services or products that tend to be the foci of attention. Hartford, Connecticut, is known as an insurance center; Pittsburgh is regarded as a major iron and steel center; Tulsa is considered to be an oil center; Washington, D.C., is the political center of the nation; Las Vegas is noted for its legalized gambling, and so on. When such specialized cities find their public images tarnished by conditions going awry, there is considerable alarm by those who live there or have financial investments there. New York City, for instance, a key financial center, has had economic problems that led to requests for federal "bailouts," an incongruity that invites humorous treatment. Los Angeles, "the City of the Angels," still regarded as the center of the motion picture film industry because of its sunny climate, has endured humorous assaults because of such current conditions as eye-irritating, throat-tickling, obnoxious air pollution called smog. According to some imaginative humorists, for instance, one man first realized how serious a problem the air pollution really was in Los Angeles when he was held up and all the robber took from him was his cough drops!

Finally there are countless jokes, jibes, jests, and humorous anecdotes about Washington, D.C., for its management or mismanagement of federal agencies and bureaus. Purchases of coffee pots for $7,000 or toilet seats for $1,000 by military buyers have been derisively treated in the press while also stimulating humorous efforts. One cartoonist used this same theme when he depicted a politician sitting on a toilet and explained in his caption, "The only time a politician in Washington, D.C., knows what he is doing!"

Crowding

Perhaps the most obvious problems of city dwelling is the presence of huge numbers of people who impinge upon each other, sometimes in uncomfortable ways. Hong Kong, for instance, one of the most crowded cities in the world, has had to improvise some fairly imaginative methods to accommodate its bustling population. Platform structures are built in restaurants, for example, to make full use of all available space. They are arranged in such a manner that persons seated at a table at floor level may find other persons seated closeby at their head-level. Thus it would appear that persons perched at higher levels can easily overhear whatever conversation may be going on privately between dining couples below them. Indeed in such close quarters, diners have found those seated nearby to take an interest in their conversation and to offer gratuitously their own ideas about the subject at hand! In certain high-rise buildings, persons who live there rarely leave because every conceivable activity goes on there such as shopping, manufacturing, schooling, entertaining, and even burials. Others spend their days on junks or water-platforms so that they rarely step onto dry land. Rooms may be rented not for day and night occupancy but only for a few hours. Whereas Los Angeles and other cities suffer from air pollution, humorists point to Hong Kong and similar places as suffering from "people pollution."

Behavioral scientists, like John B. Calhoun of the National Institute of Mental Health, have optimized conditions for a rodent population so that they finally occupied all available spaces (*The Futurist,* October, 1975). Such an experiment postulates that human populations can suffer tremendous problems that ensued in rodent populations when overcrowding led to extreme aggressiveness, apathy, and deaths. Humor appears to be one outlet unavailable to Calhoun's mice population but available to human populations who can learn to deal effectively with crowded conditions through toleration, a sense that others are enduring similar conditions as one's self, and cooperation. One cartoonist conveyed such a message when he drew a series of balconies occupied by residents of a high-rise apartment building as their day came to an end. A man on the top balcony is shown leaning over to whisper to his neighbor on the balcony beneath him, "It is a lovely sunset. Pass it on."

Urban and Suburban Pride

Crowding, pollution, traffic, or other problems do not deter urban and suburban residents from taking pride in their "hometowns." Suburbanites, for example, will go to great lengths to explain that they do not live in the central city but rather in their distinctive areas. Such people say, "I'm not from Chicago, I'm from Highland Heights!"; "I don't live in Cleveland, I live in Lakewood;" "I don't live in Los Angeles, I live in Van Nuys," and so on.

Clevelanders have responded to New York City's "Big Apple" campaign by saying that "If New York City is a big apple, Cleveland is a plum." Or a recent technique has been to refer to Cleveland as being a major port city of the "North Coast" of America.

The relative smallness of population or the fact that their hometown may be unknown gives rise to a tongue-in-cheek bit of local pride by such things as T-shirts that read, "Whereinhellis Lodi?" or "Whereinhell is Stow?" Small town or "hick town humor" frequently uses exaggeration to confront the minimal numbers of residents. Adams (1968) suggests some of the following examples: "It's a place where nothing is going on every minute."

"The town is so small - to have a village idiot we all have to take turns."

"They had a single traffic light - that changed once a week."

"You have to widen the street to put the white line down the middle."

"They hired a traffic cop and then went out to find him some traffic." (See also Lingeman, 1980)

The "Down-to-Earth" Nature of Rural Humor

One of the major differences between urban and rural people is the attitude concerning that which is "natural" and that which is "artificial." By natural, the reference is to natural phenomena such as weather conditions, soil and its fertility, water availability or the lack of it, seasonal variations, diseases affecting livestock, the growth of crops, or keeping healthy enough to carry out chores or tasks on their own. For urbanites, artificiality means the reliance upon others for such basic items as food, water, shelter, or security. Milk comes to city dwellers, as far as they can determine, in waxed cartons. Dairy herds, the care and feeding of milkcows, the arrival of calves, etc., are unknown or unimportant details as far as they are concerned. Bread comes packaged in cellophane. Fruits and vegetables arrive in the city in cans, packages, or on display tables in supermarkets. Meats are presented sliced, specially cut, in see-through packets. Sowing, weeding, harvesting crops are just not part of the urban scene. Changes in the weather or problems in animal husbandry are not urban problems because food and other supplies keep coming into cities, if not from one producing center then from other food-producers.

This difference between artificiality and naturalness is reflected in the humor of rural and urban residents. Urban dwellers are "cool," sophisticated consumers, persons who can buy and sell goods and services. They are people who feel they have control of their lives because they can pick and choose from a number of alternative possibilities. Rural people, by contrast, are more aware of how they fit into natural conditions over which they have little or no control. A frost, severe winds, a drought, or flooding can wipe out a year's effort. Disease among their animals, extreme heat or cold, blizzards, or insects can destroy earnings down on the farm. Rural persons are thus co-partners with nature. Urban people see nature as an inconvenience that merely disrupts their lives briefly.

It is within rural areas then that humor gets "down-to-earth." In a small Oklahoma town each summer, for instance, there is a "cow chip" throwing contest. In rural Ohio there is a "chicken-flying" contest that consists of measuring just how far a hen will fly when released from her coop. Many have heard of the frog-jumping contest in Calveras County made famous by Mark Twain telling of a cheat who poured lead pellets down the throat of a favored, champion jumper "to slow him down a bit." Vermillion, Ohio, stages a "woolly bear" festival annually to celebrate the amount of "fur" or "fuzz" on a black and brown caterpillar that is said to predict if the coming winter will be severe or mild.

Summary and Conclusions

Rural and urban settings are indeed major social forces that circumscribe and profoundly affect the quality of life for their resident populations. Sociologists have made major contributions to the study of urban centers and rural communities through their objective theories and thoughtful research. Their work enables persons to gain a greater comprehension of the significance of urbanization processes and the importance of rural hinterlands. What has been missing is an understanding that, from the subjective views of urban and rural dwellers, there are considerable stresses and strains involved that are relieved and made more tolerable through humor. Both urban and rural residents, with good reason, make use of humor to survive those conditions over which they have relatively little personal control. They fulfill their lives as best they can and in humor give vent to their frustrations, aspirations, and courage.

There can be no claim that a single chapter can provide a definitive analysis and complete synthesis of the place of humor in urban and rural settings. This chapter, however, does suggest that ongoing studies in different ecological settings should take into account the presence of humor and how it helps inhabitants of such settings endure.

STUDY QUESTIONS

1. What relationships between urban and rural populations lend themselves to humor? Among urban residents? Among rural residents? Which are predictable from a sociological perspective?

2. Should sociological study incorporate humor as part of investigations of city or country life or should humor be ignored in these settings?

3. How does humor function in metropolitan centers or in small towns in terms of (a) survival, (b) aggression, and (c) joyous celebrations of life?

4. What part does "urban bias" and "rural bias" play in city and country-style humor?

5. Are all or some cities subject to problems of maintaining positive images for their constituents or those who will do business with them?

6. Are there ridiculous features of life in urban and rural communities that need to be understood?

7. What socioeconomic and political changes underlie the optimism of certain urban or rural enclaves as well as the pessimism in other urban or rural locations?

8. How does humor help urban residents during the rebuilding, reorganizing, redeveloping going on in their cities?

9. In what ways does size of cities and towns, (large versus small) affect humor associated with them?

10. Aside from the stereotyped "city slicker" and "the agroikos," what other personality types are to be found in urban and rural humor?

11. In recent years a group of local residents in Burbank, California, have offered a spoof on the annual Rose Parade which they called the "Doo Dah." What rationale favors such a parody and what rationale argues against it as far as a public image of Burbank, California, is concerned?

12. What annual celebrations, festivals, spectacles, events, or parades are featured by major cities and what explains their attraction and continued support by their sponsors?

13. While competition between Frost-belt and Sun-belt cities is a serious matter, what aspects of this competition lend themselves to humorous interpretations?

14. What part does vulnerability, threats, or dangers play in urban and rural humor?

15. What are the distinctive characteristics of suburban humor when contrasted with urban or rural humor?

16. Why does mobility within major cities lend itself to humorous treatment?

17. Can humor sustain the conception of rural life as idyllic bucolic, or free from the troubles found in cities?

18. Are there identifiable humor patterns to be found in urban neighborhoods?

19. How does humor counteract sociopathic conditions within cities?

20. Would comparative analyses find unique humor patterns in the major cities of the world such as London, Paris, Madrid, Bombay, Singapore, Hong Kong, or Tokyo?

Suggested Readings

Abbott, Carl. *The New Urban America.* Chapel Hill, NC: University of North Carolina Press, 1981.

Adams, Joey. *Encyclopedia of Humor.* N.Y: Bonanza Books, 1968.

Bain, Read. "The Sociopathy of the Dog Complex." Paper read at meeting of Ohio Valley Sociological Society, Cleveland, April 29, 1955.

Blum, Jerome, ed. *Our Forgotten Past: Seven Centuries on the Land.* N.Y.: Thames & Hudson, 1982.

Bresler, Jack B. *Human Ecology: Collected Readings.* Reading, MA: Addison-Wesley, 1966.

Calhoun, John B. "Uncontrolled Population Growth: The Rise and Fall of a Colony of Mice," *The Futurist,* v. IX (October, 1975): 232.

Giddens, Anthony, ed. and transl. *Emile Durkheim: Selected Writings.* N.Y.: Cambridge Univ. Press, 1972.

Gordon, Mitchell. *Sick Cities: Psychology and Pathology of American Urban Life.* N.Y.: Macmillan, 1965.

Gottman, Jean. *Megalopolis: The Urbanized Northeastern Seaboard of the United States.* Cambridge, MA: MIT Press, 1964.

King, David C., and Marvin R. Koller. *Foundations of Sociology.* Corte Madre, CA: Rinehart Press, 1975.

Lingeman, Richard. *Small Town America: A Narrative History, 1620-The Present.* N.Y.: Putnam's Sons, 1980.

Loomis, Charles A., ed. and transl. *Ferdinand Tonnies: Community and Society.* East Lansing, MI: Michigan State Univ. Press, 1957.

Sanders, Irwin T. *Rural Society.* Englewood Cliffs, NJ: Prentice-Hall, 1977.

Sawers, Larry, and William K. Tabb. *Sunbelt/Snowbelt: Urban Development and Regional Restructuring.* N.Y.: Oxford Univ. Press, 1984.

Schwab, William A. *Urban Sociology: A Human Ecological Perspective.* Reading, MA: Addison-Wesley, 1982.

Smith, T. Lynn, and Paul E. Zopf, Jr. *Principles of Inductive Rural Sociology.* Philadelphia: F.A. Davis, 1970.

Thorns, David C. *Suburbia.* London: MacGibbon & Kee, 1972.

Untermann, Richard K. *Accommodating the Pedestrian: Adapting Towns and Neighborhoods for Walking and Bicycling.* N.Y.: Van Nostrand Reinhold, 1984.

Chapter 10:

Cross-Cultural Humor

American sociologists are commonly asked by their students how they can claim their science has universal applications and relevance when in fact the bulk of their studies has focused upon American society only. Availability of data, financial support for and social approval of scientific inquiry, and pertinence in the lives of American scholars and students alike are among the answers that can be given. But such answers cannot satisfy those who conceptualize sociology as the scientific discipline that studies human societies wherever they may be found. There is need to broaden the data base to incorporate societies throughout the world and, to this end, sociologists in America and elsewhere have raised their consciousness to do comparative analyses and to involve themselve in cross-cultural research so that generalizations can be made concerning the nature and workings of all human systems.

To escape the criticism that humor, for example, cannot be understood by reference to only a single society such as America, this chapter extends our exploration by looking at humor cross-culturally. It seeks to examine humor as it is defined in societies other than America, to compare or contrast manifestations of humor in a variety of societies, to determine what forms or types of humor are salient within specific societies, and to suggest testable hypotheses or theories that can predict what functions will be served through humorous techniques.

Without question the substantive information and treatment of humor within human societies rely heavily upon the sister science of anthropology. The forte of anthropologists has been their recognition of societal and cultural diversity. In the course of such work anthropologists have formulated a number of useful techniques and concepts that sociologists may apply when they explore modern, contemporary, urban-industrial subcultures or total cultures. In the pursuit of universal understanding of humor, both sociology and anthropology would benefit from joining hands and working together toward this common objective in the world-wide exploration of humor.

141

Selected Anthropological Sources

The Human Relations Area Files (HRAF)

Anthropological literature is replete with references to remote, distinctive societies that have been brought together in the Human Relations Area Files (HRAF). These files are repositories strategically located in various universities throughout the United States so that interested persons may have access to the wealth of comparative data they contain. A host of topics, including humor, are cross-filed by cultures. Subtopics such as tricksters, clowning, joking relationships, ridicule as a social control mechanism or ideas shared about laughter and smiling are also included in the HRAF. Such a source is an invaluable opportunity to study humor cross-culturally and was used in preparing this chapter.

Etic Humor and Emic Humor

A distinction worth considering is that between etic and emic humor. Etic humor refers to judgments by outside observers as to what constitutes humor within a given society and its culture. Emic humor refers to when and why indigenous persons, members of the in-group, think something is funny from their point of view. Unfortunately, considerable data in the HRAF consist of records of humorous events or situations as interpreted by relatively untrained field observers. What they understood to be humor was defined through the culture or cultures they represented and such humor was essentially etic humor or humor seen through an outside cultural filter. Whether they actually found and understood emic humor is still open to question.

The HRAF, however, also has data supplied by skilled anthropologists capable professionally to represent faithfully and accurately the feelings, attitudes and perspectives of other cultures as members of the in-group do. They have not lost their objectivity in their studies. They have not preselected or manipulated their data for preconceived goals. They are able to use rapport, demonstrated integrity, and scientific honesty in noting and discussing what they have found in the field. Their studies are the most reliable and valid sources of emic humor available. Fortunately, the quality of these field reports have met stringent criteria and can be examined with great profit (Apte, 1985).

Connections Between Humor and Play

Anthropologists have also observed and analyzed play as a phenomenon worth investigating. In 1974 the Association for the Anthropological Study of Play was established and its annual meetings have produced papers of considerable significance for students of humor (Lancy & Tindall, 1976; Salter, 1978; Schwartzman, 1980; Cheska, 1981; Loy, 1982; Manning, 1983). Since play like humor is manifested in almost infinite styles and nuances, there does appear to be connections between humor and play. It will be recalled that one of the major functions of humor is expressiveness, exhuberance, or as the French say it, a certain *joie de vivre*, a delight in being alive, a celebration in survival. Play is particularly notable in children's behavior throughout the world, but it extends far beyond the earliest years of life to become a matter of great fascination and concern to adults. Sports humor, for example, receives attention herein in a later chapter, and has become an important societal activity transcending the bounds of mere child's play.

Apte (1985) points out that humor is involved in play as long as it "is accompanied by or results in smiling or laughter." Humor is an integral part of unstructured play from this perspective as well as games that "do not involve competition." Within folk societies that promote cooperation, play consists of sharing and their games lack a competitive tone except in trying to excel in physical activities that benefit group survival such as spearthrowing, accuracy with arrows, or the stalking of game. Within urban societies, however, competition and personal prowess are serious matters which tend to detract from whatever humor might be possible during the play of games. Games taken too seriously have resulted in scenes of sports violence in which people are wounded or killed to the dismay and sorrow of the political entities represented on the playing fields (Lewis, 1982).

Ethnographic Reports and Comparative Studies

Ethnographic reports are essential building blocks in anthropological knowledge in that they are in-depth monographs on a single society and its culture by a technically trained anthropologist or a team of similarly qualified scholars. Such reports examine the full cultural inventories of their respective societies. The classic ethnographies that are regarded as models of field studies are *Kwakiutl Ethnography* by Franz Boas (Codere, 1966) and *Argonauts of the Western Pacific* by Bronislaw Malinowksi (1961). Comparative studies, on the other hand, take a topical approach and are able to find similarities or contrasts between societies and their cultures on selected subjects, topics, or areas of concern. Humor then deliberately selected from cultural inventories in an array of societies can be studied with profit as Apte has done.

One hypothesis proposed for future cross-cultural research is that humor is a universal phenomenon and consequently should be found in every society and its culture. One qualification in this proposition, however, is that there are degrees of humor emphasis and saliency between cultures so that most likely some societies will tend to be very sober and serious and deny and suppress humor whereas other societies will not. The lack of available data, however, from known ethnographic reports does not necessarily mean that humor was somehow minimal or lacking. This dearth may well be a function of the failure of observers to identify humor as significant enough to record or to analyze in comparison with other matters to which they were more sensitized.

Australian and American Humor

Renwick (1980) has provided a useful comparative study of Australian and American humor that demonstrates that, despite considerable similarities, there are enough differences to account for contrasting humor styles between the two societies. Both Australians and Americans consist of populations founded by immigrants, mainly from the British Isles. Both peoples have a history of rugged frontiersmen and pioneering women who struggled against great odds in a new land. Both share a deep concern for democratic solutions to social and political issues. Both speak the same language, have similar religions, are mainly Caucasoids, and have similar habits of eating, drinking, dressing, and greeting one another.

Nevertheless, the two societies differ in significant ways, and such differences account for different perspectives on what is or is not humorous to them. For example, Australians consider friendship to be extremely important whereas Americans rate work far above friendship. Australians are prone to speak of "mateship" and to set high value on the concept that "we are all in this together." Americans by contrast focus on individual leadership, competitiveness, or the idea that persons with exceptional abilities can and should be identified as superior to fellow workers. In this context Americans can be said to be "achievers" while Australians can be said to be "levelers."

Renwick noted that this difference between togetherness or individuality manifests itself in work settings, and this is particularly evident when Australians and Americans work together on some common project.

A hero in Australian folklore is a "bludger," a person much admired who has perfected the art of appearing to do a prodigious amount of work while actually doing very little. Americans too recognize that there are "freeloaders," "gold bricks," or those who earn their wages unfairly because they know how to conceal their nonproductivity. From the American point of view, however, given their concern for honest work, ideally such workers would not be viewed as heroes as much as they would be antiheroes.

Americans then tend to take seriously those who are performing far below their potential on a job that needs to be done. Australians, however, tend to be laughing, uproarously and approvingly, at successful bludgers who can make fools of their employers. Work, of course, needs to be done, but comradery is more valued to Australians and consequently the humor reaction is more supportive of clever bludgers. Once again the presence of bludger humor reaffirms in-group solidarities. It exists among American workers but not necessarily in the form found among Australians.

Comparisons Between British and American Humor

Similar to the Australian-American commonalities, the British and Americans share strong traditions but differ in their particular emphases in their ethos. Most would agree that the British are concerned with fairness, fair play, and dry understatement (Mikes, 1970). American humor by contrast tends to be more concerned with individual freedom, raucous or gross exaggerations, and a certain contempt for social class distinctions. Both, however, use humor to assault those social orders that fail to respect human dignity.

Lewis Carroll's *Alice in Wonderland,* for example, might be classified as "nonsense humor," but the theme of legitimate protest against the foolishness of pompous authorities was not lost among the British nor their American cousins. The same applies to the nonsense tale of a man who meets another man and asks, "Didn't we meet in Newcastle?" "Never been to Newcastle," replies the second man. The first man then says, "Neither have I. Must have been two other fellows." Such a tale does not provoke unrestrained laughter among Americans and consequently could be enjoyed only for its absurdity. For British audiences, however, the reaction to be expected is one of quiet thoughtfulness and covert amusement in sensing that a common man has triumphed over the normative order of things by using a logic of his own.

Class consciousness has not disappeared either among Americans or the British people. In Great Britain, however, class consciousness is much more evident, particularly because of the sustained respect for royalty and the mystique of the landed gentry.

The ability to resort to wordplay rather than to swordplay as former nobility might have done is much admired among the British. The quick, witty reply, the repartee, wins high marks among the British. It exhibits for them the value of restraint, civility, and intellect. Lord Churchill and Lady Astor, for example, were reputed to have held each other in deep contempt. During a session in Parliament, Lady Astor was reported to have said to Churchill, "If the Right Honorable Gentleman were my husband, I'd put arsenic in his coffee." Churchill was said to reply without hesitation, "If the Honorable Lady were my wife, I would drink it." On another occasion Churchill is said to have chanced to meet Lady Astor and forthrightly stated, "You are ugly, Madam." "You are drunk," replied the shocked Lady Astor. "But," Churchill straightened up to say, "*I* shall be sober tomorrow!" Such word mastery won him the admiration and approval of the British public.

On the other hand, clumsiness or error in oral communication can elicit a humorous response among the British. Spoonerism, named after W.A. Spooner, an English clergyman who was noted for such slips, consists of the transposition of an initial or sounds by accident. One such spoonerism occurred during the public announcements made by a very nervous curate at St. Peter's Church. He astounded his audience by saying, "Ladies and Gentlemen, Thursday night there will be a peter-pulling contest at St. Taffy's Church" (Feinberg, 1978).

A casual visitor to London can encounter a number of other examples of British preoccupation with wordplay and its witticisms. The London subway system is locally and fondly known as "The Tube." During a wait for the next train on the platform of the London subway, a sign warning passengers, "Wet Paint," would not escape the attention of passing travelers because some English wit had added as a precautionary measure, "...but, not when the train is standing at the station." Just outside Westminster Abbey a teenager was wearing a T-shirt with the message, "I Like School" in bold letters. Underneath the message, however, was appended the disclaimer, "...during vacations and holidays." Finally, there was a street seller of ice cream who won the approval of his customers with his modest observations, "You can lick our ice cream cones."

Such understatements or refinements strike the British as very funny. Maintaining their public composure, the British may enjoy the inward laughter that their particular style of humor evokes.

Irish Wit

Ireland holds a special place of its own in the cross-cultural study of humor. The Irish people are world renowned for their unique style of humor known as "blarney." Blarney has to do with a wide variety of subjects among the Irish; it is a whole style of humor, a sly style that elaborately sings the praises of people while at the same time suggesting that things are not quite right.

Anthony Butler (1969)focused upon this style when he offered a book to prepare unwary tourists for their future visits to the Emerald Isle. He demonstrated the gifts of flowing and flowery eloquence that comes from the glib tongue of the truly Irish. For example, Butler wrote; "On any day in Dublin's public houses you will find large numbers of strong silent men who, faced with the fact that they can't afford to drink, are comforting themselves with glasses of Irish whiskey." He added that it is only a legend that the Irish are heavy drinkers of whiskey, but opines that because there is one oasis for sustaining liquid refreshments for every five imbibers in most towns, there is only a slight danger of the natives dying of thirst.

Blarney not only applies to waxing poetic over the constant and bountiful presence of Irish whiskey, but another popular theme refers to the virtue of Irish women. Butler cautions, "In Ireland, it is well to remember that sex is an eight-letter word spelt M-A-R-R-I-A-G-E." He goes on to state, "The truth is that all Irish women have the instincts of some species of spider. The man, they plainly indicate, is only a stepping stone on the road to motherhood and that's the Irishwomen's true vocation."

Butler pokes fun at the overt modesty of Irish women when he described the undressing techniques of wives retiring for the night in the presence of their husbands. Again, using the blarney he hoped his readers would understand, he alleges that women put on voluminous nightgowns over their clothing first and then, having made a tent, they toss their clothing out through the necks of their nightgowns, a wonderful piece of gymnastics that keeps their husbands guessing as to whether or not females really exist in Ireland.

The "Irish Connection" is strong in the United States. Some fifteen per cent of the signers of the Declaration of Independence were Irish. Almost a third of the presidents have been of Irish origin and such renowned figures in American history as Davy Crockett, Stephen Foster, Edgar Allen Poe, Sam Houston, and Horace Greeley were also Irishmen. There were times, however, when in certain sections of the nation Irish immigrants were demeaned and held to be useful only in menial, lower-class tasks. Those times are long past and it is fairly accurate to state that most Americans admire and appreciate their fellow citizens of Irish origins, and "wear-the-green" each year in celebrating St. Patrick's Day as a symbolic tribute.

The Presence of Clowns

Clowns are typically associated with traveling circuses in which they provide comic relief to the death-defying feats of acrobats and animal trainers. Clown origins, however, predate these traveling extravaganzas by many centuries. In Europe their specialized characters were developed in traveling shows staged for the entertainment and edification of local populations. Unlike the court fools who were sponsored by nobility and other powerful figures, clowns played to the masses, the commonfolk who could recognize their kinship in the clowns' broad, down-to-earth styles of humor.

The presence of clowns is not limited to European cultures. Clowns are also found in Asia, Africa, and among Amerinds. Their worldwide presence suggests that they do help meet some fundamental needs of human beings universally. Of particular value are the clowns' abilities to show that certain cultural expectations or norms are absurd. Clowns also show when cultural norms are abrogated there are sometimes hilarious results and sometimes serious consequences.

Frequently found in sodalities, clown associations consisted of brotherhoods or subsocieties that called for a life apart from others in order to instruct the remainder of their people. One of the most remarkable sodalities was the Contraries of the Dakotas who behaved in manners opposite of cultural expectations so that they could present a mirror image of what would happen when folkways and mores were transgressed. Such men would pretend to feel cold in summer and dressed in buffalo robes, where in winter they would pretend to be warm and stand naked in the snow. Contraries would walk backwards, ride horses by facing the rear, took dust baths rather than bathe in rivers, and courageously advanced on enemies in the midst of battle while others were in hasty retreat. Such men would say "No" when they meant "Yes" and would approach others when signaled to go away.

Arapaho clowns would groan loudly under the weight of light objects and would pretend not to notice when truly heavy burdens were placed upon them. Koshari clowns perfected the art of talking backwards and knew how to babble outright nonsense. Clowns among the Mayan took extreme fright at inconsequential events and fell to the ground regularly when confronted with small obstacles. During religious ceremonials, Papago clowns begged for food from audiences through squeaks and signs. Hopi clowns were frequently beaten and often pretended that they were castrated by their fellow dancers. By such actions clowns served as persons who suffered humiliation when they violated cultural codes.

To teach through laughter appears to be the specialized talent of clowns wherever and whenever they are found. In a sense clowns invite misfortunes upon their heads so that "normal" people may see for themselves what troubles may ensue if customs are not followed faithfully.

Klapp (1962) offered an analysis of the social functions of Hopi clowns:

"Normally, the Hopis are sober and decorous and deem immoderate laughter a disgrace, but during the sacred Kachina rituals, clowns represent everything that a Pueblo Indian is not supposed to be — filthy, idiotic, deformed, bad-mannered, obscene, gluttonous, silly, talkative, uproarious, malicious, violent, cruel. ...They play a very important role to act out the suppressed side of the Pueblo personality; more important, perhaps, they function as a social conscience which sees into every fault."

From Bali, a clown trained in the arts of Topeng, a masked-dance theater, confirmed this instructive function of clowns when he wrote:

"I must teach something with my joking or the laughter will be hollow. In our village, many men are becoming lazy and do not want to work for the temple. When they see everyone laughing at the lazy clown (who has refused to serve his King) maybe tomorrow they won't be so lazy themselves. There is much that the people can learn from our play, but if there is too much seriousness, they will grow weary and forget. If we make them laugh, the happiness locks the lesson strong in their memories."(Jenkins, 1980).

Clowns around the world would seem to be silly or trivial characters to casual observers, but they do have their profound lessons to teach. Ibn al-Jawzi, an Islamic theologian and historian, has suggested three reasons why persons should pay attention to allegedly foolish clowns: (1)More intelligent persons can thank their Creator that they were not made to behave as clowns; (2) Some people are put on guard against foolishness itself; and (3) The humor of clowns provides much needed relaxation, a quality approved by Muhammed himself (Rosenthal, 1956).

The Joking Relationship

Perhaps one of the best known cross-cultural phenomenon associated with humor is the joking relationship. This is a widespread pattern in which certain categorical cultural ascriptions allow or encourage humorous license between individuals. Anthropological investigations have focused primarily on kinship networks in which consanguinity, affinity, or classificatory bonds either proscribe or prescribe the degrees with which joking, banter, teasing, and feigned insults are tolerated. Among members of nuclear families, for instance, the joking relationship is generally absent because the bonding between husbands and wives, parents and children, or siblings cannot be jeopardized or possibly compromised without serious consequences in terms of antagonisms and alienation. On the other hand, the joking relationship is found between members of extended kin groups, secondary and tertiary relatives, intra- and intergenerationally, particularly as these relatives are increasingly removed from the close, personal, and intimate relationships of nuclear families. These are potential sexual or marital partners and not necessarily threatening to the solidarity of nuclear family life. Much good-natured teasing, kidding, or humorous taunting can occur in these relationships such as between a husband and his wife's younger sisters or a wife and her husband's younger brothers. A certain amount of sexual-social tension is reduced, released, or dissipated through the mechanism of the joking relationship. This has been identified earlier as "social grease," the ability to slip through interactions that might otherwise be difficult, embarrassing, or dangerous if humor was not permitted or possible.

The joking relationship is not confined to preliterate, kinship-conscious societies, however. It is found in literate, industrial societies in which persons come together, particularly in work settings. Occupational humor in offices, factories, laboratories, or field settings signals a comradery, fellowship, "we-are-in-this-situation-together" type of bonding that makes tolerable the sometimes difficult, routine, or boring tasks. Chapter 16 herein on occupational humor describes and analyzes the joking relationship in greater detail for this factor, but its presence suggests that its functions apply in contemporary urbanized-industrial, high-technology circumstances as well as those of preliterates and preindustrial societies. Specific professions such as education, medicine, and sports also manifest their share of joking relationships and these will be treated in later chapters.

A variety of propositions have been advanced as to the functional usages of the joking relationship. These include the reduction of hostility, the release of tension, and the avoidance of conflict (Radcliffe-Brown, 1952/1965); social control (Lowie, 1920/1961); emotional catharsis and communication (Hammond, 1964); release of sexual and aggressive impulses (Murdock, 1949); pure entertainment and drama (Kennedy, 1970); social etiquette and screening for group membership (Malefijt, 1968); releases strenuous and dangerous work-related tension (Pilcher, 1972); symbolic indicator of strong affinal ties (Freedman, 1977); demonstration of "exclusiveness of association"(Stevens, 1978); a badge of group identity (Lundberg, 1969); and permission of the exploration of potential closeness in social relations (Howell, 1973). It was Apte's view (1985) that these theories apply to specific cultures and situations and are short of a global theory useful and valid for all societies and their cultures.

Oriental Humor

Chinese Humor

Three major personality types are discerned by Rowe (1955) among the Chinese whenever they encounter humor: the viscerotonic, the somatotonic, and the cerebrotonic. The viscerotonic are convivial, congenial extroverts. The somatotonic tend to be constrained in their reactions to humor because they seek to exert authority over others and so cannot admit to any weaknesses, shortcomings, or defects of character. The cerebrotonic, however, are the favored personality type among the Chinese because these are the intelligent, witty, thoughtful personalities esteemed by Confucian or Taoist scholars.

Face-saving or Ah Q'ism plays an essential part in Chinese humor. It is salient to maintain a public facade that persons have dignity and can be respected for whoever and whatever they are. From the Chinese perspective those who "give face" to others are judged to have humor. Those who are humorless "demand face" for themselves and so seek to stand above others whether they deserve it or not. The classic films of Charlie Chaplin, Harold Lloyd, and Laurel and Hardy were well received in China because the antics of these comics illustrated the happy salvation of small men caught in situations of gigantic proportions.

The Chinese tolerate authority, formality, and ceremony, but they also see through attempts to appear sophisticated and pretentious. Posturing is made laughable when, for example, on major festival days trained mice, dogs, or monkeys would be brought to the marketplace to perform short scenes from Chinese history or mythology, always with the overriding theme of social criticism. A monkey, for instance, would wear the cap of a high official, but one who was very inept or disgraceful in conduct. The symbolism was not lost on the Chinese for herein they showed a man with a human face but with an animal's heart.

The master-servant relationship was prominent in Chinese comedy. The master was a "ts'an chun" or high official who was forever tormented and put into awkward situations thanks to a witty clown, a "ts'ang t'ou," who was his subordinate or servant. The servant would grow bolder and bolder to the point of issuing commands to his master and finally, to the delight of Chinese audiences, hitting him to demonstrate his assumed authority. To add insult to injury, the symbol of a falcon which attacks little birds was used by the Chinese comic. His turban was called a "Ts'ang hu," the blue falcon.

Mother-in-law jokes, hen-pecked husbands, and punning provide other sources of Chinese humor. Furthermore, their curiosity about the lives of those about them draws them like a magnet to witness some hot argument over a business transaction in the marketplace. This real-life drama becomes entertainment for them and has the added advantage of observation without having to pay admission charges to a theater. Family quarrels that break out into public view produce the same effect. People gather to enjoy the tribulations of others as if the event was staged for their benefit.

John C. Wu summarizes the difference between Chinese humor and Western humor by observing, "Westerners are seriously humorous; Chinese are humorously serious." (Kao, 1946).

A Sample of Tibetan Humor

Instructive fables, legends, or stories are found in numerous cultures. Parables credited to Aesop who lived 500 years before Christ are still recited by children. Christ spoke to his disciples in parables. Abraham Lincoln was a renowned storyteller. Oral history and morality lessons are traditions among preliterate societies and are indeed the only way to pass on cultural lore to younger generations.

A legend from Tibet carries this same moral tone with a bit of humorous patina:

A monk names Duk Nyon frequently went on long walks with his students to achieve the necessary solitude and concentration for learning. During one of these excursions, Duk Nyon and a pupil came across a small stone in the middle of their path. Duk Nyon carefully and deliberately circumvented the stone by walking around it. Shortly thereafter they encountered a fairly large boulder blocking their path. Without hesitation, Duk Nyon scrambled up the boulder, climbed down the other side, and calmly continued the walk.

When the pupil inquired why his teacher had gone to such trouble to walk around a small stone and exerted such energy to climb over a boulder, Duk Nyon explained, "Small obstacles in one's path in life are, indeed, trivial and one should take care to go around them. Greater obstacles, however, cannot be avoided, and, as you saw, must be attacked directly if they are not to block your progress."

Korean Humor

Korea has a long and proud history, but it has suffered from internal upheavals and external intrusions that have affected the humorous proclivities of its people (Chang Shub Roh, 1983). Like many other former agrarian societies, Korea has been moving into the life styles of urban-industrial societies that has brought wealth to some but continues the relative deprivations of the poor as in American and other industrial societies.

Roh, for example, tells a popular anecdote of a doctor who tells an injured patient that he will soon have him walking again. The doctor, of course, succeeds in his promise because the patient has to sell his car in order to pay the doctor's bill. The humor is not lost on Koreans who are well aware that only wealthy persons own cars in Korea and that the wealthy are those few who can afford doctors' fees.

Similar to the gallows humor Obrdlik found in Czechoslovakia when his country was overrun by the Germans, Koreans developed their own brand of gallows humor when their nation was dominated by the Japanese. At that time the Koreans would tell each other that the person who would talk honestly would end up in jail. Or able-bodied persons would be sent to a government sponsored communal project as punishment for their humorous jibes at the Japanese occupiers.

In the War Between the States, the United States came close to being divided into two nations, a Northern Union and a Southern Confederacy. Unfortunately in Korean history, such a division did occur and there is a North Korea and a South Korea that are politically, economically, and philosophically far apart despite a common cultural base. As a result of these circumstances, South Koreans are fiercely democratic and have produced humor that ridicules and denigrates the North Korean communists.

Still another quality of Korean humor is the reflection of a society that is undergoing considerable change in men-women relationships. The traditional Korean view is that women are subordinate to men and should be admonished to constrain themselves particularly in their smiling, laughing, joking, and chattering when men are present. Such a view is being eroded away among better-educated, urban women in Korean society and will predictably spread to other women as they move toward more equity within their society.

Anutan Humor

Richard Feinberg represents a newer breed of field anthropologists who include humor as one of the significant areas of cultural inventories. His studies on the island of Anuta, a Polynesian island in the Eastern Solomons, included observations of humor wherever and however it was manifested to him (Feinberg, 1981).

He noted that Anutans laughed hysterically over his early ineptness in lighting a pressure lattern. Originally he thought this humor was to serve as a social corrective, to hold mistakes up to ridicule so that they will not occur again. Instead, by direct questioning, he found that the Anutan view of life was to regard happiness as a dominant value and to share laughter with a victim was to encourage that person to convert tribulations into happiness (Feinberg, 1982). Anutans would, of course, cry and share emotional anguish in cases of severe injuries or spilled blood to demonstrate their symbolic kinship, but in the main, their use of humor was internally consistent with their values and symbols.

Summary and Conclusions

Following the lead of anthropologists, sociologists are increasingly aware of cross-cultural studies that move their discipline from concentrating on their own society to a global view that takes into account socio-cultural variations and similarities. Sociologists have at their disposal a wealth of primary and secondary sources in anthropology to help them enlarge and deepen their sociological *weltanschauung*, world view, as to how and why human groups operate as they do. The universality of humor in cultural inventories lends itself to furthering these developments, and both etic and emic humor analyses have increased the data bases upon which sociologists erect their constructs to comprehend human behavior and social systems.

Ethnographic studies are the units of study in cross-cultural or comparative studies and provide glimpses into how and why societies closely related to American society or quite removed from American society deal with humor. Australians, British, and Irish persons display an approach to humor that closely resembles that of Americans, but the emphases and tone are dissimilar. Clowning and the joking relationship seem to be two subjects that lend themselves well to contrasts between and among preliterate and literate societies. Joking relationships, for example, among preliterates tend to be concerned with ways to handle the conventional styles among kinship networks. With the decline of kinship in literate societies, the joking relationship was found in nonkin occupational settings to continue to serve a variety of social needs.

Finally, a brief sampling of humor in China, Tibet, Korea, and Anuta can only suggest that generalizations concerning humor in human society are difficult to formulate without more accurate and valid cross-cultural data. This points up strikingly the need for far more effort to be made on cross -national, comparative research by sociologists together with their academic cousins in anthropology before improvements in understanding the universals in humor and society can occur.

STUDY QUESTIONS

1. Why cannot humor be understood by reference only to a single society such as American society?

2. What is the distinction between etic and emic humor and what is its significance?

3. What distinguishes ethnographic and comparative studies of humor?

4. What anthropological sources could be used to generate cross-cultural hypotheses concerning humor for sociologists?

5. What are the responsibilities of sociologists in their studies of humor in view of their discipline's applications on a global basis?

6. What are the relationships between humor and play?

7. Is Apte correct in his assessment as to when humor can be said to be involved in play?

8. Is there a dichotomy or a continuum of humor among the world's cultures?

9. What explains the Australians' proclivities as "levelers" and Americans' tendencies to be "achievers" enough to affect their senses of humor?

10.Is "blarney" a unique Irish humor or does it exist under different rubrics in other cultures?

11.What are the social functions of clowns around the world?

12.What explains the universal appearance of the joking relationship?

13.What contrasts and similarities exist between Oriental and Occidental humor?

14.Have intracultural and intercultural changes altered the nature of Chinese, Korean, or Japanese humor?

15.What are the distinctions between viscerotonic, somatotonic, and cerebrotonic personality vis-a-vis the reception of humor? Is this trichotomy applicable to other cultures?

16.What concept or concepts explain Anutan humor?

17.What strategies could sociologists employ to enlarge and deepen their cross-cultural studies of humor?

18.What "payoffs" or results are to be anticipated should sociologists give more attention to comparative studies of humor?

19.Have culture contacts and culture diffusion blurred or lost forever opportunities for cross-cultural study of humor?

Suggested Readings

Apte, Mahadev L. *Humor and Laughter: An Anthropological Approach.* Ithaca, NY: Cornell Univ. Press, 1985.

Blyth, R. H. *Oriental Humour.* Tokyo: Hokuseido Press, 1959.

Butler, Anthony. *The Book of Blarney.* NY: Bell, 1969.

Cheska, A., ed. *Play as Context.* West Point, NY: Leisure, 1981.

Codere, H. "The Amiable Side of Kwakiutl Life: The Potlatch and the Play Potlatch," *Amer. Anthropologist,* v. 58 (1956): 334-351.

Feinberg, Leonard. *The Secret of Laughter.* Amsterdam: Rodopi N.V., 1978.

Feinberg, Richard. *Anuta: Social Structure of a Polynesian Island.* Laie and Copenhagen: Institute for Polynesian Studies (Brigham Young Univ.-Hawaii campus) and the Danish National Museum, 1981.

Feinberg, Richard. "The Meaning of Laughter in Oceania: Statement of the Problem," unpubl. paper, Kent, OH: Kent State Univ., Jan., 1982.

Hammond, P. B. "Mossi Joking," *Ethnology.* v. 3 (1964): 259-267.

Howell, R. W. *Teasing Relationships.* Reading, MA: Addison-Wesley, 1973.

Jenkins, Ron. "The Holy Humor of Bali's Clowns," *Asia,* v. 3 (July/Aug., 1980): 28-35.

Kao, George, ed. *Chinese Wit and Humor.* NY: Coward McCann, 1946.

Kennedy, J.G. "Bonds of Laughter Among the Tarahumara Indians: Toward the Rethinking of Joking Relationship Theory." In W. Goldschmidt and H. Hoijer, eds., *The Social Anthropology of Latin America.* Los Angeles: Latin America Study Center, Univ. of California, pp. 36-38.

Klapp, Orrin E. *Heroes, Villains, and Fools.* Englewood Cliffs, NJ: Prentice-Hall, Spectrum, 1962.

Lancy, D. F. and B. A. Tindall, eds. *The Anthropological Study of Play: Problems and Prospects.* Proceedings of the First Annual Meeting of the Assoc. for the Anthropological Study of Play. Cornwall: Leisure, 1976.

Lewis, Jerry M. "Fan Violence: An American Social Problem." In M. Lewis, ed., *Social Problems and Public Policy, JAI Press, 1982, pp. 175-206.*

Lowie, Robert H. *Primitive Society.* NY: Harper Torchbooks, 1961. (Originally publ. in 1920.)

Loy, J., ed. *Play as Paradox.* West Point, NY: Leisure, 1982.

Lundberg, G. C. "Person-Focused Joking: Pattern and Function," *Human Organization* v. 28 (1969): 22-28.

Malefijt, A. M. de W. *Dutch Joking Patterns.* Transactions of the New York Academy of Science, Series 2, v. 30 (1968): 1181-1186.

Malinowski, Bronislaw. *Argonauts of the Western Pacific.* NY: Dutton, 1961. (Originally publ. in 1922.)

Manning, F., ed. *The World of Play.* West Point, NY: Leisure, 1983.

Mikes, George. *Humour in Memorium.* London: Routledge & Kegan Paul, 1970.

Murdock, G. P. *Social Structure.* NY: Macmillan, 1949.

Pilcher, W. W. *The Portland Longshoremen: A Dispersed Urban Community.* NY: Holt, Rinehart & Winston, 1972.

Radcliffe-Brown, A. R. "On Joking Relationships," *Africa* v. 13 (1940): 195-210.

Radcliffe-Brown, A. R. "A Further Note on Joking Relationships," *Africa* v. 19 (1949): 133-140.

Radcliffe-Brown, A. R. *Structure and Function in Primitive Society.* NY: Free Press, 1965. (Originally publ. in 1952.)

Renwick, George W. "If Australians Are Arrogant, Are Americans Boring? If Americans Are Boring, Are Australians Arrogant?" *The Bridge* v. 5, n. 2, Review of Cross Cultural Affairs and International Training, Summer (1980): 2-4; 33.

Roh, Chang Shub. "Cross-Cultural Perspectives of Humor: A Case of Korea." In Charles E. Babbitt, ed., *The Sociological Galaxy: Sociology Toward the Year 2000,* Pennsylvania Sociological Society, Beacons Publ. Co., 1983, pp. 472-482.

Rosenthal, Franz. *Humor in Early Islam.* Philadelphia: Univ. of Pennsylvania Press, 1956.

Rowe, David Nelson, ed. *China: An Area Manual.* Washington, DC: Johns Hopkins Univ., Operations Research Office, vols. I & II, 1955.

Salter, M. A., ed. *Play: Anthropological Perspectives.* 1977 Proceedings of Assoc. for the Anthropological Study of Play, West Point, NY: Leisure, 1978.

Schwartzman, H. B., ed. *Play and Culture.* 1978 Proceedings Assoc. for the Anthropological Study of Play, West Point, NY: Leisure, 1980.

Stevens, Jr., P. "Bachama Joking Categories: Toward New Perspectives in the Study of Joking Relationships." *J. of Anthropological Research* v. 34 (1978): 47-69.

Chapter 11:

Ethnic Humor

The previous chapter dealt with cross-cultural humor to indicate the global presence of humor across cultural boundaries. This chapter, however, focuses more upon an analysis of humor as it applies to ethnic groups within specific cultures of American society. Ethnic humor is essentially an intracultural or subcultural phenomenon and mirrors the give and take between and among ethnic groups who live in the same society.

The first portion of the chapter deals with the problem of defining what quality or set of attributes distinguish ethnic groups. The problem is not a simple one because ethnicity seems to have different meanings for different people due to a tangled skein of variables from which people select those factors that they believe are the most salient. Those used in this chapter may not satisfy everyone but at least it will be evident as to what factor or factors are paramount features of ethnic groups. Those elements that others assign to ethnic groups will not be neglected, however, because they will become the concern of other chapters that deal with specific groups and humor associated with them.

Ethnic grouping is not something that belongs exclusively to American society. It is found in many other societies and this chapter will have occasion to draw upon these ethnic groups in terms of their ethnic humor whenever they may be usefully cited.

Ethnic humor serves ethnic groups in a variety of ways, and these functions will be noted and discussed, particularly in the context of the overriding concern of ethnic groups to survive (Simpson & Yinger, 1985).

Finally, the rise and fall of ethnic humor will be discussed in terms of social change. Ethnic humor appears to be linked to the everchanging fortunes of ethnic groups and so is popular for a time and then declines or disappears as social histories unfold.

The Nature of Ethnic Groups

Ethnic groups are often merged with racial, religious, or political groups, but common physical features of its members, common faith, or common political aspirations are not their essential qualities. Rather, ethnic groups are characterized by cultural cohesiveness which deals with the common history of a people, their shared feelings or sentiments, their identification with common life styles, traditions, values, or heritages. Racial humor has already been discussed. Ensuing chapters will deal with religious and political humor. This chapter will focus on ethnic humor in its broader, larger, or general cultural sense. Ethnic humor reflects common hopes and fears, common symbolic ties, a consciousness of kind that seeks to preserve group identities and if possible to develop unique contributions to a larger society in which they find themselves.

There remain a number of specific hallmarks of ethnic groups that predictably will be manifested in their brands of humor. These include language and dialects, ancestral homelands, the reasons for entering a host society, the permanence of residence within a society, the processes of assimilation into a host society, and the extent to which ethnic groups seek to set themselves apart from the larger society in pursuit of their own identities and loyalties.

Language certainly is a major force in binding ethnic groups together. It effectively includes a community of speakers but also effectively excludes members of out-groups who cannot communicate in the same tongue or system of symbolic discourse.

Ancestral territories or places of origin are paramount to ethnic groups because it was within these locales that loyalties, alignments, and identities were first established (Burkey, 1978). Ancestral homelands are fondly remembered for their positive features, but are less cherished for the negative factors such as poverty or lack of opportunities that led to the emigration in the first place.

Castille and Kusher (1981) aptly described ethnic groups as "persistent people," those who will do everything in their power to preserve their identity from generation to generation. Pauline Young's classic work, *The Pilgrims of Russian-Town,* documents the irony of an ethnic group of Russian refugees who go through all sorts of tribulations to preserve their unique ways of life only to find that their children reject the old ways and accept, instead, the new American society's ways in which they now live.

It has been the same with other cultural enclaves. One cartoonist, for example, shows an American Indian couple with their small child dressed as a cowboy and playfully shooting at some Indian dolls. They ask themselves, "Where did we go wrong?"

Isaacs (1975) went beyond Castille and Kusher when he portrayed ethnic groups as those who turn inward to worship "the idols of the tribe." This entails separating themselves from outsiders to preserve those values that are essential to their ways of life. The Amish come most readily to mind in this respect, but many ethnic groups form cultural "islands" such as "Little Italies" to assure the preservation of their ethnicity. In such places they may poke fun at "out-groupers" or they may become the targets for ridicule by outsiders who do not understand why they remain apart from the larger, host society.

Length-of-stay is related to humor because some ethnic groups have entered, for example, American society much earlier than other groups. Those who came later often become the objects of laughter and derision. One humorist illustrated the point by telling about two Englishmen who wanted to leave England and settle in America. One caught the first available boat across the Atlantic while the other had to come by another boat about a week later. The late arrival was met on the dock in New York City on July Fourth by the first Englishman. When he asked about all the excitement and parading going on, the first Englishman explained, "Why, this is in celebration of the day 'we' declared 'our' independence from you Englishmen!"

Ethnic groups or their representatives, however, may also be present in a host society on a temporary basis. Brislin (1981) categorizes such persons or groups as "sojourners," those who stay a relatively short time within a given society. Such sojourners may be nationals who are students, business personnel, diplomats, missionaries, migrant workers, or military personnel. Tourists also qualify as sojourners inasmuch as their ranks are filled by a steady stream of visitors, scholars, or guests who are present in a society to take a brief look at certain attractions or concerns and then depart. Such contacts, whether brief or prolonged, constitute ethnic group encounters and can be expected to generate a certain amount of humor because of cultural differences.

In the main, sojourners tend to be conscientious about not offending the people of their host societies. They will make serious attempts to observe the mores and folkways of their hosts and so try to "fit in" as best they can. On the other hand, there is a certain number of sojourners who care little for the sensitivities of the people they are visiting and who hold themselves aloof from the indigenous people's life styles. These so-called "Ugly Americans" often are the targets of native humor in the form of ridicule, aggression or counter-aggression, and hostility.

A milder form of ethnic group encounters, particularly evident among sojourners, bears a similarity to the circumstances of children, who are also relative "newcomers" to a cultural style, when they grapple with problems of understanding the nuances and subtleties in their cultures during their early socialization. Cultural mistakes or miscues are bound to happen, but they are tolerated and excused because the individuals involved are still in the learning stages. Errors made initially could be embarrassing or even serious, but with the passage of time and from the perspective of having greater control and comprehension, such incidents become the source of much goodhearted humor and pleasurable recollections.

One such incident involved an international student at a major university who was shocked and dismayed when he was told "No need to mention it" after he had thanked an office clerk for her help in registering for classes. It took him over an hour for his advisor to calm his outrage and to explain to him the nature of the idiom he had just encountered. The student now laughs about the incident, but at the time, it was far from being a laughing matter to him.

Whether sojourners or permanent residents, ethnic groups are distinctive groups within their larger society because of their cultural differences that amount to a cultural divide or "cultural gap." These divides or gaps need to be bridged in some manner or the cultural distinctions will endure. When these distinctions continue indefinitely, ethnic humor makes much of the differences in a "we" versus "they" mentality. Feelings of superiority of the larger society and of inferiority for the ethnic group is reinforced in ethnic jibes that affirm that at least "we" are not as "they" are. Klineberg (1964), for example, noted how ridicule of ethnic differences becomes built-in reminders of superiority-inferiority themes among Italians or among the French. Italians, Klineberg observed, use the expression *fare il portughese* quite matter-of-factly because it is intended to point to behavior associated with Portugese who allegedly violate Italian sensibilities when they sneak into a theater or ride in a streetcar without paying the price of admission or fare. In a similar vein, a Frenchman might preface his remarks by saying *Je suis un paysan du Danube* (I am a peasant from the Danube), when he wishes to point out that he is rather ignorant about the subject being discussed.

Of particular significance in assessing the nature of ethnic groups, and consequently humor associated with them, is the type of contacts that brought them together in the first place. The movement from points of origin to permanent or temporary settlement is generally explained by the "push-pull" theory, which holds that some social forces operated within native lands to alienate, exclude, or force people out while simultaneously there may have been attractions or potentials for a more fulfilled life within a new society. Such theory does apply to those societies with immigration policies calculated to control the flow of newcomers to their shores. America, for example, takes pride in its past history of welcoming newcomers. The Statue of Liberty in New York Harbor symbolizes this policy, but it is ironic that this open door to immigrants is closed and both the statue and nearby Ellis Island are now historical monuments with the floodtides of immigrants to America largely over. Now and then, as with Cubans or with southeast Asian "boat people," there may be a relaxation of restrictions and large numbers gain entry once again.

What remains are the problems of assimilation and amalgamation that continue to challenge both ethnic groups and their host society to reach some acceptable level of accord. Humor emerges from such a setting because it serves both ethnic groups and their larger societies in their various needs.

Functions of Ethnic Humor

Aggression

The first of these functions of humor with regard to ethnic groups is to attack the control system that denies ethnic groups full access to participation in the life of their host societies. Those barriers to full participation take a variety of forms, but chief among them may be the ascription of certain attributes alleged to reflect the nature of ethnic peoples that are in sharp contrast to those allocated to the majority or dominant groups. Ethnic groups may be stereotyped as stupid, ignorant, unclean, given to criminal, antisocial, repugnant, outlandish behaviors, and qualified only for limited types of menial employment. Ethnic groups themselves view outsiders as possessing the same traits ascribed to them and their humor derides the negative features of people who give lip-service to high ideals, but who do not practice them in reality. "They simply do not know any better" is the reigning ideology that directs and guides their humorous barbs against each other.

Social Control

Underlying aggressive ethnic humor is the desire to gain control over those who are threats to the *status quo*. On the one hand, the ethnic groups seek to prevent or stop undesirable actions that bar them from achievements. On the other hand, majorities wish to keep ethnic groups in line so that their presence or participation does not interfere or disrupt older, familiar, or established ways. Within social limits, ethnic differences are tolerable. This is to say that ethnic peoples are acceptable as they serve the purposes of dominant groups. However, when they step over these limits and seek their own benefits, then ethnic groups are targeted for humorous assaults on their audacity.

To Portray One's Own Group as More Desirable

A more specific function of ethnic humor is to project an image that one's own group is characterized as worthy of support and consideration. Ethnocentrism calls for using the value criteria of one's own group as justification for existence and for improvements upon that existence. The in-group's foods, clothing, dances, rituals, ceremonials, mannerisms, values and attitudes, behavior, or preferences are held in special regard. As one commercial puts it, "Now that's Italian!" Or as bumper stickers proudly proclaim, "Thank God I'm Polish!"

To Diminish Disadvantages

The difficulties and disadvantages of ethnic loyalties can be diminished through humor. The attitude that being an ethnic person is "not-so-bad" is advanced by such humor. Such humor does not sidestep the notion that ethnicity may be a handicap in reaching desired goals, but that rejections and barriers serve to sharpen self-respect and to enhance the ethnic identity. Social upward mobility may take more time and more investment of energy and talents, but this does not detract from the willingness to move forward. Ethnic groups will point with pride to those among them who have overcome the foolishness and animosities of outsiders whose very actions energized or mobilized their strengths and motivated individuals to accomplish great deeds in their lifetimes. Disadvantages are thus transformed into advantages and become the focus of celebrations in humor. Such persons build on their ethnic base and rise to positions of prominence within the larger society.

Symbolic Reversal of the Social Order

While the transformation of ethnic disadvantages into advantages can occur realistically, humor does not have to wait upon reality. It may imaginatively and playfully suggest what might happen if there were to be a reversal of the social order and ethnic minorities were to take over from formerly dominant groups. Such humor would delight certain ethnic peoples or could shock outsiders from their complacencies that such social changes would never occur.

To Turn Tragedy into Comedy

Reference has already been given to gallows humor, the type of humor which expresses that despite great tragedies there is still room for comedy. This function of humor is to build morale for ethnic groups who have suffered so much through the actions of others. Nevertheless, they must hold their heads high rather than give way to dark despair and defeatism. Far from home and forced to adjust to strange ways, ethnic groups have dug deep into their psyche and found that their sorrows are not insurmountable. The resilience of the human spirit is also found among ethnic groups, and they are still able to laugh and hope for the best regardless of their trials and tribulations. They choose laughter over tears and it helps them over the rough times to encourage them to look forward to "better times to come."

To Express and Handle Self-Hatred

One of the fascinating aspects of ethnic humor is its function in terms of giving voice to self-hatred or group-hatred and so bringing it under control. In this instance ethnic group members tend to agree with outsiders that their subcultural group leaves much to be desired. Being privy to ethnic ways, they turn with considerable relish to the vulnerabilities and short-comings of their former identities. By setting aside their former affiliations, they can possibly benefit by their acceptability into majority groups. Name changes, for example, can help former ethnics to "pass" or to promote the illusion that they are members of the majority and conceal or mask their ethnicity. They hate their own kind and all that it has earned them in terms of treatment and become adept at holding their former identity in contempt. With great glee, they can use humor to shed their past and be free from any of its impediments.

To Accommodate the Out-Group

Without taking the stance of self- or group-hatreds, there is some willingness to change enough to be able to live harmoniously with those outside one's ethnic group. This is the posture of the moderate ethnic individual, who can laugh about the ways of his people but never in a judgmental or negative manner. The ethnic humor in this genre is more gentle and pokes fun at surface manifestations of ethnicity and avoids being overly critical of fundamental values or ethos that are at the heart of ethnicities.

To Blur the Lines That Keep Groups Apart

Ethnic humor that shows the same human features found in all human relationships helps reduce the actual or potential hostilities between ethnic groups and their host societies. Such humor displays for all to see that there are rigidities and absurdities among all peoples. Ethnics then are not so different from all humanity and consequently through humor merit compassion. Larry Wilde (1974), a specialist in ethnic humor, suggested that if certain ethnic humor is offensive, the solution is to remove the name of the ethnic group and replace it with another one. Thus ethnic shortcomings are interchangeable among many groups including one's own ethnic origins.

In-Group Solidarity: To Present a United Front

Finally, ethnic humor allows a group to laugh about its own predilections. It is well within the experience of many observers that certain forms of ethnic humor used by outsiders are demeaning or repugnant to the targeted group but are much more acceptable when members of the same group offer them or even invent them. Such groups acknowledge their u-niqueness or ethnic distinctiveness to themselves and so increase their willingness to stand together against all external critics. It does not matter if the substance of the humor is accurate, distorted, or far off the mark. What matters is that ethnic groups can laugh together and so strengthen their own solidarity.

Assimilation

The assimilation process calls for the gradual blending of cultural differ-ences within a single cultural framework. Its acceptance or rejection de-pends upon how willing ethnic groups are in joining with others in proce-dures that either diminish or destroy their ethnic uniqueness. In America, the expectation that ethnic peoples will eventually adapt or shed their ways in favor of becoming totally immersed in American ways has been going on for some years. The American "melting pot" has been effective through the public schools and because adults must join with others in pursuit of employment, housing, health care, and cordial relationships. Its alterna-tive is pluralism in which ethnic groups maintain some of their own quali-ties by preserving as much of their ethnic heritages as possible. In a sense both assimilation and pluralism have been taking place in American society and the end is not yet in sight.

There is little doubt that the American culture is an amalgam of bits and pieces of cultures from all over the world. Sociological texts have turned re-peatedly to Ralph Linton's satire, "One Hundred Per Cent American," (1937) to dissuade students from ethnocentric notions that Americans made their own culture. Linton's citizen's bed, pajamas, bathtub, toilet, mirror, soap, razor, towel, clothes, shoes, tie, chinaware, breakfast foods, newspapers, coins, cigarette, language, and deference to the Diety are all shown to have originated through the genius of non-Americans scattered over the face of the globe.

Assimilation and pluralism are processes that do not make headlines, at least not in contemporary American society. Elsewhere, however, ethnic conflict is tragically evident (Horowitz, 1985). At this writing, virulent eth-nic clashes occur in Northern Ireland, Chad, and Lebanon; secessionist warfare occurs in Burma, Bangladesh, the Sudan, Nigeria, Iraq, and in the Philippines; there are Somali incursions in Ethiopia and Turkish invasions in Cyprus; Uganda and Syria are locales for Army killings along ethnic lines and civilian slaughter occurs in India-Pakistan, Burundi, and Indone-sia. Terrorism from Sikhs, Basques, Corsicans, or Palestinians dominate the international news. Ethnic riots occur in India, Sri Lanka, Malaysia, Zaire, Guyana, and many other countries. Less dramatically, political par-ties and trade unions are organized ethnically. There are movements to expel ethnic traders and workers who are said to compete unfairly with members of the host society. Separatism between the French and the English in Canada and division in Belgium for Flemings and Walloons are further examples of ethnic hostilities of a serious nature. Whereas ethnic differences in American history sometimes flared into outright conflicts, they are relatively absent in modern times. Elsewhere, however, ethnic struggles continue unresolved, and the serious nature of these ethnic clashes puts a damper on ethnic humor. Only in America, where ethnic differences are subdued and slowly being worked out through assimilation and pluralism, can ethnic humor be welcomed and appreciated. In the American setting, ethnic humor gets a sympathetic hearing. In a nation originated by immigrants, ethnic pride is understood as each successive generation becomes more and more "Americanized" and less and less passionate about their ethnic uniqueness or distinctiveness.

Learning the language of their adopted country is one of the central tasks for successive waves of immigrants. It is a fundamental step in the assimilation process and did not escape the attention of perceptive humorists. The classic work of Leonard Q. Ross (1937), *The Education of H, Y, M, A, N, K, A, P, L, A, N,* refers to a Jewish immigrant who attends a night school for adults who seek to learn English, Civics, and other subjects in their quest for naturalization as future American citizens. Mr. Kaplan is portrayed as a man with a prodigious amount of ego-strength and hubris, but his multiple mistakes in learning the English language become the bane of patient Mr. Parkhill, his instructor while providing some hilarious humor. Mr. Kaplan is the prototypical immigrant who twists, mangles, and confuses English because he is still enmeshed in his older ethnic thoughtways.

Whole professional careers in ethnic comedy have been carved out by such performers as Jack Pearl, Bert Gordon, Bill Dana, Weber and Fields, Myron Cohen, Smith and Dale, and Lou Holtz. Jack Pearl created the lovable exaggerator, "Baron Munchhausen," who spoke in thick German accents. Bill Dana portrayed "Jose Jimenez," whose Spanish ancestry led him to confuse the sounds of "j" and "h." Bert Gordon was "The Mad Russian" on Eddie Cantor's long-running radio show. Weber and Fields made comedic history as "Dutch" characters in vaudeville. Myron Cohen developed an eloquent delivery in English but could captivate his audiences when he would break into an ethnic dialect. Smith and Dale specialized in fractured English and Leonard Marx, "Chico" of the Marx Brothers, spoke his lines with an Italian accent. Modern equivalents are harder to identify currently possibly because ethnic assimilation no longer holds center stage for Americans.

Resistance to assimilation, of course, is also evident in American society and is defended vigorously indeed by both ethnic groups and those who applaud ethnic groups for their courage and tenacity in clinging to cultural styles associated with their ancestral past. Kephart (1982) documents the case of the Rom or gypsies who regard all outsiders, people they call *gadje,* as fair game for *bujo,* flim-flam or outright misrepresentation. Rom will also turn to fortune telling to coax as much money as possible from gullible *gadje.* The Rom, of course, do not resort to *bujo* or fortune telling among themselves. Their explanation, often accompanied by good natured laughter, is that the Rom are too intelligent to be taken in by such foolishness whereas *gadje* are made-to-order fools and easy marks who figuratively ask to be exploited.

The Amish stand in sharp contrast to the Rom. Whereas Rom are colorful and audacious in their clothes and manners, the Amish stress plainness and modesty. Whereas the Rom resort to fair or foul means to make a living, the Amish strive to be scrupulously honest. The Rom are nomadic while the Amish are settled farmers (Hostetler, 1980). Within their enclaves, they can enjoy their own brand of humor, particularly when it reflects their dedication to their life style. Despite the abundance of Millers, Yoders, Stolzfuses, Fishers, Troyers, Swartzes, Hershbergers, or Bontragers in their midst, they delight in quick identification of individual members by reference to personal habits or preferences, humorous incidents that may have occurred to them, occupations, residences, or by putting the names of parents before the first names of a person such as calling brothers "Nancy John" and "Nancy Jake" because John and Jake's mother's first name was Nancy.

The Rise and Fall of Ethnic Humor

Ethnic humor apparently is subject to the same forces that collectively bring about fads and fashions. Some are like fads that are ephemeral and quickly pass away. Some are like fashions and endure for considerable amounts of time. This rise and fall of ethnic humor gives rise to speculation that its appearance or disappearance are causal and not chance events.

In this chapter it has been noted that ethnic humor is almost absent in virulent cases of ethnic loyalties. It flourishes in places like America where ethnic backgrounds are merged or blended in the nonviolent processes of assimilation and pluralism. Wherein stereotyping is institutionalized, certain ethnic groups are targeted for humorous references to their alleged traits, i.e. the Italians are musical, the Scots are thrifty, the Germans are methodical, the French are romantics, the Latins are lovers, the English are conservatives, and so on.

But these stereotypes run their course and prolonged joking about one ethnic group or another begins to lose its appeal when suspicions are aroused that, after all, there are numerous exceptions to the so-called general rule. The Polish joke, for instance, was a very popular bit of ethnic humor for a time. It lost much of its punch, however, when Polish people demonstrated before the world that they possessed courage in organizing their Solidarity movement and standing by their convictions despite the harsh measures imposed by the ruling military regime. Their symbolic leader, Lech Walesa, suffered house arrests, humiliating interrogations, and harrassments designed to intimidate him, but he has been honored with a Nobel Peace Prize. Paralleling these events in Poland, a Polish pope was elected to the Throne of St. Peter and has since proved himself as a charismatic personality filled with courage, wit, charm, and humility. His triumphant visits throughout the world carries the message of respect for ethnic differences and constant vigilance in behalf of peace and harmony. Attacked by a would-be assassin, Pope John Paul II earned deep admiration and sympathy as untold millions watched over his recuperation and applauded his return to an active life of compassion that included his forgiving his would-be assassin. Polish jokes lost much of their punch in the aftermath of these events and surface less frequently ever since.

The demise of the Polish joke and similar ethnic humor about one people or another occurred in the social context of the times. Topical humor depends heavily upon the changing social scene so that humorists respond to whatever conceptions people hold concerning the fortunes or misfortunes of a given ethnic group. When the butts of jokes can no longer be portrayed as fools, new targets are needed for humorous treatment.

Summary and Conclusions

Ethnic humor focuses upon intracultural or subcultural differences. It emerges out of the movements of people as culture carriers who enter host societies as permanent residents or as sojourners. Their ethnicity includes their abiding loyalties and adherence to a common history, shared feelings or sentiments, and their close identification with common life styles, traditions, values, or heritages. While racial homogeneity, religious commonality, and political longings play a part in ethnicity, these are not necessarily the key variables, particularly when the focus of ethnic humor is on their acceptance of or resistance to assimilation efforts. Standing apart from the host society, ethnic groups may be appreciated for their uniqueness and quiet contributions to the larger society or they may be seen as intrusive, competitive, or threatening enclaves to the *status quo*. Their ties to their former homelands may be very strong, moderate, or dissolved, but outsiders continue to associate ethnic groups with their places of origin and what is happening to those people who still live there.

In a sense, ethnicity concerns the right to exist, to continue, to survive, to maintain an identification distinct from others, and it is in these strong desires for continuity that ethnic humor comes into play. Ethnic humor expresses aggression, serves as a social control mechanism, favors one group over another, suggests that disadvantages are tolerable and even advantageous, can permit fanciful reversals of the social order, can turn tragedies into comedy, allows for self- or group-hatred, works to accommodate out-groups, helps blur cultural distinctions that have kept people from understanding each other, and finally, encourages in-group solidarity by the sharing of laughter.

Ethnic or subcultural groups face the dilemma of assimilation within the larger society. There is strong pressure to join with all others in the meeting of daily needs and future developments. On the other hand, ethnic groups are being asked to commit social suicide by abandoning cultural styles that have sustained and distinguished them from all other groups for generations. Ethnic humor deals with these matters such as their difficulties in comprehending the language of their host societies or their insistence on clinging to life styles that contrast too sharply with the overall mores and folkways of generalized others. Some ethnic humor is downright vicious. Other forms of ethnic humor are tolerant and appreciative of the ways of ethnic people. Depending upon the social milieu, ethnic humor ebbs and flows or moderates. Ethnic humor then mirrors social histories and thereby falls within the legitimate interests and concerns of sociologists.

STUDY QUESTIONS

1. What are the distinctive qualities of ethnic humor?

2. Is the survival thesis applicable to ethnic humor?

3. What are the social differences between intracultural and intercultural humor?

4. Does the humor of American ethnic groups differ remarkably from that of other ethnic groups in other societies?

5. How does humor serve the needs of ethnic groups or those who stand outside ethnic groups?

6. What part does language acquisition play in ethnic humor?

7. How can errors in adaptations to strange, new cultures provide the substantive matters for ethnic humor?

8. What "idols of the tribe" become the targets for humor?

9. Would ethnic humor in places like the U.S.S.R., Nigeria, or elsewhere be similar to, or stand in sharp contrast with ethnic humor in the American context?

10. Are there differences between humor directed to ethnic sojourners and those directed at those in permanent residence?

11. Is ethnic humor essentially aggressive or does it also involve considerable empathy for ethnic people?

12. In what ways do differences in "push-pull" factors that brought ethnic groups into a host society change the nature of ethnic humor that refers to them?

13. Has ethnic humor increased or decreased in American society in recent decades?

14. What is accomplished by ethnic humor of the self-hatred or group-hatred types?

15. Is ethnic humor focused on relationships between various ethnic groups or is it directed more towards ethnic groups' relationships with those who are ethnic outsiders in general?

16. What part does superiority-inferiority play in shaping the nature of ethnic humor?

17. Is ethnic humor directed against groups that are not as easily assimilated as other ethnic groups, those that resist assimilation, or those that are eager to assimilate?

18. Do contributions of ethnic representatives to host societies help modify demeaning messages contained in ethnic humor?

19. Is ethnic humor absent or relatively rare in locales where there is a history of sustained ethnic conflicts?

20. Have professional comics in America begun to abandon the persona of ethnic individuals who struggle to master a second language?

21. What explains the rise and fall of certain fads or fashions in ethnic humor?

Suggested Readings

Becker, Howard S., *Outsiders: Studies in the Sociology of Deviance*. NY: Macmillan, 1963.

Brislin, Richard W. *Cross-Cultural Encounters: Face-to-Face Interaction.* NY: Pergamon Press, 1981.

Burkey, Richard M. *Ethnic and Racial Groups: The Dynamics of Dominance.* Menlo Park, CA: Cummings, 1978.

Castille, George Pierre, and Gilbert Kushner, eds. *Persistent People: Cultural Enclaves in Perspective.* Tucson, AZ: Univ. of Arizona Press, 1981.

Clinard, Marshall B. *Sociology of Deviant Behavior.* NY: Holt, Rinehart & Winston, 3rd ed., 1968.

Grove, D. John. *The Race Versus Ethnic Debate: A Cross-National Analysis of Two Theoretical Approaches.* Denver, CO: Univ. of Denver, Center on International Studies, Studies in Race & Nations, v. 5, Study No. 4, 1973-74.

Horowitz, Donald L. *Ethnic Groups in Conflict.* Berkeley, CA: Univ. of California Press, 1985.

Hostetler, John A. *Amish Society.* Baltimore: Johns Hopkins Univ. Press, 3rd ed., 1980.

Hunt, Chester L. and Lewis Walker. *Ethnic Dynamics: Patterns of Intergroup Relations in Various Societies.* Homewood, IL: Dorsey Press, 1974.

Isaacs, Harold R. *Idols of the Tribe: Group Identity and Political Change.* NY: Harper & Row, 1975.

Kephart, William A. *Extraordinary Groups: The Sociology of Unconventional Life-Styles.* NY: St. Martin's Press, 2nd ed., 1982; 3rd ed., 1987.

Klineberg, Otto. *The Human Dimension in International Relations.* NY: Holt, Rinehart & Winston, 1964.

Linton, Ralph. "One Hundred Per Cent American," *American Mercury* v. 40 (April, 1937): 427-429.

Miller, Wayne C., ed. *Minorities in America: The Annual Bibliography.* University Park, PA: Pennsylvania Univ. Press, 1976, 1977, 1978.

Polenberg, Richard. *One Nation Divisible: Class, Race, and Ethnicity in the United States Since 1938.* NY: Viking Press, 1980.

Ross, Leonard Q. *The Education of H,Y,M,A,N K,A,P,L,A,N.* NY: Harcourt, Brace, 1937.

Royce, Anya Peterson. *Ethnic Identity: Strategies of Diversity.* Bloomington, IN: Indiana Univ. Press, 1982.

Simpson, George E. and J. Milton Yinger. *Racial and Cultural Minorities: An Analysis of Prejudice and Discrimination.* NY: Plenum Press, 5th ed., 1985.

Wilde, Larry, ed. *The Official Polish Joke Book - The Official Italian Joke Book.* NY: Pinnacle Books, 1974.

Wilde, Larry, ed. *The Official Irish Joke Book - The Official Jewish Joke Book.* NY: Pinnacle Books, 1974.

PART III:

Social Structure and Humor

The social structures, institutions, or complex organizations of societies provide significant settings for manifestations of humor. They do so not necessarily in a static, mechanical sense, but in an active sense. They not only "house" or give "shelter" to humor but they lend substance to humor, meaning and relatedness to humor, and are themselves involved in humor that helps such structures to work and to fulfill their reasons for existence.

Some of the chapters in this section focus on what some have called the fundamental, basic, "major" social institutions such as religion, education, polity, and family. Other chapters relate humor to social structures such as the military, which is closely associated with the dominant political systems of society; occupations, which is a generalized set of activities that flows from the overall economy of society, and medicine and sports, which are more specific occupations. No single chapter in Part III is comprehensive, exhaustive, definitive, or gives complete coverage to humor in these settings because of space limitations. These chapters are designed to offer suggestions that humor penetrates such social forms and services their needs and the needs of their participants while also continuing our exploration into the sociology of humor.

Chapter 12:

Religious Humor

Introduction

Religion and all that it entails is normatively associated with the spiritual, mystical, awesome nature of life and not directly with humor. It consists of three major elements: ideology, emotions, and propitiation. None of these aspects of religion calls for humor or a nonserious approach or treatment (Nottingham, 1971; Bedell, 1975; Hargrove, 1979). They are serious, sober, solemn facets of religion and not to be taken lightly by participants or observers. Humor would seem to be out of place and unwelcome, but as will be noted, it does penetrate religion and its practices and becomes in fact deeply appreciated, useful, supportive, and effective for faithful followers.

Religious ideology is composed of idea and belief systems. These systems provide the intellectual substance of faiths that probe, explain, reason, logically organize, and thoughtfully deal with the purposes and nature of life and death. Historical events, personages, and values are weighed in the balance and found to be guides to the conduct of human affairs and to appropriate personal behaviors.

Once convinced, confirmed, or consecrated to some all-embracing religious ideology, profound emotions are aroused and called into play. These run the gamut from love to hate. They can become a dedication and devotion that transforms selfishness into sacrifices and services intended to ennoble humanity or they are capable of calling out moods of extreme distaste, dislike, and contempt for those who do not share the religious ideology of believers. While kind deeds are motivated by religious emotions, in the name of these same religions, holy wars and crusades have been mounted against those called "infidels," "pagans," or "nonbelievers."

Finally propitiation, those acts of religious conduct done in the name of an ideology and the emotions they arouse, occurs in every religion. The rationale of an ideology and the inspiration of a set of emotions brings people together so that they behave as a community of believers. Such people

177

will feast and fast, sing and speak, share their ideas, feelings and inter-pretations, genuflect, sit, stand, or prostrate themselves before symbols of their faith, and engage in countless rituals and ceremonials that constitute the worship and acceptance of a faith. Such a community of believers re-ceives abundant, assuring, and reinforcing evidence that their religion is "the correct one." When and if necessary, these "true believers" will give tremendous amounts of their properties, incomes, and energies and, under extreme conditions, even their lives in support of their religious feelings and beliefs.

Religion then is not something to be lightly approached, something triv-ial, or something to be facetiously treated. Rather, humorists need to inject humor into religious matters with some awareness that their efforts may not be well received and could be seen as serious affronts or mockery of ideologies held in esteem. Under certain circumstances, among the believ-ers themselves, humor may be acceptable. Those who are outsiders, how-ever, lack such credentials, and their humorous thrusts, antics, or judg-ments about a religion are labeled hostile and defamatory.

The root of the term religion is *religare,* meaning "to be bound together." It should remind those who deal in humor that religion is a so-cial construct developed out of firm convictions of "true believers" that they have made proper sense out of the mysteries of living and dying. Their solid front can lead them to be humane, loving, and caring. Or there can be outrage and violent reactions against those whom they judge to be their re-ligious enemies, detractors, or antagonists. Collectively and individually, religion can bring out the best in humanity while it is also capable of inspir-ing the most vicious cruelties. To poke fun at religion or to followers of some particular brand of religion is indeed an act that requires the humor-ist to do so with a certain amount of restraint and believers to exercise a certain degree of forebearance.

Sacred and Secular Religions

The usual expectation, when religion is the center of discussion, is to fo-cus upon sacred, spiritual, mystical, awesome, holy, almost ineffable mat-ters. Persons expect to concentrate on the omnipresence and omnipotence of deities or the Deity, the veneration of spirits or all-powerful forces that can determine the fortunes of mortals in life and their disposition in death for eternity, and to engage in the appropriate thoughts and actions that guide, inspire, and give meaning to life and its struggles.

Religion, however, does not necessarily concern that which is sacred or is bound up with the supernatural. Rather, religion may well focus on how men and women are themselves creators of social philosophies to which they pledge allegiance. "Secular "belief systems" include, for example, such overriding ways to conduct human affairs as communism, capitalism, nationalism, socialism, internationalism, democracy, monarchy, anarchy, humanism, or scientism, and possibly other "isms." Closely resembling their sacred counterparts, secular religions have their ideologies, emotional appeals, and propitiary acts. Devotees or those under the sphere of influence of such secular systems of thought must think, feel, and behave with some conformity or suffer the consequences of being charged with disloyalty and enmity of the prevailing social order (Wallace, 1966; Bellah, 1975; Mead, 1975).

In this chapter, however, humor associated with *sacred* religions are central to the exposition. In the chapters to follow, *secular* religions and humor related to them will be analyzed. Humorous treatment of political, economic, or educational matters do merit attention, but their distinctive humors are temporarily set aside so that both sacred and secular religions are given their due. What follows selects Judaism, Roman Catholicism, and Protestantism as the major Judeo-Christian faiths in American society and seeks to analyze and illustrate humor within them. Similar treatment might apply to other faiths such as Islam, Buddhism, Hinduism, and Shintoism, but such analyses and illustrations await the effort of other scholars and lie beyond our purview here.

Jewish Humor

The Jewish Paradox

Judaism is the oldest faith in the Western World, approximately six thousand years old. It has sometimes been called "The Mother Faith" because it antedates two "daughter" faiths, Christianity and Islam. These "daughter" faiths have prospered and grown by leaps and bounds in numbers and influence whereas their "mother" remains the sacred faith of a small remnant of peoples throughout the world. With the exception of modern Israel, there is no nation-state on earth in which Judaism is the major faith.

There are those who equate Judaism with ethnicity. This perspective fixes on characteristics that are held to be life styles or manners and customs alleged to be followed by people of the Jewish faith. Judaism itself, however, falls within the rubric of religion and those who follow it are, of course, influenced by its precepts, philosophies, history, and preferences. Furthermore, the reactions of those who stand outside the religion affect how faithful, loyal, or devoted Jews will be towards themselves, their religion, and what is asked of them because they identify with Judaism. Thus this chapter looks at Judaism as a religion and uses the term *Jewish* to refer to matters associated with Judaism. Being Jewish is intended to mean that persons associated with Judaism tend to determine for themselves what portions of Judaism they will follow, what ideologies they support and what ideologies they reject, what norms they will meet and what expectations they refuse to accept. In short, as in many faiths, adherents pick and choose those elements that please them and ignore or modify those elements that displease them.

Jews are "the perennial minority" in terms of numbers and proportions within most populations. Being in the minority means that Jews must adapt as much as possible to the ways of the majority, a requirement that frequently calls for some adjustments as to how closely they identify with Judaism itself. It is ironic that even in Israel where they have a clear majority, this small land is hotly contested since its inception in 1948 with internal upheavals with neighbors, with terrorism, with external wars with unfriendly nations, and with seige-like living conditions. It would seem that there is no place on earth for Jews that has remained safe, secure, and fully receptive to their ancient faith. America appears to be the rare nation-state that has given its Jewish people the advantages of a free, open, pluralistic society. Other nation-states also deserve credit for their fair and just treatment of Jews and Judaism, but their ranks are relatively few in number.

The overall history of the Jewish people is marked with sadness, rejection, tragedy, misunderstanding, and seemingly relentless persecution and suffering (Dimont, 1962; Sachar, 1967). There has been defeat in ancient Israel and Judea, expulsion, enslavement, dispersion, derision, torture, the Inquisition, false charges of disloyalty and treasonable plots to overthrow or undermine authorities and scapegoating of monstrous proportions as evidenced by Russian pogroms, the ostracism and indignities of restrictions to separate quarters of cities or ghettos, and the deliberate, insane genocide of "The Final Solution" of Hitler's Holocaust.

Conscious of such a tragic background, the expectations would be that Jews and Judaism would be quite sober, bitter, ill-humored, and filled with self-pity and grief. Such a finding, however, is not supported by the facts. Judaism has long taught that there is a time for tears and a time for laughter (Eccles. 3:4). Judaism is highly aware of suffering and sadness, but it is also conscious of an eternal plan, a dialectic, or a divine balance to seek out and savor joy and happiness.

Fully aware that Jews are in the minority in the world's population, that they are a miniscule proportion of the world's religions, that they are sometimes treated with disdain and suspicion and cruelties, that their belief system may be an embarrassing reminder to majority faiths of their debts to Jews and Judaism and how often other religious people fall short of their own ethics, there are places like the United States of America in which Jews and Judaism are publicly received with great goodwill.

Harry Golden expressed such gratitude in *Only in America* that Jews and Judaism have found a real haven of refuge from the painful events of the past (Golden, 1958). Other nations have shown their respect for Jews and Judaism and persons are free to practice their religion without fear of comment, but in America Jews and Judaism have truly prospered in many ways. Many have called America "The Promised land" rather than Israel, because Jews and Judaism are found therein to be contributors to the cultural mosaic that is the American way of life.

From the ranks of the Jewish minority in America have come an amazing array of comic talent. Many are legendary figures in comedic history and the following list should be regarded as a partial listing because hundreds of writers and creators of comedy are omitted:

Joey Adams, Woody Allen, Morey Amsterdam, Joe Ancis, Phil Baker, Sandy Baron, Belle Barth, Jack Benny, Gertrude Berg, Milton Berle, Shelly Berman, Joey Bishop, Ben Blue, Victor Borge, David Brenner, Fanny Brice, Marshall Brickman, Albert Brooks, Mel Brooks, Lenny Bruce, Art Buchwald, George Burns, Abe Burrows, Red Buttons, Sid Ceasar, Eddie Cantor, Jack Carter, Bennett Cerf, Myron Cohen, Irwin Corey, Rodney Dangerfield, Marshall Effron, Stanley Elkin, Jules Feiffer, Totie Fields, Phil Foster, Bruce Jay Friedman, Rube Goldberg, Harry Golden, Shecky Green, Dan Greenburg, Milt Gross, Sam Gross, Buddy Hackett, Goldie Hawn, Joseph Heller, Harry Hirschfield, Abbie Hoffman, Lou Holtz, Willie Howard, Lou Jacobi, George Jessel, Mickey Katz, Danny Kaye, Georgie Kaye, Alan King, Robert Klein, Arthur Kober, Paul Krassner, Harvey Kurtzman, Bert Lahr, Louise Lasser, Norman Lear, London Lee, Fran Lebowitz, Jack E. Leonard, Jerry Lester, Sam Levenson, David Levine, Jerry Lewis, Robert Q. Lewis, Wallace Markfield, the Marx Brothers, Jackie Mason, Lou Mason, Bette Midler, Henry Morgan, Zero Mostel, Jan Murray, Lou Myers, Nichols and May, Parkyakarkas (Harry Einstein), S.J. Perelman, Gilda Radner, Carl Reiner, Don Rickles, the Ritz Brothers, Joan Rivers, Leo Rosten, Philip Roth, Mort Sahl, Soupy Sales, Dr. Seuss, Dick Shawn, Al Shean, Allan Sherman, Max Shulman, Phil Silvers, Shel Silverstein, Neil Simon, Smith and Dale, Arnold Stang, David Steinberg, Saul Steinberg, the Three Stooges, Barbra Streisand, Larry Storch, Gerald Sussman, Calvin Trillin, Sophie Tucker, Betty Walker, Nancy Walker, Ira Wallach, Billy Wilder, Gene Wilder, Paul Winchell, Ed Wynn, and Henny Youngman (Novak & Waldoks, 1981).

Such names on this unbelievably long list of professional humorists indicate that somehow their Jewish heritage did leave its mark on such personalities and that their Jewish affiliation helped shape their careers in literature, music, stage, screen, art, radio, and television. Some built directly on their Judaic resources for the wellsprings of their humor; others drew only indirectly from Judaism. Still others took a different tack and disassociated their public performances from their Judaic origins.

Jewish Attitudes Toward Humor

Jews and Judaism welcome humorous perceptions of the human condition because there is recognition that suffering, sorrow, and abject sadness is not the total range of experiences for humanity or for themselves. Pain, wretchedness, and rejection represent only one end of the continuum of feeling-states, and Jewish sages constantly point to the other end of human emotions that celebrate life lived to its fullest. In the eighteenth century, for instance, Israel Baal Shem Tov initiated the Hasidic movement in Judaism. Hasidism stressed joy in the love of God (Roth, 1959). Dancing, religious ecstacy, and sheer exuberance of the human spirit dramatized for Hasidics that the purpose of humankind was to redeem the evil that is in nature and to conquer it.

In the late nineteenth and early twentieth century, Shalom Rabinovich writing under the pseudonym of Shalom Aleichem, a Hebrew greeting meaning "Peace unto you," underscored the primary need of a person to be a happy individual and not a perpetually gloomy or sad personality. It was Aleichem who created the character of Tevye, the milkman who was a lighthearted pauper who drove his rickety milkcart around the village of Kasrilevke and who was given to speaking directly to his Maker as a powerful friend who could help him in his moments of despair.

Popularized in stage and film versions of Aleichem's writings, *Fiddler On the Roof* made theatrical history with its message that even a precarious position calls for courage and enjoying the beauty of life. One simply must never give up, takes whatever blows come into one's life and goes on from there. This is the stance of the eternal optimist who believes that even in the darkest moments God has not deserted him or her and that happiness and satisfactions are still within reach. This is the survivalist theme embedded in humor that sustains and uplifts sagging spirits to press on past life's adversities to reach better days to come. Barbara Myerhoff's *Number Our Days,* a study in the lives of Jewish old people in an urban ghetto (1978), quotes one of the major informants, Shmuel, as saying, "Our writings bring us out of the morbid parts of life by laughter. The Jew has a joyful life regardless of the oppression he walks through, because he is a good swimmer. He always comes back to the surface. He tries to reach the other side, with his humor and irony. Great humor is based on pain and grief. And in this, the Jew proved to be the expert." (Myerhoff, p. 193)

Jewish Comic Types

There are a number of Jewish comic types, but chief among them are "the schnorrer," "the schlemiel," and "the schlemazzel" (Rosten, 1968).

The "schnorrer" is the butt of much humor because such a person would go to extreme lengths to get something for nothing. He or she is perpetually seeking someone who will provide him or her with a free ride, drink, favor, or some kind of support. Other terms that might explain who a schnorrer really is are beggar, panhandler, moocher, cheapskate, chisler, bum, drifter, bargainer, and impudent indigent. A schnorrer, for instance, once knocked on the door of a rich man's house at 6:30 in the morning. The rich man was outraged to be called to his front door at so early an hour.

"How dare you wake me up out of a sound sleep!," he screamed. "Listen," calmly replied the schnorrer, "I don't tell you how to run your business, so don't tell me how to run mine."

The "schlemiel" is a true fool, a simpleton, a born loser, a klutz, a clumsy, butterfingered, sloppy, gauche type who cannot seem to do anything right. The schlemiel does not fit into any social situation, has no ability to be convincing, and frequently falls into his or her own trap or will be making some foolish agreement or wager. Some examples of this ineptitude include the following: It is said that when a schlemiel falls on his back, he breaks his nose. Or when a schlemiel takes a bath, he forgets to wash his face. There is the story of the schlemiel who is very worried and so went to his rabbi for advice. "Rabbi," he said, "you've got to help me. Every year my wife has a baby. I have nine children now and I can hardly make enough money to feed and clothe them. What can I do?" The rabbi thought a moment and then said, "Do nothing." Another schlemiel is alleged to have come home from the steam baths without his shirt. His wife scolds him, "You schlemiel! Where is your shirt?" The schlemiel thought a moment and said, "Aha, I have it. Someone at the baths must have taken my shirt by mistake instead of his." "Well then," said his wife, "so why didn't you take his shirt?" The schlemiel scratched his head and replied, "Well, the fellow who took my shirt forgot to leave his!"

Finally, there is the "schlemazzel," the individual who has bad luck or misfortune haunt him or her or dog his or her footsteps. Like the cartoon character who always is the sole person who seems to have a perpetual rain cloud over his head, the schlemazzel just never has events occur as they should. For example, when a schlemazzel winds a clock, it promptly stops. When he kills a chicken, it walks away from him. If a schlemazzel would go into the manufacture of umbrellas, the sun would shine for an entire year. If such a type went into the funeral business, people would stop dying.

These classic types are familiar to many peoples, but they have been immortalized by Jews over the centuries. Endless yarns are spun among Jewish people using these typologies. The overall attitude is, "Oh well, so what else is new?"

Yiddish, Yinglish, and Other Jewish Influences on English

The formal language of Jewish people is Hebrew, sometimes called "the language of prayer" because traditional worship services are conducted in Hebrew. The dispersion of Jews, however, particularly in Europe, led to a vernacular tongue known as Yiddish, a combination of German, Slavic, and Hebraic vocabularies and idioms. In America, Yiddish-speaking Jews encountered speakers of English and the results were what Leo Rosten (1968) called "Yinglish."

As was noted in the chapter on ethnic humor, comics have built whole careers out of the laugh-getting values of speaking "Broken English,"

"Fractured French," "Pseudo-German," or with an "Italian" or "Spanish" accent. Yiddish is among the many languages or language forms that have been borrowed or adopted by English speakers. Some five hundred terms have become part of the English language according to Kogos (1969). Many English speakers use such words as gezundheit, schmo, kibbitz, kosher, shiksa, meshuga, schnook, mishmash, halavah, bagel, schmegge, megillah, kvetch, lox, schmooze, schmaltz, ganef, schlepp, schmear, yenta, and chutzpa without necessarily associating them with Yiddish.

Mel Brooks is one Jewish comic who never forgot his Jewish roots. He is dedicated to the proposition that any means to squeeze humor out of situations is legitimate. In the movie *Blazing Saddles,* he is dressed as a war-painted, full-feathered Indian chief and encounters some hapless black settlers driving their wagons across the plains. His response is to promptly yell out to his assembled warriors, "Lazem Gain!" (Let them go!) in the spirit of true Jewish forgiveness or compassion for a suffering people.

Other Judaic influences can be found in a host of idioms to which many resort at an opportune moment. There are probably countless times when, in humor, persons use some of the following expressions:

Get lost.
You should live so long.
Who *needs* it?
Al*right* already!
I need it like a hole in the head.
It shouldn't happen to a dog.
O.K. by me.
He knows from nothing.
From that he makes a living?
Do him something.
He is a regular genius.
Go hit your head against the wall.
Excuse the expression.
Go fight City Hall.
On him it looks good.
Wear it in good health.
You should live to a hundred and twenty.
I should have such luck.
Listen, bubele, ...?
Smart, he isn't.
It's time, it's time.

(Rosten, 1968)

The Money Connection

Jews and Judaism have long been associated in the public's mind with money and money-making enterprises. The rise of Christianity as the established religion of the Western World was accompanied by declining opportunities for Jews to make a living in whatever profession or business they chose. One enterprise, however, was particularly open to Jews and that was money-lending or banking.

Financing was held to be tied to usury, the taking of interest at high rates, a practice that was held by many Christians to be sinful or evil and thus to be shunned. This conception of money-contamination did not deter many Christians from seeking profits on business transactions nor did it mean that Jews exclusively became money-lenders, but it did help to fix in stereotypic form the notion that Jews were particularly sharp business operators whereas Christians were not.

Perhaps one of the oldest Jewish jokes on record that affirms this alleged Jewish dedication to money-making is the one about an elderly patriarch on his deathbed who has his family gathered about him to pay their last respects. The old man asks if his wife is present and she confirms her presence. He then asks if his sons are in the room and is assured that they are. He asks if his daughters are in the room and again is told that they are there. Finally he asks if all the kinfolk are there. Again, he is told that everyone was with him. Suddenly the old man sits up in alarm. "Then who is minding the store?" he demanded to know.

The "Great Salesman" Theme

Not only are Jews associated with money-making stereotypically, but they have also been held to be experts in sales. Such is the thrust of the story of a highly successful Jewish insurance agent who worked for a firm whose management was entirely composed of staunch Catholics. The Catholics wanted to promote the Jewish agent as an official of the company but to elevate a non-Catholic to such a high status was unthinkable. They decided the best strategy would be to convert him to Catholicism so they called in a priest and the two of them were closeted for several hours. When the priest finally walked out of the Jewish agent's office, the company officials crowded around the priest to ask if he had indeed converted the Jew. "No," replied the priest, "but he did sell me a ten thousand dollar policy!" (Spalding, 1969, pp. 494-495)

Jewish Emphasis upon Family Life and Education

Finally, Jewish humor frequently reflects a dual concern for family life and education. Being kept marginal in most societies dominated by other religions, Jews found refuge, dignity, solace, and overall comfort only in the midst of their families. Jewish families have been called "the fortress of the faith" because in Jewish homes forms of persecution and rejection from the outside world were temporarily suspended. When Jewish comics write or speak of their families, they do so with great warmth and draw heavily upon their family life for considerable amounts of their humorous materials (Cantor, 1959; Levenson, 1966, 1973; Marx and Barber, 1974).

Jewish families also promote education as the means by which upward social mobility can occur. Traditionally education among Jews concentrated upon being educated in the intricacies of Judaism itself, so that the Jewish scholar was an honored figure among them. The effort, skills, and dedication in religious studies, however, also apply in secular studies. Formal education, particularly in major professions, is regarded as a valued channel to reach the highest social stratum and consequently to serve society and bring acceptance for their expertise. Training then in respected professions was assumed by families for their children. This matter-of-fact attitude is demonstrated in the significant story of a Jewish mother walking with her two little sons, one being five years old and the other seven. A passing neighbor admires them and says that they are handsome and bright-looking. The pleased mother promptly asks, "Which one do you mean? The 'doctor' or the 'lawyer'?"

It was Sam Levenson who observed that anti-Semites do not necessarily have to like Jews but pointed out that they would be foolish to reject Jewish doctors' contributions to medical science such as the Wassermann test for syphilis; digitalis, discovered by Dr. Nuslin; insulin discovered by Dr. Minofsky; chorhydrate for convulsions, discovered by Dr. Lifreich; the Schick test for diptheria; vitamins discovered by Dr. Funk;,streptomycin, discovered by Dr. Woronan; the polio pill, from the work of Dr. Sabin; and the polio vaccine by Dr. Salk. To these medical breakthroughs, many Jewish humorists would add "Jewish penicillin" — chicken soup.

Christian Humor

The central figure of Christianity is Jesus Christ. Normally Christ is revered, sanctified, held to be the Messiah, the Savior, the Redeemer, the Only Son of God, the Spirit-Made-Flesh, the Sacrificial Lamb who pointed out the way to live on earth and to find eternal salvation for His followers. To search for those bits of evidence that demonstrate Christ's association, recognition, and use of humor would seem to be absurd and would appear to yield nothing of consequence. Yet Christ was aware of humor and is to be credited with numerous instances of employing it in His earthly life according to scriptural accounts (Webster, 1960; Vos, 1967; Hyers, 1969; Guillet, 1972; Cormier, 1977; Kissinger, 1979; Borowitz, 1980; Stein, 1981;

Hyers, 1982; Piccolantonio, 1983). Christ mediated between the divine and the human nature of the world and in so doing resorted to humor to accomplish His ends. His humor was gentle, loving, considerate, and always designed to instruct rather than to harm, to find fault, or to reject even His most severe critics. In rebuking the Pharisees, Christ pointed out how they strain a fly from their drink but swallow a camel, an incongruity that could be seen and understood as ridiculous by His audiences. His reference to pouring new wine into old skins, a procedure that would burst the containers, was understood to mean that the older Mosaic Law no longer could contain the new morality and spiritual thrust of His message.

Christ has been rated as an excellent story teller, an amusing raconteur, who could hold His audiences spellbound and whose anecdotes were unforgettable lessons in the arts of social harmony. His parable of ten girls who waited for a bridegroom to come and for the wedding feast to begin is a case in point. Five of the girls had sufficient oil for their lamps and could stay for the festivities. The other five did not have sufficient oil and, consequently, had to leave early. One must be prepared for His coming, never knowing how long it may take, a lesson in patience and understanding. In a number of instances Christ acted out by word and deed His brilliant wit that captured the sense and intensity of the moment. One of the most telling was His rescue and compassion in the case of a prostitute about to be stoned to death. His challenge that "those who were without fault" should cast the first stones was a remarkable insight into human fallibility and the projection of guilt and punishment upon others rather than upon one's own self.

Christ made full use of humor, not so much to be hostile, mocking, or aggressive against those who would not or could not listen, but to attack symbolically those conditions that blind, hamper, or prevent people from being true to the highest moral and ethical conduct possible. It was Christ who asked that others assist Lazarus so that he may be unbound from his graveclothes. It was Christ who helped a thief "steal" into Heaven. It was Christ who asked that fishermen become "fishers" for men. It was Christ who cautioned those who clung to worldly possessions rather than to morality when He spoke of a camel passing through the eye of a needle compared to a selfish, wealthy person gaining eternal salvation. Such a record speaks to the humanity of Christ and His recognition of humor as an effective means to achieve both personal and social harmony.

Roman Catholic Humor

The establishment of the Roman Catholic church was the great "breakthrough," a major accomplishment for the long-rejected and struggling faith of Christianity. Centered in Rome, the Roman Catholic church is a marvel of complex organization that has global significance. It has managed to survive centuries of social ferment by clinging to its principles and values but showing that it can change, slowly and carefully, so as not to lose sight of its foundations and purposes.

Emulating the wit and wisdom of Christ, those priests who could combine their spiritual dedication with human concerns would win the affection and devotion of their parishioners. One such priest was Father Arlotto who was asked to deliver a sermon at the funeral of a man named Don Lupe, a surname that means wolf. Father Arlotto obliged as follows:

"Fear God and obey His Commandments. It is customary to say a few things in praise of the departed when he has left a good name behind in the world. Among the animals, there are four that have this merit and characteristic:

One is good alive but not dead - the donkey.

Another is good dead but not alive - the hog.

Another is good both alive and dead - the ox.

The fourth is neither good alive or dead - the wolf.

The body that lies before us was named Lupe. I really do not know what good I can say of him and therefore I shall say nothing and will bring my sermon to an end. Pax et benedicto, amen." (Speroni, 1964, pp. 100-102)

Ascending the Throne of Peter is the highest position in the Roman Catholic church and the pope becomes the key administrator of policies. There have been many popes whose senses of humor were notable, but Pope John XXIII is singled out as one of the most memorable. It was John the XXIII who greeted a delegation of two hundred Jews with the statement, "Welcome, I am Joseph, your brother!," a reference to his former name of Joseph Roncalli and to the biblical account of a meeting between Joseph, the brother sold into slavery, and his brothers who were amazed to see him alive and in a position of great power and responsibility (Fesquet, 1964). When a diplomat accredited to the Holy See asked the pontiff how many persons worked at the Vatican, John XXIII promptly replied, "Oh, no more than half of them!" At the Hospital of the Holy Spirit in Rome, the Mother Superior was deeply stirred by the pope's visit. She introduced herself by saying, "Most Holy Father, I am the Superior of the Holy Spirit." John XXIII replied, "Well, I must say you're lucky. I am only the Vicar of Jesus Christ!"

Pope John XXIII left his imprint on the Roman Catholic church as it continues to reconcile its long-established tenets with the contemporary values of personal fulfillment. Just as John XXIII's sense of humor mirrored his grasp of human realities that fall short of spiritual ideals, so those who advocate greater changes within Roman Catholicism turn to humor as one means to prod the church into action. Thus in a telling moment in Jean Anouilh's *The Lark,* a drama about Joan of Arc, the Earl of Warwick comments, "Our Holy Mother Church takes her time when she is asked to give birth to a small matter of policy." In the scene wherein a stern inquisitor demands to know why Joan did not pray for God's help rather than lead her army into battle, she responds, "God likes to see action first, My Lord. Prayer is extra."

Protestant Humor

Protestants acquired their name by being associated with "protests" against the authority of the Roman Catholic church, with the notable exception of the Orthodox Catholics of Eastern Europe. The term *Protestant,* however, should not be used as a blanket term to cover all those Christian faiths whose origins or purposes are not necessarily linked with objections to Roman Catholic dogma or authority. Nevertheless, many do overlook fine distinctions and unique histories and assign the label to religionists who are neither Jewish nor Roman Catholic, at least in American society. The category *Protestant* is used in this chapter in the popular sense as a catchall term so as not to be mired down in drawnout distinctions that are irrelevant to this discussion. While the Roman Catholic church provides a cohesive, comprehensive structure that units the faithful worldwide, Protestants follow the precept, "Every person is his/her own priest." This is to say that the intercession of an official priesthood is not essential for Protestants' salvation. In a sense, one may characterize Roman Catholicism as dominated by an international bureaucracy whereas Protestantism focuses upon individualism.

This personal independence that guards the right to interpret faith as one sees fit is illustrated in the case of a student who asked to examine a pamphlet entitled "What Methodists Believe" after a lecture on the topic. After looking it over carefully, the student was seen to write something on the cover and hastily beat an exit from the room. Curious, the lecturer checked the cover and discovered the student had amended the title to read, "What *Some* Methodists Believe." This same independence of thought applies to the relationships between Protestant ministers and their flocks. The ministers are the designated leaders but must bend in many ways to take into account the wishes and thought of their congregants. Accordingly, Protestant leaders are aware that while they promote religious ideals, their people are only human and will often not quite measure up — the "spirit is willing, but the flesh is weak."

One minister who is aware of this incongruity between the sacred and the profane has collected a number of examples from various church bulletins (Rev. Stanley Conover, *Modern Maturity,* Feb.-Mar., 1978, p. 68), as follows:

This afternoon there will be a meeting in the South and North ends of the church. Children will be baptized at both ends.

The Service will close with "Little Drops of Water." One of the ladies will start quietly and the rest of the congregation will join in.

On Sunday, a special collection will be taken to defray the expenses of the new carpet. All those wishing to do something on the carpet please come forward and get a piece of paper.

The ladies of the church have cast off clothing of every kind and they may be seen in the church basement on Friday afternoon.

Thursday at 5:00 PM there will be a meeting of the Little Mothers Club. All wishing to become little mothers will please meet with the minister in his study.

Wednesday, the Ladies Literary Society will meet. Mrs. Johnson will sing "Put Me in My Little Bed," accompanied by the preacher.

In a similar vein, there was the minister who was being transferred to another church. A little old lady saying her farewells to the minister she liked so well burst out with the astounding declaration, "I'm sorry to see you go. I never knew what sin was until you came to our church!"

Ministers, of course, cultivate a sense of humor in order to sustain themselves in their need to maintain a certain decorum in the face of the public. One spiritual leader retained his ability to not take himself too seriously when he developed two different file systems. One he marked "Sacred" and the other he marked, "Top Sacred."

The mundane affairs of keeping churches financially solvent keep many ministers busy. Depending heavily upon offerings of followers, it is commonplace to exhort congregants "to give to the Lord so that His work shall go forward." Noting the lower-than-usual collection in the plates one Sunday morning, one minister turned to his congregation and said, tongue-in-cheek, "I let it be known that the poor are welcome in our church. I also see by the collection plates that they have come!"

Finally there are various life cycle ceremonials such as baptisms, weddings, and funerals. One minister was quite surprised to find a 92-year old gentleman and an 82-year old lady in his study one afternoon. Longstanding members of the church, the couple was seeking his help in getting married. When he inquired why, at this late time in their lives, did they want to get married, they told him they wanted to have children in order to make them heirs to their joint estates. Trying to be as tactful as ever, the minister explained, "My dear friends, you may well be heir-minded but, at your ages, you are simply not heir-conditioned!"

Humor on Religious Rivalry or the Non-religious

Two other sources of religious humor worth noting are religious rivalries and the presence of atheists, agnostics, or disbelievers. Both matters have provoked serious, sometimes tragic, reactions among those who take a religious stance. Humor, however, can serve as a safety valve to let off steam that might otherwise be used destructively. Protestant denominations, for example, do not always agree theologically or on church structures. There are major schisms between Protestants and Catholics that prevent ecumenical movements. Judaism and Christianity share much common ground but stand apart from each other on numerous matters. Theists and atheists are poles apart. All of these become the sum and substance of humor associated with religion because they lend themselves well to the expression of symbolic aggression or criticism, or as an opportunity to require persons to think a bit more about the significance of their views of the supernatural and spiritual.

For instance, there is the story of a person who died and was admitted to heaven. The new arrival was escorted down a long corridor that connected numerous side-rooms or large assembly halls. Each one seemed to be filled with people who were singing, praying, resting, eating, or otherwise enjoying themselves. The guide identified each group's room such as the halls for the Baptists, Presbyterians, and Methodists. When the guide and the new arrival came to the last room, the guide cautioned the persons to speak in whispers. "Why so?" asked the individual. "Well," replied the guide, "this room contains the .... (insert the name of whatever religious group one wants to use as the butt of the joke.) They think they are the only ones up here!"

Concerning atheism, there is the story of the atheist who died and was immediately sent to be judged as to where he would spend eternity. God asked him if he believed in Him when he was alive. The atheist persisted, "I led my entire life in the belief that there is no God." The Almighty pondered His reply and then graciously declared, "To go through all the vicissitudes of life without believing or relying upon God took a great deal of courage and personal fortitude. Such virtues are to be recognized and rewarded. You may take your place in Heaven." Such a portrayal of the Diety that stresses forgiveness, understanding and compassion is a far cry from conceptions of supreme powers that are fearsome, impersonal, and vengeful. Religious humor in this instance stresses the positive rather than the negative.

Summary and Conclusions

Humor and religions suit each other well. While religion deals with ideologies, emotions, and propitiation of serious, sobering matters of life and death, humor can and does ameliorate some of the potential problems of different beliefs, feeling-states, and actions that have kept people apart, suspicious, uninformed, and hostile toward each other. Religious humor can be derogatory, but can also affirm the freedom to worship as one pleases, to preserve ideas as to the nature of matters that are essentially extra-scientific, and to recognize that there can be tolerance, acceptance, and appreciation of multiple ways to approach sacred and secular phenomena.

Above all, humor supports communities of believers as they take distinctive ways to cope and survive against any and all threats to their existence.

Novak and Waldoks (1981) concluded their humor anthology with an illustrative story of the coming of a new flood in three days that will wipe out the world. A Buddhist leader appears on television and pleads with everyone to become a Buddhist so that at least they may find salvation in heaven. The Pope goes on television with a similar message: "It is still not too late to accept Jesus." The Chief Rabbi of Israel then takes his turn on TV and says, "We have three days to learn how to live under water."

STUDY QUESTIONS

1. How does humor serve as a safety-valve to allow different religious systems to exist without violence and hostility toward each other?

2. Are there elements in all religions that make religion particularly receptive to humorous interpretations?

3. Are secular religions any less volatile than sacred religions in insisting on the validity of their views? Do secular religions, perhaps, need the leavening effects of humor even more than sacred religions?

4. What is the Jewish Paradox?

5. What explains the overrepresentation of Jewish humorists among professional comics in American society?

6. What is Hasidism and why does it welcome a humorous treatment of life?

7. Does Jewish humor give evidence in support of the theme of surviving against all odds?

8. Are schnorrers, schlemiels, schlemazzels exclusively Jewish comic types or are they universal types found among all faiths and peoples?

9. What gives Yiddish a strong humorous patina?

10. What do studies of the life-histories of legendary Jewish comics reveal in terms of explaining their successes?

11. What are the repetitive themes in Jewish humor? Is there a sociological explanation for the frequency with which factors appear in their particular forms?

12. Why is Jewish humor generally well-received by persons of other faiths?

13. Was Christ, Himself, essentially a comic or a humorist? Was it because He, too, was a Jew?

14. What are the contrasts between Roman Catholic and Protestant humor?

15. Does humor continue to play a major role in Christianity or is it kept relatively under control when it is applied within Christianity?

16. What is accomplished when the sacred and the profane are mixed within a humorous framework?

17. What part does humor play in interfaith discourse?

18. What study design would verify that humor has survival value for a religion or for people faithful to that religion?

19. What precautions must be taken to guard against religious humor being ill-received?

20. What are the elements in humor and in religion that make them compatible?

Suggested Readings

Ausubel, Nathan, ed. *A Treasury of Jewish Humor.* NY: Doubleday, 1951.

Bedell, George, *et al. Religion in America.* NY: Macmillan, 1975.

Bellah, Robert. *The Broken Covenant: American Civil Religion In Time of Trial.* NY: Seabury Press, 1975.

Borowitz, Eugene. *Contemporary Christologies.* NY: Paulist Press, 1980.

Cantor, Eddie. *The Way I See It.* Englewood Cliffs, NJ: Prentice:Hall, 1959.

Cormier, Henri. *The Humor of Jesus.* NY: Alba House, 1977.

Dimont, Max I. *Jews, God, and History.* NY: Simon & Schuster, 1962.

Fesquet, Henri. *Wit and Wisdom of Good Pope John.* NY: P.J. Kenedy, 1964.

Golden, Harry. *Only in America.* NY: World Publ., 1958.

Guillet, Jacques. *The Consciousness of Jesus.* NY: Newman Press, 1972.

Hargrove, Barbara. *The Sociology of Religion.* Arlington Heights, IL: AHM Publ., 1979.

Hyers, Conrad, ed. *Holy Laughter.* NY: Seabury Press, 1969.

Hyers, Conrad. "A Funny Faith," *One World* No. 78 (July, Aug., 1982).

Kissinger, Warren. *The Parables of Jesus: A History of Interpretation and Bibliography.* Metuchen, NJ: Scarecrow Press, 1979.

Kogos, Fred. *A Dictionary of Yiddish Slang and Idioms.* NY: Coronet Communications, 1969.

Levenson, Sam. *Everything But Money.* NY: Simon & Schuster, 1966.

Levenson, Sam. *In One Era and Out the Other.* NY: Simon & Schuster, 1973.

Marx, Harpo, and Rowland Barber. *Harpo Speaks!* NY: Freeway Press, 1974.

Mead, Sidney. *The Nation with the Soul of a Church.* NY: Harper Forum Books, 1975.

Myerhoff, Barbara. *Number Our Days.* NY: Simon & Schuster, 1980.

Nottingham, Elizabeth K. *Religion: A Sociological View.* NY: Random House, 1971.

Novak, William, and Moshe Waldoks. *The Big Book of Jewish Humor.* NY: Harper & Row, 1981.

Piccolantonio, Sister Linda. "The Humor of Christ." Unpubl. ms., Nov. 21, 1983.

Rosten, Leo. *The Joys of Yiddish.* NY: McGraw-Hill, 1968.

Roth, Cecil, ed. *The Standard Jewish Encyclopedia.* NY: Doubleday, 1969.

Sachar, Abram Leon. *A History of the Jews.* NY: Knopf, 5th ed., 1967.

Spalding, Henry D., ed. *Encyclopedia of Jewish Humor.* NY: Jonathan David, 1969.

Speroni, Charles. *Wit and Wisdom of the Italian Renaissance.* Berkeley, CA: Univ. of California Press, 1964.

Trueblood, Elton. *The Humor of Christ: A Bold Challenge to the Traditional Stereotype of a Somber, Gloomy Christ.* San Francisco: Harper & Row, 1964.

Vos, Nelvin. *For God's Sake, Laugh!* Richmond, VA: John Knox Press, 1967.

Wallace, Anthony. *Religion: An Anthropological View.* NY: Random House, 1966.

Webster, Gary. *Laughter in the Bible.* St. Louis: Bethany Press, 1960.

Chapter 13:

Educational Humor

Formal or public education in the broadest sense is approached sociologically as a relatively young social institution that is charged with the responsibility of instructing ongoing and upcoming generations within societies in the nature, substance, value, objectives, and applications of their cultures. The relative youthfulness of formal education as a basic or autonomous social system is emphasized because this overall charge has been among the functions of much older social systems such as the family, religion, economy, or the polity of societies. Each complex social system requires its participants to know enough about how the system works and how individuals are to play their respective positions within it. In this sense families, religions, economic and political units have instructed participants in what is required of them in order to perpetuate themselves. While generations come and go, compliant, convinced, and "well-schooled" generations are needed in steady supply if social institutions are to continue indefinitely. Should they fail in this essential task, social systems falter and collapse for want of "educated' culture-carriers. To this day, perhaps the greatest educational trainings occur within family units, within religious organizations, on-the-job, or within the structures of political agencies.

Nevertheless, education in the narrower, formal sense as used in this chapter refers mainly to those agencies openly and consciously set aside to instruct students in both the basics and refined information and skills needed to enter more fully into the life of human societies. Families, religions, economic enterprises, and political agencies continue to educate their memberships, but they have also recognized that education of participants is not their exclusive concerns nor do they propose to be deterred from their more primary tasks such as, in the case of businesses or industry, to produce, distribute, and consume goods and services. There is simply too much to learn, and accumulated knowledge has become the particular province of educators and the complex social institution called education.

195

From the sociological perspective, socialization is the process by which individuals acquire the ways and means to participate in their society. As just discussed, socialization occurs within each social institution, but when it is formalized as the central function of schools at various levels of complexity, it has come to be identified as education. In this chapter the focus is on formal schooling from primary and secondary levels to college and post-graduate levels devised to prepare individuals to take some effective statuses within their respective societies. Further, the concern of the chapter is to determine the extent humor is present in schools at various levels, wherein humor is consciously a part of the repertoire of students, teachers, and administrators, and what purposes are served by its usage. A search of the literature over the past fifteen years or so that explores the interfacing of humor and education indicates that there is indeed a rich vein to be mined and utilized to test theories and conclusions concerning educational humor.

After an overall view of the relationship between humor and education, more specific situations will be questioned and discussed such as humor in the classroom, humor as a part of educational measurement, humor within selected topics in the curricula, the presence of class clowns, humor within various levels of education, humor as a survival tool among teachers, and the adaptation of humor to changing circumstances in educational settings such as alternative schools or the problems confronting integrated school systems. Such a format is not regarded as an exhaustive coverage of possible topics in educational humor, but is varied enough to suggest the multiple ways in which humor and education are interrelated and further to suggest that there are other areas that have yet to be studied and analyzed if educational humor is to be more fully understood and appreciated.

An Overview of Educational Humor

Tracing the history of education as it was portrayed in cartoons that were published in the *National Education Association Journal* between 1920 and 1967, Weaver (1970) was able to find that changing ideologies were indeed reflected in these humorous drawings. For example, in the 1920s and the 1930s, cartoons appeared treating "schools" and "education" as synonymous terms or concepts designed to preserve American ideals. There was no criticism of schools or education as failing or coming up short in achieving its objectives of making good citizens of its students. Furthermore, those who worked in education were idealized as well-motivated, satisfied instructors who devoted themselves to their students, their community, and their subjects. By the 1950s and 1960s, however, criticism and cyncism were prominent features of the times, and such topics as poor working conditions and challenges to educational professionalism were portrayed in comical fashion in the educational cartoons of the day. The relatively low pay scale of teachers that was taken as a matter of fact in the 1920s and '30s became the topic of concern in the '50s and '60s. One cartoon of more recent vintage, for instance, carried the comment of one of its characters that "I know your occupation is a teacher, but what is the source of your income?"

The *NEA Journal*'s cartoons of the 1960s dealt with the generation gap between parents and their school-age children who were being exposed to topics and theories quite unknown to students in their times. One cartoon showed an elementary school child telling his father, "With *that* explanation, you need a refresher course!" Teachers too are shown in the cartoons as adapting themselves to the new technologies that have become part of educational professionalism. One teacher is shown in a cartoon with a screwdriver and a pair of pliers and asking her class brightly, "Class, does anyone need any help?"

Pointedly, Weaver noted that black children and black teachers did not appear in the *NEA Journal*'s cartoons until the late 1960s. It was as if they did not exist in the educational scene, were unworthy of special attention, or possibly were regarded as "no laughing matter" and so were left in limbo for fear of adverse comment.

The earlier cartoons portrayed schools as the sole means to achieve economic and social status. There was little doubt that school attendance and conformity was the road to upward vertical mobility. The cartoonists, however, knew that the road was not always smooth and the travelers upon it were not necessarily enthusiastic. They drew heavily upon stereotyped portraits of naughty schoolboys, reluctant teenagers, reprimanding principals, and straight-laced female teachers who looked like candidates for a retirement home.

Of particular significance in Weaver's study was the seemingly endless conflict between schoolboys and their female teachers. Boys were the targets of teachers' disdain because teachers rewarded compliance with academic rules of conduct, tended to de-emphasize aggressive behavior, and favored those students who facilitated the easy administration of aggregates. Given such a profile of expectations, schoolgirls fit the pattern much better than schoolboys and consequently won high approval from their mentors. Over the years the cartoons showed the boys becoming bolder and asserting themselves. One cartoon, for example, has a schoolboy confront his teacher by saying, "Think Miss Whitlow — surely there must be some way to make me behave!" Or another cartoon presents a schoolboy who audaciously explains his failing grades by saying, "Obviously, teacher is failing to recognize my style of learning."

Sherman (1979) took a different tack toward education in general when he discussed the way in which Seba Smith, a journalist with the *Portland Courier*, utilized the fictitious character of Major Jack Downing. Legend has it that the figure of "Uncle Sam," a symbol of America, was really Major Downing with a beard. Through Major Downing, Seba Smith was able to offer some choice comments on education. Uneducated himself but clever enough to use "horse sense," this spokesman for "ordinary people" was not bookish but drew his lessons from life itself. By horse sense, Downing meant common sense that drew upon life experiences to understand what motivates people and how people make use of that motivation. Educational "nonsense" such as the notion that everyone has an equal chance to succeed was humorously attacked by the Major Downing character. Formal schooling was portrayed as overly abstract, too often ambiguous, unduly organized, painfully formal, and dominated by a concern for pretense and status. For the many who did not go to school in the nineteenth century, Major Jack Downing represented the "self-made man," an outsider who had above-average intelligence, the informal learner who could make his way in the world, the person who could use humor to ridicule formal training because that person was just as effective without it.

Humorous assaults on education are nothing new. They have been going on for ages. Ressing (1975) documented what he called "Education's Bad Press." Seneca observed the charge that educators live in ivory towers when he said of instructors, "We learn not for life, but for the lecture room." Lucien referred to the painful aspects of teaching when he insisted, "Whom the Gods hate, they make school-masters." Montaigne wrote, "Certainly no one would boast of having a teacher included among his ancestors." Martin Luther had a dim view of teachers and schools when he spoke of them as "knowing only how to beat and torment" their students. "Schools are dungeons and hells" and teachers are "themselves, tyrants and jailers." Ben Johnson cynically wrote of schoolmasters who "sweep their living from the posteriors of little children." Henry Thoreau assailed education for its insistence on order when he noted, "Education makes a straight-cut ditch out of a free-meandering brook," and perhaps the *coup de grace* was delivered by George Bernard Shaw, who offered one of the most frequently quoted comments about teachers in general, "He who can, does. He who cannot, teaches."

Webb (1981) saw humor itself as a teacher. Drawing mainly from political humor, Webb pointed to the social correction function of humor in which deviation from unspecified norms is pinpointed but which allows considerable latitude for change because persons are not quite certain as to which expectations were not met. Humor can also be used with considerable effect for institutional and ideological changes, said Webb, when the normative order is held to be deviant and its symbols are degraded.

Webb is not alone in his thesis that humor has tremendous instructive powers. Baughman (1973) took the stance that humor has been absent far too long in formal education or has been sorely neglected. He describes teachers as pallbearers and opposed the somber, funeral-like atmosphere in schools that almost buries whatever enthusiasm students and teachers may have had. Writing to social science teachers, Langer (1984) recorded an interview with columnist-humorist Art Buchwald who expresses the strong need for humor to survive the demands of formal training, especially in military schools where, aside from difficult and technical subjects designed for serious applications in warfare, discipline and attention to detailed regulations are prominent. Woods (1983), writing to British sociologists, concurred that humor is a coping mechanism in schools and merits more attention than it has received.

Humor in the Classroom

While the latent functions of education are particularly noticeable in the informality of corridors, offices, cafeterias, gymnasiums, or lunchrooms, the manifest functions of education occur in classroom settings. Here is where the transfer of knowledge occurs. Here is where students can ponder, debate, question, clarify, challenge, or consider the knowledge to which they have been exposed. Classrooms are "the frontlines where the battle is joined," as one administrator put it. With the classroom sessions playing such a central role in the educational process, the question arises as to how much humor, if any, should be brought into classrooms or, if it is acceptable, just how should humor be handled in the learning situation? There is apparently no agreement among educators concerning these questions. Some are enthusiastic about the presence of humor in the classroom, some are cautious, and some are opposed on the basis of their findings.

An anonymous report in *Nation's Schools and Colleges* (1975) noted the doctoral research of Murray Weinberg, Yeshiva University, in which he investigated the facility with which humor can help students learn. Allegedly the use of humor reduces anxiety and its presence should thus increase the ability of students to retain new material. Weinberg's study showed just the opposite. Those students who were very anxious and who had relatively low intelligence tended to retain less after hearing a lecture spiced with humorous examples. Humor thus interfered with concentration and even created an unfavorable attitude toward the lecturer's presentation. Furthermore, less nervous but more intelligent students were better able to tolerate departures from serious to humorous examples. Weinberg also found that there was no significant differences in the use of humor with either the very anxious, very intelligent students or the less anxious, less intelligent students. In sum, Weinberg's study does call into question the idea that humor is *always* conducive to learning.

Sudol (1981) also cautioned educators about the dangers of classroom humor. He was aware that educators do not want their classroooms to resemble prisons with sullen "captives," but on the other hand, careless use of humor in classroom situations can convert them into "playrooms," "circuses," or "zoos." Exaggeration, playing the fool, teasing, and sarcasm are useful humorous devices, but there can be unwanted, distracting, and even dangerous effects if humor is not used judiciously. Kaplan and Pascoe

(1977) found in their test-retest of students exposed to serious and nonserious lectures that retention and comprehension were not facilitated through the humorous examples. Zillman and his associates (1984) turned their attention to the educational television programs designed to enhance children's learning. They were aware that these popular programs such as the Electric Company, Mister Rogers, and Sesame Street thrive on visual and attention-getting devices that emphasize presocial and nonsense humor. They found that such techniques led children to overestimate the properties of new objects to which they had been introduced. Distortions of reality did not help the children understand its nature, and further, the distortions they perceived remained uncorrected for a considerable length of time.

Such findings notwithstanding, educators are encouraged by their peers to bring humor into classrooms because its merits outweigh some of its negative effects, provided, of course, that it is used cautiously and thoughtfully. Rogers (1984) argued strongly for teachers to adopt a humorous frame of mind at times because humor, by its very nature, has the qualities of flexibility, spontaneity, unconventionality, playfulness, humility, and shrewdness. Shrewedness, Rogers explained, is the refusal to believe that things are precisely what they appear to be. These are qualities a good teacher would want to encourage in his or her students. As Rogers noted, "Thus it is all right to laugh in school. All of us make mistakes occasionally; all of us do silly things, become hopelessly confused, misuse words, give outrageously wrong answers, forget to zip up zippers, call Wednesday Thursday. Developing a humorous outlook depends on the teacher recognizing this condition, accepting it, valuing it as a way to make teaching and learning more fully human." Rogers told teachers that they must become more conscious of the students they have temporarily and to bring humor into their lives before it is too late. He noted that John Hinckly, President Reagan's would-be assassin, was said never to have laughed after reaching age 21.

Ziv (1976) investigated the influence of humor on creativity and found that his experimental group of adolescents did significantly better on a creativity test than his control group. This finding confirms Koestler's view that humor offers a keener alertness to utilize incidental cues. As Ziv wrote, "Laughter accepted and shared in the classroom could possibly bring forth free, less conventional forms of expression on the part of the students." "Humor," from Ziv's perspective, "should be a good part of the armamentarium of a teacher."

Bleedorn (1982) agreed with Ziv and suggested strongly that humor is an indicator of giftedness. Humor is one method to recognize creative talent and to develop that talent. She supported her rationale with assumptions that laughter is natural and necessary, that humor enhances learning because learners are in a relaxed and receptive mood, that one's sense of humor is an important mark of personal identity, that there are different levels of complexity in humor that call for a broad base of knowledge, and that learning is encouraged in an emotional climate in which there is some spirit of fun and playfulness. Undoubtedly some scholars accept these ideas on face validity, but others are prone to probe deeper and to require more empiric evidence before employing them with greater confidence.

Bleedorn's assumptions and conclusions do have the support of Bryant (1980), Ziegler (1985), and Powell and Andersen (1985). Bryant, for example, found that humor helped in the teaching of sensitive subjects, improved students' abilities to think, reduced classroom tension, made lessons easier to grasp, made learning more personable and enjoyable, and established a more efficient learning climate. Powell and Andresen noted that humor increased students' attention and interest, and urged teachers to learn how to use humor effectively.

Humor and Testing

Teaching in the long run may or may not be as effective as many teachers would like to believe. Many years or an entire lifetime must unfold before one could be certain that students have truly learned what has been taught. In the short run, however, teachers evaluate their students during the course of an academic term and provide them with some measurement of progress, comprehension, and ability to apply or relate information in some meaningful way. Particularly in the American educational systems, grading is serious business and represents some return on the educational investments being made. Failure or ineptitude are not funny to students or to those who care for them. Success and even brilliance in achievement of high grades are reasons enough for rejoicing but not until test results are made known.

Normatively one would expect to find tests to be sobering affairs and far removed from humor. The time to laugh and joke and have fun while learning is acceptable under some of the qualifications discussed earlier. But in examining students for mastery of subject matter, humor would be noticeably absent. When it comes down to testing for skills and knowledge, the process is fundamentally serious and non-humorous. Nevertheless, educators have begun to wonder if humor would not be out of place during testing sessions. Accordingly, some have begun to experiment by incorporating a bit of humor within a testing complex.

Roger Terry and Margaret Wood (1975), for example, studied the effects of humor on the test performances of elementary school pupils. They found that humor on tests depressed the performance of third-graders. They had mixed results for fifth-graders, which meant that humor seemed to have both positive and negative effects at that age-grade level. If increasing sophistication and maturity are among the variables affecting such results, it may be hypothesized that further studies at highr grade levels could possibly indicate humor in testing may have more positive than negative effects on learning. McMorris (1985) has looked into the matter and has reported that students exposed to humor on tests generally favored its inclusion. One enterprising teacher sparks interest in his students by incorporating their names in various problems. He reported they look forward to his tests because they wonder if their names will be selected for various test items. A personalized, lighter touch works for this teacher in testing situations and warrants testing at other schools.

Humor in Diverse Subjects

While humor in tests is being studied, there appears to be growing numbers of educators who find that humor has distinct possibilities for their subject-matter field. Teachers in biology, physics, aerospace, English, economics, counseling, and communication have become advocates of humor within their specialties (Gilliland & Mauritsen, 1971; Adams, 1972; Klein, 1974; Dunn, 1975; Doyle, 1976; Bryant, 1980; Colwell, 1981; Beck, 1982; Wandersee, 1982; and Keenan, 1985).

Wandersee is a strong advocate of humor for biology teachers, but he warned that it must be used as a teaching strategy with great care. "Humor," he observed, "is like a stick of dynamite. In an expert's hands it can blast away obstructions between subject matter and student. But in a novice's grasp, it may destroy a lesson just as easily." Aside from this caveat, Wandersee urged biology teachers to use his "humor generator" which provides more than 2,880 possible combinations for adaptation of humor to biological phenomena.

Adams knew that many students find the study of physics to be a formidable area with which to cope. He found that humor on a test in physics *does* distract the student but mostly from his or her nervousness rather than on ability to respond to the questioning or the problem-solving. By cutting down on fear inhibitions, he was able to relax his students enough to raise their test scores by about 20 per cent (see also I. Peterson, 1980).

Colwell found humor to be very effective with students who are suffering from a variety of motivational or remedial problems in reading and language arts. In the main the presence of humor reduced their hostilities and allowed them to experience success, the best motivator of all. Clark (1978) corroborated Colwell in affirming that the use of humor in school newspapers increases their readability for students.

The field of communication which includes speech and rhetoric is also highly conscious of humor as a vehicle for interpersonal contact and understanding (*Journal of Communication,* 1976). Bryant (1980) investigated the humor content of some 90 communication textbooks and found that 88 per cent of them contained at least one humorous item. Content analyses revealed an average frequency of six humorous references per chapter, and this amount of humor used some four per cent of the space. He noted that much of the humor was verbal (jokes, puns, riddles, limericks, anecdotes, and cute expressions) and not necessarily visual such as cartoons, photographs, or illustrations. Bryant's concern was to determine if humor was to be used mainly for attention or to entertain rather than to teaching something of substance. He found that humor was indeed used to teach and not merely to attract the attention of students. More humor was used in interpersonal speech texts than mass communication texts which is further evidence that humor lends itself well to persons being able to understand and work well with each other on a primary group level rather than secondary group levels which involve intervening media of a technical nature.

The Weisses (1981) concurred that humor has serious applications in the field of English. In general, humorous writing increases social consciousness and particularly makes readers much more aware of human values that underlie human behavior.

Still another example was the work of Keenan (1985) in the field of economics. She offered the imaginative dialogue between Karl Marx and Adam Smith as they "debated" whether an economy should produce designer jeans and who should own MacDonald's chain of restaurants. Such a scenario is meant to be suggestive of how teachers of economics may add a little more sparkle to teaching of the "dismal science."

Humor as a Coping Procedure for Educators

Those who work in education, whether they be teachers, principals, counselors, school board members, or college professors, have all used humor to balance out the stresses, strains, pressures, or responsibilities they carry. To make light of their burdens, educators do turn to humor now and then and share such humor among themselves. Kelman and Dunne (1971), for example, offer an ingenious, imaginative, and hilarious scheme to solve the rapid burnout problems of reform-minded teachers. Rather than suffer the anguish of trying to make schools far more effective than they are, such teachers may turn to a "rent-a-martyr" company who will supply those who can stand in their place. Lewis (1976) suggested "self-abuse as a teaching device." By this, she satirically observes that young people will turn away from alcohol and drug abuse if they see themselves in the disgusting behavior of their teachers.

Bird (1978) addressed the needs of principals and, like Kelman and Dunne, observed that "dead heroes lead no more." After all, wrote Bird, "Many martyrs are successful, but few survive. Principals should never say I," he advised, but should instead include everyone by saying 'we" want or need this or that in order to make the educational machinery work. By being "the second fastest gun in the West," namely, by sending in an assistant or an underling to perform some unpopular educational task, the principal is less likely to be shot down because of his or discretion in having someone else be the target of outrage when new procedures are initiated.

Finally he suggests that principals should "always leave the back door open" to permit a face-saving retreat from policies that might be disastrous (see also McIntyre, 1971).

Fleisher (1976) offered humorous solace to substitute teachers. Substitute teaching, he noted, is "almost teaching" and not "real teaching." Unfortunately, much depends upon others being ill, seriously ill, or dying. Permanent teachers and staff do not know the stranger in their midst or ask "Who are you today?" Students' reaction to substitute teachers invariably brings on an unaccountable loss of memory as to previous studies or as to how their "real teachers" let them do things. Fleisher demonstrated his empathy when he concluded, "A substitute must tread the razor's edge between sanity and unemployment."

Clark (1972) took note of the pomposity of departments of English; Klein (1974) discussed the usages of humor for school counselors; Sellers (1984) proposed that school board members learn how to appeal to their community by adding "sizzle" to their speeches; Petersik (1981) struck a responsive note among college professors when he explained the differences between what a professor says and what is meant. In all these publications is the message that humor does have a service to render to educators and that they do take advantage of it in order to not take themselves too seriously and so endure over time.

The Presence of Classroom Clowns

Students too seek relief from the tedium that formal educational procedures can become. What frequently occurs is the emergence of one or more students in the classroom who take leadership roles in inserting unexpected humor into the formal learning situation. Damico and Purkey (1978) and Damico (1980) suggested that teachers can deal most effectively with the presence of classroom clowns by recognizing those that are hostile and disruptive in contrast to those that are creative or constructive. From the perspective of students, classroom clowns are generally appreciated by converting what might be a boring session into a more interesting one. On the other hand, if classroom clowns are allowed to run rampant, they may well detract from the business at hand and be resented for their foolishness by those students who do want to understand and use knowledge being made available to them.

Clowns in the classroom themselves may discover that they have been identified with a reputation that they must sustain. It is a difficult position to be in because even clowns like to be taken seriously at times and this intention may never be realized.

A number of classroom clowns eventually become professional comedians. The classroom was one of their earliest stages. They found approval for their deeds or actions in humor rather than risking disapproval in matters in which they could not excel. Most, however, learned how to control themselves as they matured by retaining a lively sense of humor without letting their humor consciousness run rampant or dominate their actions. In this context it is useful to recall that Meredith (1958) in his analysis of comic characters explained, "Any individual is comic who automatically goes his own way without troubling himself about getting in touch with the rest of his fellow-beings. It is part of laughter to reprove his absent-mindedness and wake him out of his dreams." In this sense classroom clowns may like to disassociate themselves from situations but find eventually that they too must join with others in real-life situations and deal seriously with them.

Humor at Various Educational Levels

It is instructive to turn to Tamashiro (1979, 1980) who postulated that humor develops in children in five stages: (1) Presocial/Symbiotic Stage, in which tickling, body contact, and body noises are key stimuli; (2) Impulsive Stage, dominated by clowning, nonsense, chanting, and slapstick; (3) Self-Protective State, which involves hostility, insults, and practical jokes; (4) Conformist Stage, in which conventional jokes, moron jokes, riddles, ethnic humor, and wordplay come to the foreground; and (5) Conscientious Stage, in which original, good-natured humor, social satire, and tongue-in-cheek humor are preferred.

Tamashiro's schema offers a possible framework that assumes that the social development of young students parallels and probably determines humor preferences. It does omit, however, developments for adults or for those in later life. He does say that few adolescents reach the fifth stage of sophistication, but he leaves it for others to theorize about when social maturity in humor is finally, if ever, reached or if adults who use the humor of earlier stages have regressed into childish behaviors. Sociologically, socialization is a lifetime process and it is undoubtedly operative in whatever humor seems to characterize the educational levels reached by individuals.

Certain scholars have preferred to focus upon specific educational levels and the humor that appears at these levels. Groch (1974), for example, studied humor among preschool children and found no significant correlation between responsive, productive, and hostile humor. Responsive humor referred to that which evoked a smile or laugh in the presence of surprising, unexpected, or mildly anxiety-provoking stimuli. Productive humor called for the use of a joking framework or a deliberate violation of meaning and included silliness or teasing. Groch did find that the little girls displayed more responsive humor than the boys and the boys tended to turn to hostile joking more than the girls. In a sense, the girls acted more as an audience while the boys acted more as the entertainers or initiators of humor. Herein one sees differential treatment of the sexes having its effects in the earliest stages of socialization.

McGhee (1983) investigated humor at the elementary level and found white children thought it was funnier to see nonwhite victims whereas nonwhite elementary children had no humor preference that depended upon victims' affiliations. In this instance, subtle or not-so-subtle racism was beginning to manifest itself in the hostile humor that showed up earlier at preschool levels. Weiss (1981) based his studies on junior high and middle school children and found that their humor did indeed show that they were much more socially aware than nursery or elementary school level children in being more sensitive to persons or groups targeted as victims in hostile remarks or actions.

Hollifield (1973) is concerned more with the humor at high school levels and concocted a scenario in which a computer completely takes over a high school. The increasing rigidity and unrelenting social control encountered by adolescents who are near adulthood but who have not yet been emancipated, provides a seedbed for humor that helps these particular youngsters cope with the formal schooling they still endure.

Finally there is the college level of humor. Graeven and Morris (1975) provided a useful study of college humor that uses a humor diary technique. Drawing upon humor diaries kept by students at Vassar College in 1930 and by students at California State University at Hayward in 1972, they found remarkable similarity between the two time-periods and between quite different locales and different types of college students. Mass-produced humor, spontaneous humor, responses to memorized jokes, and recollections of past events were all found in the diaries. Most frequent, however, was humor derived from spontaneous reactions to situations or predicaments and least frequent were humorous reactions to events long past. The pattern held over time and locales and suggests that while college students of the present are different than those of past generations, in the area of humor, however, there is still laughter and amusement over the same genre of collegiate experiences.

Humor Adaptations to Educational Changes

The educational enterprise does make changes motivated either by internal criticism or by external social forces that require long-standing procedures to give way to newer systems that tend to reflect the directions in which society appears to be moving. Alternative schools as opposed to traditional schools and integrated schools as opposed to de facto segregated schools are cases in point.

Humor plays a reactive or passive part in the case of alternative schools because while there is enthusiasm for alternative schools among those who believe in providing considerable latitude for experimentation and exploration by inquisitive students, there remains a great deal of skepticism among those who prefer the traditional educational frameworks. English

(1974), for example, satirically portrayed an alternative school, "Freedom Hall," in which "non-classes" devote their attention to trivial topics underwritten by the eccentric widow of a shoelace king.

Humor, however, can take a more active role in educational changes. Peterson (1975) has written an insightful article on how black-white joking relationships have worked effectively among newly integrated faculty, for example. One-sided joking in which white males admitted to their own mistakes and problems opened the way to learning how to become more effective under the tutelage of experienced black colleagues. White female, inexperienced teachers, however, took a more circuitous route before they would enlist the help of black female, experienced teachers. First, the white women had to establish meaningful relationships with their black pupils. Only then could hostilities give way to more relaxed, two-sided joking relationships among the women that allowed them to draw upon the expertise of the black women teachers. Through humor then teachers were resocialized to operate more effectively in predominantly black settings. In this instance, the function of humor to bring about smoother, more cooperative milieus was demonstrated.

Summary and Conclusions

The emergence of education as the complex social system that processes individuals to qualify them to enter their society is one of the hallmarks of modern times. Youngsters spend the bulk of their formative years from preschool and nursery levels to college, graduate, and professional levels before they are certified or acknowledged as mature adults ready to begin their respective careers. Hosts of cadres remain in place to move students along educational channels according to their preferences, aptitudes, and demonstrated abilities. Whether from the perspective of students, teachers, or concerned communities, humor is operative and relied upon, consciously or unconsciously, to enable all participants to get on with their work.

When educational changes were made, humor smoothed the way by helping to reconcile differences or antagonistic viewpoints. Through humor, those opposed to formal schooling can and do resort to tactics designed to support their contentions. Formal education has been entered into with great reluctance over the ages. Shakespeare's schoolboy who "creeps to school in snail-like fashion" is endlessly portrayed in humor. Education's "bad press," however, is not the whole story, and humor has constructive parts to play within the educational matrix.

Humor itself is seen as instructive in terms of its social correction function. It is effective in showing when deviations from norms occur. Further, it has the ability to aid and abet classroom learning situations through relaxation, attention-getting, reduction of anxieties, and acceptance of the shortcomings of humanity. To be sure, humor is not the be-all and end-all in educational settings and can disrupt or interfere with serious learning. Empirical studies have resulted in equivocal findings that humor is effective in the learning processes. Nevertheless, used cautiously or prudently, humor does have the support of many educators to enrich their professional efforts in their classrooms, in their examinations, in diverse subject matter, in dealing with classroom clowns, in various educational levels, and in coping with frustrations or stresses in their special educational settings. As educational changes occur, humor adapts itself both as a reactive agent and as an active agent in bringing about constructive reconciliations to move forward the objectives of a sound educational system.

STUDY QUESTIONS

1. What explanations are there for the "bad press" of formal education?

2. How does humor reflect the different evaluations given education by those who are parents and those who are their children being "processed" currently in formal educational settings?

3. In what ways does educational humor confirm the perception that females make better students than males, at least, at the primary and secondary school levels? Would educational humor sustain the same brief for men and women in colleges and universities?

4. Has college humor changed drastically over the years?

5. Do anti-intellectuals or anti-school individuals continue to use humor to support their antagonism, criticisms, or objections to formal educational training?

6. What makes teachers prime candidates for targets in tendentious educational humor?

7. Just how does humor prove to be instructive in its own right?

8. Is humor really needed more in certain types of schools than in others? I.e. military schools in contrast with civilian schools?

9. Does humor disrupt or aid classroom situations?

10. Under what circumstances is humor appropriate in learning situations and when is it unwelcome?

11. What services and disservices are performed by class clowns?

12. What criteria apply to "judicious use" of humor and what criteria apply to circumstances in which humor is carried beyond acceptable limits?

13. What part does intelligence, creativity, or giftedness play in effective usage of humor in schools?

14. Is humor a useful safety-valve to reduce test-anxiety or the fear of failure in schools?

15. Can humor carry substantive information in schools or does its value rest more in encouraging students to master subject matter?

16. Does humor appreciation and usage parallel increasing socialization of students? Is this association correlative or causative?

17. What further refinements would enhance Tamashiro's schema of humor development in children? Wherein is the schema faulty?

18. Is humor effective in all subjects or does it lend itself more readily to only certain scholarly subject matter fields?

19. How is humor used by educators as a coping mechanism?

20. Is planned or spontaneous humor more effective in educational situations?

21. Wherein is humor an active agency in education and wherein is it essentially reactive?

Suggested Readings

Adams, Richard C. "Is Physics a Laughing Matter?" *Physics Teacher* v. 10 (May, 1972): 265-266.

Anderson, Ronald E. and Elaine Jolly. "Stereotyped Traits and Sex Roles in Humorous Drawings," *Communication Research* v. 4 (October, 1977): 453-484.

Armour, Richard. "Humor in the Classroom," *Independent School Bulletin* v. 35 (October, 1975): 61.

Baugham, M. Dale. "Down with the Pallbearer School of Pedagogues," *Today's Education* v. 62 (Sept.-Oct., 1973): 62-64.

Beck, James P. "Graffiti: The Vulgar Blackboard's Wit," *English J.* v. 71 (March, 1982): 73-74.

Behrens, Roy P. "Beyond Caricature: On Types of Humor in Art," *J. Creative Behavior* v. 11 (Third Quarter, 1977): 165-175.

Bird, Daniel. "The Key Word is Survival," *NASSP Bulletin* v. 62 (November, 1978): 12-15.

Bleedorn, Bernice B. "Humor as an Indicator of Giftedness," *Roeper Review* v. 4 (April-May, 1982): 33-34.

Bryant, Jennings. "Relationship Between College Teachers' Use of Humor in the Classroom and Student Evaluation of Their Teachers," *J. Educational Psychology* v. 72 (August, 1980): 511-519.

Bryant, Jennings. "Humor in Communication Textbooks," *Communication Education* v. 29 (May, 1980): 125-134.

Chapel, Gage Williams. "Humor in the White House: An Interview with Presidential Speechwriter Robert Orben," *Communication Quarterly* v. 26 (Winter, 1978): 44-49.

Chesser, Barbara J. "Reflections from a University Marriage Course," *College Student J.* v. 14 (Summer, 1980): 133-134.

Clark, Jeff. "Humor Increases Readability of School Newspapers," *Quill and Scroll* v. 52 (Feb.-Mar., 1978): 18-21.

Clark, John R. "Faculties At Large," *College English* v. 33 (February, 1972): 571-577.

Colwell, Clyde. "Humor as a Motivational and Remedial Technique," *J. of Reading* v. 24 (March, 1981): 484-486.

Damico, Sandra Bowman. "What's Funny About a Crisis? Clowns in the Classroom," *Contemporary Education* v. 51 (Spring, 1980): 131-134.

Damico, Sandra Bowman, and William W. Purkey. "Class Clowns: A Study of Middle School Students," *Amer. Educational Research J.* v. 15 (Summer, 1978): 391-398.

Dodge, Bernard J., and Allison Rossett. "Heuristics of Humor in Instruction," *Performance and Instruction* v. 21 (May, 1982): 11-14, 32.

Doyle, Charles C. "Joking and the Study of Literature," *English Quarterly* v. 9 (Spring, Summer, 1976): 87-90.

Dryli, Odvard. "Tools of the Teaching Trade," *Learning* v. 9 (Spring, 1980): 44-48.

Dunn, Harold. "Classics from the Classroom," *J. of Aerospace Education* v. 2 (December, 1975): 20-21.

English, Fenwick W. "Freedom Hall: An Alternative School," *Phi Delta Kappan* v. 55 (June, 1974): 683-684.

Fleisher, Paul. "The Fun Subs Have," *Today's Education* v. 65 (Nov.-Dec., 1976): 30-31.

Gilliland, Hap, and Harriett Mauritsen. "Humor in the Classroom," *Reading Teacher* v. 24 (May, 1971): 753-756.

Graeven, David B., and Susan Johnson Morris. "College Humor in 1930 and 1972: An Investigation Using the Humor Diary," *Sociology & Social Research* v. 59 (July, 1975): 406-410.

Groch, Alice S. "Joking and Appreciation of Humor in Nursery School Children," *Child Development* v. 45 (December, 1974): 1098-1102.

Gruner, Charles R. "Advice to the Beginning Speaker on Using Humor: What the Research Tells Us," *Communication Education* v. 34 (August, 1985): 142-147.

Hall, Clifton. "Humor in Teaching," *Peabody J. of Education* v. 47 (July, 1969): 3-5.

Hauck, William, and J. W. Thomas. "The Relationship of Humor to Intelligence, Creativity, and Intentional and Incidental Learning," *J. of Experimental Education* v. 40 (Summer, 1972): 52-55.

Hollifield, John H. "The Fully Computerized High School," *Phi Delta Kappan* v. 55 (December, 1973): 258-260.

Hoppe,,Arthur. "The Teaching Implications of Being Sinful," *Learning* v. 5 (October, 1976): 52-54.

Kaplan, Robert M., and Gregory C. Pascoe. "Humorous Lectures and Humorous Examples: Some Effects Upon Comprehension and Retention," *J. of Educ. Psy.* v. 69 (Feb., 1977): 61-65.

Kelman, Peter, and Faith Dunne. "Rent-a-Martyr, Inc.: An Interview in the Future," *Phi Delta Kappan* v. 53 (December, 1971): 236-237.

Keenan, Diane. "Economics with a Sense of Humor," *Social Studies Review* v. 24 (September, 1985): 22-26.

Klein, Joel. "On the Use of Humour in Counseling," *Canadian Counsellor* v. 8 (October, 1974): 23237.

Krogh, Suzanne. "He Who Laughs First: The Importance of Humor to Young Children," *Early Child Development and Care* v. 20 (1985): 287-299.

Langer, Howard J. "Man With a Hunting License: An Interview with Art Buchwald," *Social Education* v. 48 (February, 1984): 103-106.

Larson, Greg. "Humorous Teaching Makes Serious Learning,," *Teaching English in the Two-Year College* v. 8 (September, 1982): 197-199.

"Laughing Matter: A Symposium of Studies on Sexual and Ethnic Humor," *J. of Communication* v. 26 (Summer, 1976): 102-204.

Lewis, Florence C. "Self-Abuse as a Teaching Device," *Phi Delta Kappan* v. 57 (April, 1976): 533-534.

McGhee, Paul E., and Nelda S. Duffy. "Children's Appreciation of Humor Victimizing Different Racial and Ethnic Groups: Racial and Ethnic Differences," *J. of Cross-Cultural Psychology* v. 14 (March, 1983): 29-40.

McIntyre, Kenneth. "How to Interview a Prospective Teacher," *National Elementary Principal* v. 51 (October, 1971): 69-71.

McMorris, Robert F. "Effects of Incorporating Humor in Test Items," *J. of Educational Measurement* v. 22 (Summer, 1985): 147-155.

Meredith, George. *Comedy: An Essay on Comedy.* Garden City, NY: Doubleday, 1956.

Mindess, Harvey. "The Limits of Laughter," *Humanist* v. 43 (July-August, 1983): 27-29, 40.

Parsons, Jim B. "Computer-Based Teacher Education Model No. 2499 on Classroom Humor," *Contemporary Education* v. 48 (Winter, 1977): 110-111.

Peterson, I. "Humor in the Physics Classroom," *Physics Teacher* v. 18, No. 9 (1980): 646-650.

Peterson, John H. "Black-White Joking Relationships Among Newly Integrated Faculty," *Integrated Education* v. 13 (January & February, 1975): 33-37.

Petersik, J. Timothy. "What the Professor Really Means," *Chronicle of Higher Education* April 27, 1981, p. 48.

Powell, J. P. and L. W. Andersen. "Humour and Teaching in Higher Education," *Studies in Higher Education* VIONI, 1985: 77-90.

Ressing, Clinton. "Education's Bad Press," *Phi Delta Kappan* v. 57 (December, 1975): 272-273.

Rogers, Vincent P. "Laughing with Children," *Educational Leadership* v. 41 (April, 1984): 46-50.

Schoel, Doris R., and Thomas V. Busse. "Humor and Creative Abilities," *Psychological Reports* v. 29 (August, 1971): 34.

Sellers, Jim. "Add Sizzle to Your Speeches," *Amer. School Board J.* v. 171 (November, 1984): 28-29, 44.

Sherman, Robert R. "The Education of Major Jack Downing: Humor as a Foundation of Education," *Educational Studies* v. 10 (Summer, 1979): 175-188.

Sudol, David. "Dangers of Classroom Humor," *English J.* v. 70 (October, 1981): 26-28.

Tamishiro, R. T. "Children's Humor: A Developmental View," *Elementary School J.* v. 80, N. 2 (1980): 69-75.

Terry, Roger L., and Margaret Wood. "Effects of Humor on the Test Performance of Elementary School Children," *Psychology in the School* v. 12 (April, 1975): 182-185.

Weaver, W. Timothy. "Humor and Education," *Phi Delta Kappan* v. 52 (November, 1970): 166-168.

Webb, Ronald G. "Political Uses of Humor," *ETC, A Review of General Semantics* v. 38 (Spring, 1981): 35-50.

Weiss, Jerry N. "The Serious Nature of Humor," *English J.* v. 70 (October, 1981): 72-74.

Weiss, Helen and Jerry, eds. *More Tales Out of School: Humor From the Classroom.* NY: Bantam, 1980.

Woods, Peter. "Coping at School Through Humor," *British J. of Sociology* v. 4, N. 2 (1983): 111-124.

Zeigler, Virginia. "Humor, Leadership, and School Climate," *Clearing House* v. 58 (April, 1985): 346-348.

Zillman, Dolf. "Effects of Humorous Distortions on Children's Learning from Educational Television," *J. of Educational Psychology* v. 76 (October, 1984): 802-812.

Ziv, Avner. "Facilitating Effects of Humor," *J. of Educational Psychology* v. 68 (June, 1976): 318-322.

Chapter 14:

Political Humor

Introduction

As students of society, sociologists have an abiding concern over how societies achieve and maintain the social order, how authority and power are used to avoid, nullify, or control social conflicts so that, through social consensus, persons and groups can operate together in some semblance of accord. Such concerns are shared by other social scientists, especially political scientists who have developed their discipline along lines a bit different from that of political sociology. Lipset (1959) held that political science had matured as a "'state' discipline, the field concerned with positive and manifest functions of political institutions." Political sociology, by contrast, "has been the 'radical' discipline, stressing social conflict and social change and focusing on latent functions, informal aspects, and, to a greater extent than political science, the dysfunctional aspects of politics." Furthermore, Lipset noted that political science has been concerned with public administration in terms of making governmental organizations efficient whereas political sociology has been more interested in bureaucracy, particularly in its inherent stresses and strains (see also Orum, 1983).

In this chapter, drawing more upon political sociology than political science, the exposition deals with how the humor framework is applied to political systems so that such treatment can express the views of different, often conflicting, constituents who seek some redress of their grievances. Like the surgeon's scalpel that lays bare some troublesome, often hidden spots, humor gets at the body politic with an eye to either their removal or modification.

Power refers to the ability to control one's own life and the lives of others. It is operational in a wide variety of social settings such as in family life, in educational organizations, in businesses and industries, in religious orders, or in voluntary associations such as friendships. In large measure, however, power is heavily vested in the polity, that social institution in which legitimate authority is given to lawmakers, to executives and administrators to carry out the laws, and to those who serve as judges to adjudicate or resolve legal disputations. Such authorities determine overriding

215

policies such as declarations of war or peace, who may be imprisoned or executed, who and what may be taxed to support the regime, who may have citizenship, what social welfare programs will be formalized, and how various jurisdictions shall conduct their affairs. These are awesome powers and reach into the lives of everyone inside a society as well as others who stand outside a given society. Political power looms too large to escape the purview of humorists. Thus political humor functions to scrutinize power politics lest its excesses become intolerable or unacceptable. This "watch-dog" function carries with it the need to socially correct abuses of power and, consequently, to move agencies in directions more acceptable to those affected by the exercise of political powers.

The critical function of political humor is not necessarily exclusive of those who wield political power. It includes both those who stand outside political agencies and those who work within political organizations. Those privy to the inner workings of political entities and, in some form or other, have responsibilities within its bureaucracies are just as prone to resort to humor to achieve their ends as those persons who are outside the complex

The critical function of political humor is not necessarily exclusive of those who wield political power. It includes both those who stand outside political agencies and those who work within political organizations. Those privy to the inner workings of political entities and, in some form or other, have responsibilities within its bureaucracies are just as prone to resort to humor to achieve their ends as those persons who are outside the complex organization of power politics but who are subject to political decisions and political policies. Both the rulers and the ruled resort to humor to promote their causes at auspicious moments. Political machinery, in a variety of circumstances, seems to work more effectively when the social grease of humor is used to help the cogs turn a bit more smoothly.

Aside from "watchful" and "critical" usages of political humor, there is an application of humor that allows the social imagination to enter into fanciful construction of political forms and procedures that may caricature political realities, exaggerate the political milieu, or suggest political constructs that counter the directions currently in vogue by political authorities. Political humorists may thus conjure up utopian societies that are polar opposites of the political *status quo.*

Depending upon how one constructs social realities, political power may or may not corrupt those who hold political offices. In a number of ways political humorists suspect officeholders to abuse their powers, to violate plic trust, to excuse their mistakes, to promote their own advantages rather than those they are supposed to represent. In short, political figures are generally more maligned, satirized, or attacked than praised or esteemed. Officeholders themselves, however, can use humor to reaffirm their basic humanity, their alignment with common private citizens, their refusal to be corrupted by the political powers temporarily placed in their hands.

In what follows namely a look at humor in totalitarian societies, in utopian societies, and in more democratic, representative societies, one can determine for one's self the nature of political humor and its potential effects upon societal consensus or dissensus.

Political Humor in Totalitarian Societies

In a democratic society, humorists are relatively free to do as they please without fear of serious repercussions. This does not mean that humorists are not held accountable for their efforts in a democracy. They run the risk of finding their humor is ill-received, has offended some people and their groups, and will be rejected, disqualified, or overlooked by political audiences.

In a totalitarian society, however, the jokester, the satirist, the critical political humorist is running a serious risk and may well be severely punished or even executed for criticizing the political system. Political humor may "go underground" and appear as graffiti or be privately and carefully shared among trusted peers. A Hitler, a Mussolini, a Hedeki Tojo, an Amin, or an Ayatollah cannot tolerate being held up to ridicule. Those who dare to use political humor against absolute rulers are hunted down and silenced in some ruthless manner. The "sword" of humor cannot be tolerated in totalitarian regimes. It must be placed in the "right" hands.

In the Soviet Union, for instance, where the prevailing political-economic philosophy is promoted by a single political party, political humorists must be highly conscious of the limits to which they may go in pursuit of laughter. Officially political humor that supports the regime is highly approved and in fact is underwritten by the USSR in the *Krokodil*, a satirical journal that is published in Russia three times a month with a circulation of some 5.6 million copies. There are in addition 19 other satirical magazines with a combined printing and circulation of about 5 million copies, daily columns of humor in central and local newspapers, satirical programs on radio and television, hundreds of satirical books published annually, numerous theatrical and film comedies, variety shows, circuses, wall newspapers in factories, and art exhibitiions that utilize political humor. This volume and variety of media for political humor, however, is not directed against the Soviet system. Rather the targets for ridicule are whoever and whatever fails to live up to the standards, norms, or expectations of the political-economic policies of the communistic Russian political regime.

Alexander Vikhrev, assistant editor of *Krokodil* explained, "What is the target? Everything that obstructs, makes more difficult, complicates the development of a socialist society, in a word, all social, economic, and cultural relations. Everything that challenges communist morality is grist for the critic's mill. Neither high official position nor relative obscurity can insulate anyone from criticism where errors, illegal or immoral activities, ignorance, selfishness, vanity may damage Soviet society either materially or spiritually."(Vikhrev, 1975)

One cartoon from *Krokodil*, for example, shows a laborer hard at work with his pickax. That is the reality portion of the cartoon. By virtue of artistic license, however, his shadow is imaginatively drawn to be sitting down, taking its leisure, and relaxing with a cigarette. The cartoonist thus makes his point that while hard labor of workers and farmers symbolized in the hammer and sickle of the USSR is constantly glorified for the people of Russia, there are the temptations to consider only one's individual creature comforts and not the collective needs or objectives of the state. Such a cartoon won approval among the editors of *Krokodil* and was published because it was on target against those who would subvert the policies of state socialism.

Gallows humor was identified by Obrdlik (1942) as a morale builder for those who are oppressed. It acknowledges that political power is in the hands of oppressors, but it also affirms that those who are dominated never abandon their own determination to be free to pursue their own destinies. Bardis (1982) has reported that the Poles living under Russian domination and the imposition of military law continue to circulate gallows humor directed against the USSR. A few samples are:

"Where were you born? St Petersburg. Where did you go to school? Petrograd. Where do you live now? Leningrad. Where would you like to live? St. Petersburg.

"Polish economist: We export our coal to Russia and in exchange they take our steel.

"Intourist advertisement: Visit the Soviet Union before it visits you.

"A politburo member who disagreed with the regime commited suicide. His last words were: 'Don't shoot, comrades'!"

Humor then can be used in support of political-economic systems or it can be used to counterbalance those who oppose them. In totalitarian societies characterized by one-party systems, one-policy positions, suppression of counterviews, both those who accommodate official policies and those who oppose such policies turn to humor to advance their causes.

Utopian Humor

The search for the "perfect" political order was epitomized by the work of Sir Thomas More whose fictional island of Utopia was in his view the locale where a perfect political order existed. Perfection, however, depends upon consensal criteria and a single-minded or a few likeminded persons' agreement does not necessarily constitute perfection. Thus there are infinite possibilities for utopian political orders from the perspective of those who create or endorse them.

Political humorists find the vehicle of a utopian society lends itself well for their purposes. They may fabricate whatever pleases their fancy, offer it to larger audiences, and hope for approval and acceptance among a sizeable number of people. Some have had long-lasting effect in world literature and are consequently immortalized for their fictional accounts. Two examples: one is Jonathan Swift's *Gulliver's Travels* and the other is George Orwell's *1984,* can be cited as cases in point (Orwell, 1949; Swift, 1958).

Gulliver's Travels

Most persons first encounter *Gulliver's Travels* as a piece of children's literature and tend to treat it merely as a fanciful tale designed to amuse the very young. It was, however, a satirical piece written to alert adults to the foolishness and absurdities of their political systems.

Swift was the Dean of St. Patrick's Cathedral in Dublin, Ireland, and as a scholarly churchman hoped to offer *Gulliver's Travels,* as he put it, "to wonderfully mend the world by vexing it." Through the adventures of the seagoing surgeon, Gulliver, readers encounter political orders that contrast sharply with political systems in their own societies. Through subtle or not-so-subtle humor, Swift deftly wove the fabric of alternative political regimes to correct what he saw as serious flaws in existing usages of political power. In successive voyages to the lands of Lilliput, Brobdingnag, Laputa, Balnibarbi, Luggnagg, Glubbdubdrib, and Houyhnms, Gulliver recorded for posterity the nature of political styles calculated to stimulate readers to question how political powers are handled within their own cultural and societal contexts.

Gulliver's Travels is replete with examples of Swift's wit in exposing the follies of politics. A single example is selected to illustrate why Swift's work has endured. Swift had Gulliver discuss politics with the King of Brobdingnag who holds a rather low opinion of politicians. He sees them as overrated individuals who take a great deal of credit for their efforts when in reality he sees them as contributing very little to the common good. The King praises instead the unknown, unappreciated, unheralded individual citizen who performs such deeds as making two ears of corn or two blades of grass grow on a spot of ground where only one grew before. In sociological terms, it is the followers who make a leader successful and not necessarily the leader who makes followers successful.

1984

Eric Arthur Blair, writing under the penname of George Orwell, wrote some of the most telling political satires of the twentieth century. His earlier work, *Animal Farm* (Orwell, 1946) was another fable concocted to reach adults to warn them of the dangers of the spread of communism among freedom-loving citizenry. In the name of democracy, persons might be persuaded to give up their liberties for the sake of the so-called common good. There would be broken pledges, clever deceptions, and mind control in order to achieve these ends. In *1984,* a novel that lent special aura to a year that came to be known as the "Orwellian Year," Orwell (or Blair) engaged in his "war of words" against repressive regimes that promised much but delivered little. The utopias such regimes envisioned would consist of people divided against themselves with "Big Brother" keeping everyone under constant surveillance and control.

The major means for thought control, as Orwell portrayed it, would be accomplished through "Newspeak," the official language of the totalitarian regime. Its vocabularies were developed for three levels of discourse. The "A Vocabulary" consisted of words of common usage, few in number but rigorously defined to purge all ambiguities or nuances from them. The word *thought,* for instance, was displaced by *think* which was to be used both as a noun and a verb. The "B Vocabulary" was composed of terms that not only had political implications, but were intended to impose a desirable mental attitude upon the persons using them. The word *goodthink,* for example, meant orthodoxy or, used as a verb, to think in an orthodox, approved manner. The "C Vocabulary" consisted of scientific and technical terms to be used exclusively by specialists. Pointedly Orwell noted there was no vocabulary expressing the function of science as a habit of mind or a method of thought. Indeed there was no word in the "C Vocabulary" for science.

In sum, Orwell's satiric genius was brought to bear on his thesis that the so-called utopian societies toward which certain political figures were steering people would come about at the expense of individual freedoms.

Humor in Representative, Democratic Societies

Aside from humor within tyrannical regimes or applied to imaginative experiments in utopian systems, there are those societies in which humor may range widely and relatively unchecked because representation of different constituencies or views are given considerable latitude. In such a society, humorists will select officials, their policies, the bureaucratic structures, or whatever ineptitudes they deem worthy of attention as their "fair game" or targets. Furthermore, officeholders themselves will resort to humor to demonstrate their identity with their constituents rather than a defense of those who temporarily hold power. Humorists in representative, democratic societies will tear away any attempts to conceal whatever may be going on in the polity with minimal fears of reprisal for their efforts. Those who enter politics in such a social atmosphere can anticipate being viewed with suspicion and being held accountable. As George Washington Plunkett put it, "Men ain't in politics for nothin'; they want something out of it" (Riordan, 1963).

The Work of Mark Twain

Second to none in his vitriolic denunciations of the blunders and posturing of political *poseurs,* Samuel Clemens, under his penname of Mark Twain, wrote some of the most scathing, aggressive forms of humor directed against the excesses of political systems. As an avowed misanthrope, Twain struck out, for example, at the political scene of his day in an essay entitled, "The Damned Human Race" (DeVoto, 1967):

"The higher animals engage in individual fights, but never in organized masses. Man is the only animal that deals in that atrocity of all atrocities, War. He is the only one that gathers his brethren about him and goes forth in cold blood and with calm pulse to extermine his kind. He is the only animal that for sordid wages will march out, as the Hessians did in our Revolution, and as the boyish Prince Napoleon did in the Zulu War and help slaughter strangers of his own species who have done him no harm and with whom he has no quarrel.

"Man is the only animal that robs his helpless fellow of his own country — takes possession of it and drives him out of it or destroys him. Man has done this in all ages. There is not an acre of ground on the globe that is in possession of its rightful owner, or that has not been taken away from owner after owner, cycle after cycle, by force and bloodshed.

"Man is the only Slave. And he is the only animal who enslaves. He has always been a slave in one form or another, and has always held other slaves in bondage under him in one way or another. In our day, he is always some man's slave for wages and does that man's work; and this slave has other slaves under him for minor wages, and they do *his* work. The higher animals are the only ones who exclusively do their own work and provide their own living.

"Man is the only Patriot. He sets himself apart in his own country, under his own flag, and sneers at the other nations, and keeps multitudinous uniformed assassins on hand at heavy expense to grab slices of other people's countries, and keep *them* from grabbing slices of *his*. And in the intervals between campaigns he washes the blood off his hands and works for 'the universal brotherhood of man' — with his mouth."

The Style of Will Rogers, Cowboy Commentator

While Mark Twain used a heavy hand in his humorous assaults on power politics, Will Rogers took a totally different tack. He ingratiated himself among the very people he used for his humor and earned the title of "Ambassador of Good Will." Using the media of stage, screen, the lecture circuit, or newspaper columns before television was developed commerciall, Will Rogers was a beloved humorist to millions. He is the only professional humorist to have a statue in the halls of Congress, the major target of his good-natured comments. It was Will who frequently declared that the United States Congress was the greatest assembly of comedians ever gathered together in one place. At some point in time, Will would wryly explain, the senators and representatives would be forced to retire and return home to make an honest living like everyone else.

Never hiding his partisan politics, Will identified himself as a devout Democrat whose sacred duty included keeping a watchful eye over the shenanigans of Republicans. He used to say that every now and then he would have to go down to Washington, D.C., to visit Congress to spread a little salt around "to keep their population under control."

Humor in Will Rogers' hands was not a sword but a healing balm that brought people together to resolve their differences. His comment that "he never met a man he didn't like" was a model of diplomacy and tact in both political and nonpolitical circles (Ketchum, 1973).

The Work of Art Buchwald, Columnist

Art Buchwald is representative of political humorists who have essentially used the medium of syndicated newspaper columns to convey their messages of social correction. Like Rogers, Buchwald publicizes any and every attempt by public servants to cover up their actions, to appear to be something that they are not. Unlike Rogers, however, who played the part of a down-to-earth country lad, Buchwald is a sophisticated urbanite who takes on any and all political parties, issues, or officeholders whose words, deeds, or conduct seem to him to need the spotlight of humorous treatment. Buchwald notes that he enjoys seeing changes in administrations in Washington, D.C., because, as he explains it, a whole new cast of characters now come before him from whom he can earn his living.

A typical column will take a political issue of the moment and Buchwald will develop a conversation between himself and some outlandish, unknown personality with a faintly familiar but absurd name. The dialogue reveals the humorous twist Buchwald wishes to give the issue at hand.

For example, concerning the proposal to reinstate the drafting of young men for military service, Buchwald reported on a conversation he had with Leo Haak of East Lansing, Michigan. It seems that Mr. Haak had a formula that would resolve the standoff between young and old men. The Haak Plan proposed to not only draft young men for military duty, but also to draft the money of men too old to go to war to pay for it. Young men under 26 would sit on boards to draft the money of those over age 26. They would settle cases of "conscientious objectors," those who objected to having their money taken from them. In such cases the conscientious objector's funds would not go to support the war effort but would be donated instead to a hospital or an educational institution. And, of course, *all* their money would be taken from those in "a dollar draft" just as younger men are called upon to give up everything for their country. This "straw-in-the-wind" to sense public opinion would surely end all talk of a military draft, Buchwald noted, because nobody would tolerate losing their entire fortune for the common good (Buchwald, 1972).

Garry Trudeau, Cartoonist-Defender of Antiheroes

Garry Trudeau represents a new breed of cartoonists who take direct aim at political affairs. The *Doonesbury* cast of characters of Trudeau's comic strip have been so controversial in their political views that a number of newspapers decided that it does not belong on the funny pages but rather should be published on the editorial pages.

A typical Trudeau tableau will show a picture of the White House in each cartoon frame. Trudeau will then make his point in a series of ballooned conversations that show the duplicity of its residents over some political policy or problem. The only outward sign of shock would be a fallen signpost in the final frame of the strip.

Jeff MacNelly, Exposer of Bureaucratic "Gobble-de-Gook"

As Lipset noted, political sociologists have paid particular attention to bureaucracies, those complex organizations charged with responsibilities to carry out legitimate services on behalf of the governed. Alleged to be as efficient in their specialized tasks as possible, these complicated agencies touch the lives of the general public in sometimes frustrating and unbelievable ways. Of particular concern is the mountain of paperwork needed to expedite an individual case through the bureaucratic maze. The IRS, Internal Revenue Service, is only one bureau in the federal government but it holds awesome powers over the mental and emotional stabilities of honest taxpayers. Each year there are self-flagellation rituals in which taxpayers try to decipher instructions in filing their income tax returns and settling their accounts either with tax payments or refunds.

It was Jeff MacNelly who won a Pulitzer Prize in cartooning when he drew the ink-spattered, horribly garbled version of Form 1040, the infamous "long form" Income Tax Return of the IRS. A few excerpts are MacNelly's way of sympathizing with usually sane and sober citizens who are trying to do their civic duty but who almost lost touch with reality when confronted with IRS jargon:

"*Filing Status:* Single? Double? Sacrifice Fly?

Married Filing Singly Joint Return (even if spouse is married separately)

Joint married singly separate spouse

Head of household filing separate but joint return (if married but jointly single)

Head of joint filing single spouse's separately, or Widower with separate dependent filing out of joint return singly

Exemptions: Regular? Yourself, spouse.

Names of dependent children who lived with you? Why? (Just first names, dummy...)

Do you weigh more than last year's tax form?

Number of parakeets subtracted from Gross Rotated Income plus Line 27... unless greater than twelve miles...

How many inches in a liter?

Total confusion (add lines 6e and f, g, fold in eggs, heat until firm.)

Enter number of boxes checked; check number of boxes entered; enter number of checkered boxes, and do nothing here...''

Other Pulitzer Prize cartoons are chronicled in *The Lines Are Drawn* (Johnson, 1958) and they too carry the theme that politicians create bureaucratic procedures that weigh heavily on law-abiding citizens. D.R. Fitzpatrick of the *St. Louis Dispatch* earned his Pulitzer Prize by showing mountains of paper laws that overshadow the tablets of the Ten Commandments. Ironic political humor in this instance reveals the talents of bureaucrats to complicate that which is essentially simple.

Officeholders' Humor

Those who hold office in political systems have turned to humor now and then to provide an insider's view of what transpires within the closed circles of politicians. Of recent vintage was the work of Senator Eugene McCarthy and his colleagues, *A Political Bestiary, Viable Alternatives, Impressive Mandates, and Other Fables* (McCarthy, 1978). Among the fanciful creatures discussed are The Mandate, the Bloated Bureaucracy, the Flexible Goal, the Filibuster, the Dilatory Motion, the Gobbledegook, the Loophole, the Pregnant Pause, the Quandry, the Paradox or Pair of Doxes, the Budgetary Shortfall, the Blind Trust, and the Vanishing Milieu. Each of these fabled entities are illustrated in artistic detail by the authors. Suffice to draw upon their description of the Budgetary Shortfall to capture an example of their publication's provocative political humor:

"Among all the species known to political ornithology, perhaps none is more familiar than the Budgetary Shortfall. This ubiquitous fellow nests wherever legislative bodies meet. You will find him in county courthouses, in city halls, in state capitals, and of course on Capitol Hill in Washington. Red-eyed, red-crowned, and red-breasted, the Budgetary Shortfall cannot be mistaken for anything else.

"In Washington, Budgetary Shortfalls ordinarily are conceived in October, at the beginning of the Federal fiscal year. They emerge as fledglings just after the April 15 tax collections. By August, they are full grown, but they are peculiar in this regard. As they become fully fledged, their ability to fly diminishes."

The highest officeholders in the United States of America are the presidents. From George Washington to the present incumbent, their ranks are few but interest concerning them runs high (see Boller, 1981; Frank & Melick, 1984). Of particular interest are their associations with humor, evidence that they too found that humor could serve them well both in and out of office. Certain to hold some place in history, they manifested their humanity whenever they resorted to humor to endure the pressures of the presidency.

The lists are too long and the published incidents are too numerous to give presidential humor its proper due herein. What can be cited briefly are some references to their all-too-human qualities that made them the unique personalities most of them were. Few would argue against identifying Abraham Lincoln as one of the first humorists to occupy the White House. Lincolnia or lore about Abraham Lincoln abounds (McClure, 1879; Stoddard, 1894; Curtis, 1902; Rice, 1907; Scott, 1908; Whipple, 1915; Scoville, Jr., 1918; Wall, 1943; Angle, 1950; Mitang, 1956; Browne, 1964; Zall, 1982; Martin, 1983). Lincoln's humor was in the style of a teacher who would illustrate his points with some anecdote that was well within the experience of students. In Lincoln's case, he used the power of laughter and wit to rise above petty differences. His personal and public life was filled with failures and tragedies but his sense of humor sustained him (Noe, 1986). Humor lightened some of his darker moments and served to bring about accord among his advisors when major public policies had to be decided. Once, for example, when an impasse developed during a cabinet meeting, Lincoln settled the matter by one of his instructive yarns. He told the story of a farmer who came across a very wet log that was deeply and hopelessly mired in the field he was cultivating. "You know what he did, gentlemen?" asked Lincoln. "Why, he just ploughed right around that log!'' The Cabinet did not hesitate. They tabled the matter and moved on to more urgent business.

Calvin Coolidge or "Silent Cal" was one of the least likely presidents to be considered as a humorist. Nevertheless, Coolidge had a wit that marks him quite favorably as a very human individual, a far cry from the usually taciturn portrayals. A few instances of the Coolidge wit suggest that he has been indeed underrated as a humorist:

He explained his widely publicized image of silence when he observed, "If you don't say anything, you can't be called upon to repeat it." It was customary to bring the newly-elected president his first paycheck. When he was asked what he said when he received it, he replied, "Come again." When asked about the residents of the White House, he once replied, "No one lives there. People just come and go." A Baptist preacher did not eat much for dinner, explaining that abstinence improved his preaching. After hearing him preach, Coolidge remarked, "Might as well et." Now and then Coolidge would press all the buttons on his desk and hide behind his office door. When secretaries, aides, military men, and Secret Service agents would come rushing in, Coolidge would emerge saying, "I just wanted to see if all of you were doing your work." Finally, when asked by newspaper reporters to say a few words to the public before he left office, Coolidge obliged by saying, "Goodbye."

The Bad Press of the Politician

In general politicians are more maligned than praised. Humor again comes into play as the means to attack them as petty personages corrupted by power. Dickson (1980) offered, for example, a series of principles, dictums, and guidelines calculated to show politicians as devious, untrustworthy beings. Dickson wrote:

"Fannie's Ganif Theory... (1) Most politicians are thieves. (2) Most politicians are slow learners. (3) Therefore, never vote for an incumbent. While the challenger's natural inclinations are equally bad, it will take him time to learn how to achieve his goals."

The characterization of politicians through humor as essentially untrustworthy, devious rascals who seek political power for their own advantages rather than those of their constituents does not deter persons from seeking political office, of course. Delegation of power continues in complex societies and those who wield it do not necessarily fit the characteristics described to them by rather aggressive humorists. Some indeed are elevated to a higher status because of their dedication to the common good and are called statesmen or some other honorific title. Nevertheless, political humor that is quicker to malign than to praise serves as one means to remind officeholders that public ridicule is a powerful force itself and not to be underestimated or dismissed out of hand.

Summary and Conclusions

Political humor does not take the position of political scientists who focus their attention on the positive and manifest functions of political structures. Rather it is more akin to the approach of political sociologists who look to the latent functions, the informal aspects, and the dysfunctional aspects of politics. It seeks out the inefficiencies, the shortcomings, the subterfuges, the stresses and strains of political agencies in their management of power. Political humor is less interested in how political systems work but more on how they do not work. It is critical and watchful of officeholders and cautions them not to abuse their constituents who have temporarily entrusted them with awesome powers. It holds up to ridicule the obstructive tangles of red-tape, record-keeping, and mountains of paper imposed by complex organizations or bureaucracies. For those who are officeholders, there is one redeeming quality. It is a safety valve to relieve the strains of office and to give vent to the human qualities of powerful officials who derive their powers from their people and who will eventually return to their people as private individuals.

The social context in which political humor operates is paramount. It matters whether the social milieu is within a totalitarian society or a representative, democratic society. In a single-minded, repressive society, dissent must be couched carefully. Chiefly political humor in totalitarian societies may attack whatever opposes the state system. It supports the regime and derides those who do not cooperate with it. It cannot attack the regime itself without serious consequences for those who perpetrate such humorous assaults. In a representative, democratic society, however, political humorists may criticize the political systems without fear of major reprisals. Sometimes gentle, sometimes hostile, political humor in such systems may prod and poke at the *status quo* to suggest social changes are in order or long overdue.

Finally, there is the political humor contained in utopian constructs that allow imaginative flights of fancy to postulate the way political power might be better handled. These concoctions are adult fairy tales, but they serve to caution those who seek to control the behavior of others that there are limits to political power or breaking points in tolerance among those who are willing to let others control their lives.

STUDY QUESTIONS

1. What are the primary and secondary functions of political humor?

2. How does political humor parallel political sociology rather than the discipline of political science?

3. What explains the predominance of negative criticism directed against office-holders by political humorists?

4. How does political humor differ in totalitarian and democratic societies?

5. What outcomes are anticipated in utopian humor?

6. Are there historical data to substantiate the hypothesis that political humor does, in fact, have significant effects upon what transpires within political systems?

7. How is humor used by office-holders themselves to endure the strains of being in the public eye?

8. Can you suggest a satirical treatment of political policies that could possibly modify or profoundly change them in some meaningful way?

9. How do the Presidents of the United States rate in terms of their humor -consciousness?

10. Are political autocrats, dictators, oligarchies, or absolute monarchs humorless?

11. How is political humor used to achieve political consensus?

12. How sensitized are bureaucrats to humor that reveals their inefficiences and ineptitudes?

13.Can political humorists in a democracy operate with impunity compared with those in totalitarian societies?

14.Critique *Gulliver's Travels* in the political context of its times. Do the political conditions under assault by Jonathan Swift still prevail?

15.What impacts have Orwell's *1984* made in the conduct of political affairs?

16.Is political humor reactive or active in terms of politics?

17.What explains the broad-based acceptability of Will Roger's brand of political humor?

18.What studies can be designed to measure the acceptability or rejection of political cartoons?

19.How does Mark Twain qualify as a political humorist?

20.Who are the contemporary political humorists who seem to influence political affairs currently? How do their styles reflect the political milieu presently in place?

Suggested Readings

Angle, Paul M. *Abraham Lincoln By Some Men Who Knew Him.* NY: Books for Library Press, 1950.

Bardis, Panos. "Poles' Secret Weapon," *Toledo Blade* Jan. 28, 1982, p. 16.

Boller, Jr., Paul F. *Presidential Anecdotes.* NY: Oxford Univ. Press, 1981.

Browne, Ray B. *Lincoln Lore: Lincoln in the Popular Mind.* Ohio: Popular Press, 1964.

Buchwald, Art. "To Avoid War, A Dollar Draft," *Akron Beacon Journal,* Oct. 31, 1972, D-26.

Curtis, William E. *The True Abraham Lincoln.* Philadelphia: Lippincott, 1902.

DeVoto, Bernard, ed. *Mark Twain's Letters From the Earth.* NY: Fawcett World Library, 1967.

Dickson, Paul. *The Official Explanations.* NY: Delacorte Press, 1980.

Dunning, Lloyd. *Mr. Lincoln's Funny Bone.* NY: Howell, Soskin, 1942.

Frank, Sid, and Arlen Davis Melick. *The Presidents: Tidbits and Trivia.* NY: Greenwich House, 1984.

Gross, Anthony. *Lincoln's Own Stories.* NY: Harper, 1912.

Johnson, Gerald W. *The Lines Are Drawn: American Life Since Its First World War As Reflected in the Pulitzer Prize Cartoons.* Philadelphia: Lippincott, 1958.

Ketchum, Richard M. *Will Rogers: His Life and Times.* NY: American Heritage, 1973.

Lipset, Seymour Martin. "Political Sociology," in Robert K. Merton, Leonard Broom and Leonard S. Cottrell, Jr., eds. *Sociology Today: Problems and Prospects.* NY: Basic Books, 1959, pp. 81-114.

Martin, Carolyn F. "Lincolnia," unpubl. ms., Nov., 1983.

McCarthy, Eugene J., and James J. Kilpatrick. *A Political Bestiary, Viable Alternatives, Impressive Mandates, and Other Fables.* NY: McGraw-Hill, 1978.

McClure, J. B. *Anecdotes of Abraham Lincoln and Lincoln's Stories.* Chicago: Rhodes & McClure, 1879.

Mitgang, Herbert. *Abraham Lincoln: A Press Portrait.* Chicago: Quandrangle Books, 1956.

Noe, John R. "In the Fast Lane to Success: Turning Obstacles into Opportunites," in *Potential,* Hyattsville, MD: Great Commission, (February, 1986): 6-7, 14.

Obrdlik, Antonin. "Gallows Humor: A Sociological Phenomenon," *Amer. J. of Sociology* v. 47 (March, 1942): 709-716.

Orum, A. M. *Introduction to Political Sociology.* Englewood Cliffs, NJ: Prentice-Hall, 2nd ed., 1983.

Orwell, George. *Animal Farm.* NY: Harcourt, Brace, 1946.

Orwell, George. *1984.* NY: Harcourt, Brace, 1949.

Rice, Wallace. *The Lincoln Year Book.* Chicago: A.C. McClurg, 1907.

Riordan, William L. *Plunkett of Tammany Hall.* NY: Dutton, 1963, p. 21.

Scott, Temple. *The Wisdom of Abraham Lincoln.* NY: Brentano's, 1908.

Scoville, Jr., Samuel. *Abraham Lincoln: His Story.* Philadelphia: American Study-School Union, 1918.

Stoddard, William O. *The Table Talk of Abraham Lincoln.* NY: Stokes, 1894.

Swift, Jonathan. *Gulliver's Travels.* NY: Random House, 1958.

Vikhrev, Alexander. "Satire in the USSR," *Soviet Life* February, 1975.

Wall, Bernhardt. *Following Abraham Lincoln: 1809-1865.* NY: Wise-Parslow, 1943.

Whipple, Wayne. *The Heart of Lincoln.* Philadelphia: George W. Jacobs, 1915.

Zall, P. M. *Abe Lincoln Laughing.* Berkeley, CA: Univ. of California Press, 1982.

Chapter 15:

Military Humor

Introduction

Military humor is a social phenomenon that is difficult to classify because it seems to be aligned with a number of different but related areas of sociological studies. It may for instance be considered to be a legitimate portion of political humor because military systems originate in the defensive-offensive needs of political states to remain in power. It may well be considered to be a subtopic of occupational humor, to be presented in Chapter 16, and at present *Sociological Abstracts* categorizes military sociology as a subtopic of complex organizations or bureaucracies.

Military life, and humor associated with it, obviously embraces all of the divergent sociological concerns. As political powers declare war or peace, the military establishment mobilizes for action or organizes itself on a standby status. Military service is the locus of occupation for profesional soldiers or it may be only a limited occupation during periods of national emergency for volunteers and conscripts. World Wars I and II brought millions of American civilians into intimate contact with military life on an unprecedented historical scale. On a prolonged, agonizingly continuing basis, the Vietnam conflict involved thousands of American civilians and sorely tested the moral fabric of American society. In other military actions, such as in Korea and the Near East, even fewer numbers of military personnel were or have been involved with the military system.

Certainly the military life style fits the sociological analysis that places it as complex organization with its multiple services and its complicated bureaucracies and administrative policies. The elaborate chains of command or layers of authority continue in place whether the military services are actively at war or are operating on a peacetime footing. Routine and standard operating procedures mark the military life in times of peace and become the source of much military humor in order to survive the boredom or tedium. Even in wartime, military humor will focus on the longer periods of inaction, the wasted hours, days and years of performing duties that are unchallenging and seemingly nonproductive.

233

In this chapter then, military humor is considered against the backdrop of the relationship of the military establishment with the larger society. It subsequently will focus on the adult socialization process through which civilian recruits are incorporated into military life. Furthermore, the changing nature of military life as reflected in selected historical periods, in decisions to include or exclude women and blacks, in policies of strict enforcement or relaxation of bureaucratic rules and regulations, in the application of new technologies, and in overall morale will be examined.

Paramount in military humor is its survival function. Perhaps in no other setting is survival so critically salient. Military personnel must endure under the most trying conditions, and military humor is one of the most readily available means to achieve it.

While popular television series like *Hogan's Heroes* were farcial in their treatment of prisoners-of-war during World War II, it took a series like *M.A.S.H.* to offer a more compassionate type of military humor that brilliantly showed how humor sustained the morale of personnel engaged in a war far removed from home. The *M.A.S.H.* series well-deserved the honors that came to it, particularly for the use of humor not only to help military personnel survive the horrors and anguish of warfare but also to poke fun at war itself as a breakdown in the rational resolution of international or national problems. The *M.A.S.H.* series apparently could have continued indefinitely even though it was clearly associated with the Korean conflict. The series was terminated (although sustained in TV reruns) on a gallant note of each character going on to a brighter future. Unforgettable was the sight of the former pompous surgeon from Boston riding off on the last available vehicle - a garbage truck!

A carryover from World War II and still appearing in cartoon form is *Beetle Bailey*. This cartoon series uses humor to show the constant efforts of military personnel to get the upper hand along the chain of command. Like the *Sad Sack* cartoon character of World War II, *Beetle Bailey* represents the common serviceman who stands at the lowest end of the echelons who must take all orders from his superiors. Beetle's constant efforts to evade and foil his sergeant or commissioned officers strikes a humorous note for many servicemen and helps explain its continued appeal to all familiar and empathic with the often unfortunate status of the "underdog."

The Military-Civilian Connection

Most persons are civilians and have minimal contact with and peripheral interest in military organizations. Nevertheless, from time to time, civilian and military life styles do interpenetrate and individuals must move from a civilian to a military way of life or move back to a civilian status after long association with being in the military service. Civilians and military personnel may have cordial and supportive relations or the relationship can turn to bitterness, rejection and hostility.

Perhaps the greatest distinction between being a civilian or being in the military services is the degree of personal freedom accorded the statuses. Stouffer and his associates (1949), through their monumental work *The American Soldier: Adjustment During Army Life,* Volume I, offered one of the most significant sociological analyses of military life when they documented the ways in which civilians are transformed and absorbed into military personnel. More contemporary analysis of the military services utilizes the sociological concepts of "compliance structures" or "total institutions" in which large numbers of individuals are set apart from their society and required to conform to a regimented, enclosed, formally administered life (see also Lang, 1972).

As civilians, persons are free to pursue their own interests. As military personnel, however, individuals must follow collective interests. Civilians may dress, eat, work, travel, live, or associate as they please. Military personnel, however, are uniformed, eat on fixed schedules, assigned to duties that range from "filling up time" to extremely hazardous activities, ordered where to live, when to move, and with whom to associate. Whereas civilians may freely choose what they want to do with their lives and how they shall accumulate and utilize their property, military personnel relinquish this freedom and are required to follow orders that may make them extremely uncomfortable and even hazardous to their lives and fortunes. These and related conditions are sufficient to bring about serious tensions, distress, and alienation for military participants, let alone threaten the collective effectiveness of the military establishment. Yet it is within this military milieu that humor works so well. Humor relieves those tensions. It acts as a safety valve to let off steam and gives vent to expressive needs under instrumental duress. Humor promotes superiority for morale purposes and assigns others to inferior and subordinate positions and roles. It manifests who is in the in-group and who is in the out-group. It allows for symbolic aggression without the penalties if actual aggression would occur. Military humor, in short, sustains individuals and groups under the most trying circumstances and helps them to do what is required of them.

One paramount connection between the military establishment and the civilian society it is purported to protect is the perception that military services are performing a legitimate, albeit dangerous task. The normative expectations are that whatever the military establishment does, it does so in the name of its society to defend it against all enemies and to promote society's safety and well-being. Thus there are so-called popular wars, wars that call upon both military and civilian forces to work together to defeat a threatening enemy, to make whatever sacrifices are necessary, and to fight those who would attempt to change drastically the nature and purposes of that society's existence. Such could be said of World Wars I and II when there was a clear identity of morale, objectives, and values between those who entered military life and those who remained in civilian society. Those in the military were honorable and appreciated and accorded considerable prestige. A grateful nation would eventually provide special benefits for returning, triumphant military veterans, make their transition back into civilian life as smooth as possible, and hold all former warriors in highest respect. While actual combat and its accompanying destruction is not a funny matter, military humor in a "popular war" carried with it a "grin-and-bear-it" patina. Bill Maudlin's tired, unkempt, bedraggled cartoon characters, Willie and Joe, epitomized such a sympathetic view of the plight of American infantry soldiers overseas in World War II.

One paramount connection between the military establishment and the civilian society it is purported to protect is the perception that military services are performing a legitimate, albeit dangerous task. The normative expectations are that whatever the military establishment does, it does so in the name of its society to defend it against all enemies and to promote society's safety and well-being. Thus there are so-called popular wars, wars that call upon both military and civilian forces to work together to defeat a threatening enemy, to make whatever sacrifices are necessary, and to fight those who would attempt to change drastically the nature and purposes of that society's existence. Such could be said of World Wars I and II when there was a clear identity of morale, objectives, and values between those who entered military life and those who remained in civilian society. Those in the military were honorable and appreciated and accorded considerable prestige. A grateful nation would eventually provide special benefits for returning, triumphant military veterans, make their transition back into civilian life as smooth as possible, and hold all former warriors in highest respect. While actual combat and its accompanying destruction is not a funny matter, military humor in a "popular war" carried with it a "grin-and-bear-it" patina. Bill Mauldin's tired, unkempt, bedraggled cartoon characters, Willie and Joe, epitomized such a sympathetic view of the plight of American infantry soldiers overseas in World War II.

Such was not the case in the Vietnam debacle. This was in time an unpopular war, one that did not mobilize all civilians in support of its armed forces, one that allowed most people to conduct their affairs without too much interference or threat from the far-away locus of military action, one that lacked a clear policy of defeating a nebulous "enemy," one that was marred by political trade-offs, one that lacked victories over an identifiable enemy, one that was marked by a breakdown in morale among the military forces and dissension at home, and one that ended in withdrawal and defeat. Military humor in such a war took on a bitter, self-depracating, shameful, critical patina. The breach between the American civilian society and its Vietnam veterans was not be healed for decades.

Such was not the case in the Vietnam debacle. This was in time an unpopular war, one that did not mobilize all civilians in support of its armed forces, one that allowed most people to conduct their affairs without too much interference or threat from the far-away locus of military action, one that lacked a clear policy of defeating a nebulous "enemy," one that was marred by political trade-offs, one that lacked victories over an identifiable enemy, one that was marked by a breakdown in morale among the military forces and dissension at home, and one that ended in withdrawal and defeat. Military humor in such a war took on a bitter, self-deprecating, shameful, critical patina. The breach between the American civilian society and its Vietnam veterans was not to be healed for decades.

The striking contrast between the optimistic humor of World War II and the pessimistic humor of the Vietnam era suggests that the perceptions of reality, shared or not shared, among military personnel and their larger civilian society is a key factor in what kind of military humor emerges, what sustains them, and what expresses the ironic and the tragic rather than the comic aspects of human folly.

Transforming Civilians into Military Personnel

Socialization as an adult civilian is one thing. The resocialization of civilians into the life of the military is another. In a sense one has to shed civilian ways and take on, in their place, a whole new set of attitudes and behaviors, a transformation that sets the stage for military humor to come into play.

Each branch of military service, Army, Navy, Marines, Air Force, and Coast Guard, have their distinctive styles of bringing in new recruits and "shaping them up" for their particular duties. Because the Army tends to take the largest number of civilians into its ranks, the Army is used herein as the most representative model of military service as they "process" newcomers to learn "to soldier." Close-order drill, care and maintenance of equipment, inspections, familiarity with weapons and supporting equipment, knowledge of ranks with their accompanying privileges and disprivileges, military courtesy, military organization, chains of command, military justice, military ceremonials, and military regulations are among the basic concerns of this socialization process. The "hidden curricula" include such experiences as sleep deprivation, loss of privacy, degradation rituals that help civilians shed their former association with nonmilitary identities, isolation, exercises such as forced marches with heavy packs and minimal food and water, and a learned dependency upon one's close unit. Note the recent television commercial in which a tough-spoken Marine drill-sergeant points out how hard he worked to make his men into Marines and then wryly faces the camera and asks, "So how come you guys don't write?!"

Whether manifest or latent objectives are to be achieved, each part of the entry process provides tremendous stress and adjustment. At every opportunity, in or out of ranks, the newcomer finds a need to react to what is happening and commonly responds with banter, verbal aggression, insults, curses, comments, asides, and some telling observations of the absurdity of the military life. Indicative of its significance is the recollection of such humor years later at reunions of seasoned veterans. Discomfiture is forgotten, but the laughter it engendered is remembered and savored, sometimes a bit more embellished with each retelling but appreciated nonetheless for the human resolve to endure and survive.

Faris (1976) verified the rites of passage from civilian to a soldier have persisted through the years and take much the same form from post to post. He pointed to "unflattering haircuts and glaringly new, ill-fitting uniforms that reduce personal dignity." He noted the "extreme isolation from civilian society on the one hand and an almost complete lack of privacy from other trainees on the other." Faris observed that "evaluation of performance in basic training is done at the group level rather than at the individual level." An entire platoon must give up weekend passes, for example, if one recruit "fouls up." Basic training includes "an emphasis on masculinity and aggressiveness." Any display of "feminine softness" is swiftly ridiculed. Finally, the trainees are put under physical and social-psychological stress.

A central figure in this level of training is the drill sergeant. As Faris noted, "Most drill sergeants use humor with great effectiveness." Its first form is ridicule in which the trainees are judged as a category and not as a unified group. Perceptively, Faris indicated the ridicule is "not intended or perceived as humorous, though the form is humor." Such assaults lead to increasing solidarity among the trainees and trainee humor serves as both a defense against the taskmaster and basic training itself. Jocular humor, sexual and scatological in nature, become the institutionalized humor familiar to those who served in the armed forces. Creamed beef on toast, for example, is known as "sh— on a shingle." Or every other word seems to require the expletive "f——-g" to verify the masculine life style of troopers. The widespread overuse of "barracks language" reaffirms the exploitation of or expendability of the common soldier or enlistee. It also signals their comradery-under-arms.

Faris expressed it aptly when he wrote: "The skillful use of humor as a socialization mechanism is an important factor in effecting the transformation from a cohesive group with oppositional tendencies to an accommodation with and adoption of values of the institution, while retaining the distinctions between the status of the private recruit and the veteran NCO (noncommissioned officer). It is a form of seduction."

The Military Life in Peacetime and in War

Military humor is further shaped by the circumstances of peacetime operations or an active state of being at war. In garrison or barracks conditions, the target or "enemy" is boredom, routinization, or "playing-at-war" in "war games." In wartime, inaction and boredom occurs frequently enough to be labeled the "hurry-up-and-wait" syndrome, but there is the everpresent stress of killing or being killed as enemy forces are close at hand.

Perhaps the key variable in military humor is the degree of closeness to danger or life-threatening possibilities. In wartime, the difference is seen between those in the frontline, combat echelons and those in the rear or supporting echelons. In more recent or modern warfare in which front and rear distinctions are blurred, in which everyone is in danger or vulnerable to enemy attacks, therein the military humor would reflect the commonality of stress under seige, the possible loss of life.

Ingraham (1984) updated the circumstances of military humor under "barracks" conditions. He documents the changes that have occurred since the times humorously treated in Hargrove (1942) in *See Here, Private Hargrove*. Starting in the 1970s, Ingraham noted the ending of the military draft resulted in more married soldiers and fewer soldiers with post-high school education. Saturday morning duties and inspections, a time when there was a flurry of activities for garrison soldiers, ceased. The old pass policy of allowing only a small percentage of soldiers to be absent from their post at any one time was displaced by a more open policy of permitting soldiers to come and go as they pleased when not on assigned duty. Open dormitories with rows of cots with no privacy were redesigned to accommodate smaller two- or three-person quarters. Relatively well paid, now soldiers could afford automobiles, portable television sets, tape decks, and civilian attire. Uniformed soldiers no longer loitered around their barracks waiting for lights out. They now could afford to eat meals away from Army mess halls, drink at places away from Army canteens, and entertain themselves in places other than the Army theatre and other facilities on the base. They even may avoid barracks living altogether by renting living quarters off the base. Ingraham noted that in more than a year of close observation he did not find any high-stakes card or dice games or any identifiable loan shark or "operator," a striking change from former days when soldiers often gambled their minimal pay for the possibility of a quick and lucrative return. These changes in daily military life will undoubtedly alter the details and thrust of current military humor.

Placed on a wartime footing, military personnel must now survive the life-threatening situations which they face. Each major conflict carries with it a distinctive aura. Yet within each, individuals and groups will turn to humor to help them make it through the potential pain and sacrifices they confront. In some instances there are collective actions reflecting high spirits that "a cause" is worth supporting and that victory will be achieved at minimal cost. The Boston Tea Party, for example, was gleefully carried out by men who "tomahawked" tea packets aboard ships in Boston Harbor and flung them into the sea in defiance of taxes imposed by the British Parliament. Troops were marched out to battlefields in colorful array and accompanied by celebrating civilians in the early days of the War Between the States. The trench warfare of World War I under primitive battlefield conditions elicited humorous references to the body lice or "cooties" that pestered the soldiers.

In self-directed, self-degrading, self-negating fashion, soldiers humorously treat their circumstances to lighten their burdens of anxiety and frustration. A cartoon in a soldier's magazine showed a medical doctor at some forward station near a battlefront checking over a number of bloodied, cut, and dazed soldiers. He is saying to the men, "Have you been fighting again?"

In World War II the Axis powers of Germany, Italy, and Japan tried to use humor on the Allied soldiers through "Lord Haw Haw" and "Tokyo Rose" to break their morale. Their efforts backfired on them and these figures became special targets for laughter by the Allies. Morale was increased rather than harmed among the soldiers as they mocked these efforts through outrageous ridicule and repartee.

In the "pocket wars," "skirmishes," "brushfires," or "police actions" of Korea, Vietnam, Beirut, or Grenada, ironic humor has emerged to put the best face possible on each military engagement. The Korean conflict ended in a stalemate. The Vietnam conflict ended in withdrawal as did the Beirut policing action. Only in the case of the brief Grenada incident was there the semblance of "victory over enemy objectives." The former three military conflicts required a certain amount of tongue-in-cheek humor to try to salvage some modicum of military morale out of the humiliation with the public expression of "investing mountains of effort and achieving an anthill of results." In the retreat of the Marines from Beirut, the action was dubbed "a redeployment" similar to Napoleon's ignominious redeployment out of Russia. The soldiers told each other, "We are not retreating. We are merely hastening to a safer place."

In the Grenada episode, there was the recovery of strategic ground, the removal of hostile troops, and a change in the political direction on the island but the exercise of such massive power against a miniscule opposition elicited satiric comments in the mass media along the lines of "Much Ado About Nothing."

Women in the Military

Military life has traditionally been the exclusive domain of men. Women were people who stayed home, who kept families together, who acted in a

supportive, morale-building, encouraging way, but who never entered into
active military action alongside their menfolk. As the men on an isolated
South Pacific post put it, "What ain't we got? We ain't got dames!"
But all this has changed, except for the continued policy of excluding
women from combat wherein possible. The incorporation of women into the
armed forces in rear-echelon supportive roles or in less hazardous situations other than direct contact with enemies in wartime or in technical services in peacetime has broken the stereotype of an all-male military life
style. Rustad (1982) noted that, between 1948 and 1972, women held about
one per cent of military jobs. Between 1972 and 1982, women quadrupled
from two per cent to eight per cent of the total enlisted employment. In
1987, some 200,000 women are serving in the armed forces with 63,000 in
the Army alone.

Rustad served in the European Division of the University of Maryland as
an instructor in sociology from 1975 to 1978 during which time he painstakingly verified the gender and sexual harrassment women soldiers endured.
Such harrassment must be understood as "an additional stress factor"
added to all the other stresses soldiers endure. From all sides, civilian and
military, and in every military rank, women in the military were visible targets for derisive humor from male soldiers particularly. Sexual and scatological humor were verbal assaults on the dignity of many women soldiers,
but now and then, certain women reversed the situation by turning the joking around so that men could begin to understand what it was like to be
judged categorically and exclusively by one's anatomy or by one's alleged
sexual and gender characteristics. Willenz (1983) supported much of
Rustad's conclusions as she offered not only an historical view of the involvement and contributions of women in the military services but provided
vignettes of numerous women who were able to survive some very trying
military circumstances by maintaining their sense of humor.

Blacks and the Military

In a sense the military forces reflect the nature of their society, and thus
one could posit that if the larger society was racially biased, so too would
the armed forces mirror those prejudices and discriminatory acts connected
with racism. The history of the military forces in the United States confirms
this general hypothesis (see, for example, Binkin, et al., 1982). But there
have been notable exceptions from the Revolutionary War on to the
present. It has taken many years but with the federal government committed to the ideals of democracy and its concomitant concern for equality, the
military forces may be said to be more integrated and more concerned with
implementing ideals of racial equity than the society it seeks to preserve
and defend. As Hope (1979) affirmed, all along the historical road the
present conditions were not achieved without strife.

Similar to the women who entered the military but not identical in the overall experiences, blacks endured the demeaning comments and treatment of white peers or superiors. It is not surprising that they fight "the sword of humor" with "the shield of humor." Brotherhood, solidarity, and close identification with each other helped black soldiers adjust to the military life style. The "dap," for example, a ritual greeting of rhythmic hand-slapping among black soldiers, served as a humorous and gleeful symbol of unity despite all the efforts of white soldiers to use "put-downs" or racial slurs against them (Shuter, 1979). Its usage was forbidden by higher commands, but the orders did not entirely eradicate the practice, particularly during off-duty hours.

William Graham Sumner once held that "state ways cannot change folkways," but as already noted, federal directives have markedly altered the fabric of military society in racial integrative terms. Perhaps instituting the Defense Race Relations Institute (DRRI) in which a cadre of race relations or equal opportunity officers were trained to be eventually located in every U.S. military base throughout the world is a useful case in point. Attendees were given an intensive course in minority studies, data from the behavioral sciences with special emphasis upon individual and institutionalized racism, taught educational techniques, and given community laboratory experiences such as visits to ghetto housing projects, migrant camps, Cuban and Puerto Rican neighborhoods, and Indian settlements. They practiced what they preached by being housed together and by having ample opportunity to exchange ideas and feelings.

Of special interest was the rise of humor among the DRRI participants: "Humor was an important ingredient in group discussions and interaction. Initially, it was regarded as an unknown quantity, perhaps a potentially destructive force; but, gradually, its use became a sign of student mastery of fears and hostilities. It permitted discussion to continue even during anxious moments of free expression" (Hope, 1979, p. 102). Singer (1968) found that controlled humor does have the ability "to arouse feelings of mastery over intolerable circumstances."

The survival thesis for humor finds solid support in the efforts of the military to carry out its missions without doing damage to the principles it seeks to defend.

Technology and the Military

Paralleling the technological changes in the larger society are changes occurring in the military. In fact, *paralleling* may not be as accurate a term as perhaps *innovating* or *initiating* technological changes in the military because, in a number of instances, the military services first used technically complex equipment before such technology saw its first civilian applications. Radar equipment, night photography, and heat-sensing devices are some examples of prior military use. But aside from whether the armed services or civilian society initially tested and used technological equipment, there is little doubt that military personnel carry out their work with the help of complicated machinery and intricate electronic devices. It is no longer a question of military forces colliding with other military forces as much as it is personnel manning expensive, complex equipment versus other personnel operating their devices to counter opponents' moves on land, sea, or air.

While soldiering connotes men-at-war, the modern armies' "arms" require disciplined technicians who can use and maintain a baffling variety of technical skills. A soldier thus has an "M.O.S.," a military occupational specialty, and it is this specialty that indicates how a given military man or woman renders the needed services that military life requires. Person-to-person and group-to-group interaction is still primary or paramount, but as noted above, the growing sophistication of equipment in the military also contains a person-to-machinery relationship that emerges in military humor. (See, for example, *The 1982 Guide to the Evaluation of Educational Experiences in the Armed Forces,* that describes in three volumes the countless occupational specialties necessary to keep the armed services operational. AR 611-3 and DA Pam 600-3 also verify the numerous work functions needed by modern armies.)

This relationship between the soldier and his or her machinery emerges in military humor whenever the machinery fails to do what it is supposed to do. Of course, human ingenuity has brought the machinery into use, but it also means that human beings are not always the beneficiaries and may indeed become "the victims of their own technologies." Military personnel are quick to resort to humor when they realize how much they rely upon some elaborate piece of equipment to work efficiently, particularly under emergency or stress situations. Helicopter pilots, for example, refer to a "Jesus nut" which keeps the rotor blade secured to the airframe. Should it ever loosen or fail to do its job, they explain, they will only have time to say "Jesus!" before disaster strikes. The old adage, "Take care of your rifle so it can take care of you," has given way to the more contemporary adage befitting a modern military force, "Take care of your equipment, understand and use it wisely, or you endanger yourself and those relying on you." It is true in civilian life as well, but it can be a matter of life or death in the military. Such person *versus* machine military humor is a hallmark of modern military forces as never before (Smith, 1985).

Summary and Conclusions

Military humor can be aligned with power politics, the sociology of occupations, or with the problems of complex organizations, but it rates chapter-length treatment because it deals with the lives of untold millions who have experienced the unique transitions between civilian and military life both in entering and leaving the armed services. Far too often, military humor is associated in the minds of persons with some particular war in history such as World War I or II. But the fluid nature of human events requires a broader view. Variables that shape military humor include consideration of military life in wartime and in times of peace, morale depending upon the larger society's views as to the legitimacy of military actions or military presence, the numbers of civilians and military personnel affected or involved, the amount of time devoted to inaction, the degree of strain and stress in routinization, ritual, or ceremonials in garrison, barracks, or standby statuses as well as in combat, the differences in the privileges or disprivileges of military rank as well as comparisons between rear and frontline echelons, and finally changes in the military establishment due to the increasing presence of women, different racial types, volunteers versus conscripts, and mounting technological specialties and complexities.

Military life is highly associated with compliance structures or total institutions that require full commitment from participants. The loss of freedom to do as one pleases sets military life apart from civilian life. In addition there may well be hazardous and life-threatening situations that raise the level of stress and strain. Military humor plays a significant part in this milieu because of its ability to help persons endure. The survival function is paramount in military action and is evident in the maintenance of morale under the most trying conditions.

The resocialization of raw recruits from civilian to military personnel is frequently the arena for military humor to operate. Cohesive, efficient groups must be formed and in-group and out-group humor helps mold individualistic civilians into cooperating, disciplined units capable of carrying out military assignments. Ridicule can come from noncommissioned or commissioned officers. Within ranks, jocular bantering, curses, and sexual-scatological references serve as escape valves in ventilating their pent up feelings in these situations. Group cohesiveness is paramount and foul-ups become the favorite targets for humor. Interestingly enough, the pain of becoming a military person is frequently forgotten by military veterans. What they savor and recall fondly and frequently is the military humor that helped to carry them through these experiences.

Designed for war, military services frequently involve long periods of peacetime, non-war circumstances. In wartime, personnel are expendable. In peacetime, personnel must wait out their enlistments. In either circumstance, military personnel frequently turn to self-ridicule and self-negation for having been unfortunately locked into such confined circumstances while others have succeeded in avoiding such a fate.

Finally social changes imposed by the larger society have profoundly affected the military life styles of personnel. The presence of women, blacks, or other volunteers as well as increasing reliance upon technological equipment and devices has brought into being a new military force. Humor is still present under these new conditions, but future research may reveal more profoundly its nature, functions and significance.

STUDY QUESTIONS

1. Is military humor a product of political, occupational, or bureaucratic variables or some combination of the three?

2. How does being on a "wartime" or "peacetime" footing affect military humor?

3. How does the relationship between the military establishment and its larger society affect what military humor emerges?

4. Why is the survival function of humor so salient under military circumstances?

5. What would a study comparing military humor associated with the wars in which the United States of America has been engaged from the Revolutionary War to the present reveal?

6. Does military humor support or subvert military morale?

7. What characterizes "front" and "rear" echelon's military humor in terms of forms or usages?

8. How is military humor changed by civilian judgments of the armed services?

9. Do the various branches of the military services differ markedly in their respective brands of military humor?

10. Does military humor add or detract from the re-socialization of civilians as they enter the armed services?

11. Why is military humor recalled so frequently and relished by military veterans?

12. How does conscription or an all-volunteer policy affect military humor?

13.Has the presence of women in the armed forces increased or decreased the use of sexual and scatological references in military humor?

14.Has military humor been modified by the integration of blacks into the former all-white military service?

15.What part does increasing technology play in reshaping the nature of military humor?

16.Would studies of military humor in the armed forces of countries other than the United States reveal quite different styles and functions?

17.Does or does not military humor strengthen unit resolve or small-unit cohesiveness within the military services?

18.How does one's rank in the military establishment affect one's style of military humor?

19.Is military humor still operational among military personnel whether on-duty or off-duty?

20.Can those interested in the efficiency of military forces afford to neglect the study of military humor?

Suggested Readings

Binkin, Martin and Mark Eitelberg, with Alvin J. Schexnider and Marvin M. Smith. *Blacks and the Military.* Washington, DC: Brookings Institution, 1982.

Faris, John H. "The Impact of Basic Combat Training: The Role of the Drill Sergeant," in Nancy L. Goldman and David R. Segal, eds. *The Social Psychology of Military Service.* Beverly Hills, CA: Sage, 1976: 13-24.

Hargrove, Marion. *See Here, Private Hargrove!* NY: Henry Holt, 1942.

Hope, Richard O. *Racial Strife in the U.S. Military: Toward the Elimination of Discrimination.* NY: Praeger, 1979.

Ingraham, Larry H. *The Boys in the Barracks: Observations on American Military Life.* Philadelphia: Institute for the Study of Human Issues, 1984.

Janowitz, Morris. *The Professional Soldier: A Social and Political Portrait.* NY: Free Press, 1960.

Karsten, Peter. *Soldiers and Society: The Effects of Military Service and War on American Life.* Westport, CT: Greenwood Press, 1978.

Lang, Kurt. *Military Institutions and the Sociology of War: A Review of the Literature with Annotated Bibliography.* Beverly Hills, CA: Sage, 1972.

Martin, Michel Louis and Ellen Stern McCrate, eds. *The Military: Militarism and the Polity. Essays in Honor of Morris Janowitz.* NY: Free Press, 1984.

Moskos, Jr., Charles C. *The American Enlisted Man: The Rank and File in Today's Military.* NY: Sage, 1970.

Rustad, Michael. *Women in Khaki: The American Enlisted Woman.* NY: Praeger, 1982.

Shuter, Robert. "The Dap in the Military: Hand-To-Hand Communication," *J. of Communication* 29 (Winter, 1979): 136-143.

Singer, J. D. and M. Small. "Alliance Aggregation and the Onset of War, 1815-1945," in J.D. Singer, ed. *Quantitative International Politics: Insights and Evidence.* NY, Free Press, 1968: 247-286.

Smith, Merritt Roe, ed. *Military Enterprise and Technological Change: Perspectives on the American Experience.* Cambridge, MA: MIT Press, 1985.

Stouffer, Samuel A., Edward A. Suchman, Leland C. DeVinney, Shirley A. Star and Robin M. Williams, Jr. *The American Soldier: Adjustment During Army Life.* Princeton, NJ: Princeton Univ. Press, vol. I, 1949.

Willenz, June a. *Women Veterans: America's Forgotten Heroines.* NY: Continuum Publ., 1983.

Chapter 16:

Occupational Humor

The sociology of occupations has developed an impressive literature upon which to draw (see, e.g., Miller & Form, 1964; Taylor, 1968; Smelser, 1969; Krause, 1971; Pavalko, 1971; and Dunkerley, 1975). This specialized field of sociology offers a firm foundation upon which to build a profound understanding of how occupations at various levels of society and economy have social dimensions and significant social consequences. Humor, however, has to date been given minimal or practically no attention in these works. This is not meant to be critical of this development, but it reflects the serious, sober approach of sociological scholars to work-related phenomena. As the significance of humor becomes increasingly recognized, future studies of sociologists will likely include humor as another factor in occupations worthy of attention and investigation from the sociological perspective.

In the previous chapter, the focus was on those whose occupations were military and how they drew upon humor to endure and survive the circumstances derived from peacetime and wartime military service. In this chapter the focus is on civilian occupations in general and what part humor plays in this work-related context. In chapters that follow, two specific occupational matrices are singled out for special treatment, namely, medical and sports personnel. Beyond this a concluding chapter deals with the career patterns of humorists or comics themselves, those who not only know the high value placed upon humor while work is being conducted but who have made a vocation out of humor itself.

In this chapter then civilian occupations generally are considered in terms of how humor operates to enable workers at all levels to cope with their work situations and relationships. First, there is recognition that occupational changes have occurred so that occupational history indicates that some kind of occupational humor is rooted more in the past than in the present. Next, it is noted that sociologists have developed a vast literature in the study of occupations and that these sources suggest the breadth and

249

depth of occupational contexts in which humor manifests itself. Also a generalized pattern of work histories indicates additional settings for humor to function. Finally, occupational humor is evaluated as an effective morale builder to sustain workers as they go about their varied tasks in service to the overall society and economy.

Occupational Humor of the Past

Occupations of the past were characterized by the need for human labor to produce goods and perform services. Individuals worked alone or in concert with others to get jobs done or to create the necessary foodstuffs, clothig, housing, or items essential to survival. Life was labor-intensive and each person lent their personal strength and skills to allow the social order to endure. Starting early in life and continuing until well into old age, each individual had to perform some useful task in order to justify his or her existence. Work itself was tedious, energy-draining, and more often than not carried on with considerable risk to life and limb (Bettmann, 1974). Under such circumstances it is difficult to explain some of the nostalgia that some people retain and preserve for former occupational types. One can only speculate that perhaps those who glorify the past neglect or overlook unpleasant factors and value instead whatever was pleasant about the working conditions in past times.

Wilson (1963), for instance, has collected a remarkable listing of occupations that have vanished from American society or have been preserved by a few historical devotees. He writes about fletchers, websters, snobscats, costermongers, perukers, shepsters, sartors, Jack Ketches, and farriers. These obsolete or displaced occupations are more recognizable as, respectively, arrowmakers, weavers, shoe cobblers, sellers of fruits, fish, and vegetables, wigmakers, clothcutters, tailors, executioners or hangmen, and horseshoers. Wilson also includes cowboys in his list of early Americans at work. These highly romanticized "waddies" are selected for examples of occupational humor of the past because these men and their work have been a major part of Americana for many years. Furthermore, cowboy humor is prominent in American lore in contrast to the failure of historians to record whatever humor existed in occupations no longer existing.

Cowboys are authentic American folk heroes and are admired characters in the mass media. While police officers and criminals have preempted the attention of the public in the mass media, cowboys were frequently portrayed as the "good guys" full of bravado and derring-do in the recent past. While Tom Mix, William S. Hart, Buck Jones, and Hoot Gibson were immortalized in early films, what remains of this mythology are "urban cowboys" replete with broad-brimmed Stetsons, colorful shirts, "western-cut" vests and jeans, ornate bolos, and high leather boots. And significantly, cowboys' affinity for humor has accompanied this preserved imagery.

Hoig (1958) noted, for example, "Someone once described the cowboy as 'a man with guts and a hoss,' but whoever said it didn't do the cowboy justice. To describe the cowboy truthfully the definition would be more apt to read, 'a man with guts and a hoss and a heckuva sense of humor.' This last best marks him for what he was."

Hoig lends credence to the theme that humor is used to survive extenuating circumstances when he wrote:

"Without his humor, it is doubtful that the cowboy could have survived, for his knack for seeing the humorous side of life was every bit as vital to him as his rope, horse, or six gun. Without an ability to laugh at troubles and hard times, the cowboy could never have withstood the pressures piled on him in a world of strenuous work and violent action. It was typical of a cowboy who had been put afoot by a rabbit-shy cayuse to respond by shaking his fist after the animal and declaring, "Jes fer that, I'm gonna walk home!' And when the waddie trudged, footsore and weary, back into ranch headquarters, he would likely be asked what in the heck he meant by making that poor animal come home all by itself. The man who felt sorry for himself out West was lost."

During cattle drives or work in the open range, the cowboys were fed through the services of a camp cook who moved with the men and the stock as they traveled the grasslands. Such a man was a prime target for much good-natured joshing by the cowboys. His hard-as-rocks biscuits or his steady serving of easy-to-prepare beans were commented upon frequently, framed always in a joking style so as to avoid alienating the outdoor cook, their major source of "vittles" while on the prairies. Camp cooks, in turn, knew the finer points of defending their culinary skills in order to practice "one-upsmanship," again using humor in such strategies. One example must suffice to illustrate:

A cowboy was constantly grumbling about the bad food or "fixin's" of the camp cook. In feigned sympathy, his foreman told the cowboy to consult the cook himself, because the cook understood the problem quite well and had laid in some medical supplies to allay gastro-intestinal upsets. The foreman assured the cowboy that with the help of the cook's "liver-regulator" he would be able to digest whatever food was offered him. When the cowboy asked the cook for the proper medicine, the cook promptly took out his cocked .45 pistol and pointed it at him saying, "This is the best darned liver-regulator I know about, and if I hear one more word outa you I'm gonna let you have a big dose of it!" Needless to say, the improvement in the waddie's health was remarkable (Hoig, 1958).

Cowboys, of course, were not alone in their reliance upon humor to relieve the tedium and constraints of their occupation. Folklore is replete with examples of ways in which workers encourage each other to pull together to get some major feat accomplished. Gandy dancers, for example, persons who manhandled long strands of steel to lay railroad tracks, were emboldened to lift their heavy loads by rhythmic chants in order to get the job done. By working in unison the load per worker was within their physical limits. The same applied to the bawdy sea chanties sung by sailors as they hoisted shipsails by ropes and pulleys or to turn a windlass to haul up heavy anchors. Long before the days of propeller-driven boats, crews of men strained at long ropes to bring river boats upstream against the current and their unison singing or shouts were designed to help them lean into their rope harness and accomplish what was a tremendous exhibition of strength. The examples are endless, but the key point is that workers have often pooled their efforts to move tremendous loads long before the days of powerful machinery, in part through morale-building techniques such as encouraging songs or humorous stimuli.

Management has known for many years that happy, contented workers are far more likely to produce a product or render a service better than if they are discontent and overburdened with monotony and isolation or shown little appreciation for their good work. This is especially true in cases where workers have to perform the same tasks repeatedly with little apparent relief or relaxation. A holdover from the days when cigars were hand-rolled from tobacco leaves, there is an interesting case in point from Puerto Rico in which humor was openly recognized, given prominence, and made a part of the production process. Workers were typically seated around a large table on which they hand-rolled so many cigars from tobacco leaves per hour. Rather than granting each worker the freedom to joke around with one another or rejecting the idea of workers being forced to remain silent while working, the management hit upon the idea that a single worker would be chosen to offset the tedium in a direct effort to improve morale and in turn production. This worker would be seated on a chair placed in the center of the large worktable and would be paid the same hourly rate as his or her fellow workers. However, this designated worker-of-the-day was freed from having to produce the daily quota of cigars. Instead, this worker had only one duty to perform - to entertain the others by reading the newspapers, by gossiping, and by light banter so that attention was more on the flow of talk than it was on the monotonous work of hand-rolling tobacco leaves. The arrangement worked very well and as management had hoped, cigar production was not only sustained but it was in fact increased by the workers.

In other work settings, depending upon limits set by management, workers are given some leeway in expressing a humorous perspective on their work or their personal preferences. While formal norms usually prevail, particularly for those work settings in which clients, customers, or the general public are to be served, there are many informal work settings not involving customers or clientele in which humor is given considerable license. Memoranda, desk or bench decorations, graffiti, door statements, or bulletin board items are openly displayed and reflect a "not-to-be-taken-too-seriously" attitude of staff and line workers. If "breaks" from work are allowable, these moments are used to relax, to refresh one's self, and particularly to draw upon humor to continue through the work sessions that lie ahead. Predictably much of the banter and light conversation revolves around the work itself and does not detract from it as much as it enhances it and makes it more tolerable.

Occupational Humor in Modern Society

While past occupations have involved humor as a relief from tedium, despair, and difficulties, contemporary occupations have their own characteristics that encourage workers to utilize humor in order to cope with their vocational circumstances. The insights of sociologists applied to occupations establish baselines in this regard. For example, the Durkheimian understanding that while there is division of labor in human societies, the mechanical solidarity of persons performing identical tasks, such as farming, has given way to organic solidarity in which specialized occupations fit together in support of the larger society. A type of independence or self-sufficiency for occupations gives way to a new interdependence of highly specialized vocations. Modern occupations are more likely to be very specialized and so fit the organic solidarity mode. More than 20,000 distinctive jobs are listed in the *Dictionary of Occupational Titles* issued by the United States Department of Labor. New occupational titles are constantly being added so that most people are unfamiliar with and far removed from unique job performances needed in modern high-technology society.

What is understood is that work may or may not be central to individual workers or employees. The Marxian view that alienation from work is characteristic of untold numbers of workers seems to have validity at the lower levels of the occupational pyramid. Workers as adjuncts to machinery was brilliantly satirized by Charlie Chaplin in his classic film *Modern Times* (McDonald *et al.*, 1965) when a worker is caught in the machinery and even fed by machinery to dramatize the relationship (see also Chinoy, 1955, and Dufty, 1969). Estrangement from work is recognizable in the various comments of workers on assembly line jobs or in the pleasure of leaving work at the end of a workday or in the receptivity to early retirement. One popular musician made a fortune out of this detachment from work with his song, 'Take This Job and Shove It.'

Terkel (1974) spent three years contacting workers in every conceivable industry, business, profession, or service in his classic *Working*. From the humblest menial laborer to the highly trained technician and sophisticated professional, what emerged was a pattern of using humor to achieve personal respect and a rejection of anything that dehumanized or demeaned them.

A spot welder on the third shift at a Ford Motor plant, offered Terkel a verbatim description of how he coped with his job through humor:

"Ford keeps its overhead down. If I had to go a few feet to get some stock that would be time I'm not working. So Ford has everything set up. If you run out, the truck will come blowing carbon monoxide in your face. But it's making sure you'll never run out of work. I mean you're *really* tied down to the job. Laughs You stand on your feet and you run on your feet. Laughs

"We get 48 minutes of break — 30 minutes in the morning and the other 18 in the evening. You always go to the bathroom first. Laughs It's three flights up. You come down, you walk to another part of the plant, and you walk up another three flights to get a bite to eat. On the line, you don't go to the washroom when you have to go. You learn to adjust your physical..... Laughs For new workers, this is quite hard. I haven't gotten used to it yet. I've been here since 1968.

"The part of the automobile I work on is before it gets all the pretties. There is no paint. The basic car. There's a conveyorlike... Mr. Ford's given credit for inventing this little....Laughs There is no letup; the line is always running. It's not like... if you lift something, carry it for a little while, lay it down, and go back - while you're going back - you're actually catching a breather. Ford has a better idea. Laughs You hear the slogan: They had a better idea. They have better ideas of getting all the work possible out of your worn body for eight hours.

"You can work next to a guy for months without even knowing his name. One thing, you're too busy to talk. Can't hear. Laughs You have to holler in his ear. They got those little guys comin' around in white shirts and if they see you running your mouth, they say, 'This guy needs more work.' Man, he's got no time to talk.

"A lot of guys who've been to jail, they say you don't work as hard in jail. Laughs They say, 'Man, jail ain't never this bad.' Laughs That's the way I feel. I'm serving a sentence..."(Terkel, 1974, pp. 164-165)

Workers like the spot welder are affirming their concerns that they be treated as human beings rather than as robots. Lewis Yablonsky (1972) coined the term, "robopaths," to identify programmed, mechanistic personality types who coldly and dutifully carry on their work just as if they were some automated mechanism. Smiling, laughter, or some signs of human warmth are missing from robopathic workers. While such types do exist, there are many others who show their humanity by adopting a more pleasing receptiveness to others as well as to themselves as they go about their tasks. One hypothesis worth testing would be to determine if there is indeed a positive correlation between humor and occupational status or between humor and occupational prestige. Sociologists have established occupational rating scales (see Nam and Powers, 1983), and these can be used to determine if there is a parallel increasing of humor as occupations increase in status or prestige.

Saunders (1981), for instance, has written at length about the social stigma attached to occupations. His studies of lower grade workers in service organizations in the United Kingdom stem in part from his own experiences in the "backstage areas" of restaurants. The lowly sculleryman or *plongeur,* for example, has the task of collecting, washing, and returning to their allocated places various pots and pans. The work is unappetizing as it involves scraping away leftover scraps of food, cleaning and scouring burnt spots, and removing greases or fats used in food preparations. Many have to wear large rubber aprons, boots, and gloves and use brushes, steel wool, and various detergents in steaming hot water to accomplish their tasks. While such work has to be done, the plongeur stands at the bottom of the occupational ladder even in the kitchen setting of major restaurants. Saunders understandably makes no mention of humor for plongeurs, albeit the dire need to help such a worker through his labors. With attention fixed elsewhere, whatever humor used by scullerymen was present, it went undetected and unworthy of notice. If, on the other hand, consciousness of humor in work settings would have been a part of the sociological study of occupations, it may very well have been detected, affirmed, and observed to be a significant part of the work experience.

For those, however, higher on the occupational scale, humor has more chance of observation because workers have more freedom of expression, more identification with their work, and more ability to articulate their ideas and feelings about their occupations. Probability suggests that humor is more likely to surface among the unsupervised than the supervised. Professionals, near professionals, entrepreneurs, and middle management stand a greater change to ventilate their feelings than do those who have constant supervision over them and expect them to do their work, however difficult, boring or demanding it may be, without the alleged "wasting of time, energy, and productivity" through humorous by-play.

In recent years American management has become increasingly familiar with the Japanese way of building the morale of their workers through regular meetings in which worker's suggestions for improvement can be heard. The Japanese schedule exercise programs during the work-day, engage workers in activities such as singing company songs to build enthusiasm, and offer their workers employment throughout their work-careers. This Japanese style may not be effective with American workers who are accustomed to individual life styles, but it has been adapted in various American work-places with quite favorable results.

Humor in the Work Career

Work careers represent a paradigm, schema, or framework within which humor manifests itself as a coping mechanism. Such careers or job histories may vary in terms of being "straight-line" or "checkered," being uninterrupted or interrupted, or being "dead-end" or unlimited in opportunities for advancement. The straight-line career refers to fixing on some occupation or profession and moving steadily toward and within that occupation. The checkered career refers to a variety of occupations and work styles that jobholders have experienced. Many different circumstances can explain the 'checkered' career. Delays in entering a career apply to women who have devoted themselves to their children and/or husbands before thinking about themselves. Such women temporarily drop out of their work and then resume the same or different type of work than they had before. Ill-health, the closing of plants, dissatisfaction with policies, or the realization that some work offers little in the way of promotions or financial rewards are other conditions that result in some workers trying out a variety of careers. For purpose of brevity, only the straight-line, uninterrupted, and unlimited opportunity work careers are considered to indicate those circumstances or phases of development in which humor emerges.

Job Entry or "Getting In"

Entering a career or work position is no small task in itself. This initial step may be blocked or thwarted by established policies that may be laughable to outside observers but most serious to those being kept away from some occupational slot. Such persons will note, however, the absurdity of the situation and use humor to plead for social corrections. A fairly familiar pattern is to call for experienced help rather than inexperienced help. For employers, this practice limits the pool of potential employees, allows for smoother assimilation of new employees into a work force, and effectively saves the need to train employees in basic skills, knowledge, or orientations. For those seeking entry, however, they plead that experience cannot even begin until someone "lets them in" and provides the necessary experience. They are willing to enter at the lower levels of the work ladder, but as they humorously address their problem, one must be allowed to begin to climb the ladder or be cut off from climbing anywhere.

Criteria for job entry are also targets for humorous assaults. Few would object to qualifying for job consideration on some meritorious basis. However, job entries frequently occur through something other than ability to perform a job well. The old saw says, "It isn't *what* you know, but *who* you know that counts." The use of "pull," "the inside track," family influences or reputation are quite often the means by which doors are opened to some and closed to others. The late Robert Kennedy's appointment as Attorney General of the United States was a clear case of nepotism which he handled with considerable wit. When students at the University of Colorado asked him how a student should prepare him or herself for a law-enforcement career, he grinned and said, "By all means, do as I did. Study hard, devote yourselves to your studies and some day, who could say otherwise, you, too, could become Attorney General of the United States if your brother ever became President of the United States first!"

Job-Satisfaction or "Getting Along" in Job Careers

Once entry is gained into some occupation, the next step is to remain there and, where possible, to climb the occupational ladder through promotions and recognition of increasing aptitude for greater responsibilities.

Laurence Peter lent his name to the principle that persons are promoted to the highest levels of their *incompetence* (Peter & Hull, 1969). The "Peter Principle" is a humorous observation of reality, that persons who allegedly do well at one level of work may or may not also be well qualified to perform work at higher levels of supervision, work they have never done and work that they therefore may not do as well as their original performance on lower-level jobs. Herein humor functions as "truth over sham," honesty over pretense or allegations.

Those who remain behind or are bypassed in the promotion process can become discouraged, demotivated, and bored with their work. Such jobs may show large turnover rates as people come and go in certain occupational positions. Or those who stand up to their assigned tasks turn to humorous ways to continue. Some will ridicule what they are doing or turn to comraderie with fellow workers caught in the same day-to-day routines. Others will resort to techniques that "look like they are working" when they are reallly not. Still others identify with the comic-strip character Dagwood, who often at the urging of his wife Blondie, nags his surly boss for a raise only to be refused, fired for assuming he is worth a raise, and then rehired. Does one "rock the boat" and "make waves" or resign one's self to life on "the treadmill to oblivion" that the radio comic Fred Allen used to to characterize much of a person's working life? As Allen's figure of speech cleverly noted, working hard is supposedly the means to get ahead, but not on a treadmill. One works hard merely "to stay even."

The assumption of effectiveness on the job provides still another opportunity for humor to emerge. Holding up the inept, clumsy, harmful-to-self-and-the-work-process employee to ridicule is a favorite procedure. The carpenter who hits his thumb instead of the nail, the painter who paints his face rather than the wall, or the worker who saws off the board he is sitting on are cases in point. Circus clowns have gotten considerable mileage out of skits in which a group of workers are supposed to build a scaffold to repair a wall but who end up knocking each other down, swinging boards into each other's head, stepping into pails of cement or water, and ending up with a sorry mess. Humor points out that things are not as they appear to be and workers can relate the pratfalls of the clowns to their own work situations. Many are witness to the sign that reads "Our staff is eager to serve you" but shows a motley crew of near-imbeciles confronting the public.

Human error creeps into every occupation despite precautions against it. When mistakes are made, both employers and employees must be willing to recognize them and to make amends to satisfy customers or consumers.

While this is understood and publicly stated, there are often attempts to make the correction of mistakes or problems rather difficult to accomplish. A fairly familiar bit of visual humor in regard to this is the large notice stating that complaints will be processed but the space provided for specifying the complaint is only about one square inch of space. While complaints, grievances, or fault-finding are declared to be legitimate, the settlement of mistakes or problems is not made an easy process. As this sort of humor suggests, there is much protectionism, much shielding of staff members, or much complicating of the system. Indeed among the occupations there are certain designated personnel such as a receptionist or office secretary who often function by seeing to it that certain messages never reach their bosses or employers or that certain messages are diverted to lower-level echelons in order not to disturb higher authorities or policymakers. Favorable messages might get through but unfavorable ones are blocked, delayed or redirected. Quality control, inspections, inquiries, and supervision help reduce product errors, but human bungling eludes some of these efforts. It is often with tongue in cheek that certain warranties or assurances are made. It is also through humor that both producers and consumers endure the nonsense that often prevails in certain work places.

Retirement or "Getting Out"

Eventually work careers are terminated. One does not simply continue forever with one's occupation or master-role. Some are pushed or forced out, while death or ill health forces their careers to end for them. Others have some flexibility about when they retire from the work force. Retirement introduces ambivalent humor because of its bittersweet nature. In one respect retirement is sad, sentimental and regretted because it means a type of "social death," the ending of occupational relationships of fairly long standing. On the other hand, retirement is pleasurable as it means freedom to fill one's own time as one pleases.

Irony exists in traditional retirement gifts of gold watches, easy chairs, or luggage. Time is no longer to be carefully measured. Retirees may not necessarily wish to sit around the remainder of their lives. Or they may never travel, thanks to health problems, high costs, lack of interest, or lack of opportunity.

It is also ironic to discover that, as Atchley noted, many retirees do not really retire from careers as much as they retire from jobs (Atchley, 1985). They take on second careers or "second jobs" and so remain part of the work force despite their identification as "retired."

For those who are "workaholics" or who thoroughly enjoyed their work, retirement is a bitter pill to swallow. They are removed from their work with a great deal of aggressive humor directed against whoever or whatever they hold responsible.

For those, however, whose work was tiresome, dirty, dangerous, uncomfortable, overdemanding, or unrewarding, retirement is a time for jubilation. It is with great good humor that they count down the minutes, days, and months remaining before they can retire happily and securely. If, however, the circumstances surrounding their retirement are less than joyous due to poor health, company reorganization, buyouts or other reasons forcing them into involuntary retirement, their separation from work takes on a negative, hostile, satirical tone and their humor is accordingly sour, dour, and embittered.

One final observation might be worth noting. It is the return of the retiree to the bosom of his or her family. Many marriages work just fine as long as the wage earner is away from the home most of the workday. Couples enjoy weekends and vacations or holidays together. But contemplation of "togetherness" seven full days a week makes some spouses shudder. One wife of a retired chemist in San Francisco, for example, has written a humorous piece to express the need for a sturdy sense of humor to cope with the constant presence of the retiree. She entitled it *Love, Honor, and Hang on* (Owens, 1976).

Summary and Conclusions

Occupation as the master status figures prominently in individual lives and provides the social milieu in which humor frequently is utilized. The stimuli for humorous responses are to be found whenever and wherever work is conducted, but there are imposed limits as to whether or not humor is welcomed or suppressed. Historically occupations were labor-intensive, involving the need for individuals to combine their efforts or for persons to carry on tasks that called for individual fortitude and craftmanship to hand-fashion articles or to render individual services. Humor eased the discomforts of either condition. The romanticized character of the American cowboy operating against great odds is a case in point. Work songs or chants and playful gossip are examples of the latter effort to maintain group morale and productivity. In the present, however, humor may or may not be encouraged during the course of a workday, and it is these conditions that call for further study and interpretation.

While occupational sociology has developed as a major specialization in the discipline, it is usually presented in a sober or totally serious fashion with minimal or no attention given to the presence of humor. As this chapter seeks to demonstrate, there are circumstances worthy of study in which humor can and does emerge in work settings. Among them is the need for humor despite alienation from monotonous and repetitive tasks associated with technical machinery. While some workers become robopathic, others use the safety valve of humor to endure and to assert their humanity on the job.

Sociologists are familiar with status and prestige ratings assigned to various occupational levels. It was proposed in this chapter that a positive correlation exists between humor and occupational status and prestige. Causal analysis can follow and the possible sources of occupational humor at various levels are suggested. Using the model of work careers, it is suggested, for instance, that each phase of work careers brings into play the need for and the use of humor. From entry into and retirement from occupations, humor is shown to be present and strongly related to modes of work via occupations.

STUDY QUESTIONS

1. Why is occupation dubbed the master status?

2. What are the functions of occupational humor?

3. What part does nostalgia play in characterizing occupations of the past as having a humorous component?

4. Why is humor so welcomed and appreciated by certain types of workers in certain types of work-settings?

5. Are there work-settings that tend to suppress manifestations of occupational humor? Why does this occur?

6. What work-settings are more emenable to occupational humor than others? Why?

7. What accounts for the relative paucity of references to occupational humor in occupational sociology literature?

8. In what sense are workers treated as adjuncts to machinery and in what sense are they acknowledged to be human beings and in need of comic relief?

9. Why and how is occupational humor likely to surface in unskilled and semi-skilled labor-settings?

10. What is the nature of occupational humor at middle management and professional levels?

11.Is there a positive correlation between occupational humor and occupational prestige? Why or why not?

12.In what ways does occupational humor differ at different stages of a work-career?

13.Is humor more likely to be manifested in highly supervised or in less supervised working situations?

14.What humor may be found in getting a work-career started?

15.Is humor more likely to be present when promotions are based on merit or on "pull" or favoritism?

16.Are job-incompetencies laughable? Why or why not?

17.Is humor present when workers artfully pretend to be busy at their labors when, in fact, they are not?

18.How is in-group humor of workers used against out groups of consumers or the public the workers are alleged to serve?

19.Is humor present in the process of avoiding accountability for work allegedly being done?

20.In what ways is retirement from work funny?

21.What humor, if any, can be found among the unemployed? Do they have unique ways to use humor to sustain them? And, does humor exist among unpaid volunteers? For what purposes do unpaid volunteers use humor?

Suggested Readings

Atchley, Robert C. *Social Forces and Aging.* Belmont, CA: Wadsworth, 4th ed., 1985.

Bettmann, Otto L. *The Good Old Days - They Were Terrible!* NY: Random House, 1974.

Chinoy, Ely. *Automobile Workers and the American Dream.* NY: Doubleday, 1955.

Dufty, N.F., ed. *The Sociology of the Blue-Collar Worker.* Leiden: Brill, 1969.

Dunkerly, David. *Occupation and Society.* London: Routledge & Kegan Paul, 1975.

Hoig, Stan. *The Humor of the American Cowboy.* Lincoln, NE: Univ. of Nebraska Press, 1958.

Krause, Elliott A. *The Sociology of Occupations.* Boston: Little, Brown, 1971.

McDonald, Gerald D., Michael Conway and Mark Ricci, eds. *The Films of Charlie Chaplin.* NY: Bonanza Books, 1965.

Miller, Delbert C. and William H. Form. *Industrial Sociology: The Sociology of Work Organizations.* NY: Harper & Row, 2nd ed., 1964.

Nam, Charles B. and Mary G. Powers. *The Socioeconomic Approach To Status Measurement: With a Guide to Occupational and Socioeconomic Status Scores.* Houston, TX: Cap and Gown Press, 1983.

Owens, Thelma. *Love, Honor and Hang On.* Pasadena, CA: Ward Ritchie Press, 1976.

Pavalko, Ronald M. *Sociology of Occupations and Professions.* Itaska, IL: Peacock, 1971.

Peter, Laurence F. and Raymond Hull. *The Peter Principle.* NY: Morrow, 1969.

Saunders, Conrad. *Social Stigma of Occupations: The Lower Grade Worker in Service Organizations.* Westmead, England: Gower Publ., 1981.

Smelser, Neil J., ed. *Occupations and the Social Structure.* Englewood Cliffs, NJ: Prentice-Hall, 1969.

Taylor, Lee. *Occupational Sociology.* NY: Oxford Univ. Press, 1968.

Terkel, Studs. *Working: People Talk About What They Do All Day and How They Feel About What They Do.* NY: Random House, 1974.

Wilson, Everett. *Early America At Work: A Pictorial Guide to Our Vanishing Occupations.* NY: Barnes, 1963.

Yablonsky, Lewis. *Robopaths: People As Machines.* Indianapolis, IN: Bobbs-Merrill, 1972.

Chapter 17:

Family Humor

Introduction

Paradoxically, families that are alleged to be initiated and bonded by love, concern, affection, and compassion are also the same intimate groups that have at times and unprecedented numbers and proportions been the scenes of malaise, disillusion, abuse, and violence. Family humor represents, at best, attempts to defuse what might otherwise become a volatile situation that destroys not only relationships but also the very characters or personae participating in domestic dramas. Rhodes and Wilson (1981), marriage and family counselors, write knowingly about "surviving family life," and document the need to recognize that this most intimate bonding between the sexes and generations calls for an ability to make light of what might otherwise be a heavy burden.

It would be foolish to claim that humor alone can resolve the distress and the strains of familial living, but there is something to be gained when humor is recognized for its usefulness as a social lubricant, as a means to expose pretense and sham, as a device to seek social correction, and as an expression of social bonding so that persons may share laughter and life together as amicably as possible. Family humor then has considerable potential worth exploring.

The term family elicits different responses from different sociologists because they are aware of the social forces such as industrialization, urbanization, and modernization that have globally revolutionized family structures (Goode, 1963; Ackerman, 1972; Streib, 1973; Young, 1973; Neuhaus, 1974; Duberman, 1977; Hutter, 1981).

Furthermore, the macrochanges have led to microchanges in intimate life styles that differ from the traditional nuclear family (TNF) of husband, wife, and biological or adopted children, and extended family networks of consanguineous or affinity-related TNF's. Included among them are single parenthood, group marriage, open marriage, cohabitation without marriage, intimate networks, and communes or intentional communities (O'Neill, 1972; Constantine, 1973; Hall, 1979; Stein, 1981).

263

Thus when "family humor" is identified as the central concern of this chapter, sociologists would want to know to which family structure or form is reference being made. The answer has to be that family humor applies to both traditional and nontraditional patternings in which men and women seek to live together, in which males and females reproduce and socialize their young, in which various generations are supported through their life courses, and in which a variety of values are fostered. Contemporary sociologists generalize about the institution of "the family," but they acknowledge the tremendous varieties of familial life by also referring to "families" (see Koller, 1974; Reiss, 1980).

Perhaps one of the most significant sociological perspectives is the view that families are arenas in which personalities come into play. These personalities may be cooperative, congenial, complemental, and supportive, but they also may be clashing, maladaptive, disagreeable, and exploitive or somewhere in between these polarities. The presence or absence of humor in personality-mixes in families signals the state of their social health and whether or not familial relationships may be damaged seriously or beyond repair.

In this chapter the heavy responsibilities of families are observed to be carried out under sometimes trying conditions. Family humor counters these circumstances by its promotion of a "grin-and-bear-it" patina on the part of participants, just as we observed among military personnel forced to live together under trying conditions. Furthermore, the various family members or personae of family dramas themselves are targeted in family humor as butts of jokes or as foils whose statuses and roles readily lend themselves to awkward, absurd, or exaggerated interpretations. The chapter also identifies those professional comedians whose stock-in-trade is family humor. Finally, the chapter concludes with suggestions for research in family humor and for their potential contributions to family theory.

Tasks Imposed Upon Families

The basic need for family humor has its origins in the almost impossible tasks imposed upon families. In TNF units, husbands and wives are asked to fulfill each other's lives emotionally, economically, socially, and spiritually. This is a long-range plan that can be sabotaged or demoralized by a host of changing circumstances, most typically from external independent variables such as the state of the economy, the polity, or social mobility within social stratification systems. Depending upon reproductive controls, the couple must decide when and if they wish to become parents. When parenting comes by choice or by chance, the same dyad add to their functions the need to socialize children so that this new generation will fit into their respective societies and subsets. In addition, the familial members must take into account other unique individuals who are cast in the kinship networks as grandparents, uncles, aunts, and cousins. The family members may themselves play their roles as siblings, uncles, aunts, and cousins to still other individuals. A Pollyannish, optimistic, idyllic, an unrealistic expectation is that everyone will work together harmoniously and happily. A more realistic and objective view is that individuals will play their roles in their own unique styles driven by inner and outer forces often beyond their understanding or control. Such behavior is bound to clash or border on the intolerable at times unless interactions are kept under control. There is much good sense in the folklore that says that persons do not choose their relatives. They are "givens" in the matrix of family life, and it is in this context that humor may relieve the tensions that might otherwise develop.

Families have been compared to magnifying glasses. All the imperfections of humanity are seemingly larger because family members are so close to each other. Marriages and families represent the minimal social distance so that little things look big because perspective is lost. Furthermore, the closeness can lead to friction rather than to close cooperation and consideration. When family members rebel against circumstances that denigrate them, that they see as intolerable, there is more heat than light, and they lash out at each other or act out their frustrations. Family members may not be responsible for what bothers them, but they are the nearest available persons and so become vulnerable targets for aggression. An old refrain observed, "You always hurt the one you love, the one you shouldn't hurt at all." It may well be that persons outside families are really responsible for whatever angers an individual but these persons are relatively immune from attacks. One kicks the family dog, for instance, rather than his or her boss who has heaped some unfair burdens upon that person. One scolds his or her spouse over family budgets when the real problem originate in rising costs, profit-taking, in planned obsolescence of products, or other aspects of the economy or occupational system beyond their control or even understanding at the time. In short, families are "acted upon" rather than being independent units that can conduct their own affairs as they please.

What other tasks are families called upon to perform? They are called upon to take care of such creature comforts as housing, food, clothing, and health. Furthermore, they are enjoined to handle education, entertainment, rest, relaxation, and encouragment of talents of various family members. They are to procreate and rear their children so that they may fit into their society politically, economically, and morally. Families are asked to be both vocational and avocational guides. They must protect family members from all dangers such as crime and corruptions and steer them instead toward wholesome, positive, constructive behaviors. In short, families are asked to perform almost miracles with human beings and their relationships. That they do not always succeed in these assignments is evident in high rates of divorce, dissolution, desertion or other indices of marital and family distress.

Whenever families do achieve some modicum of success or satisfaction, a certain presence of humor is predictably a part of the pattern. The ability to laugh at human woes or human imperfections makes the difference between toleration and defeat. Humor offers another way to perceive phenomena, and those who draw upon it in familial situations are encouraged to go forward rather than be overwhelmed by extenuating circumstances. Robert Morley's clever book, *A Book of Worries*, (1979) offers readers a suggested list of worries for those who may have overlooked some. These worries frequently are the figments of imagination and anticipation of outcomes or possibilities, but they do not occur with the frequency with which persons conjure them up. With all their anxieties and strains, families are still survivable with appropriate and judicious dosages of therapeutic, life-sustaining humor.

The Personae of Family Humor

Who are the characters in family humor? Around whom does family humor tend to focus? These are the people who are called upon to play their parts in family life in some responsible manner, but who instead fall short of normative expectations. They respond not in terms of ideal sociocultural norms but in real, human, very recognizable ways. One of the responses to family humor is to say, "How true!" One recognizes in the misadventures of family members that the way things are supposed to be and the way they actually are may be two different entities.

The Harried Housewife-Mother

If one had to single out one domestic character as the most likely candidate for family humor, the harried housewife-mother is that persona. She is the main linchpin in TNF's that holds the rest of the family together. On her shoulders fall the numerous domestic chores needed to keep a household operating in as smooth a fashion as possible. It is she who transforms the income of her spouse into economic services. It is she who has had primary responsibilities in child-care. Where she resides constitutes "the home" or domicile. When volumes of *Who's Who* books are published, the absence of women's names or their minimal representation is due to the fact that they have invested heavily in their families and not as heavily in advancing their own personal work-related careers. This is, of course, rapidly changing as women reject the housewife-mother roles and join men in the work force. Whereas in past years there was little recording of unsung heroines who labored in behalf of their families, the *Who's Who* volumes are beginning to record the names of housewife-mothers who have expanded their participation in careers outside their homes. Such persons are thus recognized and rewarded, along with men, as contributors to the larger society.

What are the harried housewife-mother's services on behalf of her family? They include providing three or more meals a day; cleaning furniture, rugs, floors, utensils, clothing, storage areas, windows, and decorations from all dust, grime, or dirt; keeping everything in its rightful place so that clutter is avoided and items can be located when needed; purchasing and paying promptly for all goods and services; watching over the health and security of all family members from the family dog to the smallest baby; acting as hostess, chauffeur, companion, counselor, confidante, and social secretary; and serving as a help-mate and lover to her spouse. Many have noted that if she were financially compensated for each specialized service that she renders, her family could not afford her. Labor-saving devices were supposed to relieve her of some of the more odious and difficult tasks, but instead her hours-per-week have increased as she raises her standards in housekeeping. As humorists have observed, she is indeed married to "a house" and not necessarily to her husband. The terms *housewife* or *homemaker* are most apt. While some men have been willing to take on a larger share of household tasks, the term "house-husband" is a relatively new concept that is far from commonplace.

Women have, of course, rebelled or been "liberated" from their traditional statuses and roles. With much good humor, they retaliate with all sorts of reactions. Bumper stickers announce that "Housework rots the mind" or "A woman's place is in the House, and in the Senate." T-shirts carry messages such as "Born to shop" or "A woman's place is in the mall." Another device is signs or plaques that state, "You can't fire me — slaves are bought and sold" or "Equal Opportunity Kitchen." Cartoonists now show the ridiculous nature of the harried housewife-mother when they show her surrounded by a howling, demanding group of small children, the kitchen in disarray, and her husband telling her, "No wife of mine is going to work!"

Strong Wives and Weak Husbands

Publicly stereotyped as weak, dependent, and unable to deal with the demands of the world, many wives are the real pillars of strength, the powerful authority figure, the insightful leader in their families. Their husbands may command considerable respect and authority outside but inside their homes, unobserved in the privacy of their domiciles, husbands consult carefully with their wives about their personal affairs. Male domination was long alleged to include powers both outside and inside homes. Humorists have been among those who knew differently and have exposed that inconsistency and the mythology of powerful patriarchs in the midst of their family empires. Indeed there have always been strong wives and weak husbands and a certain degree of delight is found by raising consciousness about that reality.

Mothers-in-Law

A well-known persona in family humor is the stereotypical mother-in-law. She is pictured as constantly interfering, intruding upon the newly established nuclear family of her son or daughter. She does not abandon her "Momism" or "Super-Mom" posture but extends it to her adult children and to their spouses and their children. She holds herself as the senior authority on all domestic matters, a sort of a female Supreme Court who has the final decision as to how things shall be. She gives advice freely and expresses her preferences whether they are requested or not. This negative image of mothers-in-law is a powerful one. Evelyn Millis Duvall, more than thirty years ago (1954), took aim on mother-in-law jokes and demonstrated that there was a positive side to mothers-in-law that was well worth investigating.

Duvall's work notwithstanding, the negative image of mothers-in-law persists in family humor. One can still hear stories such as the one about a husband who meets a crony who asks where he has been. The husband enthusiastically replied, "I've just come back from a great trip. I took my mother-in-law to the airport!"

The Zany or Competent Servant

Collins (1985) pointed out that household servants are a relatively rare breed compared to their former prominence in middle as well as upper-class homes. Nevertheless, servants such as a maid, cook, butler, chauffeur, gardener, or handyman can still be found in families and become the source of much family humor.

The tradition of household help being a figure in family comedy dates back to Italian street theatre when an assistant to the main character was known as a *zanni,* a down-to-earth buffoon who delighted audiences by an ability to unmask his pompous master. In a sense the zany appealed to common men and women because he or she told the truth whereas others covered it up or were even unaware of what was the truth or heart of the matter.

Whatever humble service was rendered, the family servant performed competently, cleverly, and with considerable dispatch. In emergencies, the zany would save the day and would earn respect, appreciation, gratitude, and laughter from employers. Former characterizations of competent servants who drew laughter were Arthur Treacher's portrayal of a haughty butler in films, Zazu Pitts' performances as a maid, or the valet in *The Admirable Crichton* who would organize a hapless assembly of upper-class gentry when they were shipwrecked. In modern times, the maid in the television sit-com *The Jeffersons* brings the egomaniac Jefferson to confess his shortcomings, the handyman in Bob Newhart's New England inn TV-series evokes sympathetic amusement for his integrity, or the maid in *Maude* can match wits with her acid-tongued employer. By such personae, the superiority of persons in lowly statuses is not lost on audiences of the viewing public.

Mischievous Children

Still other personae of family humor are to be found in young children. These youngsters can get into mischief, particularly when unwatched or unattended, within sseconds. Still too young to be fully committed to the ways of society or aware of the consequences of their acts, children can innocently or not so innocently change a peaceful household into a war zone rather quickly. The Katzenjamer Kids was a popular comic-strip cartoon series of the past that portrayed the boisterous antics of children capable of absolute mayhem when they wanted their way. The *Our Gang* film comedies offered similar fare. In modern times, Keane's syndicated cartoon series *The Family Circus* frequently illustrates, with hyphenated trails, the circumvolutions or roundabout paths taken by children in carrying out simple tasks for parents. In *Dennis, The Menace,* the boy is constantly pestering his neighbor with his presence and eternal questioning. Dennis comes home one day to tell his mother that he has been told by the neighbor that he gives him great pleasure — when he goes away.

Weird Neighbors

Families, of course, do have neighbors who may or may not be similar to them in the way they conduct their own family affairs. At any rate, the idiosyncracies of nigh-dwellers make excellent foils in family life experiences, sometimes comically and sometimes sorely testing a family's patience.

In the halcyon days of radio comedy, Fred Allen used the people who lived in "Allen's Alley," and Jack Benny used his famous neighbors for humorous episodes. Dagwood and Blondie are constantly bothered by neighbors who borrow but never return household equipment. Bob Newhart's family has neighbors, three brothers, two with the same name and one who never speaks. Neighbors are frequently shown to be dropping in on a family at the most inconvenient times. In brief, the contrast between the way one family conducts its affairs and the way surrounding families conduct theirs is strikingly different and form the bases for much family humor.

The Senex Iratus

A *senex iratus* was the figure in ancient Roman comedy who was an old man who stood in the way of what other family members wanted to do. He would rave and rant to insist that he was the center of family authority, even though he was often ridiculous or absurd in his mental gyrations or in his mannerisms. In the play *Life With Father*, the *senex iratus* was the father who assumed that he was totally in charge of his family when in reality he is frequently undermined and outwitted by his artful wife and children when they conspire against him.

In the classic television series *All in the Family*, Archie Bunker plays the *senex iratus* to the hilt by objecting vociferously to the challenges to his authority by his daughter, his son-in-law, and even his eager-to-please wife. He blocks or stands in the way of other family members but to no avail except to show observers his unabashed loyalty to old-fashioned or anachronistic values. He is a fool but does not know it. Such a character may be funny to those unaffected by him. To those who have lived with a *senex iratus* or a man out of step with his times, such a personality type is far from funny. It is only by contemplating the *senex iratus* at a later date or by removing one's self from the family context that such a character can be appreciated for what he really is in terms of family humor.

Sibling Rivals

Children born of the same parents may enter into what sociologists call sibling rivalry. While they share much in common, they may compete with each other for their parents' love or adulation. Tom Smothers' lament that "Mom always liked you more than she liked me" to his brother Dick was a trademark of their comedy. Brothers and sisters are frequently said to engage in "cat and dog" fights over toys, clothing, or special privileges. It may take many years to mellow out so that they may learn that love can be shared and is not the exclusive province of one sibling over another. They have learned to distance themselves from their childish perspective and in later maturity laugh at how they "used to be."

The scars of invidious comparisons between and among siblings may remain a long time. The humor that emerges from such an interaction takes on a more bitter, aggressive, hostile style. One woman, for instance, refers to her sister as "Miss Goody Two Shoes" despite her considerable maturity as a middle-aged woman. She continues to remember how her sister was judged "to have never been wrong" while she herself was found filled with faults, blame, and guilt.

Miscellaneous Family Personae

The listing of personae above does not exhaust the possibilities for those who play their parts in family humor. The list is more suggestive than exhaustive. Certainly grandparents who refuse "to act their age," aunts and uncles with bizarre tastes, and cousins with a host of predilections in extended family networks cast a wider net of personae to become the characters in family humor.

The variety of other familial forms in contemporary settings adds other possibilities. For example, in blended families, those in which each spouse brings to a second marriage their children from their previous marriage, the complications of "her children," "his children," and later on "their children," those who are born out of the new union, confuse and befuddle those who are trying to understand the relationships. When adopted children speak of their mother, they distinguish between their "birth mother" and the "rearing mother." When cohabiting but unmarried heterosexual couples deal with outsiders, they have to know how to pose as "marrieds" to some but not to others. Or in group marriages in which numbers of men have sexual access to a number of women and all share their economic resources, there are still other possibilities for humor. A film, for example, showing just such a group marriage focused on one man who remained behind all the others as they kissed him goodbye, taking their children to schools and themselves to work. He heaves a sigh of relief at their departure, arranges himself comfortably in his chair, and looks the camera squarely in the eye and comments, "Here you see a perfectly contented man!"

Professional Family Humorists

A number of performers have made family humor their stock in trade. As a result they have earned the support and acclaim of those audiences that regard them as able to articulate family life conditions with which they are most familiar. Witty, entertaining, and often right on target with their portrayals of family life, these family humorists do not have to exaggerate too much to win the approval of those they wish to reach.

Erma Bombeck

Author, lecturer, and columnist Erma Bombeck is closely identified with family humor as the harried housewife-mother persona. Her booklength sallies whose titles indicate their humorous content include *Just Wait Till You Have Children Of Your Own!*, *I Lost Everything in the Post-Natal Depression*, *The Grass Is Always Greener Over the Septic Tank*, *If Life Is A Bowl of Cherries, What Am I Doing in the Pits?*, *Aunt Erma's Cope Book*, *How To Get From Monday to Friday in Twelve Days*, and *The Second Oldest Profession*. In *At Wit's End* (1967), she explains why she writes about the American housewife. She observed,

"Very frankly, I couldn't think of anyone in the world who rated a better press. On television she is depicted as a woman consumed by her own bad breath, rotten coffee, underarm perspiration, and irregularity. In slick magazines, she is forever being brought to task for not trying 'to look chi chi on her way to the labor room,' for not nibbling on her husband's ear by candlelight, and for not giving enough of those marvy little intimate dinner parties for thirty or so.

"In cartoons, she is a joke. In erudite groups, an exception. In the movies, the housewife is always the one with the dark hair and the no-bust. Songwriters virtually ignore her. She's the perennial bad driver, the traditional joiner, the target of men who visualize her in a pushbutton world."

"If she complains, she is neurotic. If she doesn't, she's stupid. If she stays at home with the children, she is a boring clod who is overprotective and will cling to her children till they are forty-eight years old. If she leaves home to work, she is selfish, ambitious, and her children will write dirty words in nice places."

As champion and spokeswoman for the harried housewife-mother, Erma Bombeck is a professional humorist with considerable insight into what has been identified in this chapter as "the impossible tasks" foisted upon "the little woman."

Sam Levenson

As a raconteur, author, educator, and loving family man, Sam Levenson devoted some forty years to reminding others of the importance of family life. With wit and charm, he instructed his audiences about real-life families in which caring lives are led. In personal correspondence dated May 25, 1979, Levenson wrote, "Throughout my work I have felt a philosophic need to 'prototype' rather than stereotype the people I write about. My father becomes a special private father at the same time that he was *a* father; *my* mother is *a* mother, etc., all finally epitomized in the universal idea of fatherhood, motherhood, etc. Each is placed in his or her personal environment which ultimately reflects the environment of humanity. We need to talk a lot about this."

One of the remarkable qualities of Levenson was his breaking of one of the cardinal rules of stand-up comedians - he would laugh heartily at his own jokes or descriptions. By doing so he demonstrated his close communion with his audiences. Like so many others, he drew his strength from his own family of eight brothers and sisters who contrasted sharply with those homes in which there was a paucity of love and an abundance of permissiveness and materialism. He was a product of his times, but above all, an individual who reflected some of the strengths of traditional nuclear families.

Phyllis Diller

Sam Levenson's laughing at his own humorous material was matched in the way Phyllis Diller would "break up" over her portrayal of a married woman who could do nothing right. Clutching a long-stemmed cigarette holder and wearing a coiffure that made her look like she just touched an electric circuit, she would violate every rule of good grooming in a fruitless effort to show sophistication. The persona she projected was the image of the inept housewife, the scatterbrain who missed the mark everytime she tried. Now and then to counterbalance her lack of self-esteem, she would refer to Fang, her husband, the long-suffering man who was not exactly a bargain in the marketplace of loving spouses.

She once pointed out to a receptive audience that her husband was recently arrested for fleeing from the scene of an accident - herself! She told another audience that everyone she meets tells her that she is really a beautiful person - *inside*. "Leave it to me," she moans in mock despair, "to be born inside out!" On another occasion she told fascinated listeners that she used to bury her ironing out in the backyard until she discovered the secret of their neighbor, Mrs. Clean, whose laundry was so much whiter than hers. She washes it! (Franklin, 1979).

Interestingly enough, Phyllis Diller has transformed her persona by going through a series of cosmetic surgeries. She has been regarded as one of the best spokeswomen for this type of surgery by her willingness to "go public" in contrast to the more usual stance of protecting personal privacies. She has become a role model for women who are willing and able to endure much in order to achieve both external and inner beauty in sociocultural terms.

Eddie Cantor

Still another professional who specialized in family humor was Eddie Cantor. He was a dominant force in American show business for some fifty years. Married to his beloved Ida, he was a devoted family man who parlayed his fathering of five daughters into decades of laughter. When Dr. Dafoe, the attending physician at the birth of the Dionne quintuplets, met Eddie, he quipped that Eddie was merely Papa Dionne "in slow motion!"

Perhaps Cantor's greatest talents were in his ability to move from celebrations of life to the sadness and tragedies of life and back again to laughter and exhuberance. One moment he would be rolling his eyes, clapping his hands, and prancing all over the stage and in another moment would move his audiences to tears or to sentimental contemplations (Cantor, 1959). This is the view of life as both tragic and comic and one in which people must learn to survive.

Danny Thomas

Like Cantor, Danny Thomas worked well in different media whether it was on stage, in films, radio, or television. His trademark was humor that family members of all ages could enjoy. His *Make Room for Daddy* television show, for example, was a pioneering "sit-com," situation comedy, in which a father is doing his best to keep his family safe, secure, and content.

Thomas rates as a family life specialist in still another way. He has set an example of an entertainer who does far more than entertain. Thomas has acted constructively and effectively when, at a low point in his career, he prayed for help from St. Jude, patron saint for those without hope, to find his place in life. He vowed to build a shrine to the helpless and the poor. True to his word, Thomas built the renowned St. Jude's Hospital for Children near Memphis, Tennessee, at a cost of some 2 million dollars. He set the pattern that others have followed in which laugh-makers and other entertainers have used their charisma and stage-presence to enlist the financial support for those who suffer from disease, poverty, famine, or economic hardships. Playing "benefits" for worthy causes has become one of the activities in which many celebrities participate.

Others

Again the list of humorists and performers who specialize in family-type humor is only suggestive and not exhaustive. One could point to others such as Lucille Ball who played the part of a scheming but hilarious wife in the long-running *I love Lucy* television series. One could also point to Bill Cosby who is known for his caricatures of children and for his renewed popularity in a TV series devoted to the fortunes of an upper middle-class black family. The list could include Danny Kaye who became a sort of world Pied Piper whose work in UNICEF was devoted to the needs of children everywhere.

Suffice to say that family humorists are a special breed who not only mirror some of the silliness, absurdities, and incongruities of families, but who offer meaningful messages in human endurance in coping with family systems. More than that, they encourage practical help for individuals caught up in the shortcomings of families to meet human needs.

Suggested Research and Theory in Family Humor

There was a time when family study was said to be a patchwork of topics loosely connected by a common thread of concern over family life. At present there are a number of theories, frameworks, or conceptual approaches from which to build a coherent body of sociological knowledge on the family (see Nye & Berardo, 1966; Burr, Hill, Nye & Reiss, 1979; and Lee, 1982). The concern herein is not to dwell on their nature, but to focus upon family humor and to suggest what might be done in terms of more research and theory building than has heretofore existed. As with any pioneering, exploratory effort, the studies would be tentative at the outset, but refinements will come as data bases are established to weave findings into some appropriate theoretical constructs and systems.

While family forms and functions have shifted rapidly away from traditional nuclear families (TNFs), much family humor still reflects TNFs. What is needed is more study on humor as it operates within the numerous alternatives or options to TNF. While it may well be that humor will still be used as a coping mechanism or as a survival technique, the newer intimate life styles may serve other purposes.

Furthermore, the personae of family humor should reflect the human experiments in familial living now ongoing. Are the characters in family humor any different from those in traditional nuclear families or extended families? Will mothering or fathering be different as greater usages are made of surrogate parents or fertilizations in vitro? Is family humor unchanged when people act together in quasi-families or in relationships "as if" they were somehow a family unit? What distinguishes the humor of single parents from those of parents with partners? What family humor applies to homosexual couples who consider themselves "married?" These are but a few of the research questions that might be answered.

Summary and Conclusions

Family humor no longer focuses strictly on traditional nuclear families (TNF). It needs to acknowledge that a wide variety of intimate life styles exist and to take them into account. It has started to do so with references to single-parent households, to communes, to living together without being married. But regardless of what forms families take, humor plays a part in the art and skills of two sexes and numerous generations living together in the close proximity of a shared household.

The need to be bonded, the need to deal effectively with serious and sobering dilemmas that come from familial living provides a case for humor to become an additional source of help. Humor can help people in families ease past each other with a minimal amount of pain and a maximal amount of pleasure. Families are arenas of clashing personalities. Through the mirror of humor, family participants can learn the arts of accommodation and cooperation. Professional family humorists are experts at showing how family humor works and helps families to survive. Most people, however, are not professionals in family-life humor. These are the amateurs in family humor who do draw upon their senses of humor, as expressed philosophically, "to go one day at a time."

STUDY QUESTIONS

1. What are the unique characteristics of families that make family humor distinctive from all other types of humor?

2. Is the assumption that, despite macro and microchanges in family life styles, family humor still provides the same services it did for traditional nuclear families a valid one?

3. What is meant by the "grin-and-bear-it" patina of family humor?

4. How does humor help families in the less-than-perfect performances of their responsibilities?

5. In what ways does family humor reduce tensions generated by close sexual and generational ties?

6. Can family humor provide a perspective that counters the tendency to magnify trivial events that can hamper or even destroy families?

7. How valid is the claim that humor might help defuse potentially abusive or violent behavior among family members?

8. What insights are to be gained by understanding the nature of those things that worry families?

9. Of all the personae in family humor, which are the most likely candidates to become butts of jokes or targets for derision?

10. What makes mothers-in-law rather than fathers-in-law, the most frequently mentioned personages in family humor?

11. What explains the humor of strong wives having weak husbands?

12. Does the competent family servant speak for himself/herself or for the larger society?

13.What explains the appeal of competent family servants when they comment openly about the families they serve?

14.Is humor concerning mischievous children instructive for parents?

15.What makes neighbors excellent foils in family humor?

16.Why has the senex iratus prototypes continued to appear over the centuries in family humor despite massive changes in the ways families conduct their affairs?

17.What humor could arise as men and women turn with increasing frequency to alternatives to traditional nuclear family life?

18.Is humor concerning sibling rivalry always aggressive or could it have other themes?

19.Have professional family humorists added or detracted from an understanding of family life?

20.Why do some professional humorists specialize in family humor and others do not?

21.What questions need to be answered through empiric studies about families and the way they are treated in humorous fashions?

22.Does structural-functionalism, conflict, control, exchange, and symbolic interaction theories explain family humor? If so, how?

Suggested Readings

Ackerman, Nathan, et al. Marriage: For and Against. NY: Hart, 1972.

Bombeck, Erma. At Wit's End. NY: Doubleday, 1965.

Burr, Wesley R., Reuben Hill, F. Ivan Nye and Ira L. Reiss, eds. Contemporary Theories About the Family. Vols. II & II. NY: Free Press, 1979.

Cantor, Eddie. The Way I See It. Englewood Cliffs, NJ: Prentice-Hall, 1959.

Collins, Randall. Sociology of Marriage and the Family: Gender, Love, and Property. Chicago: Nelson-Hall, 1985.

Constantine, Larry L. and Joan M. Group Marriage. NY: Macmillan, 1973.

Duberman, Lucille. Marriage and Other Alternatives. NY: Praeger, 2nd ed., 1977.

Duvall, Evelyn Millis. In-Laws, Pro and Con. NY: Association Press, 1954.

Franklin, Joe. Encyclopedia of Comedians. Seaucus, NJ: Citadel Press, 1979.

Goode, William J. World Revolution and Family Patterns. NY: Free Press, 1963.

Hall, Francine S. and Douglas T. The Two-Career Couple. Reading, MA: Addison-Wesley, 1979.

Hutter, Mark. The Changing Family: Comparative Perspectives. NY: Wiley & Sons, 1981.

Koller, Marvin R. Families: A Multigenerational Approach. NY: McGraw-Hill, 1974.

Lee, Gary R. Family Structure and Interaction: A Comparative Analysis. Minneapolis, MN: Univ. of Minnesota Press, 2nd ed., rev., 1982.

Levenson, Sam. Everything But Money. NY: Simon & Schuster, 1949.

Morley, Robert. Book of Worries. London: Weidenfeld & Nicolson, 1979.

Neuhaus, Robert and Ruby. Family Crises. Columbus, OH: Merrill, 1974.

Nye, F. Ivan and Felix M. Berardo. Emerging Conceptual Frameworks in Family Analysis. NY: Macmillan, 1966.

O'Neil, Nena and George. Open Marriage. NY: M. Evans, 1972.

Rhodes, Sonya and Josleen Wilson. Surviving Family Life. NY: Putnam's Sons, 1981.

Reiss, Ira L. Family Systems in America. NY: Holt, Rinehart & Winston, 3rd ed., 1980.

Stein, Peter J., ed. Single Life. NY: St. Martin's Press, 1981.

Streib, Gordon F., ed. The Changing Family: Adaptation and Diversity. Reading, MA: Addison-Wesley, 1973.

Young, Leontine. The Fractured Family. NY: McGraw-Hill, 1973.

Chapter 18:

Medical Humor

Medicine and humor would appear to be antipodes. At one extreme is the field of medicine, a profession that deals with disease, pain, suffering, illness, disability, and a host of morbid difficulties that threaten, interrupt, debilitate, undermine, and eventually destroy lives. At the other extreme is humor, that social product and social process that seeks out the joy in life, the fulfillment of living, the savoring of fun, laughter, and frivolity, all of which would be understandably the opposite to the morbidity of the medical world.

Yet there are associations and relationships between medicine and humor that merit serious consideration. This chapter will suggest a number of these associations, relationships, or interactive patterns that elicit, under certain circumstances, considerable humor. They will be found, for instance, in the various status and role ascriptions of medical personnel, particularly in connection with those they serve, the patients. The serious, sobering, social systems or settings in which medicine is administered on behalf of individual patients and public health have their lighter side and so carry with them opportunities in which humor will be manifested. In short, humor and medicine, while appearing to be polarities, do mix and bring into being phenomena that have considerable sociological significance.

Status and Role Ascriptions in Medical Humor

The position and behavior of persons involved in some way with the field of medicine set the stage for medical humor. Each status and role carry with them the potential for humor to emerge and to make itself felt.

Unquestionably medical doctors hold the highest status in the medical hierarchy. It is the physicians who have been carefully selected from a pool of high quality potential candidates who have endured years of demanding training and who have been qualified to diagnose and treat a tremendous, overwhelming array of diseases and disabilities afflicting humans. They are the carriers of awesome life and death information, and have been granted a relatively exclusive status by society to be the ultimate authorities in medical decisions. They select from among a wealth of data, know-how, and medical expertise the precise materials and techniques to be used to combat disease and to restore health. It is also a lucrative career, rewarding not only financially but also in prestige and esteem from those who serve with them and from those being served.

Such a posture, however, makes medical doctors vulnerable to humorous assaults. Humor, for example, is frequently used to attack pomposity, to bring down those who may hold too exalted a view of themselves and their offices. Humor will cut through sham, posing and pretense in order to reveal whatever may be closer to reality. Humor will expose the humanity or shortcomings of human beings. It will seek superiority of those who promote humor and will take careful aim on the inferiority of those they wish to bring down.

Medical humor then may be "pro-doctor," but it is more likely to be "anti-doctor" (see, e.g., Tushnet, 1971; Illich, 1976; Lambert, 1978; and Mendelsohn, 1979). Such diatribes reflect what many believe is closest to the true nature of humor itself, namely, to be hostile, aggressive, and negative about something that displeases in order to reach what humorists would call "a socially corrected order."

Three examples are selected to illustrate wherein physicians and their patients potentially are at odds and consequently become the foci for medical humor. One topic is the seemingly interminable and exorbitant amount of time patients spend waiting to see their physicians. The second subject refers to the doctor-patient relationship as either trusting, friendly and cooperative or possibly becoming one of distrust, dissatisfaction, or antagonism. The third example concerns the high costs of medical care and how these rising costs alienate patients or make it almost impossible to obtain needed medical treatment.

The silent suffering and the deep-seated frustrations of patients waiting their turn for medical attention is given voice in humor complaining about the problem of doctor-patient ratios. There are many in need of a physician's care and too few doctors to serve them as promptly and as efficiently as might be desired. As patients, they learn "patience" and often even tolerance.

"If time is money," declared one patient, "I propose to send my doctor a bill for all the hours I invested in waiting for him." "Do I have the *year* right?" asked another annoyed patient. Volumes could be filled with humorous examples of the prolonged waiting of patients. Sociologically, the inordinate amount of time spent waiting for the services of physicians may be explained by exchange theory. Simply put, an exchange takes place in terms of resources. Medical doctors have the medical resources that patients desire. Patients have their time and their money. Medical resources are scarce whereas time and money are relatively abundant. The cost in time for patients is exchanged for the limited time of medical doctors. There is no conspiracy to disregard the needs of patients, but on the other hand, patients have to delay gratification until they can receive the resources of the medical professionals. The satire of the waiting-room syndrome, nevertheless, reminds those who dispense medical resources that services should be rendered as speedily and as efficiently as possible.

The first instance of doctor-patient humor in terms of prolonged waiting is related to the second instance of the changing nature of the doctor -patient relationship. The older, more traditional view is one of compassion, humanitarianism, deep understanding on the part of physicians as to what their patients endure (see Pellegrino, 1979; Culver & Gert, 1982; and Kastenbaum, 1982). A newer perspective is that patients are "consumers" of medical services. Haug and Lavin (1983), for example, provide considerable evidence that there has been a "consumers' rebellion" directed against the authority of physicians. The formerly unchallenged view that medical doctors knew what was best for patients has given way to demands for more doctor-patient communication, for more dialogue, and for "informed consent" (see Lander, 1978; Barber, 1980; and Pendleton & Hasler, 1983).

Malpractice lawsuits have proliferated and physicians are distressed over the high costs of premiums to insure them against litigation. With every patient a potential litigant, doctors and patients are now involved in "antagonistic cooperation," an oxymoron or bit of wordplay that has signifiance for both. Medical humor in this vein is "directed laughter" against former assumptions that medical professionals are immune to error. The old saw that doctors used "to bury their mistakes" has lost much of its relevance.

Finally, there are the rising costs of medical care. Jokes about doctors wearing masks during surgery because they were "robbing" patients and did not want to be recognized have been around for a long time. Observing that the "real surgery" in operations consists of "separating patients from their money" is still another example of medical humor with this type of referent. "If patients are not ill before they see physicians, they will be when they see their bills" goes another punch line. Behind such humor is the hard truth that high quality medical care is very expensive to the patient, at least in the United States under its current system of medical economics. The advancement of sophisticated medical technologies and medical specializations is applauded, but they must also be funded from some source. Should patients in need of costly treatment be charged because they are the key beneficiaries? Or should there be a sharing of costs by spreading them over time to communities or to the larger society? Protest humor that takes as its target the rising costs of American medical care performs a practical function by signaling the need to correct socially the situation before it becomes intolerable (see Babbie, 1970; Jaco, 1972; McKeown, 1979; Glasser & Pelto, 1980; and West, 1984).

In the mass media there have been a remarkable number of presentations that purport to show the caring, conscientious, concerned medical doctors such as Dr. Kildare, Marcus Welby, Trapper John, and Quincy, M.E. While humor forms a part of these portrayals, few could match the prominent humor that marked the television program known as *M.A.S.H.* This series dealt with the officers, staff, and personnel in a military field hospital in Korea during that war that received wounded soldiers fresh from combat zones. The key scenes consisted of surgeons and nurses joking with each other during side-by-side operations under primitive conditions. In the midst of these life and death settings, the various doctors would wisecrack and make crude jokes to balance out the suffering, loneliness, and deaths they were forced to witness. Always in this humor was an undercurrent of hope, compassion, and conciliation among themselves and their patients. While still popular and rated well with competing TV programs, *M.A.S.H.* was brought to an end with each doctor maintaining a gallant dignity as he rode out of sight to a new assignment. To be sure, the series was fictitious, contrived, and sentimentally pro-doctor, but its humor juxtaposed pain and suffering with life and its fulfillment. *M.A.S.H.* earned a place in comic history using the survival thesis very well. It showed a facet of medical humor worth remembering.

Nurses

Sometimes called "the handmaidens" of medical doctors, albeit that males have entered their ranks and are often designated as "male nurses" to counteract the traditional feminine identity, nurses have been targeted for their share of humorous treatment. Nurses are invariably accused of using rusty or blunt needles, of being excessively slow in responding to a patient's bedside call, or of treating patients regardless of age as if they were helpless infants incapable of bathing, eating or relieving themselves.

Nursing and physicians interact in the same social milieu as do medical doctors and their patients. Traditionally the status and roles call for subordination of nurses to the superordinated physicians. Nurses carry out doctors' orders. It is their "hands on," nurturant, round-the-clock presence that is appreciated by grateful patients. However, when this rather idyllic and traditional pattern is disturbed, the stage is set again for hostile and negative humor. Nurses, for example, have challenged the authority of physicians by demanding a larger share of the consulting and decision -making aspects of patient care. Nurses may even become officious in demanding that certain routines be followed by patients. Like the doctors, nurses carry heavy workloads and schedules and cannot always be available precisely when patients have needs or make demands. Such circumstances are a far cry from the Florence Nightingale image that patients and doctors formerly held of the nursing profession. Anti-nurse humor emerges in this context just as anti-doctor humor emerges when people believe the exchanges are unfair or unbalanced. Nurses are cast as witches who do not sail around on brooms but who use twisted needled syringes or administer medications and cold instruments hard-heartedly. Exaggeration thus looms large in this form of medical humor. Nurses can do little about it except to defend themselves against "burnout." It is noteworthy that a national organization of nurses is called Nurses For Laughter with its motto of "Laughter can be hazardous to your illness."

Dentists

Doctors of Dental Surgery (D.D.S.'s) are specialized physicians who concentrate on the healthy or unhealthy state of patients' teeth. Humorists refer to them sometimes as doctors who spend their professional lives "looking down in the mouth." They have been targeted for humor on a number of premises: allegations that dental procedures are relatively painless, the discomfort of submitting one's self to holding one's mouth wide open while instruments and other equipment are inserted to carry out necessary dental procedures, or the overall fear of dentists because of past painful experiences or reputations.

Dentists, of course, are prepared to administer anesthetics of various kinds and dosages. The reduction of anxiety aids both patients and dentists and whatever gets the job done is welcomed. Humor helps along these lines when judiciously applied. More than likely, humor serves as a means to reduce tensions preceeding dental work and as an expression of welcome relief once the tasks are accomplished. Considerable dental humor portrays patients as submitting themselves to indignities of various sorts, in a sense martyrs, while dentists are stereotyped as unaware and unconcerned about the feeling-states of their patients. Dentists, however, are far more aware than their patients often credit them, and they can defend themselves with the "shield" of humor. For example, dentists are humorously pictured as stuffing their patients' mouths with ten different metallic instruments together with untold quantities of cotton wadding and then regaling them with a prolonged and erudite discourse on topical issues of the day. Their patients are effectively denied immediate responses, or may be asked for more elaborate answers than the muffled, unintelligible responses.

A pro-patient, anti-dentist example of humor cites the case of a dentist who pulled the wrong tooth. "Don't worry," says the dentist, "I'm coming to it!" A pro-dentist, anti-patient example tells about a young lady who was very hesitant about getting into the dental chair. She admitted that her tooth hurt badly and she wanted relief but, on the other hand, she could think of other things she'd rather do. She told the dentist, "Your know, Doctor, I'd almost rather have a baby than go through with this." The dentist is then alleged to have calmly replied, "Make up your mind, please. How do you wish me to adjust this chair?"

In whatever specific context, the dentist-patient relationship is a mini-drama of pain versus pleasure and both participants find comfort and refuge in the humor to deal with it.

Psychiatrists

Medical doctors with special expertise in the relationships between body, mind, and emotions attract a large share of special humorous attention. The mental gymnastics involved have long fascinated those interested in the intellect or the workings of human minds. Schizophrenia and delusions have particularly been popularized to provide a broad social base upon which psychiatric humor can build. One example involves the understanding that conventional language is a symbolic system and that one has to dig deeper to find appropriate referents: Two psychiatrists greet each other in a hospital corridor by saying, "Good morning." Both, however, are also shown coming away from that brief greeting muttering to themselves, "Now I wonder what he meant by that?" A similar variation on the theme of hidden meanings and psychiatric subterfuge is the story of two psychiatrists who meet on the street and one says to the other, "You're fine. How am I?"

The removal from social reality is featured in much psychiatric humor. It is especially amusing when transference is alleged to have occurred between a delusional patient and the psychiatrist. There is the tale of a patient who tells a psychiatrist that his troubles stem from the fact that he prefers bow ties to long ties. The psychiatrist tells him not to worry, "Why, many people prefer bow ties to long ties and that includes me." The patient brightens up at this remark and replies, "Oh good! How do you like yours, fried or boiled?"

Humor That Focuses on Patients

Medical doctors, dentists, nurses, psychiatrists, and other medical professionals do indeed occupy the central attention in medical humor. As has been shown, a considerable portion of this humor deals with their relationship to their patients, clients, "consumers," or the general public. Patients, clients or consumers of medical services, however, come in for a fair share of humorous treatment in their own right.

Hypochondriacal Patients

Hypochondriacs are individuals who are troubled by various conditions that do not easily yield to medical skills. In the past, when efforts to treat such patients failed, the tendency was to dismiss them as persons who did not need medical attention and who were beyond the services of medical

professionals. The more modern approach is to accept them as persons
sorely in need of compassion and sympathy and that physicians may be of
help in providing what society or social "others" have not provided in
terms of individual support. It has long been observed that many patients
visit physicians in search of persons who will simply listen to what they
have to say or how they feel who also may not be truly hypochondriacal.
Moliere used this as a basis for his comedy *The Doctor In Spite of Himself.*
In this satire Moliere showed how patients recovered from ailments regardless of the ministrations of their physicians. In his play, a woodcutter succeeds in a case that has baffled medical doctors. The woodcutter correctly
diagnoses the condition of a lovesick woman who cannot speak because she
has been denied the company of the man she loves by the *senex iratus,* her
domineering father. When the woodcutter brings the lovers together, the
lady's speech is miraculously restored and of course, the woodcutter is
hailed as a medical genius. The close relationships between social and
physical health are thus highlighted in Moliere's comedy. For those who
continue to dismiss the hypochondriacal patient or the patient they suspect
of this malady, one humorist noted the case of a patient who apparently got
some satisfaction by having carved on his tombstone, "See, I told you I was
sick!"

The fine line between needing and seeking attention is not always easy
to discern. The patients who enjoy the attention of others are the comical
types. There are, of course, those who are not-so-comical types and these
do merit the sympathetic support and concern of others. Which category
fits the late President Lyndon Johnson is a matter of interpretation.
Johnson once impulsively displayed his scars from gallbladder surgery to
press reporters. It was an altogether human action and reflected Johnson's
down-to-earth nature, but the incident was humorously assaulted because
many felt that the dignity of his high political office required more
restraint.

It is well within the experience of many people to know patients will provide the most intimate details of their ailments and how they were medically treated if they encounter any person who displays the slightest interest
in their experiences. Apparently, like many war veterans who endured life
-threatening episodes of combat and who thoroughly enjoy reminiscing
about their battle scars to others, so too are there patients willing to provide more information about their medical histories than even their closest
friends may want to hear, and thereby becomes the source of much humor.

Mental Patients

Mental illness is, of course, no laughing matter like other forms of illness. Mental patients, however, are frequent subjects of humorous treatment, perhaps because their lack of touch with reality strikes some people

as funny. At one time it was believed that the bizarre behavior of such patients was due to the various phases of the moon. Thus "lunacy" and
"lunatic" seemed to aptly describe and explain their actions. A popular
film cartoon series was called "Looney Tunes," and some may refer to
psychiatric facilities as "looney bins," essentially holding pens for the
mentally disturbed. Other imagery, regarded as harmless joking by some,
is to refer to mental patients as "not playing with a full deck of cards,"
"not having all their oars in the water," "not having all their marbles,"
"operating with bats in the belfry," or "off their rockers."

Sociologists are fond of pointing out that social facts do not speak for
themselves but are to be interpreted. Social psychologists say something
similar when they observe that what is more important than an individual's
social situation is that individual's *perception* of the situation. What is
calmly accepted by one person may make another individual highly disturbed. This fairly common principle, however, when applied to the
strange perceptions of the mentally disturbed is judged to be absurd,
amusing, or hilarious. Such is behind the humor of a story that tells of a
group being escorted around the facilities of a mental hospital. When the
tour was over, the group thanked their guide for his excellent services.
They remarked how normal the patients appeared to be. The guide promptly corrected them, "They are all here for good reasons, but some are more
out of touch with reality than others. Take that fellow over there. He thinks
he's Napolean Bonaparte!" Then the guide came closer to his audience
and confidentially whispered, "Of course, he isn't Napoleon Bonaparte. I
am!"

Subintentional Patients

Hypochondriacal and mentally ill patients appear frequently in various
forms of medical humor. But subintentional patients constitute a third category of patients that requires a bit more analyses than has heretofore
been given. Subintentional patients occupy the middle ground somewhere
between intentional and unintentional patients. Intentional patients are
those who deliberately set about to harm themselves and when they
succeed, they require medical attention. Would-be suicides may bungle
their attempts and the results may call for years of therapy. Unintentional
patients are those who become the victims of accidents, injurious crimes,
or some unwanted disease. Like the intentional patients, they too must be
medically treated over prolonged periods. Subintentional patients are
those who participate in bringing about their own difficulties but who did
not really believe that anything unhealthy or harmful would eventuate from
their actions. In a sense they victimize themselves by underestimating the
dangers to which they are subjugating themselves. A number of these self-
inflicted damages come from such self-indulgent habits as smoking, drinking, overeating, or relying upon drugs to solve their problems. Jokes

abound about smoking, being drunk, being obese, or being "stoned." They make light of a serious matter and add to the rationalizations used to excuse poor health habits or practices. For example, subintentional patients respond to the warnings on cigarette packs that "the Surgeon General of the United States has determined that this product may be hazardous to your health" with questionable humor of their own by saying, "What else is new? Food is fattening, drinking helps drown sorrows, and living leads to death! I enjoy what I'm doing and I intend to keep on doing it. It's my life and I'll live it any way I please!"

Overeating is in the same category as the self-indulgent smoking habit. Eating is, of course, a generally pleasurable act. Eating is also a social act and many often eat more than they really need when in the company of others. The fat person is often stereotyped as being "jolly," but people are also becoming more aware that obesity is a life-shortening condition. Dieting or eating sensibly is a recommended way to avoid the dangers of being overweight. This too becomes the substantive topic of further joking or more humor. In response to those who caution persons to watch what they eat, overeaters say they do exactly as they have been told — they "watch what they eat" and then they eat it! A company specializing in sight gags, for example, offers dieters a spoon with a large hole in it, a knife with three-fourths of the blade missing, and a fork with all the tines missing. Another entrepreneur makes signs to be strategically placed on refrigerator doors such as one in the form of a pig that reads, "One pig in a household is enough." A comic takes another stance by admitting that exercise will take off unwanted pounds and so recommends his "pushaway exercise." He explains that the exercise he has in mind is "to push-away-from-the-table" as often as possible.

The stumbling, fumbling, fuzzy-minded, unsteady drunk comes in for a lion's share of humor dealing with subintentional patients. Indeed some comics make drunken behavior a major part of their act to convince audiences that they are inebriated and so are to be excused for their slurred speech, lack of coordination, and their violations of norms. It is a pose that does bring laughter to certain audiences, particularly those who regard themselves as "social drinkers" fully in control of their alcohol intake, see themselves as superior to drunks, and "know better" than to let alcohol dominmor in that it may be funny to some but it exacts serious penalties in damaging the lives of too many people to be humorous to others.

Hospital Humor

Hospitals are major settings for the delivery of medical care and thus play a significant role in the medical world. Most physicians are affiliated in one way or another with hospitals in order to practice medicine. But in what ways do hospitals lend themselves to the generation of humor?

Dependent Patients

One source is the need to maximize efficiency in handling large numbers of patients in terms of their diagnostic needs. Patients must be identified, admitted, tagged, and entered into hospital regimens in order to make the system work. The "good" patient is the cooperative, docile, dependent, passive, "patient" patient who submits his or her self to hospital care. There are schedules to meet in terms of feeding, cleaning up, visiting hours, diagnostic tests, periodic medications, surgery, or special therapies. The patient is expected to go along with stated and unstated, clear and vague rules or to be labeled the "bad" patient who fails or refuses to cooperate. There is little room for individuation but, instead, maximum effort to "take care" of the medical problem. In such a processing of medical cases, humor emerges. It rebels against the dehumanizing procedures that treats patients as so many "-ectomies" or as patients whose personal identities have been lost in the medico/administrative pigeonholes of diagnostic categories. Such humor ridicules the notion that patients are "a field of concentration" calling for medical expertise, but tries to remind everyone that patients are whole persons in need of maintaining their unique individuality and their personal dignity.

Hospital Gowns

Humorists can select among a host of devices those items that symbolize the dependence and the submission of hospital patients to medical treattients in traction, hospital beds that change shapes depending upon which gears or buttons are touched, or enormous sized hypodermic needles are among the targets that help but also disconcert those who endure them. Hospital gowns are particularly chosen as objects of laughter. It is true that some hospitals mercifully excuse patients from the requirement to wear the special hospital gowns and allow patients the option of wearing their own nightgowns, pajamas, and robes. On the other hand, when it serves the hospitals' needs better, patients are issued hospital gowns with characteristics designed to facilitate medical procedures than to provide comfort.

These gowns are typically white, starched by overzealous laundry workers, and styled in such a manner that covers one's front but neglects any assaults from the rear. Hospital gowns allow nurses, doctors, aides, and sundry attendants to have easy access to patients' bodies, but such garb plays havoc with norms of modesty, privacy, and decorum. Symbolic of the surrender of the self to whatever esoteric actions are required medically, hospital gowns come in for their fair share of medical and hospital humor.

Hospital Roommates

Humorists have also delighted in pointing out "the shared hospital room syndrome." These are the "semi-private" room accommodations or the "wards" that gather together patients with similar difficulties but who may have little else in common. Fortune may smile upon patients and they may well have congenial, cooperative, and accommodating roommates. Unfortunately in a number of cases, chances are that roommates may be more bothersome than the problem requiring hospitalization in the first place. Talkativeness, over-curiosity about one's life, or other inconsiderate conduct are among their obnoxious qualities that provide typical sources of hospital patient humor.

Hospital Visitors

Hospital visitors, like roommates, are another specific target for satirical humor. They are usually welcomed and are allegedly in hospitals to express concern, sympathy, and support and even to speed recoveries. Again, from a humorous perspective, there are negative as well as positive attributes of certain hospital visitors. They may sometimes "get-in-the-way" of recovery or cause more troubles by their very presence. Some will recite, for example, how well family members or fellow workers are getting along *without* the patients. Others will completely ignore patients' problems and use their visit to unburden themselves of their own problems. Satirists seize upon such circumstances and concoct ways and means to retaliate. They offer, for instance, "the art of being tactful, namely, to make people feel at home when you really wish they were"; there is need to tell people "Do come again when you can't stay so long" or to display a sign which reads, "Do not disturb. I am disturbed already."

Maternity Wards

Finally there is one so-called happy section of hospitals and that consists of the maternity wards or the suite of rooms reserved for bringing new life into the world. Whereas other patients may suffer the painful removal and repair of organs or the loss of life itself, maternity patients are usually hospitalized for more joyous occasions for such "blessed events." Indeed a common joke is the question: "Is giving birth to a baby really a 'disease'?"

Summary and Conclusions

Medical humor brings together antithetical ideas of pain and pleasure, of life and death, of illness and disease with well-being, health, and restoration of the sick back to society. It is aware of the serious, sobering side of medical care, but it is also aware of the need to find relief, hope, and changes of a positive nature.

Medical and hospital humor pays close attention to the status and role ascriptions of medical personnel and particularly to how these social ranks and behavioral patterns apply to those being served, the patients. Furthermore, medical humor looks to health care delivery systems or settings with a view to modify or correct them into providing such care in a more humane, personal way.

Medical humor may well be pro-doctor, but it is more likely to be anti-doctor because hostility and aggression are well-suited to joking frameworks or directed laughter against selected targets. Nurses, dentists, and psychiatrists are frequently singled out for special treatment in medical humor because of their singular qualities, but in the end, it is the patients representing the need for society to have persons maintained at their fullest vigor and potential who receive the lion's share of humorous attention.

Hypochondriacal, mental, and subintentional patients are specific types of patients around which a considerable amount of medical and hospital humor has developed. As dependent patients who must conform to hospital regimens in order to make these systems work, humor allows them to assert their personal humanity and to insist on constant vigil to protect their dignity.

STUDY QUESTIONS

1. Is humor out of place or a discordant idea in the field of medicine?

2. In what ways should medical humor be welcomed and in what ways should it be rejected?

3. Why are medical doctors vis-a-vis their patients given such prominence in medical humor?

4. Do you agree that considerable amounts of humor are more "anti-doctor" than they are "pro-doctor"?

5. Is there room in medical humor to appreciate the strains, tensions, and heavy investments of time, energy, money, caring, intelligence, and stamina that medical personnel endure?

6. What ends are served by medical humor?

7. Is the exchange between doctors and their patients fairly presented in medical humor?

8. What explains the past popularity of the television comedy series *M.A.S.H.*?

9. Does medical humor dwell unduly upon stereotypes or does it make certain that whole-truths are balanced against half-truths?

10. What characteristics of the nursing profession are selected for comic treatment and why are these qualities selected for humor rather than others?

11. What constitutes "the funny side" of dentistry? What would a study of the in-group behavior of dentists reveal in terms of their usages of humor?

12. Why have psychiatrists been marked as targets for humor?

13. Does medical humor pay much attention to the responsibilities of patients to maintain their own health?

14. Does medical humor portray patients as foolish?

15. To what extent are social variables cited in medical humor as causative factors in poor health habits?

16. Is medical humor accurate in noting the dependency of hospital patients?

17. What, if any , is "a happy side" of hospitals?

18. What explains why medical humor does deal, in part, with mental health?

19. Can medical humor assist in distinguishing between reality and the perceptions of reality?

20. Does medical humor provide substance for the survival thesis or not?

21. Who or what is supported and who or what is attacked in medical humor?

Suggested Readings

Babbie, Earl R. *Science and Morality in Medicine: A Survey of Medical Educators.* Berkeley, CA: Univ. of California Press, 1970.

Barber, Bernard. *Informed Consent in Medical Therapy and Research.* New Brunswick, NJ: Rutgers Univ. Press, 1980.

Culver, Charles M. and Bernard Gert. *Philosophy in Medicine: Conceptual and Ethical Issues in Medicine and Psychiatry.* NY: Oxford Univ. Press, 1982.

Glasser, Morton and Gretel H. Pelto. *The Medical Merry-Go-Round: A Plea for Reasonable Medicine.* Pleasantville, NY: Redgrave Publ., 1980.

Haug, Marie and Bebe Lavin. *Consumerism in Medicine: Challenging Physician Authority.* Beverly Hills, CA: Sage, 1983.

Illich, Ivan. *Medical Nemesis.* NY: Pantheon Press, 1976.

Jaco, E. Gartly, ed. *Patients, Physicians and Illness: Sourcebook in Behavioral Science and Health.* NY: Free Press, 2nd ed., 1972 ; 3rd ed., 1979.

Kastenbaum, Victor, ed. *The Humanity of the Ill: Phenomenological Perspectives.* Knoxville: TN: Univ. of Tennessee Press, 1982.

Lambert, Edward C. *Modern Medical Mistakes.* Bloomington, IN: Indiana Univ. Press, 1978.

Lander, Louise. *Defective Medicine: Risk, Anger, and the Malpractice Crisis.* NY: Farrar, Straus & Giroux, 1978.

McKeown, Thomas. *The Role of Medicine: Dream, Mirage, or Nemesis?* Princeton, NJ: Princeton Univ. Press, 1979.

Mendelsohn, Robert S. *Confessions of a Medical Heretic.* Chicago: Contemporary Books, 1979.

Pellegrino, Edmund D. *Humanism and the Physician.* Knoxville, TN: Univ. of Tennessee Press, 1979.

Pendleton, David and John Hasler, eds. *Doctor-Patient Communication.* NY: Academic Press, 1983.

Rosengren, William R. *Sociology of Medicine: Diversity, Conflict and Change.* NY: Harper & Row, 1980.

Tushnet, Leonard. *The Medicine Men.* NY: St. Martin's Press, 1971.

West, Candace. *Routine Complications: Troubles with Talk Between Doctors and Patients.* Bloomington, IN: Indiana Univ. Press, 1984.

Wolinsky, Frederick D. *The Sociology of Health: Principles, Professions, and Issues.* Boston: Little, Brown, 1980.

Chapter 19:

Sports Humor

Sports humor is embedded in a social matrix that has challenged the "sociological imagination," an ability to make connections between the "larger historical scene" and the "individual's inner life and external career" (Mills, 1959; see also Theberge and Donnelly, 1984). A single chapter cannot do justice to the broad sweep of sports history nor to a complete social psychological analysis that explains the relationships between sports and individualistic responses, but it is possible to select a few areas that are pertinent to sports humor itself.

These specific areas include an understanding of the origins and development of play, games, and sports, the elements involved in sport behavior, the purposes served by participation and observation of sports; and finally the emergence of humor in selected sports' settings.

Origins and Development of Play, Games, and Sports

Playfulness is a quality found in all higher social animals including *Homo sapiens* and gaming is held to be a refinement of play (see Laughlin, Jr and McManus in Pankin, 1982). Indeed, Huizinga (1949) proposed that wisdom or intelligence was not the central characteristic of human beings but rather playfulness and so coined the more apt *Homo ludens.*

Nixon (1984) offers some useful distinctions between play, recreation, games, and sport and yet sees them as a socio-cultural developmental continuum from high to low autonomy, expressiveness, spontaneity, and separation from daily life. Play is defined as "voluntary, nonutilitarian activity characterized by the freedom to innovate, spontaneity, and a lack of external regulation." Recreation is defined as "mostly voluntary activity that tends to be separated from the concerns of daily life and is aimed at refreshing the mind and/or body." Games are "relatively rule-bound and formalized activities that take on collective representations and are based on a combination of elements which include competition, skill, chance, strategy, physical exertion, and/or pretense." Sport is the refinement of

295

gaming which Nixon defines as "institutionalized competitive activity involving two or more opponents and stressing physical exertion by serious competitors who represent or are part of formally organized associations."

Thus, from sheer exhuberance, free expression, and nonutility there is increasing movement and development toward social organization, external regulation and constraint, and mounting seriousness, formalization, rationalization, bureaucratization, and focus upon instrumental tasks as seen in intercollegiate athletics, major league baseball, professional football, or Olympic competition. While sports like hockey, boxing, football, soccer, baseball, and basketball pit opposing individuals or teams against each other, there are rules by which to abide and designated authorities to enforce them for the protection of participants. It is ironic that sports violence is a major topic of concern in the sociological study of sports (see Dunning, 1971 and Goldstein, 1983). Not only the "players" may harm each other, but also those who observe them or identify with them as spectators. Huizinga's "playful species" have apparently at times shifted their concerns or values to individual, team, school, regional, or national loyalties that enable them to forget why games and sports are conducted in the first place. Unruly crowds or mobs have destroyed property and clashed with each other over their unabashed outrage or over their celebration of sporting outcomes.

Sport itself has a long, cross-cultural history (see Mandell, 1984 for a general but fascinating coverage; see also Rader, 1983 for a history of American sports.) Such histories suggest that some universal needs are being met and that certain common elements are operative.

Elements Common to Games and Sports

Roger Caillois (1962) suggested that there are four main elements, qualities, or factors at work in games and sports. These are identified as *agon, alea,* mimicry, and *ilinx.*

Agon is roughly translated as competition in which adversaries confront each other allegedly with equal chances to triumph, one over the other. Each sport or game tends to test one or more qualities such as speed, endurance, strength, skill, ingenuity, alertness, determination, or memory. By emphasizing equal opportunity, by stressing competitors who have no special advantage over others, by "fair play," winners are said to be clearly superior to losers in terms of their exploits during contests. But as Caillois was quick to acknowledge, equal chances to win are difficult to operationalize. There are special advantages in being permitted to make the first moves at the outset of a game, in having a better starting position on a circular track than others, in having the sun at one's back during certain plays, or in having the wind blow from a certain direction. By compensating for these unintended advantages or disadvantages, certain sports require that runners take turns in starting positions or in defending one side of a playing field or in the usage of special equipment. In horse racing, certain weights are added. In golfing, certain "handicap" points are added or subtracted.

What has been called "the competitive edge" presumes that prior to any contest there has been appropriate training, careful preparation, sustained attention to details, and a determination to do the very best of which one is capable. In the end, champions must depend upon their own abilities to excel and so prove beyond the shadow of a doubt that they are superior to all other competitors.

The presence of the second element, however, somewhat negates this proof of superiority and tremendous effort on the part of competitors. This element is *alea*, the Latin name for dice. Caillois employs it because he wishes to point out that there is always an element of pure chance in the playing of games and sports. These are the fortuitous circumstances, "the breaks" about which players and observers alike speak, when they know that things did not work out quite the way they were planned or anticipated. A slip of the foot, an unexpected collision with a fellow player, or being caught off-balance may make the difference between defeat or victory.

The third element in all play is *mimicry*, according to Caillois, by which he means the agreement to play out an illusion, in a sense, creating an imaginary milieu in which participants "make believe" that they are someone other than themselves and so, during the course of a game or sport, temporarily suspend their personalities in order to act according to the mandates of the game (Berger and Luckman 1967). This is the persona or the mask that players adopt while the sporting activity is in progress. Similar to actors or actresses, their uniforms or paraphernalia are costumes that help construct the illusion and give it substance.

Finally, there is the element of *ilinx*, derived from the Greek word for whirlpool. This is the pleasure found in subjecting one's self to a certain amount of disorientation or the possibility of losing control and yet emerging safely and in control in the end. Perhaps diving from heights, acrobatics or gymnastics, pole-vaulting, or controlling a race horse or fast racing car come closest to illustrating the presence of *ilinx* in sporting activities. Those who have witnessed the possibility of vertigo in winter sports such as tobogganing or ski-jumping can agree with Caillois' analysis. Caillois himself points to *ilinx* in the attraction of various rides in amusement parks such as roller coasters, Ferris wheels, water slides, or airplane swings. In each contraption, persons submit themselves to the possibility of danger, but having escaped it, they exalt in their triumph and rush to do it all over again. Survival, once again, manifests itself as a core reason for derived pleasure, satisfaction, or humor.

Purposes Served by Sports Participation or Observation

Sports humorists are fond of poking fun at the absurdity of chasing a small ball around a golf course, the dropping of balls through hoops, the driving of a puck into a net, or the carrying of a ball across a goal line, yet these sports generate tremendous enthusiasm among players and spectators alike and represent heavy investments in land, real estate, equipment, and travel. What ends are being served? What services or functions are being met?

Stevenson and Nixon (1972) suggest *social functions* of sport: (1) the socioemotional function, (2) socialization, (3) integration, (4) the political function, and (5) social mobility.

The Socioemotional Function

There are at least three different aspects that seem to cluster around the socioemotional function of sports. The first of these is the cathartic effect of sports to defuse tensions, aggressions, and frustrations. For both players and observers, joy, hate, sadness, or other emotions are expressed, directed, or ventilated in socially nonthreatening ways. There is pleasure to be obtained by managing tension, conflict, and frustrations. There is aesthetic pleasure for performers and spectators alike to skillful conduct. Elias and Dunning (1970) identify this function as "the search for excitement in unexciting societies." In an otherwise drab, dreary, boring, routinized everyday live, individuals can find sufficient excitement to make life tolerable.

A second aspect is the ability of sports to set up opportunities for community, comradery, belongingness, friendship, and companionship. That it may not always do so is evident in the intense rivalries, fan fanaticisms, or excesses of team loyalties. On the other hand, sports does bring people closer together or minimizes social distances when they might not have otherwise met or known each other.

The third aspect of the socioemotional function of sports refers to their ritualistic, religious, or 'magical' overtone. In sports events, there is a reaffirmation of a commitment to the existing social structure, the system of cultural beliefs, and their continued stability.

In sum, tension and conflict are managed by catharsis and aesthetics, community and comradeship are made possible, and there is reassurance that through ritualistic performances individuals and their society are on the correct paths of behavior.

Socialization

Sports are excellent socializing agents in the sense that they both reinforce and model the cultural mores and beliefs of host societies as well as uphold those personality attributes said to be the most desirable for societal members. For Western societies, for example, character-building in the form of learning leadership, initiative, cooperation, sportsmanship, self-control, respect for rules, achievement drive, and team loyalty are esteemed and validated through participation in sports. The most successful athletes are held up as models to emulate, and being among "the best" a society can produce; they have been frequently paid well for promoting ideas or for selling products and services.

Integration

The integrative function of sports refers to the close identification of team or club members not only with their respective groups but also with who and what that team or club represents in a larger sense. It includes recognition that sport organizations represent an entire city, a college, a regional enclave, or an entire nation. Players and fans alike, for example, proudly display trophies or wear symbols that leave no doubt as to their affiliation, connectedness, or belonging to a significant group or larger collectivity.

The Political Function

Sports become political instruments for the entities they represent. Victories for sports teams or superior performances by individuals demonstrate triumphant effectiveness of the larger collectivity or sponsorships.

The Olympic Games, for instance, backed by nationstates are supposedly designed to promote international peace and goodwill. Refusal to participate by nationstates in the Olympics is a political gesture to make clear the displeasure with certain policies and the lack of accord and accommodation among major political powers. The cathartic function of sports to defuse combativeness fails or falls short when the political function of sports becomes salient and dominant. Under such circumstances, sport opponents are not seen to be playing out an illusion or a ritual but are seen as "the real enemy" who must be defeated.

Social Mobility

Finally, outstanding ability in sports becomes the means for upward social mobility with all its attendant socioeconomic rewards. Those with aptitudes and talents in sporting activities are not only climbing upward on the sporting ladders but are using a major societal channel for upward social mobility within the social class structure.

Social mobility, however, may be negative as well as positive. Many individuals fall by the wayside and never succeed in sports. Others are excluded, set aside, or denied access. Race, sex, and age barriers have existed for decades in sports reflecting the nature of host societies. While these barriers have been breached as systems changed, the vision of an open-class society in which upward social mobility occurs on sheer merit continues to elude most societies.

Recapitulation in Terms of Sports Humor

The leitmotif that sports are embedded in a social matrix is basic to understanding and "getting at" sports humor itself. From basic playfulness found in all higher-order social creatures, human beings have developed recreations designed to refresh both minds and bodies, have made further refinements by rule-dominated games, and culminated in sports itself with elaborated organization, bureaucratic systemization, and accompanied infrastructures and suprastructures. Humor is found in this context because the incongruity of taking seriously that which is, in itself, nonserious is laid bare.

Furthermore, the elements of *agon, alea,* mimicry, and *ilinx,* competition, chance, pretense, and controlled imbalance, respectively, found in games and sports become the ingredients for humor because it exposes the degree to which humanity constructs elaborate social webs that entangle, befuddle, and bemuse.

Finally, the functions of sports in terms of socioemotional expression, socialization, integration, political usages, and social mobility become the substantive materials for humor that reveal the centrality of continuity and survival against all odds, real or imagined. When sports humor pokes fun at the millions of dollars invested in playing fields, arenas, swimming pools, golf courses, race tracks, or stadiums, at the dedication, preoccupation, and mesmerization of multitudes with sports, at the antics of adults playing childish games, and at the absurdity of exalting over such actions as dropping a ball into a net, carrying a football over a goal line, driving a puck into a net while on iceskates, or being able to reach a finish line before others, there is more sense than nonsense behind it. Just as there is a growing specialization in the sociology of sport, there is a sociology of humor that connects them because both are social products and social processes.

Humor in Selected Sports

Baseball

It is fairly easy to start an argument as to which sport is "*the* American sport" as far as popularity is concerned or as far as being "most typical" of American society. Many would say that football, basketball, or some other sport has edged baseball out of its past prominence. Nevertheless, baseball still rates very high in terms of American interests. Baseballmania culminating in the World Series is inescapable to the most casual observer of the

American scene. Further, baseball has been diffused to other societies, such as Japan, who have adopted it with even more fervor than many Americans.

Baseball rates very high when it comes to humor. There is something about players trying to hit balls out of reach of opponents, running bases, or making spectacular catches or moves that harkens back to the playfulness found in observers and participants alike. Gregory and Lewis (1983) capture this humorous *aura* when they describe major league baseball players as "adult men, acting like teenagers, playing at a child's game."

Childlike in acting out their aggressions, some baseball players have furiously attacked the nearest available inanimate object. Joe Garagiola and Martin Quigley (1980) agreed that baseball is "a funny game" and offered as proof such memorable performances of outrage as Pitcher Fred Hutchinson's feat of smashing 45 light bulbs in the Detroit runway after being ousted from a game or Solly Hemus and Ken Boyer of the St. Louis Cardinals who took out their spleen on some innocent protective helmets lined up ouside their dugout. Others have ripped out drinking fountains or broken bats into splinters to suggest that they were a trifle disturbed by some decision on the playing field. This is *agon* carried to extremes.

It was baseball that inspired the hilarious "Damn Yankees," a classic musical comedy in which a fan sells his soul to the Devil in order to win the World Series for his beloved baseball team.

Philip Roth (1973) chose to make baseball the centerpiece of his *The Great American Novel.* In it, Roth chronicled the exploits of the Ruper Mundys, a team, that plays all of its games away from home because the War Department appropriated its ball park for an embarkation camp near Port Puppert, New Jersey.

The Mundys are a wonderfully inept team that lost 120 out of the 154 games they played that season. Their roster included an unbelievable array of nontalented misfits such as a one-legged catcher, a one-armed right fielder, a fourteen-year old second baseman, a left fielder whose specialty consisted of crashing into outfield walls, a fifty-two-year old third baseman, and an eighteen-year old center fielder who is contracted to be at the bottom of the batting order in order to learn something about humility.

The character of "Nickname Damur," the fourteen-year old second baseman, suffers the indignity of not being given some nickname, an honor conferred upon all true baseball players. Such names as Hank, Dutch, Whitey, Ohio, Twinkletoes, Lightening, Flash, Dusty, Cappy, Rube, Goose, Gabby, and Kid, for example, are rejected. Damur is finally saddled with "Nickname" just to be merciful and to put an end to his humiliation. Garagiola confirms that nicknames are the hallmarks of baseball players. He himself was never called Joe, Joey, or even Mr. Garagiola. Instead, he was called Dago, Wop, Spaghettie Bender, Ravioli Wrestler, and other descriptive names, not so much to demean his national origin but rather to display the "Americanism" of red-blooded baseball players who poked fun at all nationalities.

Ethnicity was not the only target. Bald-headed players were called Skinhead, Onion Head, or Knob Head. Fat umpires were unceremoniously dubbed Whale Belly. Players wearing glasses might be called Captain Midnight, Cyclops, or Sealed Beam. Peewee Reese was called "The Champ" not because he was a great baseball player but because he was a marble champion as a child. Skoonj was Carl Furillo's nickname, derived from an Italian snail. Rube Walker was called "Coconut" because his head was alleged to resemble one. Gil Hodges was "Moony" because of his round face. Billy Herman was known as "Banjo Eyes." One look at his eyes confirmed the reason for the label.

Joshing baseball players is standard operating procedure, but the favorite targets are the baseball umpires. These lonely "men in blue" have the thankless task of applying rules before partisan crowds and fiercely competitive players. Even when photographs have proven them wrong, their decisions still stand (Kahn, 1953). Their eyesight, of course, is always in question. At one time only three umpires officiated at major league games. Gladys Gooding, organist for Ebbets Field in Brooklyn, once drew high approval from the fans when she greeted the moment the three umpires took the field with an enthusiastic playing of "Three Blind Mice." The razzing of the visual acuity of baseball umpires continues in the tradition of baseball. In a game between the San Diego Padres and the Atlanta Braves, the famed "Chicken Man" mascot delighted the crowd by holding a gigantic eye chart inches from the face of first base umpire Nick Colosi.

Team managers are the field generals of baseball but they, like everyone else, must defer to the infallibility of umpires or suffer the possible consequences of being ejected from the game. As a manager Billy Martin, for example, has acquired a reputation for a quickly angered, disgusted, dirt-kicking mentor when it comes to some decisions directed against his players. In a well-designed television commercial, Billy touts his pursuit of peace and tranquility in using his pipe tobacco while a part of the television screen shows an insert of his outrage over some umpire's call. Other managers made baseball history by their diplomacy in dealing with the omnipotent umpires. Frankie Frisch, when managing the Pittsburgh Pirates, once came out of his dugout holding an umbrella to suggest not too subtly that perhaps it was raining too hard to continue the game. Jimmy Dykes, then manager of the Chicago White Sox, once conspicuously placed a portable radio outside his dugout and then went into a mime act for the benefit of everyone to show his disbelief that the game being broadcast was the same game played out before his eyes.

Fans, of course, often disagree with managerial tactics as well as with umpires. Warren Giles, when managing the Cincinnati Reds, once received a telephone call at 3:30 a.m. asking if he really was the general manager of the Cincinnati Reds. When Giles affirmed that he was, the fan quietly responded, "Why?" (Carlson, 1940).

The players themselves are frequently first-rate comedians. Two of the most famous baseball comics in thc sport's history were Nick Altrock and Al Schact. Altrock took delight in imitating every move of the umpires. Schact would put on an act of actually "stealing" a base by picking it up and running off the field with it. Not to forget the great athletes of the day in other sports, the two would put on a boxing match in an improvised ring in midfield to give their version of the fights of Jack Dempsey against such opponents as George Carpentier, Luis Firpo, and Gene Tunney. Schact would pretend to be Gertrude Ederle swimming in the English Channel across the ballpark. Or the two of them would dress up as the reigning tennis queens, Helen Wills and Suzanne Lenglen, and hilariously swat th ball back and forth ending with a swoon at the net.

Not to be unfair to baseball itself, Schact would be called in from the bullpen to face the one and only Babe Ruth impersonated by Altrock. He would courageously warm up and then watch, just as courageously, while the pitched ball sailed, in his imagination and that of the crowd's, over the outfield fence (Spink et al., 1951).

Flaunting the rules, of course, would be particularly delightful to mass audiences. Herman "Germany" Schaefer, an earlier partner of Altrock, just for laughs would not only steal second base but when he had the opportunity, would steal back to first base. His "reverse steal" led to the need to specify in baseball regulations that players must run the bases only in one direction (Spink et al., 1951).

In the ancient tradition of court jesters who were kept as part of the entourage surrounding monarchs because of their unique physical appearances, so sports figures have relied heavily upon their own physical attributes to appeal to fans. Tremendously tall basketball players can use their natural heights to neatly "dunk" the ball through the hoop to insure its going in for the score. In boxing, memorable pugilists were ponderous "Two-Ton" Tony Galento and the giant Primo Canera. Such types have been called "body freaks," a term coined by Stanford Gregory, Jr. and Jerry M. Lewis, specialists in the sociology of sports. "Body Freaks" are naturals for humorous reactions because they not only go along with the rules of the game but can turn them to their advantage such as height in basketball or weight in boxing.

Max Patkin, a sideline coach in baseball, got a lot of mileage out of his scarecrow appearance. He happened to be six feet three inches tall and weighed only 165 pounds. Being double-jointed or, as the fans described it, "snake-hipped," and with a nose to rival that of Jimmy Durante, Patkin would stretch out his "turkey neck" to twist it in every direction and make unbelievable facial grimaces over whatever ensued during a baseball game. To add to these assets as a natural clown, he would wear a tent-sized uniform and a cap two sizes too large for his small head (Spink et al., 1951). The masking, illusion, or mimicry of sport was thus deliberately held up to ridicule.

In one of the most memorable incidents in the history of baseball humor, Bill Veeck, then owner of the St. Louis Browns, secretly contracted a Chicago midget, Eddie Gaedel, three feet seven inches tall, to come to bat at a crucial moment in a game against the Detroit Tigers. Needless to say, beside the uncontrolled laughter, Gaedel was walked on four straight pitches due to the opposing pitcher's understandable inability to keep the ball within the tiny strike zone. Gaedel was immediately replaced, of course, by a pinch-runner (Spink *et al.*, 1951). While certainly the existing rules were followed, a body freak had been used to play havoc with the assumption that baseball athletes are normally proportioned. And the veil of that illusion was lifted and shredded humorously. Veeck was fully aware of what he had done and showed his innovately entertaining skill through the power of exaggerated humor.

Baseball does lend itself to the practices of humor (for further examples see Russell, 1944; Lardner, 1947; Lomax & Stanley, 1950;, and Hollander, 1967). While these are from past eras, humor will undoubtedly continue in the future. Television's "Baseball Follies" is a current development in showing a humorous display of playing errors and "goofs." Not necesszarily a body-contact sport, baseball seems to have a gentility and an appeal to people of all ages and abilities. Most recent evidence comes from Florida where teams of eighty-year-old men sedately wear white shirts, bow ties, and caps, solemnly line up to sing the national anthem before each game, and then politely play baseball on a regular schedule. Playfulness, recreation, games, sports, and good humor are thus joined. We focused on the sport of baseball, a uniquely American game herein to develop the topic, while the reader can easily exploit one or more types of sport as a subject of such humor.

Football

In football, the raw fodder for humorous treatment is found in the rugged, bone-crushing, huge mountains of flesh and bones, carefully packaged or suited in protective gear, known as "the players." They tackle each other, use their bodies as battering rams to block potential tacklers, or physically assault opponents, usually within the established rules of the game. On the playing field, their job is to fool the opposing teams by clever plays, feints, or strategies (see Merchant, 1971). Off the field, however, they seek to be known as "gentle giants" who would not hurt a fly. One rugged football player sells bouquets of flowers on television commercials and another peddles cologne and encourages his image as a romantic ladies' man.

In what has to be the most lopsided scoring of a game in football history, Georgia Tech clobbered Cumberland by a score of 220 to 0. During that almost unbelievably one-sided game, a Cumberland quarterback had fumbled the ball and it bounced toward the left halfback. Three gigantic Georgia Tech monsters bore down on the poor fellow while he declined to have anything to do with the lost pigskin. "Pick it up," yelled the Cumberland quarterback. "Pick it up, my foot!" yelled back the halfback, "I didn't drop it!" (Maslin, 1974). Once more, survival manifests itself in humor.

Basketball

Height, body coordination, speed, and talent for endurance and teamplay constitute some of the factors that make great basketball players. It was Coach Larry Costello who once claimed that a person could cut seven feet four inches tall Kareem Abdul-Jabbar into two persons and he would still have a pair of All-American guards (Maslin, 1974).

Nate Archibold, only six feet tall, is still regarded as a midget in the professional ranks of basketball. It is reported that Archibold stood around the first two weeks of his career as a professional basketball player watching six feet ten inch professionals pluck rebounds off the roof. When his coach asked how he liked professional basketball, Nate is reputed to have replied, "I don't know, coach. The ball hasn't come down to me yet." (Maslin, 1974).

Other Sports

There are many other sports that provide the milieu for humor. Wrestling, golf, tennis, swimming, or track come to mind in this regard. It is well within the experience of participants of aficionadoes of such sports to recall, with renewed zest, those incidents and circumstances that incite them to laughter. Suffice to say, these sports can be sociologically analyzed for their distinctive brands of humor and will predictably affirm the factors and patterns just presented and discussed.

Summary and Conclusions

Sports humor is part and parcel of a social matrix that is well worth exploring. It can be appreciated and understood even better as sociologists exercise what C. Wright Mills called the "sociological imagination," an ability to make connections between the broad sweep of history and the external and internal lives of individuals.

In this chapter the universal and cross-cultural qualities of play, recreation, games and sport are basic variables in phenomena that eventuate in sports humor. By progressive restrictions on free play, high autonomy, expressiveness, spontaneity, and removal from the burdens of daily life, societies develop their recreational pursuits to re-create or refresh minds and bodies in order to cope with social responsibilities, further refine their recreations through games that are rule-bound and formalized, and finally bring into being sports characterized by low autonomy, conformity to game rules, competitive activity between serious opponents, emphasis upon physical skill and exertion, and symbolic representations of social collectivities.

Elements or factors operative in games and sport are *agon, alea,* mimicry, and *ilinx:* competition which makes painstaking efforts to assure that no unfair advantages are granted to participants as they test spscific qualities such as speed, endurance, strength, skill, agility, ingenuity, alertness, determination, or memory; chance which may negate superiorities, determination, and serious preparations; illusion or "making believe" that certain behaviors are essential; and the taking of controlled risks that disorient, temporarily threaten, or even harm or endanger life and limb.

Through sports, both individuals and their society are well served. Some five major functions can be delineated: (1) a socioemotional function wherei tension and conflict are managed or controlled by catharsis and aesthetics, community and comradeship made possible, and there can be reaffirmation that individuals and their respective societies are correct in following some appropriate, for them, cultural agenda; (2) socialization that reinforces and models mores and beliefs so that sports figures represent the epitome of their society; (3) integration in which participants and observers alike closely identify with social collectivities ranging from teams to nation-states; (4) a political function in which victory for teams or superior performances by athletes demonstrate and verify the strength, vitality, and promise of political sponsors; and (5) social mobility for those favored in society or its denial through exclusion or barriers for those disfavored.

Sports humor is found in these social contexts because it becomes the means by which persons can apply the full range of services that humor makes possible. In brief, sports can be understood as a microcosm of society because all the qualities that make up the larger society are mirrored in it. The "little errors in everything," the absurdity and incongruity of human machinations such as taking games and sports too seriously, and the desire to enjoy life to its fullest despite its burdens encourage humorous expressiveness. Ever mindful of the need to survive and laugh at its ability to create its own environment, humanity embraces humor whether at work or at playing games.

STUDY QUESTIONS

1. How does "the sociological imagination" apply to sports phenomena?

2. To what extent is humanity more playful than intelligent?

3. What is the progressive connection between play, recreation, games, and sport?

4. Why is sports characterized by low autonomy to such an extent that humor is used to counterbalance it?

5. How does humor point out the absurdity of taking games and sports too seriously?

6. What pleasure, fun, or satisfaction is derived from breaking sports rules?

7. Is sport a release from social productivity and social responsibility?

8. In what ways are sports capsulizations of society, subject to all of its problems, and consequently amenable to the social correction functions of humor?

9. What humor is found in the operation of chance in games and sports?

10. Is sports competition a serious or non-serious activity?

11. How do sports play out illusions?

12. How does humor reveal the illusions promoted through sports ?

13. What pleasure is to be found in techniques that threaten equilibrium or physical well-being?

14.Does sports humor help individuals throw off the stifling effects of imposed social constraints?

15.Why do players and spectators alike exalt over sports victories or personal sports triumphs?

16.Is it possible to ban or exclude humor from sports?

17.Is sports humor a legitimate area of study for sports sociologists?

18.Is one sport more likely to encourage humorous targeting than other sports?

19.Is professional wrestling an example of ludicrous illusion?

20. How are sports cathartic in effect?

21.Wherein does sports humor support or fail to support the thesis of human survival?

Suggested Readings

Ball, Donald W. and John W. Loy. *Sport and Social Order: Contributions to the Sociology of Sport.* Reading, MA: Addison-Wesley, 1975.

Ball, Donald W. "Failure in Sport," *American Sociological Review* v. 41 (August, 1976): 726-739.

Berger, Peter and Thomas Luckmann. *The Social Construction of Reality.* NY: Doubleday - Anchor, 1967.

Caillois, Roger. *Man, Play, and Games.* Chap. 3, publ. in London, 1962, Meyer Barash, transl., and reprinted in Eric Dunning, ed., *The Sociology of Sport.* London: Frank Cass, 1970.

Carlson, Stan W. *Baseball Banter.* Minneapolis, MN: 1940.

Garagiola, Joe and Martin Quigley. *Baseball Is A Funny Game.* Philadelphia: Lippincott, 1960.

Goldstein, Jeffrey H., ed. *Sports Violence.* NY: Springer-Verlag, 1983.

Gregory, Jr., Stanford and Jerry M. Lewis. Unpublished paper on Sports, Kent State Univ., Dept. of Sociology & Anthropology, 1983.

Hollander, Zander, ed. *Baseball Lingo.* NY: Norton, 1967.

Huizinga, Johann. *Homo Ludens: A Study of the Play Element in Culture.* London: Routledge & Kegan Paul, 1949.

Kahn, James M. *The Umpire Story.* NY: Putnam's Sons, 1953.

Lardner, John. *It Beats Working.* Philadelphia: Lippincott, 1947.

Laughlin, Jr., Charles D. and John McManus. "The Biopsychological Determinants of Play and Game," in Robert M. Pankin, ed., *Social Approaches to Sport.* East Brunswick, NJ: Assoc. of Univ. Presses, 1982.

Lomax, Stan and David Stanley, eds. *A Treasury of Baseball Humor.* NY: Lantern Press, 1950.

Mandell, Richard D. *Sport: A Cultural History.* NY: Columbia Univ. Press, 1984.

Maslin, Herman L. *The Funniest Moments in Sports.* NY: M. Evans, 1974.

Merchant, Larry. — *And Every Day You Take Another Bite.* NY: Doubleday, 1971.

Mills, C. Wright. *The Sociological Imagination.* NY: Oxford Univ. Press, 1959.

Nixon, Howard L. *Sport and the American Dream.* NY: Leisure Press, 1984.

Rader, Benjamin G. *American Sports: From the Age of Folk Games to the Age of Spectators.* Englewood Cliffs, NJ: Prentice-Hall, 1983.

Roth, Philip. *The Great American Novel.* NY: Holt, Rinehart & Winston, 1973.

Russell, Fred. *I'll Go Quietly.* Nashville, TN: McQuiddy Press, 1944.

Spink, J.G. Taylor, Fred Lieb, Les Bierderman and Bob Burnes. *Comedians of Baseball Down the Years.* St. Louis, MO: Charles C. Spink & Son, 1951.

Stevenson, Christopher L. and John E. Nixon. "A Conceptual Scheme of the Social Functions of Sport," in *Sportwissenschaft* 2 (1972): 119-132; reprinted in Andrew Yiannakis, Thomas D. McIntyre, Merrill J. Melnick and Dale P. Hart, eds., *Sports Sociology: Contemporary Themes.* Dubuque, IA: Kendall/Hunt, 2nd ed., 1976.

Theberge, Nancy and Peter Donnelly, eds. *Sport and the Sociological Imagination.* Fort Worth, TX: Texas Christian Univ. Press, 1984.

Ward, Gene and Dick Hyman. *Football Wit and Humor.* NY: Grosset & Dunlap, 1970.

PART IV:

Sociology and Humor

Having looked at humor in general by considering its significance, its treatment sociologically and social psychologically, its history, and its media, attention was paid to social variables and social structures or contexts that give humor its forms, its substance, its functions, and its specific objectives and purposes.

There remains two other facets to be considered. The first concerns those unique individuals who follow a professional career in the performance of humor, the comics or the comedians and comediennes. These are the persons or persona who stand center stage in the spotlight and captivate mass audiences or publics, sometimes only briefly and sometimes achieving legendary, mythical, and possibly even immortal status as purveyors of humor.

The second is offered in the epilogue that suggests the possibility of developing a specialized field of inquiry for sociologists and the discipline of sociology — a sociology of humor. While the topic provides closure for the text, it looks forward to the development of this sociological specialty much in keeping with general epistemology and the more specific sociology of knowledge and aesthetics.

Chapter 20:

The Social Role of Professional Humorists: Comedians and Comediennes

For humor to exist in human society, two fundamental categories of human activity must be actively in operation which are different in terms of personnel and the roles played, yet are mutually dependent upon each other. The first category comprises those persons who enjoy humor, use it in many ways knowingly or unknowingly, who serve as audiences, resonators and affirming publics, the key receptors and appreciators of humor to those who provide humor in its many ever-changing forms and to a great extent are dependent on the second category of providers of humor. The second category thus comprises those persons who create humor, disseminate it to those in the first category, the receptive audience in its many forms and receive positive rewards in many forms such as personal satisfaction in making another person laugh or smile or please and delight large audiences in an auditorium or theater or a vast largely unseen audience reached through some form of mass media, a radio or television network, a film, a recording, or a silent book, or a column syndicated for a newspaper or magazine.

A distinction worth noting is the difference between those who enjoy humor, employ it consciously or unconsciously in almost every aspect of their lives, who serve an audience, resonators and affirming publics, and those who create humor, perform it, make it their livelihood, and carve out a career for themselves that sometimes reaches legendary, mythical, and perhaps even immortal heights of achievement. The first category applies to almost everyone, to whole societies, to participants in specific socio-cultural systems, social institutions, or organizations because humor is omnipresent, ubiquitous, almost irrepressible on the basis of its usefulness to humanity in promoting its survival, its continuance, its ongoing needs. The second category, however, applies to a select category of persons who stand apart from others because they devote their lives to the promotion of humor, to use themselves as humor carriers, to earn their living by physical

313

action, words, deeds, or expressive symbolism in humor, and to personify a humorous perspective on an otherwise sad, sober, somber, serious, and sometimes tragic world. They win hearts and minds, capture attention, and earn approval among those socially attuned to their comedic messages.

This chapter does not offer a definitive, encyclopedic coverage of all professional comics. It is aware of the vast literature on professional comics and leaves that coverage to be explored by students of the historical record. It does, however, seek to probe certain aspects that appear to be paramount in explaining the nature of humor performers, namely, what factors, processes, or characteristics seem to persuade them to have enough hubris to stand out from the crowd and to enact humor in some form or other. Furthermore, it suggests there are facilitators or facilitating circumstances that operate to bring certain men and women into professional comic careers. It notes that certain styles, trademarks, or persona strike a responsive chord in various publics receptive to comic performers because of the prevailing modes of the times. It observes the appeal of interactive teams of professional comics. Finally, it selects a few professional comedians and comediennes to extract pertinent sociological strands that illustrate and help explain why these individuals are so meaningful (Cahn, 1970; Franklin, 1979; Allen, 1982).

Social Forces That Shape Professional Comic Careers

One of the most useful studies of professional comics was made by Seymour and Rhoda Fisher (1981). Their primary sources were intensive, often open-ended depth interviews with some forty professional comics. Their secondary sources were an additional analysis of forty biographies of professional comedians. Thus, about eighty past and present comedians and comediennes formed samples of the larger universe of professionals of the comedic field.

The Fishers used two projective psychological tests, the Rorschach Inkblot and Thematic Apperception Tests as well as statistical analyses to study what social forces were at work to attract these individuals into a professional comic career and to give the careers their distinctive features.

The hypothesis that many professional comics begin their lives in families of lower socioeconomic status finds support in the findings of the Fishers' study. The Fishers readily agree that such a beginning is not a prerequisite for comic talent because there are highly successful professionals whose origins are in both middle and higher socioeconomic strata. Proverty or near-poverty does not in itself create laughmakers with superb or unusual proficiencies in projecting humor. These conditions, however, are conducive seedbeds that have encouraged would-be comics to find relief from their circumstances and to distance themselves from their origins by being or acting funny. Out of impoverishment came enrichment for certain comic performers. Some never forgot their modest origins and gave generously of themselves on behalf of the less fortunate. Others embraced the wealth and fame that their careers brought them and, in a sense, never came back even psycho-socially to their former roots.

The Fishers found that there was considerable admiration for the fathers of these future professional comics, but this did not exclude room for a healthy respect for their mothers. The fathers were often quite funny themselves, but the moral codes were reinforced by the mothers who were eager to help their children mature and to take on adult responsibilities as soon as possible.

While some received considerable approval from their parents as they moved toward their comic careers, most encountered opposition or disapproval. One could surmise that some of the objection stemmed from familiarity with the difficulties of pursuing such a career successfully, from a perception that comic performers are not necessarily in high-status work, and from knowledge of the instability of such careers. Nevertheless, parents and relatives who were already actively involved in show business were facilitators for these budding comics. There was considerable modeling, reinforcement, and familiarity with comic performers as in the case of professional circus clowns, for instance, because almost half of their fathers were themselves established professional circus clowns.

In the discussions on humor media, it was observed that musical training, proficiency, and aptitude were powerful means to convey humor. Reference has already been made to the enhancement of such performers as Victor Borge, Jimmy Durante, Jack Benny, Morey Amsterdam, and Harpo Marx through musical talents. The same applies to Peter Schickele who parlayed his schooling in musicology into a comic career by violating its rules and mocking concert decorum. In each instance, music becomes the excuse or extrinsic device to get at the real objectives which are to grapple with life's problems through humor.

The Fishers also found that many professiional comedians surfaced early in their childhood through their escapades in neighborhoods, informal play, and in schools as "class clowns." Not particularly dedicated to formal education, these future professionals would garner approval and acceptance from their peers through humor. Bill Cosby, for example, had a reputation as a class clown, was a failure in most of his school work, but was also known to have a high native intelligence (Cohen, 1969). Cosby was adept at sports, at comical performances, and at developing his career. The former class clown has achieved a doctorate in education, an accomplishment of great personal pride to him and one that he proudly parades. Cosby's work with children and family life is well known, and while he is an accomplished master of comic performances, he often uses that talent to promote the importance of education to young students. Cosby confirms the finding of the Fishers' study that professional comics have a strong need for attention and acceptance. When people laughed at him, Cosby insightfully was aware that "that meant they liked me, they accepted me" and that was sufficient motivation to continue to hone his native talents.

Aside from this inner drive to be liked and accepted by others, the Fishers found that professional comics had a tremendous need to defend their "self-goodness." By presenting themselves as inept, inadequate, or foolish, the professional comics would win the sympathies of numerous people because tremendous numbers know what it means to be powerless, somewhat defenseless, or overwhelmed by conditions beyond their control. The comic performers are not innately "bad," but are "good" characters who are doing the best they can in their social milieu. Many in their audience see comics as they see themselves, protecting their personal integrity despite the machinations of others.

Perhaps one of the highest achievements to which a comic performer aspires is the creation of a persona, a believable and acceptable illusion or mask that represents human personality types. In a sense the comic gives life, form, and substance to intangible qualities such as humility, self-serving aggrandizement, or conformity to expectations. Charlie Chaplin's "Little Tramp," Jack Benny's "stingy employer," or Woody Allen's "Little Drip" are cases in point. Once established in audiences' minds, the characterizations could be made to fit whatever settings, times, or situations could be contrived.

Not all forces against which comics strived were sociogenic. Some were physical forces such as gravity. One does not ignore it, fight it, or destroy it. One adapts to it and so preserves life. Harold Lloyd, for example, tested out a number of persona before he fixed upon what he called the "glasses character" which was a normally dressed young man who wore a pair of over-sized horn-rimmed glasses "which gave him the slightly owlish appearance of an innocent-minded, guileless young fellow" (Schickel, 1974). When things began to happen to such a persona, particularly when confronted with the pull of gravity from great heights. Lloyd was unforgettable, for instance, in the film "Safety Last," a film that showed the desperate efforts of his persona to keep himself from falling off the hands of a department store's huge clock on the face of a twelve-story building. The same principle was at work in Laurel and Hardy's roles as piano movers or in Chaplin's "The Gold Rush." Laurel and Hardy try valiantly to move a piano up a long flight of stairs on a hillside only to have it escape their clutches many times and end up at the bottom of the hill. Chaplin's Little Tramp fights hard to keep his balance while a wooden shack totters perilously over a steep precipice, shifting back and forth until in the end he manages to get himself on to firm ground just before the shack crashed to the depths below. These actions of feeling small, of falling down, or of being taken in by some unyielding, unforgiving physical force are comedic devices of great import. They symbolize the common experiences of humanity as it struggles to keep its balance much like the "Fiddler on the

Roof'' who makes music while the world around him is threatening to collapse.

Finally, the Fishers' study led them to believe that one of the profound services rendered by professional comics is their moral relativism. Something is good or bad depending upon, or relative to, one's times, culture, or society. Moral absolutism, the contrary view, insists that there is a universal morality applicable to all persons, all cultures, or all societies. Sociologists and anthropologists are among those social scientists who essentially favor the concept of moral relativism or pluralism and are more skeptical about a stance that some ethical principle is universally valid.

Professional comics do not consciously study moral or normative relativism as much as they "show" that mores are a part of social controls imposed upon them by fallible human beings acting in concert. It is altogether possible to dare to be different or "to get in step with a different drummer" at times, and the rest of the world will still go on as before. Like the ethnomethodologists, by taking the actions they do, professional comics reveal the assumptions, premises, and taken-for-granted formulations by which people interact and take each other into account. Some are laughable, petty, and unworthy of support as far as they are concerned. On the other hand, some of the assumptions are useful, and without them, the social order becomes a shambles. Professional comics demonstrate what can ensue when there is no consensus about what is appropriate and what is not.

The Fishers' study of professional comics is summarized as:

1. Being funny is intended to soothe and 'heal' people and, perhaps, to win them over.

2. The comical is a means of attacking existing standards, exciting anarchy, and creating an ambience in which the difference between good and bad is blurred.

3. The comic approach permits the simultaneous exposure and integration of contradictions.

4. Being funny probably serves to vent hostility, but in a fashion that conceals its intent; and even implies 'I am nice and good rather than angry or threatening.' Concealed communication is often an important intent of the comic.

5. To appear as the comedian is to depreciate one's self and yet to occupy a unique status with special powers.

(Fisher & Fisher, 1981, pp. 216-217)

Comic Teams

The greatest proportion of professional performers of humor develop their own style, aura, or persona as soloists. They often spend years searching for characterizations suitable for them and, more importantly, effective with audiences in achieving the results they so desperately want to achieve. They are never far removed from others because the very nature of humor as a social product requires them to relate to others. But, in the main, their performances rely upon their own capacities and not upon colleagues or partnerships.

There is a remarkable number of professional comics, however, who are part of comedic history because of the give-and-take, the contrasts, the complemental-supplemental, the interplay, and the resonance or sounding-board effect of comical partnerships or relationships. These comic teams were more dyadic and triadic, although occasionally three or more performers could enhance or heighten the team with each other's characterizations enough to achieve stardom or top billing. The Marx Brothers, Leonard, Adolph (later known as Arthur), Julius, Herbert, and Milton, or better known by their stage names as Chico, Harpo, Groucho, Zeppo, and Gummo, respectively, played madcap lunatics for many years with tremendous success. They eventually trimmed their acts to a threesome by removing Zeppo and Gummo. Al, Jimmy, and Harry Joachim became the Ritz Brothers while a fourth brother, George, stayed in the background as their manager. The team of Moe, Shemp, and Jerry Howard and Larry Fine was eventually trimmed to a successful comical triad known as The Three Stooges, Moe, Jerry (better known as Curly), and Larry. Essentially the Three Stooges were clowns who carried their act for fifty years from vaudeville to movies and television (Maltin, 1985).

The more balanced comical twosomes were more frequent than larger numbered teams because the additional members often created a dissonance that tended to disrupt rather than blend the group. The dyad, it is true, is vulnerable to breaking apart if the interchange or tradeoffs do not succeed or are too confining or restrictive to one or both members. The breakup of Jerry Lewis and Dean Martin came as a surprise to many. The Bud Abbott and Lou Costello team operated on a precarious basis, a condition unknown to many of their fans (Thomas, 1977). George Burns and Gracie Allen gave memorable performances until death tragically removed the truly remarkable and more talented partner, Gracie (Burns, 1955; see also Harmon, 1970).

Such teams as Gallagher and Shean, Smith and Dale, Weber and Fields, Olsen and Johnson, Laurel and Hardy, Lum and Abner, Wheeler and Woolsey, Amos and Andy, Rowan and Martin, Edgar Bergen and Charlie McCarthy, Moran and Mack, Bob and Ray, and the Smothers Brothers were all-male comedians who stood in contrast to each other. One member might act "straight" while the other acted "weird." Like the cartoon characters Mutt and Jeff, one might be tall and the other short; one might be fat and the other thin; one might be "normal" and the other "deviant." As foils, they enhanced each other's image. As competitors, they extended themselves. As "sympaticos," they harmonized with each other's patterns so that one built upon the other's actions.

The mixed teams of Fred Allen and Portland Hoffa, Sid Caesar and Imogene Coca, Fibber McGee and Molly, Jack Benny and Mary Livingston, Mike Nichols and Elaine May, Ford and Hines, or Meara and Steller allowed gender differences to become a significant feature of their performances.

The rarest type of comedic teams were those that were all-female. Perhaps one of the best known in films was the combination of Thelma Todd and Zasu Pitts and, later on, Thelma Todd and Patsy Kelly. Feminine wiles or departures from behavior ascribed for women could be played out skillfully with humor by these teams. Comediennes performing singly have existed for many years, but the dominance of males as comics marks the female comic as a rare breed indeed. Belle Baker, Lucille Ball, Kaye Ballard, Gertrude Berg, Fanny Brice, Carol Burnett, Judy Canova, Carol Channing, Joan Davis, Phyllis Diller, Marie Dressler, Gracie Fields, Totie Fields, Charlotte Greenwood, Goldie Hawn, Judy Holliday, Helen Kane, Beatrice Lillie, Moms Mabley, Bette Midler, Mary Tyler Moore, Martha Raye, Joan Rivers, and Lily Tomlin rate among the better known comediennes and inescapably use their versions of womanhood to reach their respective audiences or publics. Franklin (1979) identifies them as "comedians," in conformity with the traditional generic usage of "mankind" to apply to both men and women. Far outnumbered by male comics, the few comediennes could use their ascribed gender status to greater advantage in the course of their acts than the men. As soloists, both male and female comics relied upon their unique talents or flair for the comedic, but the women had the special advantage of using the magnified absurdity of sexual ascriptions in telling ways. When they teamed together, their unity or bonds as "sisters" geometrically increased their comedic messages that equity of treatment continues to elude society.

The Greatest Professional Comic of the 20th Century

When it comes to naming the greatest professional comic of the twentieth century, a century filled with social changes, an era that is a part of living memories, one is hard-pressed because much depends on preferences, values or tastes that are subjective in nature. One could easily set up *a posteriori* or *ex post facto* criteria, or be accused of consciously doing so, but it is an exercise worth doing because it helps to crystallize ideas and factors as to a possible "ideal type" or what specific elements enter into the making of excellence in a professional comedic career.

Such criteria worth considering are: (1) a global or worldwide appeal that transcends social and cultural differences, (2) an ability to excite deep emotions, (3) a presentation that encourages people to think about human conditions, (4) the creation of a persona that demonstrates the resilience of humanity to meet the vicissitudes of life with courage and to bounce back with determination and personal dignity, (5) sustained performances that cover decades rather than brief time periods, (6) versatility in terms of adaptations to changing media or new technologies, and (7) multidimensionality that symbolizes the many-sided nature of human personality.

The professional comic who most closely and admirably meets these criteria was Charles Spencer Chaplin. There may well be others to be nominated or there may be judges who would exclude Charlie Chaplin, but he would certainly stand out as a giant among giant performers of humor *par exellence.*

The "examined life" is useful because there are lessons to be learned in every life history. In the life course of individuals, it becomes possible to detect those strands that make up the fabric of an individual's accomplishments. Professional careers, whether they be in comic performances, art, education, business, medicine, sports, or religion, all have their origins and development in the circumstances that have shaped the ultimate outcome. The use of biographies, both self-perceived or interpreted by observers of the human record, need not be neglected by those interested in understanding what culminated in the unforgettable performances in humor. In Chaplin's case, referred to by many as "the best of best" in comedic history, there are certain highlights worth recalling (see Chaplin, 1964; McDonald, Conway & Ricci, 1965).

Born in London, April 16, 1889, Charles was the son of stage performers. His father was notable because of his acts of omission rather than of commission. He did very little for his wife and children and died an alcoholic at age 37. Charles' mother did her best to maintain herself and her children but soon began to falter on the stage as a coquettish soubrette and eventually sank into poverty and serious mental illness. Charles and his half -brother Sidney were forced to spend a part of their young lives in a workhouse for orphans and the indigent, an experience that Charlie never forgot. In such a life one sees the elements that the Fishers' study confirmed that can lead to an intensive search to find satisfaction to balance out the pains of the past.

Chaplin soon found that he could evoke laughter from rough, rowdy audiences and could win the approval of others by his comical schoolboy recitations. Thanks to contacts made by his father, one of his few positive actions, Charles joined a vaudeville act as a clog dancer in a troupe known as the Eight Lancashire Lads. His career was launched. From his child-acting he became a veteran vaudevillian and eventually found maturity in a troupe called Karno's Company. Extended tours in America brought Chaplin to the attention of Mack Sennett, the founder of the Keystone Company that had begun to make films for the fledgling cinema industry.

His arduous years of struggling as a relatively unknown but highly effective performer of comic routines were soon over. He improvized his characterizations in accord with the techniques of the early filmmakers which consisted of fleshing out some general scenario that the producer

-director wanted to follow. At that time, there were no elaborate scripts or major preparations made for the overall film projects, and the company relied upon setting up some conflict between a hero and a villain, some violations of social norms, and the concluding scenes of an orchestrated "chase." Chaplin's background stood him in good stead and he soon created the figure of "The Little Tramp," a baggy-pants, homeless wanderer, a cane-twirling, derby-hatted, mustached, polite-mannered champion of women, a graceful and courageous image of a man who met adversity and social rejection with dignity and aplomb.

What Chaplin had done was to put before the public a complex, multi-faceted, appealing image of an individual who personified qualities of profound import. His costume, for example, quickly showed that here was a man of little material wealth or power, but herein were also the accoutrements of the upper social classes and signs of aspirations for upward social mobility. His character was certainly not part of the mainstream but always that of an outsider who could, by his very actions, demonstrate that there is much to be corrected in the way people treat each other and the way they organize and conduct their affairs. His rootless, harmless, caring, little tramp was always searching for love and acceptance and what he received instead was heartbreaking rejection. Whenever misfortune came, the little man could pick himself up, shrug off the discomfiture, and move on. Hope and promise would triumph and help him to carry on. Out of the most commonplace, this wanderer could, ballet-like, find grace, beauty, and artistic timing. In short, Chaplin had found a persona that gave him the means to mix tragedy with comedy, to give sentimentality full play in the midst of laughter and humor.

There is no evidence that Chaplin deliberately sat down and designed his artful characterization. He himself indicated that much was fortuitous. He was astounded at the adulation and acclaim that masses of people accorded him. Much, however, was due to his background and pioneering in a new technology that brought him to the world stage.

In the year of his debut, 1914, he made thirty-five unprecedented one- and two-reel short films and one six-reel film called "Tillie's Punctured Romance." Between 1915 and 1918, Chaplin made fourteen short films for Essanay Company and a four-reeler called "Carmen." He also worked in twelve shorts for Mutual Company in 1916 and 1917 in such classics as "The Floorwalker," "The Rink," "Easy Street," "The Cure," and "The Immigrant." Between 1918 and 1919, nine film comedies featuring Chaplin were released by First National and included such works as "Shoulder Arms," "The Kid," and "The Pilgrim," all based on American themes of the times. Through the United Artists which he helped found, full-length comedies were made that brought him to the zenith of his performing career. "The Gold Rush" was made in 1925, "The Circus" in 1928, "City Lights" in 1931, "Modern Times" in 1936, and "The Great Dictator" in 1940. He continued to direct and appear in films up to 1966. Chaplin died at age 88 on December 25, 1977, having achieved knighthood in his native England, along with the highest awards and recognition from fellow professionals, and global acclaim for his wistful clowning. In Chaplin's own words, he had carefully brought to life a comic spirit in which an underdog prevails despite a societal system beset by overbearing policemen, snapping mongrels, and Yukon blizzards: "One cannot do humor without great sympathy for one's fellow man." While some would focus on his private life that was sorely troubled and at odds with conditions for which he had contempt, it was the professional comedic expertise in creating a meaningful persona that places him at or near the pinnacle of professional comics.

Summary and Conclusions

This closing chapter sets apart those special men and women who devote their professional lives to the performance of humor from all others who draw upon humor to see them through the trials and tribulations of living as best they can. They make humor come alive by drawing attention to their deeds and characterizations and at the same time thereby make their living. All others, by contrast, are amateurs, audiences, and responsive publics who deeply appreciate and reward professional comics for what they do. In a sense, professional comics stand in the spotlight by fixing attention to themselves and their representations and all others stand in the background seeing before them much that mirrors back to them what is going on in human lives. Much of what they see are social environments that are made tolerable by being able to take a humorous perspective or interpretation of them.

The history and tradition of the professional fool goes back to antiquity and was traced in an earlier chapter. This final chapter was devoted more to the contemporary times in which modern technologies make more accessible the artistry, skillful ways, and symbolic messages of comic performers. They are brought "up close," and they seem to be in everyone's primary groups because they possess familiar hallmarks, behaviorisms, and features in the privacies of homes or in darkened theaters in which one can find personal communion with them.

Professional comics, of course, do not "just happen" but are products of their backgrounds in conjunction with their overall social milieus. Most often they have origins in lower socioeconomic families, are more likely to be men than women, have a strong need to earn acceptance, tend to reveal the numerous shortcomings in social life by acting them out, blur the distinctions between the approved and the disapproved ways of behaving, and favor a more optimistic than a pessimistic view of the human condition. They are undaunted, irrepressible men and women who know the powers of humor and so encourage others to draw upon it frequently. They often work alone, but sometimes through dyadic, triadic, or even larger groupings or teams, they interplay with each other to reach even greater performances than they could do as soloists. The social nature of humor calls for a give-and-take relationship whether among amateurs, between comic performers and audiences, or within the ranks of professional comic artists.

Their greatness rests upon symbolism and the use of a persona that identifies who they represent and what is to be gained by seeing them in action. When they are most effective, professional comics reach legendary, mythical, and almost immortal status because they have profoundly touched the emotions and intellects of their publics. Perhaps the greatest of the professional comics in the twentieth century was Charles Spencer Chaplin who rose from poverty and rejection to knighthood and lavish acclaim among his peers.

STUDY QUESTIONS

1. What interactive patterns exist, or need to exist, between humor professionals and their audiences or publics?

2. Why are there more professional comedians than comediennes?

3. What social factors shape comic careers?

4. What are the advantages and disadvantages to be weighed in opting for a professional comic career?

5. What talents need to be developed in preparation for a, professional comic career?

6. Is comic performance a high or low-status occupation?

7. How does study of professional comics inform sociologists or contribute significant information to the field of sociology?

8. What are the hallmarks or distinguishing features of a great career versus a mediocre career in comedy?

9. What social factors determine comic popularity?

10. Are opportunities in comic careers today increasing or decreasing? Explain.

11. How do professional comics teach their audiences or publics?

12. What do professional comics teach or promote of social significance?

13. What supportive teamwork is necessary for professional comics?

14. Do professional comics rely upon their own resources or talents for their public performances over a lifetime career?

15. While the author nominated Charlie Chaplin as "the greatest comic of the 20th Century," do you agree or disagree? Why? Whom would you select? Why?

16. What are the strengths and weaknesses of comic teams?

17. To what extent are professional comics self-elected?

18. Is Charlie Chaplin correct in asserting that "one cannot do humor without great sympathy" for humanity? Why or why not?

19. What refinements would you add to the Fishers' study of professional comics?

20. What social functions are performed by professional comics?

Suggested Readings

Allen, Steve. *More Funny People.* NY: Stein & Day, 1982.

Burns, George. *I Love Her, That's Why! An Autobiography.* NY: Simon & Schuster, 1955.

Cahn, William. *A Pictorial History of the Great Comedians.* NY: Grosset & Dunlap, 1970.

Chaplin, Charles. *Charles Chaplin: My Autobiography.* NY: Simon & Schuster, 1964.

Cohen, Joel H. *Cool Cos: The Story of Bill Cosby.* NY: Scholastic Book Services, 1969.

Fisher, Seymour and Rhoda L. Fisher. *Pretend the World is Funny and Forever: A Psychological Analysis of Comedians, Clowns, and Actors.* Hillsdale, NJ: Lawrence Erlbaum Associates, 1981.

Franklin, Joe. *Encyclopedia of Comedians.* Secaucus, NJ: Citadel Press, 1979.

Harmon, Jim. *The Great Radio Comedians.* Garden City, NY: Doubleday, 1970.

Maltin, Leonard. *Movie Comedy Teams.* NY: New American Library, rev. & updated, 1985.

Marx, Harpo and Roland Barber. *Harpo Speaks!* NY: Freeway Press, 1974.

McDonald, Gerald D., Michael Conway and Mark Ricci, eds. *The Films of Charlie Chaplin.* NY: Bonanza Books, 1965.

Nathan, David. *The Laughtermakers: A Quest for Comedy.* London: Peter Owen, 1971.

Schickel, Richard. *Harold Lloyd: The Shape of Laughter.* Boston: New York Graphic Society, 1974.

Thomas, Bob. *Bud and Lou: The Abbott and Costello Story.* Philadelphia: Lippincott, 1977.

Weales, Gerald. *Canned Goods as Caviar: American Film Comedies of the 1930's.* Chicago: Univ. of Chicago Press, 1985.

Epilogue:

Toward a Sociology of Humor

Every ending has a beginning. Looking over what this book has attempted, it should be clear that this work has merely introduced the subject matter. It constitutes an "exploration" into the sociology of humor and suggests what this specialization might investigate or consider. Thus the ending signals the possibilities of developing a sociology of humor just as historians, psychologists, philosophers, anthropologists, artists, or communicators in a variety of media have done in their respective areas of competence.

Humor has not escaped the attention of scholars in the social and behavioral sciences. There are sociologists who have already brought their expertise to bear upon humor and have made significant contributions in understanding it and seeing its ramifications. This book has attempted to bring together some of the salient accomplishments to date and suggests that far more work and a finer treatment sociologically can build upon this.

As the information, discussions, and analyses suggest, there are many questions yet to be answered that would further our understanding about humor. By studying humor from a sociological perspective some of these questions may be answered. What has been presented in these pages would seem to warrant sociological concentration upon humor because of its social and cultural relevance. A sociology of humor holds high potential for sociologists to consider. A fully developed sociology of humor is a specialization that will take many years to accomplish, but as this work suggests, there are many avenues to explore.

How is a sociology of humor to be accomplished? A major effort is needed to research a variety of ideas, theories, and empirical propositions that may be developed from the ideas, data, and substantive material presented in this work as one beginning. These and related material need to be disseminated to sociologists, faculty, students, and other channels of instruction in academia to establish the specialty within the regular curriculum in sociology. Undoubtedly there must be sociology faculty to introduce

327

courses in this specialty. The author has done so within his own department and university and has found that students, faculty, and administrative officers have been most supportive. This knowledge should also be introduced and promoted outside the campus to organizations and publics in the "real world" off campus. This author has found that organizations in communities within his region have welcomed discussions and presentations on the nature of a sociology of humor. Furthermore, there have been a number of professional forums in and outside of sociology that afford opportunities to present and discuss critically what a sociology of humor has to offer.

Humor is omnipresent in all human societies and is recognized and expressed in art, music, drama, and literature. Sciences, too, have appreciated the constant presence of humor in human lives and have gone beyond aesthetic and affective expression toward cognition of its significance. A sociology of humor would be a welcome addition in this effort to ground the data firmly through scientific research and theory.

This book develops the theme that humor can best be understood as a means to survive the vicissitudes of human life. The data and analyses presented herein have generally supported this proposition. But this and many other hypotheses and theories given throughout this exploration are in need of far more research and analysis before they can be accepted as valid. Such research could also contribute to the modification or even displacement of this and other ideas presented in this volume. Indeed it is our hope that this work will stimulate and provoke sociologists to put the salient ideas and propositions to the scientific sociological test and thereby join in the scholarly development of this new sociological specialty. It is by such collective scholarly and scientific efforts that new trails are blazed in the discipline and a new body of knowledge is legitimately developed.

Humor involves those matters that are central to sociology. Social interaction, social processes, social systems, and social products are to be found in abundance in the phenomenon known as humor. A Sociology of Humor can therefore verify and affirm that the discipline has much to contribute of significance and value. We hope that this volume will contribute significantly toward this development.

INDEXES:

NAME INDEX

SUBJECT INDEX